T0281152

Lecture Notes in Computer Scit

Commenced Publication in 1973
Founding and Former Series Editors:
Gerhard Goos, Juris Hartmanis, and Jan van Leeuwen

Alessandro Garcia   Ricardo Choren
Carlos Lucena   Paolo Giorgini
Tom Holvoet   Alexander Romanovsky (Eds.)

Software Engineering for Multi-Agent Systems IV

Research Issues and Practical Applications

 Springer

Volume Editors

Alessandro Garcia
Lancaster University, Computing Department, InfoLab 21, Lancaster, LA1 4WA, UK
E-mail: a.garcia@lancaster.ac.uk

Ricardo Choren
SE/8, IME, Praça General Tibúrcio 80, Urca 22290-170, Rio de Janeiro/RJ, Brazil
E-mail: choren@de9.ime.eb.br

Carlos Lucena
Pontifical Catholic University of Rio de Janeiro, Computer Science Department
Rio de Janeiro, RJ - 22453-900, Brazil
E-mail: lucena@inf.puc-rio.br

Paolo Giorgini
University of Trento, Department of Information and Communication Technology
Via Sommarive, 14, 38050 Povo (Trento), Italy
E-mail: paolo.giorgini@dit.unitn.it

Tom Holvoet
K.U. Leuven, Department of Computer Science
Celestijnenlaan 200A, 3001 Leuven, Belgium
E-mail: Tom.Holvoet@cs.kuleuven.be

Alexander Romanovsky
University of Newcastle, School of Computing Science
Newcastle upon Tyne, NE1 7RU, UK
E-mail: alexander.romanovsky@ncl.ac.uk

Library of Congress Control Number: 2006923375

CR Subject Classification (1998): D.2, I.2.11, C.2.4, D.1.3, H.3.5

LNCS Sublibrary: SL 2 – Programming and Software Engineering

ISSN	0302-9743
ISBN-10	3-540-33580-3 Springer Berlin Heidelberg New York
ISBN-13	978-3-540-33580-1 Springer Berlin Heidelberg New York

Springer is a part of Springer Science+Business Media

springer.com

© Springer-Verlag Berlin Heidelberg 2006
Printed in Germany

Typesetting: Camera-ready by author, data conversion by Scientific Publishing Services, Chennai, India
Printed on acid-free paper   SPIN: 11738817   06/3142   5 4 3 2 1 0

Foreword

With the integration of computing and communication into the very fabric of our social, economic, and personal existence, the manner in which we think about and build software has become the subject of intense intellectual, scientific, and engineering reexamination. New computing paradigms have been proposed and new software architectures are being examined. The study of multi-agent systems (MAS) is one important movement energized by a growing awareness that application development may need to follow radically new paths. Fundamentally, MAS denotes a new software specification and design paradigm. Moreover, when viewed in the context of large-scale deployment, it emerges as the embodiment of the quintessential concerns facing the software engineering community today. As computing and communication permeates the essential aspects of the societal infrastructure, software must become more nimble, slimmer, more natural, and more discrete. Software must integrate itself in an organic way into the activities it serves and the resources it exploits.

Technological changes and their societal implications clearly impacted the evolution of MAS research. The starting point was the wired network that facilitated the development of distributed applications for which MAS appeared to offer a novel design strategy. The introduction of base stations and wireless communication (with devices that move along the fringe of the wired network and can disconnect unexpectedly for extended periods of time) highlighted the importance of disconnected interactions, highly decoupled computing, and migration across the wireless link. MAS proved to be particularly well suited to respond to the requirements of the new environment; for example, it seems natural for a disconnected host to rely on an agent migrated to the wired network to carry out work on its behalf. The advance of ad hoc networks offered still new opportunities and also new challenges for MAS research. Structuring applications as communities of agents that can float over a physically mobile infrastructure is clearly an intellectually exiting possibility to consider, but finding applications that match well to this environment remains a contentious point among researches and practitioners. Finally, MAS made its presence felt even in the newly emerging field of sensor networks. The flexibility of the basic MAS paradigm is indeed remarkable and all indicators point to its continuing evolution towards enabling application developers to achieve increasingly more effective utilization of the deployed computing and communications infrastructures.

The most visible MAS contributions can be attributed to successful abstraction and conceptualization efforts that demonstrate the expressive power of the various embodiments of the basic paradigm across multiple technological substrates. However, only the combination of exciting conceptual frameworks with analytical power, design methodology, and engineering practice will lead to achieving a truly high impact on the society at large. These concerns should be formative elements for the MAS research agenda. Interestingly enough, the content of this volume matches well with this perspective on the field. Papers on context awareness, coordination, and modeling continue to focus on strengthening and deepening our understanding of conceptual frameworks having both scientific and practical significance. Papers addressing requirements, architecture, and dependability capture methodological and engineering concerns. Analysis alone receives somewhat more limited coverage in this volume.

MAS research is well positioned in terms of technical coverage of the field and promises to lead to the deployment of nimble and responsive user-centered applications. However, the community needs to recognize that in today's environment the marketplace has a greater than ever voice in determining research relevance and impact. This is not due to the evolving patterns of research funding, but due to the high degree of integration of computing and communication into the workings of a modern society. Acknowledging this should lead to the emergence of a research paradigm that focuses on the creative integration of conceptual, engineering, and application concerns in the shaping of the next generation of MAS. I view this volume as an important step along this path.

December 2005

Gruia-Catalin Roman
Washington University in Saint Louis

Preface

Software is becoming present in every aspect of our lives, pushing us inevitably towards a world of autonomous distributed systems. The agent-oriented paradigm holds great promise for responding to the new realities of large-scale distributed systems. It is strongly rooted in the theories underlying multi-agent systems (MASs) and, as a result, offers appropriate software engineering abstractions and mechanisms to address issues such as context-awareness, openness, coordination, ubiquity, mobility, adaptation, and cooperation among heterogeneous and autonomous parties. Not surprisingly, multi-agent software development is one of the most rapidly growing areas of research in academia and software industry.

Nevertheless, the complexity associated with software agents and MASs is considerable, posing new challenges to software engineering community. Without adequate development techniques and methods, MASs will not be sufficiently dependable, trustworthy and extensible, thus making their wide adoption by the industry more difficult. Commercial success of MAS applications requires scalable solutions based on well-understood software engineering approaches that ensure effective deployment and enable reuse.

A large MAS is complex in many ways. When a set of agents interact over open heterogeneous environments, several problems emerge. For example, openness requires appropriate abstractions and mechanisms for supporting context-awareness. In addition, it makes their coordination and management challenging and increases the probability of exceptional situations, security holes and unexpected global effects. Moreover, as users and software engineers delegate more autonomy to their MASs and put more trust in their results, new concerns arise in real-life applications. Yet many of the existing agent-oriented solutions are far from ideal; in practice, systems are often built in an ad-hoc manner, are error-prone, not scalable, not dynamic, and not generally applicable to large-scale environments. If agent based applications are to be successful, software engineering approaches will be needed to enable scalable deployment.

The main motivation for producing this book is the Software Engineering for Large-Scale Multi-Agent Systems (SELMAS) workshop series, which focuses on bringing together software engineering practitioners and researchers to discuss the several issues arising when MASs are used to engineer complex systems. SELMAS 2005[1] was the fourth edition of the workshop, organized in association with the 27th International Conference on Software Engineering (ICSE), held in Saint Louis, USA, in May 2005. The theme of this particular workshop edition was "Software Everywhere—Context-Aware Agents." To produce the book based on this workshop edition, we decided to extend the workshop coverage, and to

---

[1] Garcia, A. el al.: Software Engineering for Large-Scale Multi-Agent Systems - SELMAS 2005 (Workshop Report). ACM Software Engineering Notes, Vol. 30, N. 4, July 2005.

invite several of the workshop participants to write chapters for books based on their original position papers, as well as several other leading researchers in the area to prepare additional chapters. Thus, this book is a continuation of a series of three previous ones[2−4].

This book brings together a collection of 15 papers addressing a wide range of issues in software engineering of MASs, reflecting the importance of agent properties in today's software systems. The papers in this book describe recent developments in specific issues and practical experience. At the end of each chapter, the reader will find a list of relevant references for further reading. The papers in this book are grouped into five sections: Context-Awareness, Coordination, Dependability, Modelling, and Requirements and Software Architecture. The first section is especially dedicated to the SELMAS 2005 theme. The other sections contain high-quality contributions on other important complementary concerns in MAS development. We believe that this carefully prepared volume, describing the most recent developments in the field of software engineering for MASs, will be of particular value to all readers interested in these key topics.

With a comprehensive selection of case studies and software engineering solutions for MASs applications, this book provides a valuable resource for a wide audience of readers. The main target readers for this book are researchers and practitioners who want to keep up with the progress of software engineering of MASs, individuals keen to understand the interplay between agents and other software development paradigms, and those interested in experimental results from MAS applications. Software engineers involved in particular aspects of MASs as a part of their work may find it interesting to learn about application of software engineering approaches in building real systems. Some chapters in the book discuss the transitions involving different MAS development phases, such as requirements, architecture specifications, and implementation. One key contribution of this volume is the description of the latest approaches to reasoning about complex MASs. We are confident that this book will be of considerable use to the software engineering community by providing many original and distinct views on such an important interdisciplinary topic, and by contributing to a better understanding and cross-fertilization among individuals in this research area. Our thanks go to all our authors, whose work made this book possible. Many of them also helped during the reviewing process. We would also like to express our gratitude to the members of the Evaluation Committee who were generous with their time and effort when reviewing the submitted papers. We specially thank all people involved—authors, workshop participants, and

---

[2] Garcia, A., Lucena, C., Castro, J., Zambonelli, F., Omicini, A. (eds.): Software Engineering for Large-Scale Multi-Agent Systems. LNCS, vol. 2603, Springer-Verlag, April 2003.

[3] Lucena, C., Garcia, A., Romanovsky, A., Castro, J., Alencar, P. (eds.): Software Engineering for Multi-Agent Systems II. LNCS, vol. 2940, Springer-Verlag, February 2004.

[4] Choren, R., Garcia, A., Lucena, C., Romanovsky, A. (eds.): Software Engineering for Multi-Agent Systems III. LNCS, vol. 3390, Springer-Verlag, February 2005.

reviewers—for making this book series and the SELMAS workshop editions a high-quality scientific joint project.

December 2005   Alessandro Garcia (Lancaster University, UK)
Ricardo Choren (IME-Rio, Brazil)
Carlos Lucena (PUC-Rio, Brazil)
Paolo Giorgini (University of Trento, Italy)
Tom Holvoet (K. U. Leuven, Belgium)
Alexander Romanovsky (University of Newcastle, UK)

Organization

Evaluation and Program Committee

N. Alechina (University of Nottingham, UK)
E. Alonso (City University London, UK)
R. Ashri (University of Southampton, UK)
B. Bauer (Universität Augsburg, Germany)
C. Bernon (IRIT, France)
M. Brian Blake (Georgetown University, USA)
P. Bresciani (IRST, Italy)
J-P. Briot (Université Paris VI, France)
G. Cabri (Università di Modena e Reggio Emilia, Italy)
J. Castro (UFPE, Brazil)
M. Cossentino (ICAR-CNR, Italy)
S. Cost (University of Maryland Baltimore County, USA)
J. Debenham (University of Technology - Sydney, Australia)
J. Dix (University of Manchester, UK)
C. A. Fernández (Universidad Politécnica de Madrid, Spain)
M. Fredriksson (Blekinge Institute of Tech., Sweden)
C. Ghidini (ITC-irst, Italy)
M-P. Gleizes (IRIT, France)
Z. Guessoum (Université Paris VI, France)
B. Henderson-Sellers (U. of Technology - Sydney, Australia)
K. Henricksen (University of Queensland, Australia)
J. Indulska (University of Queensland, Australia)
C. Jonker (Vrije Universiteit Amsterdam, The Netherlands)
M. Kolp (Université Catholique de Louvain, Belgium)
J. C. Maldonado (USP - So Carlos, Brazil)
V. Mascardi (Università di Genova, Italy)
H. Mouratidis (University of East London, UK)
J. Odell (Agentis Software, USA)
E. Oliveira (Universidade do Porto, Portugal)
A. Omicini (Università di Bologna, Italy)
S. Ossowski (Universidad Rey Juan Carlos, Spain)
L. Penserini (ITC-irst, Italy)
G. Rossi (Universidad Nacional de La Plata, Argentina)
A. G. Serrano (Universidad Politécnica de Madrid, Spain)
J. M. Serrano (Universidad Rey Juan Carlos, Spain)
O. Shehory (IBM Research Center in Haifa, Israel)
J. Shepherdson (British Telecommunications plc., UK)
A. von Staa (PUC-Rio, Brazil)
M. Stal (Siemens AG, Germany)

Table of Contents

Context-Awareness and Coordination

Modeling

Requirements and Software Architecture

Dependability

Policy-Driven Configuration and Management of Agent Based Distributed Systems*

Anand R. Tripathi, Devdatta Kulkarni, and Tanvir Ahmed

Department of Computer Science,
University of Minnesota, Minneapolis, MN 55455, USA
{tripathi, dkulk, tahmed}@cs.umn.edu

Abstract. In this paper, we demonstrate a policy-driven approach for building and managing large scale agent based systems. We identify different classes of policies for agent based component integration. We also identify the system services and mechanisms that are required for policy-driven integration of components and their management. Policies are derived from the application level requirements and are used in dynamic configuration of agent based systems. Through case studies of two applications we demonstrate the utility of the policy-driven component integration approach in distributed agent systems.

1 Introduction

Building and managing large distributed component systems is becoming an increasingly challenging task. Continuous intervention by system administrators is generally limited in large-scale distributed environments. System support is needed for reconfiguration and reorganization when systems evolve with the addition of new components.

Component based approaches for structuring distributed systems have sufficiently matured and are widely used today [1]. New challenges in using the component technology are concerned with building systems using dynamic integration of active components such as agents [2]. Policy-driven approaches have been used previously for managing distributed systems [3]. In this paper we propose a policy-driven approach for building *distributed agent systems*. We identify the policy classes and the essential services required in building distributed agent systems.

Policies are derived from an application's functional and non-functional requirements. The functional requirements of an application may require certain components to be present on an agent or certain agents to coordinate towards some common goals. The non-functional requirements of an application may state that all the agents and components should be monitored for failures. In the policy-driven integration approach, the agent composition and the inter-agent interactions are driven by the policies which are derived from the high level requirements. The policies act as a glue in creating a dynamic configuration of

* This work was supported by National Science Foundation grants 0087514 and 0411961.

A. Garcia et al. (Eds.): SELMAS 2005, LNCS 3914, pp. 1–16, 2006.

the system in order to satisfy the functional and non-functional requirements. Since the application requirements are realized through a set of policies hence it is important to monitor events indicating policy violations (*policy-events*) and perform *policy-actions* to ensure that the requirements are not violated. Such an event and an action pair forms a *rule*. These rules are derived from the policies and form the basic mechanism for building policy-driven systems.

An agent is an active object encapsulating other components and is considered as a *first-class component*. It serves as an execution environment with security privileges; representing some principal in the environment. Moreover, an agent may be capable of migrating in the network. In this paper we use the term *component* to refer to objects that are contained in an agent; these objects may be active or passive. This agent model is supported through the Ajanta mobile agent programming framework [4, 5].

In policy-driven distributed agent systems, there are intra-agent policies for component integration, inter-agent policies for agent-to-agent interactions, and policies to ensure system robustness. Based on these policies, rules are derived for dynamic integration of agents and components in the system.

Agent based distributed computing models provide an ideal foundation for policy-driven component integration. Agents are autonomous entities that can encapsulate and enforce local policies. Autonomous agents are capable of learning and adapting to the new or modified global policies that dictate the interactions among distributed agents. Mechanisms of self-configuration, self-monitoring and recovery can be built using agent's capabilities.

In this paper we identify policy classes and present essential services and mechanisms for building distributed agent systems. We use two case study examples to elaborate on this policy classification. One of these systems is targeted towards network monitoring using mobile agents [6] and the other is targeted towards building secure distributed collaborative applications from their high-level specifications [7, 8, 9]. Both these systems are based on the Ajanta mobile agent programming framework.

These two applications lie at the opposite end of the spectrum of building policy-driven distributed agent systems. Network monitoring represents the class of systems that are open and evolving. Such systems do not have any limit on the number of agents present in the domain. There can be spontaneous arrival or departure of agents in the domain. Network monitoring system is targeted towards large domains where hosts, agents, or components may get added or removed over a period of time. Network monitoring policies are related to the configuration, monitoring, and failure-recovery of agents and components in the domain. On the other hand the specification driven secure distributed collaboration framework is used for synthesizing collaborative application by integrating a set of agents and components having specific collaboration and security requirements. Only a fixed set of agents can participate in the collaboration. External agents cannot join the collaboration spontaneously after the collaboration environment has been instantiated. In this way the secure distributed collaboration system represents a closed agent system.

Section 2 discusses the central concepts of the policy framework. We discuss the policy classification and the core set of services and mechanisms required for building policy-driven agent based systems in that section. In Section 3 we use the two representative applications (network monitoring, and secure distributed collaboration) to elaborate on the policy framework and show its utility in developing real systems. In Section 4 we compare the policies in network monitoring and distributed collaboration systems and conclude in Section 6.

2   Policy Framework for Agents in Distributed Environments

Figure 1 shows an agent immersed in the environment and interacting with other agents and services in the environment. Associated with each agent are two kinds of attributes: *intrinsic and extrinsic*. Intrinsic attributes of an agent are determined by the application level requirements. These include agent's functional role, components present in the agent, and the associated component policies. An agent acquires extrinsic attributes when it enters an environment. These are determined by both application and domain level requirements. The extrinsic attributes of an agent include the external context information for the agent, information about other agents of specific attributes present in the environment, and agent interaction policies related to other agents in the domain. Other components may also need to be deployed on the agent, depending on the extrinsic attributes.

Policies related to intra-agent components and inter-agent interactions determine the behavior of the agent. These policies depend upon the functional and

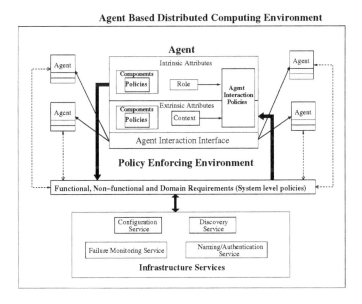

Fig. 1. Agent immersed in the environment

non-functional requirements of an application and the domain specific requirements of the application domain. Below we present policies classes for building
distributed agent systems.

2.1 Policy Classification

Related to any software application there are three kinds of requirements: functional requirements, non-functional requirements, and domain requirements [10].
Functional requirements capture the application's essential functionality and services it should provide. Non-functional requirements capture aspects of security,
performance, and fault-tolerance of the application which are orthogonal to the
application's core functionality. Domain requirements address the restrictions
imposed on the application by the domain of usage of the application.

We use *system level policies* to represent the above three kinds of application requirements. These policies include functional requirements such as which
agents or components should be installed for the required functionality, how
many instances of various agents are required and agent-to-host mappings. These
policies also include non-functional requirements such as failure monitoring and
timely recovery of agents in the system. In order to satisfy system level policies,
we refine them into *agent interaction policies* and *component integration policies*.

- *Agent Interaction Policies:* These policies determine the set of agents with
  whom an agent with a given set of attributes should communicate and interact with in some specific ways. Policies may also enforce certain constraints
  on these interactions based on security requirements. For example, an agent
  may be restricted to communicate only with the agents residing in a specific
  domain or owned by some designated set of users. The interaction relationships among agents, as determined by policies, are dynamic in nature as
  agent attributes and functionalities may change with time.
- *Component Integration Policies:* These policies are related to the components
  deployed within an agent. Constraints on component behavior or relationship between different components deployed within an agent are captured by
  these policies. They also include the list of local and remote events that will
  invoke the component, access to any system resources required by the component, and co-location of other components for proper functioning. These
  policies also relate to other component attributes such as what state of the
  component should be checkpointed, how often checkpoints should be taken,
  and if the component gets deleted then which other local and remote components should be informed about this. These policies can be defined at the
  component design time or can also be modified dynamically later.

2.2 Services for Policy Enforcement in Agent Based Distributed Systems

We have identified above different policy classes for realizing the application level
requirements in distributed agent systems. In such an approach it is important
to monitor policy violations and perform policy reinforcement actions to ensure

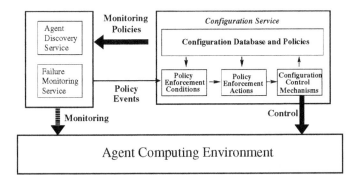

Fig. 2. Policy Driven Configuration Management

that the application requirements are not violated at any time. System level services and mechanisms are required for performing such policy monitoring and configuration control activities. In our framework these actions are performed by the following services: *agent discovery service, failure monitoring service*, and *configuration service*. Figure 2 shows these essential services and the interactions between them.

- *Agent Discovery Service:* This service is required for integrating new agents in the system. Its function is to detect the presence of new agents and notify the configuration service. In some architectures, the agents may first discover the configuration service and then inform the discovery service of their presence.
- *Failure Monitoring Service:* This service performs the failure monitoring of agents, components and other services present in the domain. It generates failure events corresponding to the failure of an entity and sends these events to the configuration service.
- *Configuration Service:* As new agents and components are deployed in such an environment, they need to self-configure according to the system policies. Similarly, when a component is removed from the system due to failures, or administrative reasons, or operational conditions (such as mobility of devices), appropriate reconfiguration actions are needed to be executed to preserve the invariants implied by the system policies. Configuration service has the knowledge of the global configuration policies and is able to take suitable actions when configuration change events are detected. The configuration service knows the "configuration change events" (*policy-events*) that are considered critical for policy enforcement, and it instructs agent discovery service and failure monitoring service about its interest in the detection of such events. These services detect such *policy-events* in the system and notify the configuration service of such changes. The configuration service is responsible for evaluating policies and enforcing them when critical changes occur.

The configuration service consists of a configuration database and the policy enforcement engine. Various agent related queries can be performed on this database. Examples of such queries are, finding all agents having a particular attribute, and finding an agent having certain set of attributes. This database can also store the initial configuration information for different types of agents in the system. This can be used to restart a failed agent. For example, it may list the set of components that must be installed on an agent at the time of restart and any specific initialization that needs to be performed for such components. In our approach, an important design principle is to require each agent to perform its own recovery after it has been restarted, so the configuration service is rarely involved in maintaining any information about an agent's local state. Similarly, components within an agent should be designed to reconstruct their execution state, through checkpoints or other mechanisms such as soft-state [11, 12].

The configuration service receives configuration change events when the *agent discovery service* informs it of the addition of new agents/components in the system, or the *failure monitoring service* informs it of any agent failures or departures. On detecting agent arrival, the configuration service has to inform the arriving agent of the system level policies that determine its functionalities and interaction relationships with the existing agents. Some new components may also need to be integrated in the agent according to the system level policies. On detecting the failure of an agent, the configuration service may try to restart the failed agent on the same or a different host. Existing agents may need to be informed of the agent restart so that they can setup appropriate interaction relationships with the restarted agent.

On receiving event notifications from the *agent discovery service* and the *failure monitoring service*, the configuration service performs the following functions. It identifies the policies that depend on the change events and identifies the agents that are affected by those policies. It also executes the actions required for enforcing the policies. In some applications, the policy enforcement actions may need to be performed cooperatively by a set of distributed agents in the environment. In such cases, the configuration service notifies all those agents. These actions ensure that the resulting system state conforms to the requirements and constraints implied by the policies.

As shown in Figure 2, the above functions of the configuration service are performed by three kinds of entities namely *policy enforcement conditions, policy actions*, and *configuration control mechanisms*. Policy enforcement conditions identify the conditions under which a policy event should trigger policy actions. A policy action determines the set of agents and components that are affected by a given event according to the policies. It also determines which new agents and components need to be created and installed in the system, and how the interaction relationships among the agents in the system needs to be altered. For this, it may query the configuration database. Finally, it invokes the appropriate configuration control mechanisms to realize the necessary changes in the configuration.

Agents, and the components contained in them, may also explicitly register with the configuration service their interests in certain specific kinds of configuration change events based on their local policies. This requires the configuration service to maintain such events of interest, called call-back information, for existing agents. This call-back information is also stored in the configuration database.

3 Case Studies

In this section we provide two case studies demonstrating the utility of the policy framework for agent based distributed environments.

3.1 Network Monitoring System

Konark [6] is a network monitoring system which monitors hosts in a network for various kinds of events. In this system, mobile agents are launched to monitor each host in the environment. Each agent contains components, termed *detectors*, to detect events in the environment. New detectors can be added to an agent remotely. Examples of events in this system include user logins, program executions on a host, file modifications, and network traffic patterns related to intrusions.

Agents can subscribe to events from other agents to detect compound events based on correlation of events from distributed sources. This is supported through the event subscription/notification mechanisms provided by Konark. The subscription/notification model for communication among agents is implemented using the underlying Ajanta agent communication model based on RMI. The execution of a detector in an agent can be triggered by events generated in the same agent or other agents in the environment. Other researchers have also developed similar event based systems for monitoring distributed systems [13, 14]. In our approach we use event detection and handling as a building block for policy management functions. The list of local or remote events that can trigger a detector form a triggering relation among detectors. It is termed *trigger dependency*. This makes Konark useful for correlating events occurring at different locations in a network system. Events are also stored in databases for long-term correlations.

We illustrate the usefulness of the policy framework of Section 2 by showing its utility through three example requirements of network monitoring. The first two requirements are application level functional requirements, while the third requirement is system robustness requirement. For each high level requirement, we identify the policies and corresponding policy events and policy actions.

Requirement 1: One of the application level requirements in the monitoring system is to detect abnormally high number of root login activities (successful/unsuccessful attempts) in the entire domain in a specified period of time. Following policies and rules are derived from this requirement.

1. (System level Policy 1): All agents in the system should contain the login detector.
   - *Policy-Event:* Arrival of a new agent in the domain.
   - *Policy-Action:* Install login detector in that agent.

2. (System level Policy 2): At least one agent should be present in the system to perform root login correlation across the entire domain.
   - *Policy-Event:* Failure of root login correlator agent.
   - *Policy-Action:* Install root login correlation component on another agent.
3. (Agent Interaction Policy): All the agents should send locally detected root login events to the correlator agent.
   - *Policy-Event 1:* Arrival of a new agent in the domain.
   - *Policy-Action 1:* Establish event subscription/notification relationship between the newly arrived agent and the correlator agent.

   - *Policy-Event 2:* New root login correlator agent is created.
   - *Policy-Action 2:* Change the event notification policy for all the agents such that they start reporting the root login events to the new correlator agent.
4. (Component Integration Policy): All the components required for root login detection should be present on an agent. The component integration policies for the root login detector at each host are shown in Figure 3. A periodic timer event triggers the execution of the *Syslog Event* detector. This detector generates events based on new log entries in the system log files. A *Syslog Event* triggers executions of the *Connection Event* detector, which filters and generates any login related events. This event triggers detectors for specific kinds of login, such as *SSH*, *Telnet*, and *Rlogin*. These detectors are filters which check if a given connection event belongs to a specific class. Any of these events, both local and remotely generated, trigger the *RootLogin* detector whose function is to determine if the login corresponds to the superuser. A trigger dependency marked only as *local* implies that the triggering event detector must be co-located in the same agent with the triggered detector. Similarly, a dependency marked only as *remote* implies that the triggering

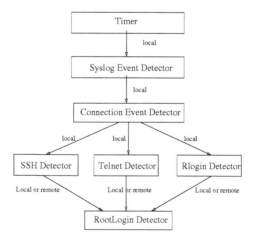

Fig. 3. Component Trigger Dependency: Root Login Event Trigger Dependency

event detector must be in an agent different from the one containing the triggered detector.

- *Policy-Event:* Failure of a required component within an agent.
- *Policy-Action:* Deploy the failed component on the agent.

Requirement 2: Network traffic should be continuously monitored for traffic using protocols and ports listed in the alerts posted in the known attack vectors on the CERT web site (*http://www. us-cert.gov/channels/techalerts.rdf*). Following policies and rules are derived from this requirement.

1. (System level Policy 1): There should be a monitoring agent in the system that should continuously monitor the CERT web site.
   - *Policy-Event:* The agent responsible for monitoring the CERT web site fails.
   - *Policy-Action:* Another agent should be started to perform the monitoring of the CERT web site.
2. (System level Policy 2): There should be at least one agent monitoring the network traffic for vulnerable port numbers appearing in the alerts posted on the CERT web site.
   - *Policy-Event :* Traffic monitoring agent fails.
   - *Policy-Action :* Restart the monitoring agent.

Requirement 3: All the agents in the system should be monitored for failures. Each agent should contain a heartbeat monitor component and should send *AgentAlive* events to the *AgentFailure* monitoring agent. Following policies and rules are derived from the above requirement.

1. (System level Policy 1): All agents should be deployed with heartbeat monitoring component
   - *Policy-Event:* Arrival of a new agent in the domain.
   - *Policy-Action:* Deploy heartbeat monitoring component on the agent.
2. (System level Policy 2): There should be at least one agent that performs failure monitoring functionality for all other agents in the domain.
   - *Policy-Event:* The agent responsible for failure monitoring of other agents fails.
   - *Policy-Action:* Designate another agent for performing failure monitoring of other agents in the domain.
3. (Agent Interaction Policy): All agents should send heartbeat messages to the failure monitoring agent.
   - *Policy-Event 1:* Arrival of a new agent.
   - *Policy-Action 1:* Establish the appropriate event subscription/notification relationship between the new agent and the heartbeat monitoring agent.

   - *Policy-Event 2:* Restarting of the failure monitoring agent.
   - *Policy-Action 2:* Establish the event subscription/notification relationship between the restarted failure monitoring agent and all other agents.

We have tested configurations consisting of up to 1000 agents in our network test bed. It takes less than five minutes (4 minutes and 17 seconds) to perform a policy-driven configuration of the network monitoring application consisting of 1000 agents. System configuration time grows linearly with an increase in the number of agents. Each arriving agent needs to be configured according to the system level policies. In our current setup, a special agent performs the functions of the configuration service. With an increase in the number of agent arrivals, the load on this configuration agent also increases thus increasing the time required for system configuration.

3.2   Secure Distributed Collaboration System

Secure distributed collaboration framework [8] supports construction of secure collaborative activities from their high level specifications. Figure 4 shows the steps involved in creating the collaboration environment. The specification of an activity defines a set of roles and a shared object space in which collaborating users perform their tasks. Policies related to activities, roles, user context and objects are derived from the collaboration specification. The middleware contains generic manager agents for activity, role, and object management. The derived policies are given to the respective manager agents to realize a particular collaboration environment. The specification model supports expression of the desired policies for coordination and dynamic security. Users participate in a collaboration through roles by executing operations (tasks) associated with the roles. A user's membership in a role represents a set of privileges, and these privileges are dynamically constrained by associating event-based preconditions with the role operations.

Manager agents communicate and interact with each other according to the policies derived from the activity's specification. The various different kinds of policies given to the agents in a collaboration environment are related to activity

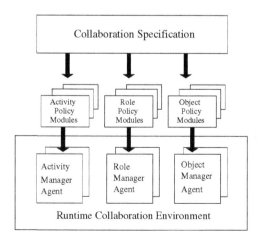

Fig. 4. Collaboration Environment Creation Process

```
1.    Activity Meeting {
2.    ActivationConstraint
3.          currentTime > 8.00 am & currentTime < 6.00 pm
4.    Object room
5.    Object projector
6.    Object presentation
7.    Role Accountant {
8.        Operation DisplayFinancialData
9.          Precondition
10.            #(Chairperson.ApprovePresentation) = 1
11.            & room.isPresent(thisUser)
12.            & room.isPresent(member(Chairperson))
13.        Action projector.display(data)
14.   }
15.   Role Chairperson {
16.       AdmissionConstraint
17.          #(members(thisRole)) < 1
18.       Operation ApprovePresentation
19.       Action presentation.approve()
20.   }
21.   }
```

Fig. 5. Context aware collaboration activity specification

and role instantiation, role admission/activation, operation preconditions, and object access control. *Policy-events* are related to activities, roles, operations and services. Examples of events include instantiation of an activity, invocation of role operation, and admission/removal of a user from a role. The details of this model can be found in [8].

Figure 5 shows an example specification of a meeting activity. The activity declares three objects (room, projector and presentation) and two roles (Accountant and Chairperson). A role provides operations through which role members can access objects. Role operations can have preconditions. A precondition is a boolean condition involving two types of events: cardinality based events and query events. Cardinality events are related to the count of role operation invocations and query events are related to the boolean queries over the objects. The operator # is used to obtain the role operation invocation count. An activity can have *ActivationConstraint* for restricting the instantiation of the activity and a role can have *AdmissionConstraint* restricting the admission to the role.

The specification in Figure 5 captures the following collaboration requirements.

1. The activity should be instantiated between 8.00 am and 6.00 pm (*lines 2-3*)
2. User in the *Accountant* role is allowed to invoke the *DisplayFinancialData* operation only if the *Chairperson* role has executed the *ApprovePresentation* operation and the members of the *Accountant* role and the *Chairperson* role are present in the room (*lines 8-13*).
3. Only one member is allowed to be present in the *Chairperson* role (*lines 15-17*).

These coordination and security requirements are enforced through the following set of policies. Requirement 1 restricts the instantiation of activity only within the allowed time. This policy is enforced at the *Activity Manager*. In this model, events are used to represent operation invocation by role members and any object related queries. As part of requirement 2, the *Accountant* role manager subscribes to the *ApprovePresentation* operation event from the *Chairperson* role manager and user presence events from the room object. Such events are conveyed to the appropriate subscribers on their occurrence. These form the agent interaction policies. For satisfying requirement 3, the role manager corresponding to the *Chairperson* role monitors user presence in the role. This policy is enforced by the *Chairperson* role manager component and involves no interaction with any other entity. This is the component integration policy for this example.

All these policies are derived from the specification of the collaborative activity an example of which is shown in Figure 5. In order to change the policies one has to write a new specification. Writing a new specification results in the creation of a new collaboration environment. It is not possible to change the policies once the collaboration environment is realized.

3.3   Policy Derivation

In the policy-driven agent based component integration approach presented here, identification of the *policy-events* forms an important step in the approach. In case of Konark based network monitoring, the *policy-events* and *policy-actions* are derived manually from the high level requirements. Policies in Konark are expressed as event handlers that are executed when *policy-events* occur. In case of distributed collaboration system, the *policy-events* are expressed as preconditions for activity instantiation, role admission and role operation invocation in the XML framework. The policies for a particular collaborative application are also verified for correctness and consistency using SPIN based model checking [15]. In our future work we will explore the specification of Konark's network monitoring policies through some policy specification language or through an XML specification framework similar to our framework for collaboration system. This will allow expression of policies in a more convenient fashion and also verification of policies for their correctness.

4   Discussion

Both the network monitoring system and the distributed collaboration system have been implemented. Details of the design and implementation can be found in [6] and [8], respectively. Both these systems extend the Ajanta programming model with application specific policies. The policy-driven paradigm provides flexibility in building the inter-agent interactions and dynamically extending the functionality of the agents in both these systems. In fact, policies give the agents the necessary autonomy in performing their tasks and managing their relationships with other agents and components in the system.

The nature of policies and the degree of agent autonomy differs between the two systems. Network monitoring is an example of open agent environment which can evolve over time with new agent arrivals, agent departures, and agent failures. In network monitoring system there are policies for configuration management of each detector within an agent, inter-agent communication and agent fail-over and restart. Agents have autonomy in deciding to whom they can report events, the rate at which events could be reported, restarting of a failed detector and maintaining event subscription and notification relationships.

On the other hand, the specification driven collaborative application construction framework is used for synthesizing new collaborative applications and is a closed agent system. The policies in the distributed collaboration system deal with event based security and coordination requirements between the participating role agents in collaborative applications. The enforcement of security and coordination constraints for a collaborative application requires that agents be supplied with strict guidelines about event generation and notification, limiting their dynamism as compared to the network monitoring system.

Policies help in specifying suitable tradeoffs for scalability of the network monitoring system at an expense of latency in detection of events of interest in the domain. For example, policies can be used to limit the reporting rate of successful root login events generated at a node to the correlator node with a possible delay in detecting whether the number of root login attempts in the domain is above a system defined threshold. The failure monitoring of the agents is also policy-driven wherein an agent can designate its monitoring peers and keep on sending regular *AgentAlive* events to them.

5 Related Work

The advantages of agent based architectures for building large scale software system are discussed in [16]. The application of agent based designs for building complex control systems are elaborated in [17] with specific concerns for diagnosis and repair functions needed in such systems to ensure robust operations. In [18] a three level model of organizational rules, organizational structures and organizational patterns is developed to address management aspects in open multi-agent environments. Policy-driven approach for building distributed agent systems presented here, reflects similar kinds of notions with specific focus on inter-agent interactions and intra-agent component integration.

IETF has been active in the standardization of the terminology [19] and the specification of policy information model [20] for network monitoring. IETF defines the following policy classes: *motivational policies (related to identifying whether policy goals are accomplished or not), configuration policies, installation policies, error and event policies, usage policies, security policies,* and *service policies*. This policy classification arises from the requirement of having declarative policy specification, a deliberate design decision by the IETF Policy Framework WG. The *agent interaction policies* and *component integration policies* defined in this paper are of procedural nature providing a binding of the application level requirements on to the agents in the domain. Policies are represented as condition-action pairs in the IETF model. In our model, policy conditions are represented as *policy-events* and policy actions are performed by event handlers. This is also similar to the approach of constraint preservation through the ECA (event, condition and action) model in active databases [21].

Other researchers have considered usage of policies in building agent systems [22]. In their approach policies related to roles, agent authorizations, and agent obligations are represented through Ponder policy language and are enforced through agent based middleware. Their policies are able to capture requirements of an open multi-agent system such as an agent based network management system. In our model, an agent's access control policies can be realized by constraining its interactions with other agents through the agent interaction policies based on the agent's role, authorizations, and obligations. Moreover, our policy framework is able to support diverse applications such as network monitoring and secure distributed collaboration.

The use of policies and their enforcement is the central concept in our approach for building autonomic system architectures. Similar concepts have been proposed in the past by others in the context of *law governed systems* [23] and *normative multi-agent systems* [24, 25]. Law based management of open multi-agent distributed systems has been studied in [26]. Policies can be viewed as a form of laws or norms. Similar to normative systems an agent's policies in our framework are based on the agent's context such as other agents present in the domain. The social pressure for enforcing norms in normative multi-agent systems is similar to our notion of policy enforcement in which policies are enforced based on the occurrence of policy events. In our work we demonstrate the utility of these concepts in a practical framework. Moreover, we identify the core set of services and mechanisms that are required for policy enforcement in autonomic configuration and management.

6   Conclusion

The design principle of separating policies from mechanisms has been known to system designers for a long time. The difficult part is to identify the policies and build mechanisms that can implement different kinds of policies. In this paper we have studied the application of this principle for building agent based distributed systems. We defined the policy classes and identified essential services for building distributed agent systems. Through two representative case studies we demonstrated the utility of this approach.

References

1. Szyperski, C.:   Component Software Beyond Object-Oriented Programming. Addison-Wesley ACM Press (1998)
2. Tripathi, A.:   Challenges Designing Next Generation Middleware Systems. Communications of the ACM **45** (2002) 39–42

3. Sloman, M.: Policy Driven Management for Distributed Systems. Plenum Press Journal of Network and Systems Management **2** (1994)
4. Karnik, N., Tripathi, A.: Security in the Ajanta Mobile Agent System. Software Practice and Experience **31** (2001) 301–329
5. Tripathi, A., Karnik, N., Vora, M., Ahmed, T., Singh, R.: Mobile Agent Programming in Ajanta. In: Proceedings of the 19th International Conference on Distributed Computing Systems. (1999) 190–197
6. Tripathi, A.R., Koka, M., Karanth, S., Pathak, A., Ahmed, T.: Secure Multi-Agent Coordination in a Network Monitoring System. In: Software Engineering for Large-Scale Multi-Agent Systems, 2002 (SELMAS 2002), Springer, LNCS 2603. (2003) 251–266
7. Tripathi, A., Ahmed, T., Kumar, R., Jaman, S.: Design of a Policy-Driven Middleware for Secure Distributed Collaboration. In: Proceedings of the 22nd International Conference on Distributed Computing Systems (ICDCS). (2002) 393–400
8. Tripathi, A., Ahmed, T., Kumar, R.: Specification of Secure Distributed Collaboration Systems. In: IEEE International Symposium on Autonomous Distributed Systems (ISADS). (2003) 149–156
9. Tripathi, A., Kulkarni, D., Ahmed, T.: A Specification Model for Context-Based Collaborative Applications. Elsevier Journal on Pervasive and Mobile Computing **1** (2005) 21–42
10. Sommerville, I.: Software Engineering 6th Edition. Pearson Education Asia (2002)
11. Clark, D.D.: The design philosophy of the DARPA internet protocols. In: SIG-COMM, Stanford, CA, ACM (1988) 106–114
12. Candea, G., Cutler, J., Fox, A.: Improving Availability with Recursive Micro-Reboots: A Soft-State System Case Study. Performance Evaluation Journal **56** (2004)
13. Rowanhill, J.C., Varner, P.E., Knight, J.C.: Efficient hierarchic management for reconfiguration of networked information systems. In: International Conference on Dependable Systems and Networks (DSN'04). (2004)
14. Mansouri-Samani, M., Sloman, M.: Monitoring Distributed Systems. IEEE Network (1993) 20–30
15. Ahmed, T., Tripathi, A.R.: Static Verification of Security Requirements in Role Based CSCW Systems. In: Proceedings of 8th ACM Symposium on Access Control Models and Technologies (SACMAT 2003), New York, ACM (2003) 196–203
16. Jennings, N.R.: An Agent-Based Approach for Building Complex Software Systems. Communications of the ACM (2001) 35–41
17. Jennings, N.R., Bussman, S.: Agent-based control systems: Why are they suited to engineering complex systems? IEEE Control Systems Magazine **23** (2003) 61–73
18. Zambonelli, F., Jennings, N.R., Wooldridge, M.: Organisational Abstractions for the Analysis and Design of Multi-Agent Systems. In: Agent Oriented Software Engineering. (2001)
19. IETF: Terminology for Policy-Based Management. In: RFC 3198. (2001)
20. IETF: Policy Core Information Model – Version 1 Specification. In: RFC 3060. (2001)
21. Ceri, S., Widom, J.: Deriving production rules for constraint maintenance. In: Proceedings of the sixteenth international conference on Very large databases, San Francisco, CA, USA, Morgan Kaufmann Publishers Inc. (1990) 566–577
22. Corradi, A., Dulay, N., Montanari, R., Stefanelli, C.: Policy-Driven Management of Agent Systems. In: Workshop on Policies for Distributed Systems and Networks (POLICY 2001). (2001) 214–229

23. Minsky, N., Ungureanu, V.: Law-Governed Interaction: A Coordination and Control Mechanism for Heterogeneous Distributed Systems. ACM Transactions on Software Engineering and Methodology (TOSEM) **9** (2000) 273 – 305
24. Lopez, F., Luck, M., d'Inverno, M.: A normative framework for agent-based systems. In: 1st International Symposium on Normative Multiagent Systems (NorMAS2005). (2005)
25. Jones, A., Sergot, M.: The characterisation of law and computer systems: The normative systems perspective. In: J.J.Ch. Meyer and R.J. Wieringa (eds.): Deontic Logic in Computer Science: Normative System Specification. John Wiley and Sons, Chicester. (1993) 275–307
26. Minsky, N.H., Murata, T.: On Manageability and Robustness of Open Multi-Agent Systems. In Lucena, C., Garcia, A., Romanovsky, A., Castro, J., Alencar, P., eds.: Proceedings of Computer Security, Dependability and Assurance LNCS, No. 2940, Springer-Verlag (2004) 189–206

Views: Middleware Abstractions for Context-Aware Applications in MANETs

Kurt Schelfthout, Tom Holvoet, and Yolande Berbers

K.U. Leuven - DistriNet - AgentWise taskforce,
Celestijnenlaan 200A, 3001 Leuven, Belgium
{Kurt.Schelfthout, Tom.Holvoet, Yolande.Berbers}@cs.kuleuven.be

Abstract. Programming applications for highly dynamic environments such as mobile ad hoc networks (MANETs) is complex, since the working context of applications changes continuously. This paper presents "views" as abstractions for representing and maintaining context information, tailored to applications in MANETs. An application agent can define a view by declaratively describing the context information it is interested in. A supporting middleware platform, called ObjectPlaces, ensures that the information represented by a view continuously reflects the agent's context information, despite the dynamic situation in a MANET. We elaborate on the distributed protocol that ObjectPlaces uses to maintain the information of views, and give an evaluation of the protocol's correctness and overhead.

1 Introduction

Given the increasing pervasiveness of networks due to the advent of wireless communication, the next generation of distributed systems presumes little network infrastructure, and is comprised of computing devices (nodes) that can be carried around, or are placed on moving vehicles. Mobile computing nodes connected in such an ad hoc way form a mobile ad hoc network (MANET) [1].

An application developed for MANETs necessarily consists of distributed agents that need to communicate among each other to achieve a common goal. Given the dynamics of a MANET, this communication between application agents is complex: the nodes on which these agents live are mobile, and can disappear from a conversation at any time. Dealing with this complexity at the application level is hard, so an application developer benefits greatly from a coordination middleware that offers high level mechanisms to manage communication among agents.

ObjectPlaces is a coordination middleware that supports a first order abstraction of an agent's context. For our purposes, an agent's context is the aggregate of all available information on currently reachable nodes in the MANET [2]. An agent's context thus changes because (1) information on a reachable node is changed, or (2) the set of reachable nodes changes. In ObjectPlaces, an agent can gather context by defining a *view*. A view is built by the middleware based on a declarative specification that describes "how far" over the network the view reaches, and in what information the viewing agent is interested.

A. Garcia et al. (Eds.): SELMAS 2005, LNCS 3914, pp. 17–34, 2006.

The most important property of a view is that it is an actively maintained structure, that changes as the agent's context changes. The agent can listen for new context events, e.g. the arrival of a new node carrying interesting information. A motivating example for such an active notion of context occurred in a real world application, wherein we are currently applying the ObjectPlaces middleware. In this application, automatic guided vehicles (AGVs) in a warehouse coordinate to transport goods [3]. AGVs communicate to avoid collisions (among other things); an AGV thus needs to be notified actively when another vehicle enters in a possible collision range. Other examples are rescue workers that want to be notified of incoming and leaving ambulances, battlefield scenarios where soldiers want to be notified of incoming transports, etc. If the middleware does not support an active context representation, the application programmer is forced to program such a representation using polling.

In the following section, we describe the ObjectPlaces middleware in more detail. Then we discuss its relation to existing coordination middleware. In Sect. 4 we describe a protocol to maintain a view in a MANET. Then, the ObjectPlaces middleware and specifically the notion of a view is evaluated analytically and empirically in Sect. 5. Finally, we conclude.

2   Views on Objectplaces

In ObjectPlaces, each agent can maintain "viewable data" in a local collection of objects called an *objectplace*[1]. The objects in an objectplace represent information that is of interest to other agents, and so contribute to the overall context information available. Other agents can gather copies of objects from objectplaces on nodes in their neighborhood using a *view*. In other words, context information is made available by putting it in a local objectplace, and can be gathered by building a view. Agents can coordinate by influencing each other's context, much like what happens in everyday traffic: when a car driver is going to take a right turn, he or she turns on the turning indicator. Other drivers can see this "context change", and react appropriately.

First we describe how an agent can manipulate its local objectplace, then views are described in more detail. The section is concluded with a discussion of ObjectPlaces in relation to existing work.

2.1   Manipulating an Objectplace

An objectplace by itself is basically a tuplespace variant: an objectplace is a set of objects that can be manipulated by operations such as put, read and take. Contrary to existing tuplespace approaches however, an objectplace has a fundamentally *asynchronous* interface: operations return control to the client immediately (an agent that uses the middleware is called a *client* of the middleware), and results are returned as they are available via a callback. This is important in order to allow views to be built efficiently and conveniently, see Sect. 3.

---

[1] "ObjectPlaces" - the middleware - is written in plural and with two capitals, "objectplace" - the software entity - is written without capitals.

For clarity, we have made two simplifications. First, although an objectplace can be manipulated remotely, for this paper the reader can assume that an objectplace is only locally accessible. Views, discussed in the next section, provide a way for clients to observe the contents of remote objectplaces. Second, although a client can create objectplaces at will, we assume that the middleware offers exactly one objectplace on each node.

Similar to tuplespaces, in order to read or take objects from an objectplace, clients indicate what objects they want to read by means of a *template*. A template is a function from the set of objects to a boolean value. Every object for which the template function returns true matches with the template.

The operations on an objectplace are the following:

put(Set, Callback) puts the given set of objects in the objectplace. Returns true to the callback if all objects were successfully added.

take(ObjectTmplt, Callback) removes the objects matching with the template from the objectplace and returns them to the callback.

watch(ObjectTmplt, EventTmplt, Lease, Callback) observes the content of the objectplace. Returns copies of objects matching the object template to the callback (the objectplace is not changed). The event template is used to indicate in what events on the matching object the client is interested in. Event template and lease are described in detail shortly.

A watch operation's event template can match with three possible events: isPresent, isPut or isTaken. If the event template matches with isPresent, the objectplace returns copies of all matching objects it currently contains to the callback, and returns the empty set if there are no matches (this is important for so-called test-for-absence operations, where the client needs to know there are no matching objects). If isPresent is the only event with which the event template matches, the watch operation is finished. However, when the event template also matches with isPut or isTaken, the objectplace must return copies of matching objects that are either put in or taken from the objectplace. In order to do so, the operation is registered by the objectplace, and when an appropriate event occurs on an object matched by the object template, the client is notified. An event template that matches with isPresent and isPut for example, first returns copies of objects currently contained in the objectplace. When new matching objects are put in the objectplace, copies of these are returned in a subsequent call to the callback. Objects returned to the callback are also annotated with the event that occurred on the object, so the client can distinguish between events.

To unregister watch operations that are waiting for an event, a watch can be provided with a Lease object. A client calls the discard operation on the Lease to unregister the corresponding watch operation. The same lease can be given as an argument to more than one watch; in that case, upon discard all these operations are unregistered atomically.

2.2   Views

A view is a local collection of objects, reflecting the contents of multiple objectplaces on reachable nodes in the network based on a declarative specification. This collection is continuously updated by the middleware, both with respect to changing contents of the objectplaces in the view, as with respect to changes in the network topology. A view thus represents the context of the viewing agent.

To build a view, a client specifies:

A distance metric and a bound determines "how far" over the network the client's view will reach. An example is a hop count-metric with a bound of three: the view will span objectplaces reachable in a maximum of three hops from the node where the view is issued.

An object template constrains what objects will be included in the view.

Given these parameters, the ObjectPlaces middleware searches the network for nodes satisfying the constraints (using the protocol described in Sect. 4). On these nodes' objectplaces, a `watch` operation with the given object template is executed. The `watch`'s event template matches with all possible events. The results of all these watch operations, which are events indicating the presence, arrival or removal of objects in an objectplace, are sent to the node issuing the view. This allows the viewing node to keep the view up to date with respect to changes in the content of the participating objectplaces. Changes in the network are handled by managing the watch registrations on the nodes in the view. When it is detected that a node moves out of the view, the view's watch on the objectplace of that node is unregistered, and the viewing node is notified; when a node moves into the view, a watch on its objectplace is registered and consequently the viewing node is notified as well, see Fig. 1. How this detection is done is discussed in Sect. 4. A view is actively maintained in this way until it is released by the client. Any client on any node can build a view, and clients can specify as many views as they want. Each client can have its own set of views to observe the context that it is interested in.

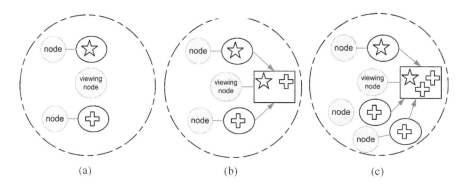

(a)   (b)   (c)

Fig. 1. Circles denote nodes, ovals denote objectplaces, and the rectangle denotes a view. The other shapes represent data objects. (a) A viewing node declares a new view. The circle denotes the bound on the distance metric and so the nodes from which the middleware will gather data for this particular view. (b) The middleware has gathered the appropriate data, and the view is built. (c) A new node enters the zone, so the view is updated with the new data object that the node carries in its objectplace.

A client can not only specify constraints on the content of the view based on its interests, the content can also be represented in a client specific way (e.g. as a sorted collection). In its raw form, a view is built out of the events generated by the watch operations on the participating nodes, as well as events generated by the middleware when a node leaves or joins the view. Users of the middleware can program their own representation using these raw events. For example, we have provided an implementation of a view as a collection, supporting a collection interface common in object-oriented API's (i.e. `java.util.Collection` in Java). This allows sorting and iterating over the collection for example. The collection is updated as `watch` events are generated, e.g. when an `isPut` is received, the corresponding objects are added to the collection. Usually, a view is described as such a collection in this paper, since it is the most common usage pattern. Other representations of a view can be an accumulation to a single value, e.g. the average of an attribute of the objects in the view, or translating objects in the view to objects the agent understands, to deal with heterogeneous agents. Both the contents and the representation of a view can thus be customized.

As an example, suppose a car arriving at an intersection wants to know the positions of other cars, since the car has to give way from the right. It builds a view on all cars within 50 meters (distance metric and bound), containing position and car id objects (object template). The car chooses a sorted list as representation, closest car first. A traffic monitor nearby also builds a view on nearby cars, and car id objects, but accumulates the car id's in a counter for traffic information purposes. In both cases, the content of the view is partly the same (car id's), but the representation is different (a sorted list, vs. a count of the unique id's).

In conclusion, a view is a powerful abstraction that can be put to good use for coordination, since it is an active representation of a agent's context. A view takes the heterogeneous nature of a MANET into account, because both the contents and the representation of a view can be tailored to each client's wishes.

3   Discussion and Related Work

The ObjectPlaces middleware can be seen as a hybrid between two well known approaches for coordination: publish/subscribe systems and tuplespaces. In order to characterize the difference between publish/subscribe (P/S) and tuplespaces (TS) systems for MANETs, we first define some terminology. The coordination middleware imposes two forms of coupling on its clients: *space coupling* and *time coupling*. Clients are considered to be coupled in space if the knowledge they have about each other's location during communication is high. For example, request/reply communication is highly coupled in space: both sender and receiver need to know where the other is (e.g. address and port number).

Clients are considered coupled in time if they need to be up at the same time in order to receive or send a message. Request/reply communication is again highly coupled in time: if one of the communicating parties is disconnected, the message cannot be delivered. Coupling in time is related to failure semantics of message delivery: the longer the receiver can be disconnected from the sender while the message can still be received, or in other words, the higher the persistence of a message, the higher time uncoupling a certain coordination model provides.

For MANETs, the middleware must be able to uncouple clients as much as possible, both in space - due to the dynamic nature, it is impossible to predict with whom to interact - and in time - nodes may join and leave the network dynamically.

Another way to contrast coordination middleware is whether a certain sender can *push* messages to a receiver (i.e. notify him) and if a receiver can *pull* messages from the sender (i.e. polling). Generally, both forms should be possible: if there is only information-push, unnecessary messages may be sent to receivers who are not interested; if there is only information-pull, there could be wasted bandwidth due to unnecessary polling by the receiver.

Now, publish/subscribe systems and tuplespace systems are described, and evaluated for MANET applications with respect to the characteristics mentioned above. Also, existing coordination models for MANETs are discussed and compared to the Object-Places middleware.

In a **publish/subscribe (P/S)** system (e.g. [4,5]), publishers send notifications of state changes to a list of subscribers. Subscribers are not known in advance but let the P/S middleware know of their interest in certain events through the use of subscriptions. The P/S middleware handles the delivery of notifications to the right subscribers.

P/S systems are uncoupled in space: a publisher publishes events, not knowing with whom it communicates; a subscriber is handed some event in which it is interested, equally unaware of the originator of the message. Senders can push information to receivers, so that receivers only get notified when necessary. P/S systems are coupled in time: both publisher and subscriber need to be active at the same time in order to transmit an event. This is especially a problem in ad hoc networks since new nodes arrive in the network regularly. Previous events were not delivered to these newcomers, which either leads to a slower startup time (waiting until the publisher changes state and sends an event), or a regular publication of events by the publisher especially for possible newcomers. These events are unnecessary since the publisher has not changed state.

This problem is implicitly addressed in various work in P/S systems. For example, [6] describes that, due to the appearance and reappearance of hosts, there is a phase immediately after reconnection in which a mobile subscriber needs to subscribe to events and wait until some events get fired until it can reassess the current state of the network. Buffers and virtual clients are introduced to subscribe to past events and events in future locations respectively. Generally, the problem of time coupling is handled through buffers which are assumed to be reliable and fixed, e.g. [7] [8] [9]. Such an infrastructure is however not available in MANETs.

STEAM [10] is a P/S middleware for MANETs where subscribers can not only filter events on their content and subject, but also on location. STEAM defines proximities that are areas around a certain publisher, where subscribers can listen to events from that publisher. Publishers need to send events periodically to account for possible newly arrived subscribers.

ObjectPlaces can be seen as a P/S variant: a view is a subscription to events on objectplaces in the vicinity of a client. Clients "publish events" by manipulating objects in their local objectplace, which triggers watch operations of views that are observing that objectplace. The resulting events are then delivered to viewing clients. However, the problem of disconnection and reconnection is solved elegantly in ObjectPlaces, since a message is always stored in an objectplace. Newly arrived clients can thus be brought up to date immediately by querying neighboring objectplaces using a view. At the same time, the view subscribes to events on the objectplace, and so keeps the viewing client up to date in the future as well. The objectplaces thus act as a buffer in which clients can store observable state. Senders are relieved of having to send events periodically.

Tuplespaces (TS) systems, with Linda [11] as a first incarnation, provide a shared collection of data, called tuples, and a set of operations (read, write, take) on the collection to manipulate the data. Throughout the years, Linda has spawned many variants, e.g. [12] [13].

Because Linda's synchronous, polling model did not provide some essential primitives for distributed programming (where asynchronous interaction is more efficient and convenient), several variants were created that add asynchronous primitives, e.g. [14][12][13]. Modern implementations thus acknowledge the information-pull problem by providing extra primitives that allow an event-based style of interaction with the tuplespace. An objectplace expands on this idea by making *all* operations fundamentally event-driven and asynchronous. This greatly simplifies the maintenance of a view. It also allows the maintenance to be done efficiently, since network messages are only sent if there was a change. No costly polling is necessary.

TS provide time uncoupling: sender and receiver do not need to be active at the same time since the tuplespace stores their messages until removed. Concerning space coupling, although sender and receiver do not need to know each other, they do have to know in which tuplespace their interaction will occur. No system that we know of tries to implement a globally shared tuplespace in a distributed system (this would be impractical since any query would have to search the complete network), so interaction is confined to a certain tuplespace on a certain host the client has to know about beforehand. Tuplespace interaction entails more space coupling between clients than P/S systems: TS only provide identity uncoupling. Space coupling is especially a problem in MANETs, since it is a priori unknown with which nodes a client will interact.

Work in tuplespace variants for MANETs has acknowledged these problems. Lime [15] is a middleware for mobile agents and mobile hosts that attaches a personal tuplespace to each agent in the application, and shares these tuplespaces transparently when two agents are on the same or on connected hosts. In ObjectPlaces, views provide better control: an agent can select exactly in which information on which hosts it is interested. Moreover, several agents can have different views, each tailored to its own wishes.

The LIME middleware was extended fairly recently in EgoSpaces [2]. In EgoSpaces, clients can (similarly as in ObjectPlaces) build a view over the locally available network, based on a distance metric. We see two improvements made in ObjectPlaces. First, EgoSpaces' view is always represented as a tuplespace (supporting primitives like in, inp, . . .). In ObjectPlaces, the representation of the view can be tailored to the client's wishes (e.g. a sorted collection), thus providing better support for heterogeneous agents. Second, an EgoSpaces view is mainly used as a one-shot query: generally, the view is not maintained actively. While it is possible to register reactions on a view in EgoSpaces, these can react "only" to incoming tuples [16]. It is unclear how an agent can be notified of a tuple *leaving* it's view (except by polling), a necessary precondition for building an up to date client-side representation such as in ObjectPlaces. Also, a quite elaborate construction has to be set up to maintain an active view in EgoSpaces [16]. ObjectPlaces provides lightweight active views that are actively maintained by default (a "one-shot view" is a special case of the views described in this paper).

TOTA [17] (Tuples On The Air) is a middleware that provides applications with the notion of a self-maintaining distributed tuple. Each node in the network hosts a tuplespace. A distributed tuple is propagated to nearby nodes, and can be changed with each propagation according to an application-specific rule (e.g. counting the number of hops from the root). This tuple is then maintained by the middleware as the network changes. In a way, TOTA does exactly the reverse of ObjectPlaces: instead of gathering objects from neighboring nodes, TOTA spreads objects (or tuples) to neighboring nodes. An important difference with ObjectPlaces is that a view is specific for every client, while a distributed tuple is the same for all observers. In other words, while in TOTA the "sender" of a message (the agent that adds a distributed tuple) determines both who it reaches and what the content is, in ObjectPlaces the "receivers" of a message (the clients that build a view) can determine both content and representation. We believe this makes ObjectPlaces better suited to deal with heterogeneous application domains.

In conclusion, ObjectPlaces takes the best of both P/S and TS systems, and so overcomes the difficulties of both approaches for MANETs. An objectplace, by offering asynchronous operations, acts as a generator of events, which get transported to interested clients through views. However, a view also gathers the current content of objectplaces, so clients building a view are immediately up to date. Clients of the ObjectPlaces middleware are thus uncoupled in time (a local objectplace acts as a buffer), uncoupled in space (building a view requires no information about agents participating in the view), offers an information-pull mechanism (a view gathers information from neighboring objecplaces), and an information-push mechanism (manipulating a local objectplace, which triggers an event on watching views). In addition, the representation of a view can be tailored to the application agent's wishes, and a view is actively maintained by the middleware automatically.

A final note about ontology. ObjectPlaces neither restricts nor supports the definition of the contents of the exchanged objects. Making sure that different agents on different nodes can understand the objects exchanged through views is the responsibility of some higher abstraction layer, or the application. For a generic approach for defining a common ontology in a tuplespace-like scenario we refer to [18].

4   View Protocol

The construction of a view in a MANET requires a distributed protocol that is able to find and maintain a set of reachable nodes in the network given a bound on a distance metric. This means that the protocol should be able to: (1) notify the viewing node when a node enters or leaves the view (2) register and deregister watch operations on nodes entering and leaving the view respectively; (3) route the events generated by the watch operations to the node where the view was defined. Existing ad hoc routing protocols (for an overview, we refer to [1]) are not adequate because they can only provide a fixed "distance metric" (usually hop count). Since the distance metric used for building the view is application specific and determined at runtime, we need a protocol that does fit our requirements. This protocol can be viewed as an alternative to the one proposed in [2].

We assume from the underlying network layer that: *(1)* a single-hop broadcast is available that broadcasts a message to all nodes within communication reach, represented by the function *broadcast (message)*; *(2)* a reliable single-hop unicast that sends a message to a designated node within communication reach, represented by the function *unicast(message, $id_{receiver}$)*. We can reasonably expect these functions to be built based on data link standards such as IEEE802.11 [19].

Algorithm 1. The view protocol

Process Root:

on timeout t_{br}

1: $removeOutdated(participants, f_p.t_{br})$

2: $broadcast(dist\_msg(id_{view}, 0, id_{root}))$

on receive content message c

3: $updateTime(participants, timestamp(c), c.id_{sender})$

4: $updateView(participants, c.events)$

5:

Process Participant:

on timeout t_{br}

6: $removeOutdated(neighbors, f_n.t_{br})$

7: $id_{parent} = findParent(neighbors)$

8: $d_{current} = calculateDistance(neighbors, id_{parent})$

9: **if** $d_{current} \leq bound$ **then**

10:    $broadcast(dist\_msg(id_{view}, d_{current}, id_{participant}))$

11:    $events = objplace.watch(object\ template, allEvents, cb)$

12:    $unicast(cont\_msg(id_{view}, events, id_{participant}), id_{parent})$

13: **else**

14:    $alive = false$

15:    $stop\ timer$

on receive distance message d

16: $updateTime(neighbors, timestamp(d), d.id_{sender})$

17: $updateDistance(neighbors, d.distance, d.id_{sender})$

18: $alive = true$

19: $start\ timer$

on receive content message c

20: **if** alive **then**

21:    $unicast(c, id_{parent})$

The data structures necessary for the protocol are depicted in Table 1, while the protocol is depicted as Algorithm 1. The protocol builds and maintains a shortest path spanning tree, starting on the node with the client issuing the view, called the root. This tree determines which nodes are included in the view - these are called the participants in the view. In the text and in Algorithm 1 the protocol is described as if there is only one view - this is only for expository purposes. In reality this protocol is executed for every view in which a node participates. That is why with each message a unique view

Table 1. Contents of data structures and communication messages

Root	Participant	Distance msg	Content msg
id_{view}	id_{view}	id_{view}	id_{view}
$participants = \{(id_{participant},$	$neighbors = \{(id_{neighbor},$	id_{sender}	id_{sender}
$\quad timestamp, \{object\})\}$	$\quad timestamp, distance)\}$	distance	$\{event\}$
distance metric, bound	$id_{parent}, d_{current}$		
object template	distance metric, bound		
	object template		

id, id_{view} is transmitted. The data structures in Table 1 are also for one single view, and are duplicated for every view in which a node participates.

The length of a path is determined by the distance metric, which is a parameter of the protocol. This allows building a shortest path based on hop count, but also on any other distance metric such as physical distance, or bandwidth. The only constraint on the distance metric is that it should increase monotonically the further it gets propagated from the root, to ensure that the distance does not grow out of bounds as it gets propagated in a loop. Such a metric can always be chosen, by including a hop count with any other metric the client chooses (e.g. physical distance) [2].

The view building process starts when a client issues a view. The node on which this client is located is responsible for building and maintaining it, and is the root for that view. The root first builds a unique id for the view, consisting of its own id and a sequence number that is unique on each node. Two activities now occur in parallel: the building and maintaining of the shortest path spanning tree, and the building and maintaining of the contents of the view. The contents of the view is maintained at the root and consists of a list of participants and the objects each participant's objectplace currently contains.

The spanning tree. To build and maintain the spanning tree, the root and all participants regularly broadcast distance messages. This allows participants to determine what their distance is from the root ($d_{current}$), given the view's distance metric. The root starts the tree-building process by broadcasting a distance message with the id of the new view, its own id and a distance of zero (line 2). Nodes that receive a distance message check whether they are participants in the view. To this end, each participant maintains a list of its neighbors - nodes from which it has recently received a distance message. Upon receipt of a distance message, the participant records the time the distance message was received from that neighbor (function $updateTime$, l. 16), and the distance that neighbor broadcasted (function $updateDistance$, l.17). The participant sets the *alive* variable to indicate it should check whether it is in a view, and starts a timer (if the participant already was in the view, these have no effect).

After every broadcast period, given by t_{br}, a participant recalculates its distance from the root based on its list of neighbors. First, neighbors for which the timestamp of the distance message that was last received is older than a given timeout, are removed (using $removeOutdated$, l.6). This timeout is given as a neighbor freshness factor f_n that is multiplied with t_{br} to determine the actual timeout. The participant then determines the neighbor that is closest to the root using $findParent$ (l.7). Based on its parent's distance, it calculates its own distance from the root $d_{current}$ using the distance metric (1.8). If it is within the bound, it broadcasts a distance message itself (1.10), and repeats the process every t_{br} time to account for changes in the tree. Otherwise, it goes to sleep, waiting for new distance messages to come in that might change the situation (1.14-15). The end result of this protocol is that each node regularly checks whether or not is in the view, and knows a parent in the tree which is the closest to the root of all its neighbors.

The contents of the view. Each node that is in the view, determines the objects it contributes to the view by executing a `watch` operation on its local objectplace. The resulting events of this `watch` are transported to the root using content messages. The *events* variable is the set of buffered events at the participant that have not been sent to the root yet (we are stretching notation in line 11, since these events are actually sent to callback *cb*). A node that receives such a content message from one of its children forwards it to its parent, so that it reaches the root (1.21). The root maintains a list of participants of the view. For each content message it receives, it updates the objects that participant contributes to the view (using *updateView*, 1.4). It also records the reception timestamp of each content message (1.3), and removes those participants it hasn't heard from for $f_p.t_{br}$ time, where f_p is the freshness of the participants (1.1). This means that participants must periodically send a content message to the root, even when there are no events to be returned ($events = \{\}$) to ensure that the root does not consider them out of the view (1.12).

This protocol tolerates mobility of any node and disappearance of participants. New nodes are discovered by the periodic broadcasting of the distance messages. Nodes that should be removed from view are detected because they discover for themselves that they don't have any more neighbors, or their distance has gone out of bounds. Changes in the spanning tree are similarly detected through exchange of distance messages.

Using the spanning tree to deliver events. When sending content messages, the spanning tree is actually used as a multi-hop routing tree to the root. Although the shortest path from participant to root may not always be known, at least some path exists (possibly temporarily containing cycles) and events are delivered as long as every node on the path forwards the content message to its parent.

However, in the case where a node that received an event goes down before forwarding the event, the event is lost. To compensate for this loss, one can choose to use a reliable link protocol from node to root, such as the alternating 1-bit protocol. Each event received by the root would then have to be acknowledged before the node can send another event. Although this makes the protocol reliable, it also induces additional overhead. One possible solution is to use unreliable best-effort event delivery, which may be tolerable for some applications where the view may be slightly incorrect or out of date. Regularly, the view may be "flushed" and current state from all nodes is sent again.

Propagation of other parameters. The parameters of the view, such as the distance metric, also need to be sent from the root to the participants. This was not discussed, but is done in a straightforward way: whenever a node receives a distance message with an id_{view} it does not know, it requests the relevant view parameters from the sender of the distance message. When the node determines it is not in the view, it may delete this information - or decide to keep it for a while longer because it might become a participant in the view later. We do not elaborate further.

5   Evaluation

The following parameters influence the correctness and the performance of the view: *(1)* the broadcast period t_{br}, *(2)* the freshness for neighbors f_n, and *(3)* the freshness for participants f_p. Instead of letting the application designer choose these experimentally, we mathematically derive bounds on these parameters, supporting the designer in making the right trade-offs.

The view protocol is influenced by uncontrollable factors concerning the dynamics of MANETs. In order to keep the presentation clear, we focus on the dynamics of the network only - in other words we assume for the rest of this section that the contents of the objectplaces stays the same. We focus on this problem because this is where any problems and bad assumptions will be revealed. Specifically, we take into account the number of nodes on a given area and the speed of these nodes. The speed influences how busy the protocol will be updating changes, and the concentration determines connectivity, or the number of nodes in the view.

We study how accurately the protocol can represent the perfect view, which is obtained by "stopping time" and comparing the view the protocol built at that time with how the view should look, given the current position and connectivity of the nodes. There are two kinds of errors: *false exclusions*, objects that are not in the view but should be; and *false inclusions*, objects that should not be in the view but are. Then, we look at overhead induced by distance messages, and describe some results from simulations.

5.1   False Exclusions

A false exclusion occurs when a node enters the view, while the view didn't notice the new arrival yet. The critical parameter to minimize this kind of false exclusion is the broadcast period. When this period is short enough, a new node entering the view receives a distance message from a neighbor early, and the view updates fast. Suppose nodes have communication range r, and relative speed v_r, and we want to detect a node when it has traveled at most distance l into communication range of any participant. The worst case scenario occurs when an undetected node moves straight at another in the view. In this case, the maximum broadcast period to ensure that a node is detected is:

$$t_{br} \leq \frac{r - l}{v_r}$$

with no transmission delay and no message loss.

Supposing a message can get lost with probability p_{loss}, then the minimum broadcast period to ensure that a node is detected at a distance l with minimum probability p_{detect} is:

$$t_{br} \leq \frac{r - l}{n.v_r}$$

with n the number of resends until a probability of receiving a message p_{detect} is reached. From the inequality $p_{detect} \geq 1 - p_{loss}^n$ it follows that

$$n \geq \frac{\log(1 - p_{detect})}{\log p_{loss}}$$

To incorporate message delays, these bounds should be tighter: one should subtract the message delay from a node to its neighbor and subtract the delay to send the contents from the new participant to the root.

Another kinds of false exclusion occurs when the root removes a participant while it should not, because a content message did not reach the root in time. We write the duration it takes to send a message i as $t_{d,i}$ (from the start of sending to the end of receiving), the time of reception of message i as $t_{rec,i}$ and the freshness of a participant as f_p. For each two consecutive content messages 1 and 2 it should be true at the root that $t_{rec,2} \leq t_{rec,1} + f_p.t_{br}$, otherwise a participant is removed in error. After some calculation, this becomes: $t_{d,2} - t_{d,1} \leq (f_p - 1).t_{br}$. This inequality gives a lower bound for both the freshness and the broadcast period. The inequality shows that the bound is dependent on the *difference* between two delays only. This means that if the delay increases fairly slowly, the protocol adapts to this increase. Only when the delay suddenly increases with a value of $(f_p - 1).t_{br}$ does a false exclusion result. In other words, the broadcast period and the freshness determine the robustness of the protocol to message delays and congestion.

The upper and lower bound described above show the tradeoff between accuracy and performance. The smaller the broadcast period, the more accurate and responsive the view becomes. However, sending more messages affects the performance, and causes congestion. Choosing a small broadcast period and freshness also causes errors in the view by decreasing the protocol's tolerance for delays. The bounds given accurately characterize the trade-off to make and so support the designer in his or her decisions.

5.2   False Inclusion

False inclusion occurs when a node moves out of range or out of distance of the view, while the view still contains the node's contents. Two parameters influence this: the broadcast period t_{br} and the freshness of the participants f_p. Two scenarios exist.

In the first scenario, a node that is in the view moves out of communication range. The time it takes to detect this is maximum $f_p.t_{br} + t_d$, where t_d is the total transmission delay to successfully send a content message from the node to the root.

In the second scenario, the node is within communication range but for some reason the network changes and the node is out of the view (i.e. it's distance becomes greater than the bound on the view distance). The node is still within communication range with other nodes in the view. The total time it takes to remove this node from the view is $t_{br} + t_d + f_p.t_{br}$, so a broadcast period longer than the first scenario since it is only after this time that the node's parent broadcasts a new distance, so the node realizes that its distance from the root has changed.

Concluding, in order to minimize errors, the broadcast period and the freshness should be as low as possible. However, as was shown in the previous section, this makes the protocol more brittle. A similar trade-off must thus be made.

5.3   Overhead

The overhead incurred by the protocol is caused by the periodical broadcasting of distance messages. Content messages are the actual objects that are transferred, and thus represent the useful content of the communication channel. How many bandwidth is taken up by content messages is entirely up to the application: an application that builds far-reaching views on large objects that are changed frequently obviously consumes more bandwidth than a close-by view on small objects. Consequently, we focus our attention on the overhead incurred by distance messages.

An upper bound for the number of distance messages broadcast dm on a shared communication channel with v views, each of them spanning maximum n nodes is:

$$dm = v.n.\frac{1}{t_{br}}$$

Given that a distance message consists of three 4 byte long data structures (see Table 1: two integers and an IP address), the bandwidth taken up by distance messages can be calculated.

As an example, suppose a 1 Mb/s (IEEE802.11 offers bandwidth between 1 and 11 Mb/s) wireless channel should accommodate 50 views, each spanning 10 nodes, where each node broadcasts a distance message twice per second. This uses 96Kb/s on the channel, representing about 10% of the channel's capacity. For a relatively low bandwidth channel with many quickly updating views, we feel this overhead is acceptable. Furthermore, as is shown in the next section, actual overhead is lower (the above formula provides an upper bound, since the number of nodes in a view varies).

5.4   Simulations

The goal of the simulations is to evaluate whether a MANET is able to sustain a view-like concept. Instead of focussing on achieving a detailed simulation that conforms to reality as much as possible, we instead opted for a more straightforward approach that exposes the reasons behind problems more easily, while still reflecting the most important realities in a MANET.

In the simulations, N nodes move around randomly on a rectangular area of size $l.w$, with a constant speed v. Each node has a predefined transmission range r. A receiver node within that range can receive messages from the sending node. Sending and receiving messages takes time, resp. t_{send} and t_{rec}. Nodes move a distance every second. All other activities occur instantly. Of the nodes moving around, one root node tries to build a view with a distance metric that increases one unit with each hop, and a bound denoted by d (in other words, we want the content of all objectplaces within d hops). All nodes have an objectplace which contains exactly one object. This never changes - we focus again on the dynamism of the network, not of the objectplaces' content. All results are obtained by doing 10 runs for t_{sim} minutes each with identical parameters, and then averaging the results. The parameters are summarized in table 2.

First, the influence of the speed and concentration of the nodes on the number of errors in the view is studied, fixing $d = 3$. In Fig. 2(a) we see the total number of seconds a view is wrong versus the number of nodes on the given area, for different

Table 2. Simulation parameters

$l.w$	size of area	$100.100m^2$
t_{sim}	duration of the simulation	30 minutes
r	transmission range of the nodes	$20m$
N	number of nodes	variable
v	node speed	variable
d	range of the view in hops	variable
t_{send}, t_{rec}	duration of send and receive	$50ms$

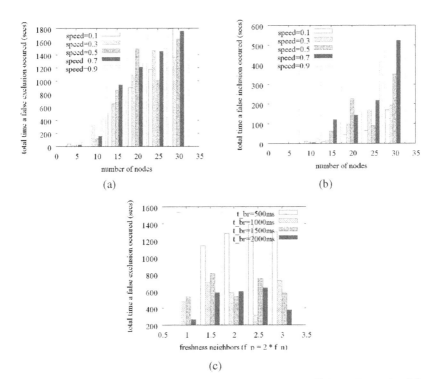

Fig. 2. (a) False exclusions vs speed, (b) False inclusions vs speed, (c) False exclusion for different broadcast periods and freshness, with $f_p = 2.f_n$

speeds, due to false exclusions and false inclusions. The speed does not influence the error significantly, but the concentration does. This is as expected, because the broadcast period was set to 500ms, which gives the view plenty of time to update given the range of speeds we are looking at. However, we see that the number of views that are wrong due to false exclusions is very high with higher concentration of nodes. The reason for this is congestion: too many nodes in the view mean that content messages are not reaching the root in time, which causes the root to remove participants in error. This is due to the fact that $f_p = 1$, which is the most unforgiving value possible (see Sect. 5.1).

To find a good trade-off, we fixed $v = 0.5\frac{m}{s}$, $d = 3$ and $N = 25$, a scenario that gave quite some errors in the previous tests. We also set $f_p = 2.f_n$, because as the content messages are multi-hop, they are more susceptible to delay. As can be seen in Fig. 2(c), the combination of freshness and broadcast period influences the correctness of the view greatly. Good values for this particular scenario seem to be $t_{br} = 2000ms$ and $f_n = 1$, or alternatively $t_{br} = 1000ms$ and $f_n = 2.5$. As was shown in the analysis, a shorter broadcast period and smaller freshness do not increase the accuracy of the view: on the contrary, they cause congestion which does more harm than good. The improvement obtained by choosing a higher broadcast period alone is remarkable, and stresses the importance of this parameter.

So far, we have looked at the total number of seconds a view is wrong, and have been able to reduce this time from 100% to about 16% of the total duration. Although these numbers don't look very promising, the criteria for marking a view as wrong are harsh: if only one object is missing, or should be missing but is included, the whole view is "wrong". However, such a view may still be accurate enough to be used for practical purposes.

In order to know *how wrong* the view actually is, we measured the total duration a node is falsely in- or excluded, and the average size of the view measured in the number of nodes included per second, for the same runs as the previous experiment. We found that the number of nodes in the view was on average 8 nodes (averaged over time). The number of falsely excluded nodes per second is 3.50. The protocol manages to build the perfect view 84% of the time, and gathers contents from 70% of the content it should gather the rest of the time. Similar results are obtained for false inclusions, where the problem was less severe to begin with.

We also measured the message overhead in the simulations. Similarly as in Sect. 5.3, we measure the bandwidth used by distance messages. For these experiments, t_{br} was set to 500ms, and $f_p = f_n = 1$. The speed of the nodes does not have any influence on the overhead (which it shouldn't, since nodes broadcast at a constant pace irrespective of their speed). The number of nodes, however, does: in Table 3, the overhead in bps (bits per second) is shown, and the percentage of the bandwidth this would use on a shared channel of 1Mbps. As can be seen, the overhead is 0,2% at the highest. This is again for only one view; for multiple views, the numbers can simply be multiplied by the number of views, since without optimizations each view sends out its own distance messages. Also note that the overhead % is pessimistic, since it assumes that all nodes send on the same shared channel, while in reality, due to sending range restrictions, two far-away nodes can be sending simultaneously without interference. For the example given in Sect. 5.3, 10 nodes with 50 views and t_{br} equal to 500 ms, the overhead on a 1Mbps second is thus $0.05\% \times 50 = 2.5\%$, significantly lower than the worst case of 10%.

The results are workable for applications where network infrastructure is not available (e.g. search and rescue scenarios) or where a best effort approach is tolerable

Table 3. Overhead of distance messages

Number of Nodes	5	10	15	20	25	30
Overhead bps	343	512	771	1169	1645	1985
Overhead %	0.03%	0.05%	0.08%	0.12%	0.16%	0.20%

(e.g. calling a cab via a PDA). The ObjectPlaces middleware was implemented in Java. An implementation in Java Micro Edition should pose no significant challenges. Also, the communication overhead induced is certainly acceptable. We believe that there are no objections to use ObjectPlaces on a wide range of resource constrained devices, to support a wide range of applications that need to be context-aware.

However, the described protocol is but one way of supporting a view; in the automatic guided vehicle application discussed in the introduction, we are actually using a wireless network with access points in order to improve the reliability of communication. Collision avoidance is an application in which a best effort approach is not adequate. The concepts ObjectPlaces offers remain the same and retain their strengths for mobile applications; only the underlying implementation differs.

6   Conclusion

This paper discussed a middleware system for MANETs that provides a powerful abstraction of context to the application. In ObjectPlaces, agents coordinate by building a view on information made available by remote agents in the network. The view is actively maintained, and is client-specific both in contents and in representation. We presented a distributed protocol that maintains such a view in a MANET, and showed acceptable performance results, mainly focussing on the accuracy of the view. While for the construction of a view we necessarily take a best-effort approach, it was shown that good insight in the working of the protocol helps performance.

An interesting direction for future work is to provide to the application using the view an indication of how good the view represents reality at this point in time - in other words, estimate the accuracy of the view and show this to the application. This estimate can for example be based on a node's location and a known probability distribution of the nodes in space, or can be learned through experience. This is useful where the accuracy of the view is important. If nodes know the view is probably wrong, they can move more slowly or change the broadcast frequency in order to increase the accuracy.

References

1. Royer, E., Toh, C.K.: A review of current routing protocols for ad-hoc mobile wireless networks. IEEE Personal Communications (1999)
2. Roman, G.C., Julien, C., Huang, Q.: Network abstractions for context-aware mobile computing. In: Proceedings of 24th International Conference on Software Engineering. (2002) 363–373
3. Weyns, D., Schelfthout, K., Holvoet, T., Lefever, T.: Decentralized control of E'GV transportation systems. In: Proceedings of AAMAS 2005 - Industry Track, Utrecht, The Netherlands (2005)
4. Carzaniga, A., Rosenblum, D.S., Wolf, A.L.: Design and evaluation of a wide-area event notification service. ACM Trans. on Computer Systems **19** (2001) 332–383
5. Segall, B., Arnold, D.: Elvin has left the building: A publish/subscribe notification service with quenching. In: AUUG 97. (1997)
6. Cilia, M., Fiege, L., Haul, C., Zeidler, A., Buchmann, A.P.: Looking into the past: enhancing mobile publish/subscribe middleware. In: Proceedings of the 2nd international workshop on Distributed event-based systems. (2003)

7. Fiege, L., Gärtner, F.C., Kasten, O., Zeidler, A.:   Supporting mobility in content-based publish/subscribe middleware.   In: Proceedings of the ACM/IFIP/USENIX International Middleware Conference. (2003)

8. Cugola, G., Jacobsen, H.A.: Using publish/subscribe middleware for mobile systems. ACM SIGMOBILE Mobile Computing and Communications Rev. **6** (2002) 25 – 33

9. Sun Microsystems, Inc.: Java message service spec. 1.1 (2002)

10. Meier, R., Cahill, V.: Exploiting proximity in event-based middleware for collaborative mobile applications. In: Proceedings of the 4th IFIP International Conference on Distributed Applications and Interoperable Systems (DAIS'03), Springer-Verlag Heidelberg, Germany (2003)

11. Carriero, N., Gelernter, D., Leichter, J.: Distributed data structures in linda. In: Proc. 13th ACM Symposium on Principles of Programming Languages. (1986)

12. Cabri, G., Leonardi, L., Zambonelli, F.: Mars: A programmable coordination architecture for mobile agents. IEEE Internet Computing **4** (2000) 26–35

13. Sun Microsystems, Inc.: The javaspaces v1.2.1 spec. (2002)

14. Rowstron, A.: Using asynchronous tuple space access primitives (bonita primitives) for process coordination. In Garlan, D., Mtayer, D.L., eds.: LNCS 1282: Coordination Languages and Models (Coordination'97), Springer-Verlag (1997) 426–429

15. Murphy, A., Picco, G.P., Roman, G.C.:   Lime: a middleware for physical and logical mobility.   In: Proc. of the 21th International Conference on Distributed Computing Systems (ICDCS-21). (2001)

16. Julien, C., Roman, G.: Active coordination in ad hoc networks. In: Proceedings of the 6th International Conference on Coordination Models and Languages. (2004)

17. Mamei, M., Zambonelli, F.: Self-maintained distributed tuples for field-based coordination in dynamic networks. In: The 19th Symposium on Applied Computing (SAC 04). (2004)

18. Blake, M.: Agent-based communication for distributed workflow management using jini technologies. International Journal on Artificial Intelligence Tools **12** (2003) 81–99

19. IEEE Computer Society LAN MAN Standards Committee: Wireless lan medium access control (MAC) and physical layer (PHY) specifications. IEEE Std 802.11-1997 (1997)

An Adaptive Distributed Layout for Multi-agent Applications

Koenraad Mertens, Tom Holvoet, and Yolande Berbers

AgentWise, Distrinet, Department of Computer Science, K.U. Leuven
Celestijnenlaan 200A, B-3001 Leuven, Belgium
Koenraad.Mertens@cs.kuleuven.be, Tom.Holvoet@cs.kuleuven.be,
Yolande.Berbers@cs.kuleuven.be

Abstract. A multiagent application consists of an environment and a number of agents. The environment contains information that the agents use and manipulate to do their work. When a multiagent system is decentralized over a number of different hosts (*i.e.* more than one execution platform is used), the environment has to be decentralized as well. The distributed layout of the environment can influence the performance of agents and of the system.

In this paper we discuss when a distributed system can dynamically change its distribution layout. Our focus is on a distributed environment in which mobile agents move around and are aware of the distributed nature of the system.

Changes to the layout of the distribution are not only triggered by the agents (like other, application-specific actions), but they can also be triggered by external events and the environment itself. A layer of meta-agents monitors those triggers. It has the ability to pro-actively change the distribution layout over the different hosts when this improves the behavior and efficiency of the application.

Using a specific application (solving distributed constraint satisfaction problems) as an example, we indicate the usefulness of changes to the distribution layout and how they can be incorporated easily into a multiagent application design. It turns out that for some problems, the improvement in efficiency can be more than 30%.

1   Introduction

Multiagent systems consist of an environment and a number of agents that are situated in that environment [1]. Because in many multiagent systems, interaction between agents [2] (one of the means to reach a goal in multiagent systems) is done through or with a dependency on the environment [3,4], the environment is an important aspect of the design of the application. Nevertheless it is only recently that more attention is devoted to the environment [5,6,7].

In multiagent systems, the term 'environment' can be used for two different software concepts:

- The execution environment: This refers to the platform used to execute the system, *e.g.* a Java VM or the Windows operating system.
- The application environment: This refers to the environment in which the agents reside, *e.g.* a grid structure when the agents are players in a strategy game or a graph structure when the agents are fire trucks and police cars in the RoboCupRescue project.

A. Garcia et al. (Eds.): SELMAS 2005, LNCS 3914, pp. 35–52, 2006.

These software concepts should not be confused with the physical setting in which the application is executed, although they can have a similar topology. In a peer-to-peer application, the execution environment, the application environment, and the physical setting consists of a network of connected nodes. In this paper, we focus on the application environment. For the remainder of this paper, we refer to it as 'environment'. To indicate the execution environment, we use the term 'execution platform'.

When a multiagent system is decentralized, the environment has to be decentralized as well: a multiagent system where the environment is located on one host and the agents are distributed over a number of hosts is not really decentralized, but rather a client-server approach. The distribution layout of the environment defines how the various parts of the environment are scattered over the available hosts. This becomes an important issue that influences the behavior and efficiency of the system. In decentralized systems, it should be possible to change the distribution layout of the environment in order to guide the behavior, or increase the efficiency of the system. One of the basic ideas in software engineering is to assign responsibilities to entities that have the required information to fulfill it (Information Expert pattern, [8]). In the case of a multiagent system, the agents and the environment collect information, so they should be responsible for detecting when and how the environment should be changed.

In this paper we list which circumstances can trigger changes in the distribution layout of the environment. Because the reactions to those circumstances are highly application dependent, we apply our findings to a specific application: a decentralized multiagent system to solve distributed constraint problems. Using this application we show how dynamic changes can be incorporated in an existing application design, without disrupting the existing functionality. We describe a selection of the results that show the usefulness of dynamic adaptation of the decentralized environment. Although not all problems are equally suited to benefit from an adapting environment layout, our tests suggest that many practical applications do.

The structure of this paper is as follows: first we define the concept of "distribution layout of an environment" in Sect. 2. The circumstances that can trigger a dynamic change to the environment and the changes that can be requested are listed in Sect. 3. Section 4 gives a short overview of the CSAA framework: this is the case we discuss in Sect. 5 to illustrate the need for dynamic adaptability of the layout of the environment. The relation of our work to existing work is described in Sect. 6. The results of this case are discussed in Sect. 7. In Sect. 8 we finish with our conclusions.

2   Distribution Layout of the Environment

The centralized version of running a multiagent system is shown in Fig. 1. There is one execution platform, running on a single processor. The environment and the agents interact with each other and are executed on top of the execution platform.

When a multiagent system is decentralized, more than one execution platform is used (Fig. 2). In order to use these execution platforms, the environment has to be decentralized as well. When doing so, the environment is split in two parts:

Logical environment: The part of the environment that interacts with the agents. In a decentralized setting, there can either be one big logical environment (a transparent

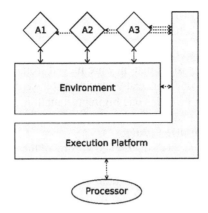

Fig. 1. Architecture of a centralized multi-agent system. The agents interact with the environment (solid arrows). Both agents and environment are executed (dotted arrows) on top of an execution platform (*e.g.* a Java VM) which runs on one single processor.

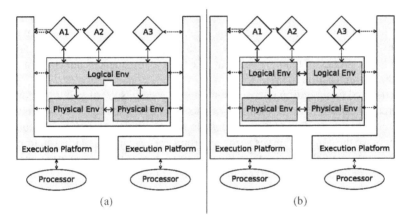

Fig. 2. Architecture of a decentralized multi-agent system. The agents interact with the logical environment. This can be (a) one logical environment for the whole application, or (b) a logical environment that is split up so the agents can be aware of the distributed nature of the application. The logical environment interacts with the different parts of the physical environment, which is always split up. The agents and environment are all executed on top of the execution platform that is located on the same processor as they are themselves.

layer, so the agents are not aware of the distributed nature of the system) or multiple small logical environments, one on each host (so the agents can be aware of the distributed nature, if their capabilities allow it).

Physical environment: The part of the environment that interacts with the execution platform. This is always split in different parts on each host because it represents the way the information is stored in the decentralized system.

The agents interact with the logical environment and are executed on top of the execution platform of the processor they are located on.

With respect to their knowledge of the decentralized system, there are two ways agents in such a system can behave:

1. The agents are unaware of the distribution. When agents move around in their logical environment, it is possible that they are moved from one host to another, but they are not aware of it (either because they do not have the capability or because the logical environment provides one big representation of the problem nature to them). The agents do not adjust their behavior when the application is ported from a centralized to a decentralized system.

   An example of this category is a distributed version of the traveling salesman problem, solved by a swarm of agents [9]. Each agent walks around in the graph structure, provided by the environment. Whether or not an agent goes from one host to another is not important for that agent. Each agent walks the path it wants to walk, it is the environment that makes sure an agent is moved to another host (and thus another execution platform) if necessary. When some subset of the nodes in the graph could be better grouped on the same host (because agents make a lot of moves inside that subset), it is up to the environment to group them.

2. The agents are aware of the distribution. When an agent moves from one host to another, it knows it has done so: the environment is presented as a number of separate logical environments to the agents. Each agent is also aware of the layout of the distribution and the consequences of distribution (*e.g.* cost of communication to other hosts, processor load,...) and can take those consequences into account when deciding which action to take.

   A distributed computation intensive multiagent system, such as solving a complex differential equation, is an example of this category: each agent is located on a different host and each agent is responsible for calculating a piece of the equation (in this case the equation serves as the environment). Agents need information from other agents (neighboring parts of the equation), but as this information has to be fetched over a network link, accessing it is slower than accessing local information. As performance is important, each agent gets as much information as possible from its own host, minimizing the (slow) use of the network link.

3   Adaptation of the Environment Layout

The goal of our system is to change the distribution layout of the logical environment. There are two categories of events that can trigger such a change: external and internal events. In this section, we first discuss those events in more detail. Next we introduce a layer of meta-agents that will perform the changes. Finally we give an overview of types of changes that can be necessary.

3.1   Events That Trigger a Change

The events that trigger a change can be divided into two categories: external and internal events. External events are directly brought into the system by the user or a separate system. Internal events are produced by entities inside the system. There are two types of entities that can gather information that justifies a change in the distribution layout: the agents and the environment.

1. External events: brought into the system when the execution platform changes (*e.g.* a new host is added when solving an equation) or a change in the problem situation is introduced (*e.g.* an extra city is added when solving the traveling salesman problem).
2. Internal events:
   - Events produced by agents: happens when an agent detects that a change in the layout of the logical environment would increase its performance (*e.g.* if some agent in the equation solving application makes intensive use of the information present on another host it can request to be transferred to that host or that the data is transferred to his own host). The agents are only able to detect performance increases for themselves, they are unable to judge if this would also increase the efficiency of the application as a whole. This type of events is only possible when the agents are aware of the decentralized nature of the application.
   - Events produced by the environment: happens when the environment detects that there is some performance bottleneck in the overall distribution layout of the system (*e.g.* one host in the distributed computation has a much higher load than another host, which could be solved by rearranging the parts to be calculated).

The agents and the different parts of the logical environment have only a partial view of the system. This implies that they are unable to judge if a change would have a positive global effect. Therefore, the events that are produced by the agents and the environment will not necessarily cause a change to happen. The events are stored as *influences* in the system. A separate entity monitors those influences and decides which action has to be taken. the layer of meta-agents we use to do this is discussed in Sect. 3.2.

This is very similar to the application-specific actions that are done by agents: they only send influences to the environment, they do not actually perform the actions [10,11]. When two agents request a conflicting action at the same time, only one or even none of them can be carried out, that is up to the environment to decide (*e.g.* two different agents request to kick a ball at the same time, in two different directions: the resulting action will be a combination of both requests). In the same manner, several influences requesting a change in the distribution layout can contradict each other. In that case, it is up to the meta-agents to decide which change to perform.

3.2   A Layer of Meta-agents

The environment itself is not a proactive entity in the system: it reacts to inputs and performs ongoing tasks such as pheromone evaporation, but it does not take itself the initiative to start new actions. Because of this non-proactive nature, the environment itself can not be responsible for interpreting the influences and changing the distribution layout. Additionally, in the applications we focus on, adjusting the distribution layout is a separate concern: it should not interfere with the correct behavior of the system, only with the performance. For that reason, we created an additional layer of meta-agents, whose sole purpose is to monitor the influences and adjust the distribution layout. For each part of the logical environment, one meta-agent is created. This is illustrated in Fig. 3.

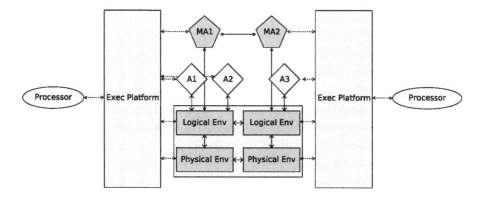

Fig. 3. Architecture of a decentralized multi-agent system with a layer of meta-agents, responsible for adjusting the distribution layout. The logical environment consists of different parts (one for each host). In each part of the logical environment a number of agents (Ax) are located. The distribution layout is managed by a layer of meta-agents (MAx, one meta-agent per part of the logical environment).

A meta-agent has a limited view of the environment. By interacting with the other meta-agents and with the part of the logical environment it is associated with, each meta-agent is able to make decisions that have a global impact. However, the meta-agents can only exchange meta-information: they can indicate what kind of information on a remote host is required by another host, but they should not exchange the information itself. The intent of the meta-agents is not to solve the application problem, but to adjust the environment so that the regular agents can solve the problem more efficiently.

3.3   Types of Requests for Changes

There are three ways in which the distribution layout of the logical environment can be changed:

1. A new part is created.
2. An existing part is removed.
3. An existing part is moved from its host to another host.

The first two types of changes are always triggered by external events: they must be carried out immediately because they influence the correctness of the application. The thirth type of change is mostly triggered by internal events.

Internal events are generated by either the agents or the different parts of the logical environment. They create the influence that requests that a part the the logical environment has to be moved from one host to another host. The most explicit manner to request such a move, it to state the three items involved in the move:

1. The part that has to be moved,
2. The host on which that part is currently located and
3. The host to which the part has to moved.

Since the agents and the different parts of the logical environment only have a local and thus limited view of the system, they do not have the ability to decide if a proposed change has a positive impact on the system as a whole. Therefore, the influences that are produced by multiple entities are gathered by the layer of meta-agents and they decide which changes to the distribution layout are made. When all move-influences are fully specified , it becomes very difficult for the meta-agents to combine the different influences. The meta-agents have more options for combining the influences if the moves are specified less strictly, *i.e.* when only one or two out of the three items are specified, or when some items themselves are specified less strictly. Some examples are:

- Only the host from which a part has to moved is specified. The meta-agents can choose which part has to be moved, and where to move it to. This can be used when one host has a high workload.
- Only the destination host is specified. This can be used when one host has a low workload. The meta-agents can choose to move one big part of a highly loaded host, or different small parts from multiple host.
- Two parts of the logical environment are specified that have to be placed on the same host. The meta-agents can choose on which host these parts have to be placed. This can either be one of their present hosts, or even a third host.
- A part of the logical environment and an agent or a group of agents are specified that have to be placed on the same host. Again, the meta-agents can freely choose the destination host.

Which requests are possible depends on the application, but in general, less strictly specified influences result in more freedom and a better combination by the meta-agents.

In Sect. 5 we give further examples of the different circumstances for and types of adaptation. The examples are extracted from a specific application: solving of constraint satisfaction problems using a distributed swarm algorithm. The next section describes in short how this application works.

4   CSAA Framework

The constraint satisfaction ant algorithm (CSAA) provides a general framework for solving constraint satisfaction problems (CSPs) using a swarm algorithm. CSPs are converted to a graph. This graph is used as the environment for a multiagent swarm application. Using an approach that is based on ant colony optimization (ACO) [12] a solution is searched.[1]

4.1   Centralized Framework

In Fig. 4 a graph is constructed for a small CSP problem with 3 variables ($A \in \{4, 5, 6\}$; $B \in \{2, 3\}$; $C \in \{2, 3\}$) and 2 constraints: ($A = B + C$; $B > C$). Each variable is converted to a main node (nodes A, B and C on Fig. 4(a)). From each main node, there are as many edges as there are other main nodes, each leading to a child node (from main node A to child nodes AB and AC in Fig. 4(b)). From each

---

[1] An implementation in Java of the CSAA framework can be found at *http://www.cs.kuleuven.be/~koenraad*

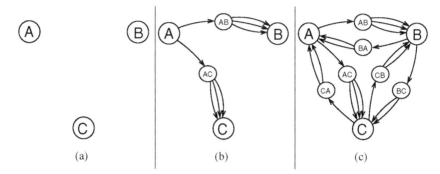

Fig. 4. Construction of a graph for a problem with 3 variables: $A \in \{4, 5, 6\}$; $B \in \{2, 3\}$; $C \in \{2, 3\}$ and 2 constraints: $A = B + C$; $B > C$. (a) Each main node represents a variable. (b) Going to the next main node is a two-step process: first the selection edge is chosen, then the value for the current variable (A has 3 possible values: there are 3 value edges from AB to B). (c) The complete graph for the problem. A reference to $A = B + C$ is stored in A, B and C, a reference to $B > C$ in B and C.

child node, there are as many edges as there are values for the variable of the previous main node. These edges all lead to the same main node (in Fig. 4(b) there are 3 edges from AB to B because the domain of variable A contains 3 values). The edges going from a main node to a child node are called *selection edges* because they select which main node will be visited next; the edges going from a child node to a main node are called *value edges* because they determine a value for a variable.

The layout of the graph imposes a few restrictions on the kind of CSPs that can be solved: each possible value has to be represented by an edge, so values must be discrete and finite in number. The total number of nodes is $n + n(n - 1)$, with n the number of variables. This makes that very big problems can not be solved by this centralized framework: the number of nodes would be too large to fit into the memory of a computer. A distributed version of the framework (see Sect. 4.2) or a modified version of the centralized framework can bypass this restriction.

The multiagent system that is used to solve the CSP is organized as a swarm of agents. Each agent of the swarm moves around in the graph, constructing a solution while doing so. In each main node, a suited selection edge has to be chosen (each main node can only be visited once by the same agent); in each child node, a suited value edge has to be chosen (values have to comply with previous chosen value: the constraints of the CSP determine which values are suited and which are not). On each edge a feedback value (in the form of synthetic *pheromones*) is stored that influences the selection process. A more detailed description of the behavior of the agents and the pheromones can be found in [13].

4.2   Distributed Framework

In [14] a distributed version of the CSAA framework was presented. The agents in the system are aware of the distribution and adjust their behavior to this knowledge. The set of variables in the problem is split up in as many parts as there are hosts and each

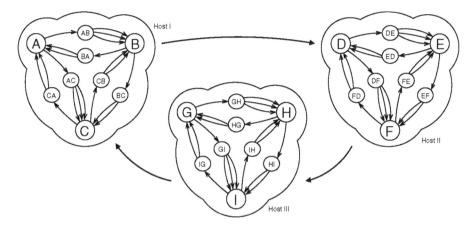

Fig. 5. Distributed graph for the CSAA. A copy of a constraint involving A and D is stored both on host I and host II. A constraint involving only variables A, B and C is stored only on host I.

part is assigned to one host. Each host builds its own logical environment, holding only variables associated with the variables the host is responsible for. The constraints are also distributed over the hosts. Each hosts gets a copy of all constraints the variables it is responsible for are involved in. If a constraint concerns several variables that are located on different hosts, multiple copies of that constraint are kept: one on each host that has such a variable.

The agents that try to solve the CSP jump from host to host. They must have visited all main nodes on a host before going to a next host. The hosts can be arranged in a loop, making the order in which each agent visits all hosts fixed. A second option is not to determine an order between the hosts, so each agent can choose for itself the order in which it will visit all hosts. A layout for a simple distributed problem with nine variables and six hosts is displayed in Fig. 5.

The goal of the CSAA framework is flexibility. This requires the environment to be flexible: it must be possible to add new variables or constraints and to delete others. Because the environment has knowledge about the work load on the hosts, one of the responsibilities of the environment is an equal distribution of the work load. When the environment detects that the workload is ill balanced, it suggests changes to the layout. Agents can also suggest a reorganization to the environment layout, when some variables can be grouped together to be able to process them more efficiently. Which variables this are can only be determined by the agents. The three types of circumstances that call for a change in the environments distribution layout that were introduced in Sect. 3 are present in this application, as well as several of the changes that can be requested. They are discussed more thouroughly in the next section.

5 The CSAA Framework as a Use-Case for Environmental Adaptation

Different types of changes to the distribution layout can be requested and there are different types of circumstances that call for a change. In Sect. 5.1 we give examples of those circumstances and requests in the context of the CSAA framework, in Sect. 5.2 we explain how the environment is able to handle those requests when it is distributed itself. The main purpose is to illustrate the opportunities that changes to the environment layout can offer and to show how multiagent techniques can be used to incorporate this functionality into an existing application design.

5.1   Different Types of Requests for Change

Changes Because of External Events.   There are several external events that can trigger a change in the environments distribution layout. The most obvious are adding or removing variables, values, constraints or hosts. Others include a change in the host capabilities or the failure of a connection between two hosts. Whenever such an external event happens the environment *must* adapt.

When a variable, value of constraint is deleted, the change to the distribution layout is rather trivial: the according part of the graph structure simply has to be removed. When an extra variable value or constraint is added, some extra edges and connections have to be added. Adding or removing such components could cause the work load to be ill distributed, but this will be handled automatically (see Sect. 5.1). When an extra variable is added, the environment has to decide which host to assign it to. The simplest option is to assign it to the host that has the lowest work load and let the agents decide if some other host is more suited with respect to the constraints that exist between the new variable and existing variables. A similar approach can be taken when a new host is added: the environment removes some variables from each host and assigns these variables to the new host. The agents are then responsible for rearranging the variables for efficiency.

All changes that are requested because of external events, must be carried out immediately: a correct solution for the problem can not be found without those requested changes (with the exception of a new host that is added). For changes that are requested by agents or by the environment, explained in the following paragraphs, this is not the case. They can be postponed because they do not influence the correctness of the solution, but only the efficiency of the algorithm.

Changes Requested by the Agents.   Agents are responsible for assigning values to variables and checking the constraints of the problem. When an agent has already assigned values to a number of variables, it can sometimes happen that a next variable can not be assigned a value. *E.g.* variables A, B and C have already been assigned a value. There exists a constraint between variables A, B and D. Because of the chosen values for A and B, every possible value for D violates the constraint.

When this happens, all value assignments between the assignment of the first variable in that constraint and the present variable were a waste of effort. In the example: the value that was chosen for C did not help in determining that no value for D could be found. To prevent this from happening in the future, all variables that are involved in the constraint should be assigned a value around the same time. In our examples this means that variables A, B and D should be placed on the same host.

In this type of change request it does not matter which of the variables are moved to another host, or which host they are moved to: as long as the variables end up at the same host, the efficiency of the system will be increased. It is even possible that other variables get moved as well (because of load balancing requirements). The request does not have to be carried out immediately: it does not influence the correct behavior of the application, it only affects the efficiency of the application.

When two agents are running, and they both request a conflicting change at the same time, at least one of the requests can not be fulfilled. Furthermore, when solving highly constrained problems, executing all requests could mean that all variables are transferred to the same host (which, in a decentralized setting is obviously not the desired behavior). How this and other conflicts that can arise from multiple change requests are handled is explained in Sect. 5.2.

Changes Requested by the Environment. The environment is responsible for grouping associated variables on the same host (the distribution layout) and providing a communication infrastructure for the agents. The distribution layout is closely related to the work load on each host. A change in work load can be caused by a change in distribution layout or because one of the hosts suddenly has to do more calculations (*e.g.* because the agents on that host gradually choose other values that require more calculations). In the CSAA framework the distribution of the workload is measured by comparing the period of time an agent needs to process all variables on the different hosts. The duration of this period needs to be the same to avoid bottlenecks. Differences in work load cause the environment to request a change in the distribution layout. As with the requests by agents, changing the distribution layout does not influence the correct behavior of the application and so the changes do not have to be carried out immediately.

5.2 Handling Requests for Change in a Distributed Setting

Because the agents only interact with their logical environment, they can only send requests for changes to the distribution layout to that logical environment. The logical environment itself also produces requests for change. Therefore, we store all information about these requests in the logical environment.

The layer of meta-agents that was introduced in Sect. 3.2 is responsible for adapting the distribution layout of the system. It takes as input external events and the information stored in the logical environment. Based on that information, it decides when and how the distribution layout must be changed.

The next paragraphs give two examples of how the meta-agents interpret the requests for changes to the distribution layout.

Transferring Data on Request of Agents. When an agent detects that a variable can not be assigned a value, it sends feedback to the environment. The agent indicates in its feedback which host contained the most restrictive variables that prohibited a value assignment. The environment stores this feedback in the node that is associated with the variable. This information is encoded under the form of *pheromones* (artificial imitations of the biological chemicals that *e.g.* ants use, [15]). For each host in the system, there is a different type of pheromone.

When a meta-agent detects that one type of pheromone for a node exceeds a certain threshold, the variable that is associated with that node is transferred to the corresponding host. Using a threshold mechanism prevents all variables to be transferred at the same time. In combination with workload balancing (described in the next paragraph) it prevents that all variables are transferred to one and the same host: because variables are only transferred gradually, the load balancing process has the necessary time to redistribute the variables that are present on crowded hosts.

Balancing Workload. When agents are transferred from one part of the logical environment to another, they are first stored in a buffer at the receiving part. When the meta-agent that is associated with this part of the logical environment detects that the number of agents in the buffer becomes too high, one of the variables in the logical environment is transferred to another part of the logical environment. Which variable gets transferred depends on the host it gets transferred to. There are two possibilities:

1. When the order of the hosts is fixed, a variable gets transferred to the part of the logical environment that is located on the previous host. The workload of that previous host will certainly be lower: the previous host was able to fill the buffer of its successor, which means more agents were processed at the same time.
2. When the order of the hosts is not fixed, a variable gets transferred to the host with the lowest number of agents in its buffer. To avoid an election process between the hosts each time a variable has to be transferred, each part of the logical environment remembers the buffersize of each other part each time an agent is transferred to that part.

The variable that is transferred is the variable whose associated node has the highest pheromone level for the host to be transferred to.

One of the drawbacks that can arise when using both a dynamic transfer of the variables and workload balancing is that variables can be transferred back and forth between hosts. To prevent oscillations in the transfer of variables, the threshold in the meta-agents are adjusted by the workload balancing process. Each time this process transfers a variable away from a host, the threshold that is needed for other variables to be transferred to that host increases.

6 Related Work

Research in the domain of resource allocation and load balancing has been active for a long time. In the last decade, research has shifted from centralized [16] and pseudo-decentralized approaches (client-server approaches, like [17]) to completely decentralized approaches. In these decentralized approaches, multi-agent systems are a natural choice for coordinating the systems resources. Both intelligent agents [18], and in recent years swarms of reactive agents [19,20,21] have proven to be efficient. The approach that is described in this paper is no new approach, but merely an instantiation of existing techniques.

According to the general model for load balancing schemes that is presented in [22] each load balancing scheme can be decomposed into four main criteria:

1. The triggering policy
2. The selection policy
3. The communication and domain policy
4. The matching policy

As described in Sect. 5.2 the agents leave information on each host about the nodes that should be transferred by preference and which host they should be transferred to. This information is stored as pheromones in the logical environment. The meta-agent layer is responsible for the distribution layout and load balancing and uses the information in the pheromones to determine the triggering (pheromone level exceeds threshold, in combination with buffer size), selection (node with the highest pheromone level) and matching policy (preferred host to transfer to). As it is implemented now, no extra communication between meta-agents is needed to determine when and where to redistribute nodes.

The advantage of this approach is that information is accumulated by the entities that are most suited to do so. The task of the agents is to search for a solution, which involves moving from host to host and taking into consideration dependencies between nodes. They are best suited to gather the information about these dependencies. The logical environment, which consists of collections of associated variables, is best suited to indicate when a host is overloaded or underloaded.

The distribution layout of the system is a separate concern and a non-functional requirement: it does not influence the correctness of the system. Therefore, the adaptation of the distribution layout is done by a layer of meta-agents: the meta-agents can be changed to implement another load-balancing algorithm without changing the correctness of the system. Using a meta-level for non-functional requirements is a well-known technique [23,24] also.

7   Results

The features of the adaptive environment, described in Sect. 5, were implemented and integrated into the existing CSAA framework. We tested this modified framework on a number of graph coloring problems, represented as partial constraint satisfaction problems. Based on the results, we distinguish between two classes of problems: completely connected graph coloring problems and partially connected graph coloring problems. In this section we give and discuss the results of one completely connected and two partially connected problems[2]. The difference between the different classes of problems allows us to define whether the use of the adaptive features is opportune for a given problem.

Figures 6, 7 and 8 are averaged *anytime* curves. An averaged anytime curve illustrates how the average of the best solutions that are found improves as time (given by

---

[2] All problems had hard as well as soft constraints. For each pair of variables and colors, 10 problems were created, each with a different number of hard constraints. The percentage of hard constraints ranged from 3% (easy problems) to 30% (more difficult problems) of all edges. The penalties for the soft constraints were chosen randomly between 1 and 50. Every problem was solved 10 times, so the figures display averages for 100 runs. We used a distribution layout of three heterogeneous hosts (ranging from an AMD 1600+ to a Pentium IV 2.6GHz). Initially the variables were randomly distributed on the hosts.

The completely connected problem that is reported on in this paper had an edge (constraint) between each pair of variables. For the partially connected problems, the probability of an edge between two variables was 0.5. The completely connected problem and the first partially connected problem had 11 variables and 3 colors, the second partially connected problem had 15 variables and 5 colors.

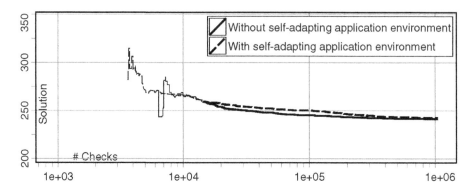

Fig. 6. Progress results of the CSAA framework without an adapting environment (solid line) and with such an environment (dashed line) on a completely connected graph coloring problem with 11 nodes and 3 colors. Executed on three heterogeneous hosts.

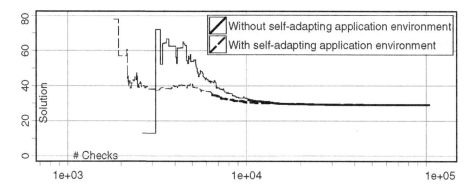

Fig. 7. Progress results of the CSAA framework without an adapting environment (solid line) and with such an environment (dashed line) on a partially connected graph coloring problem with 11 nodes and 3 colors. Executed on three heterogeneous hosts.

the number of constraint checks) proceeds. Each curve starts as a thin line. This means not all 100 runs have found a solution yet: the shown value is the average best solution for the runs that have already found a solution. Once the curve becomes a thick line, all runs have found a solution.

All three figures compare the results of the CSAA framework without an adaptive environment to the results of the CSAA framework with such an environment.

7.1 Completely Connected Problems

In the first type of graph coloring problems, each node is connected by an edge to each other node. The results that were obtained for problems with 11 variables and 3 colors are depicted in Fig. 6.

There is not a big difference in the results of the CSAA framework with and without an adaptive environment. The results with such an environment reach a first solution

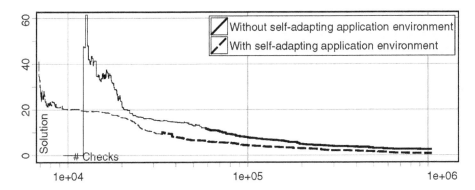

Fig. 8. Progress results of the CSAA framework without an adapting environment (solid line) and with such an environment (dashed line) on a partially connected graph coloring problem with 15 nodes and 5 colors. Executed on three heterogeneous hosts.

a little bit faster for the easier problems (the thin dashed line starts sooner than the thin solid line), but for more difficult problems (the beginning of the thick lines), the difference is hardly noticeable. The quality of the solutions is very comparable, both during the solving process as at the end of the process.

7.2   Partially Connected Problems

In the second type of graph coloring problems, the probability for two nodes to be connected by an edge (or constraint) was only 0.5, reducing the number of edges by 50%. The results that were obtained for problems with 11 variables and 3 colors are depicted in Fig. 7. The results for the problems with 15 nodes and 5 colors are depicted in Fig. 8.

In contrast with the results of the fully connected problems, there is a noticeable difference when partially connected problems are solved using the CSAA framework with or without an adaptive environment. The intermediate results of the framework using the adaptive environment are better: as well for the easier problems as for the harder problems, a solution is found approximately 30% to 40% faster. The quality of those intermediate solutions is better also: for the problem with 11 variables of Figure 7, an average best solution that is within 30% of the final solution is found after approximately 3000 checks when using an adaptive environment. That is less than half the amount of checks than when such an environment is not used (approximately 7000 checks needed).

The final solutions for both versions are approximately the same. Altough in Fig. 8, the last displayed solutions of both versions are not exactly the same yet, we expect them to reach the same value if the algorithms are allowed to run longer.

7.3   Observations

A first thing we can conclude when we look at the results, is that the final solution that is found by the CSAA framework remains unchanged whether it uses an adaptive environment or not. Because the adaptations of the environment layout (moving variables from one host to another) are only concerned with the efficiency of the algorithm (balancing workload and a more efficient use of the heuristics), this is an outcome that could be expected.

A second conclusion is that not all problems are equally suited for the use of an adaptive environment. When solving graph coloring problems that consist of a completely connected graph, there is no effect in using the proposed adaptations. The workload on the hosts will probably benefit from an adaptive environment, but the adaptations will have no effect on the effectiveness of the heuristics.

When a partially connected graph coloring problem is solved, the heuristics can be made more efficient by adapting the environment: in most partially connected graphs, there are some highly connected subgraphs. Putting those subgraphs on the same host will result in better heuristics and a faster convergence to the final solution.

8   Conclusions

In this paper we presented a number of circumstances that cause the dynamic adaptation of the environment layout. A layer of meta-agents reacts upon triggers from the agents, the environment or external triggers to change the distribution layout of the system.

To illustrate the different types of circumstances and requests, we used a distributed swarm algorithm for constraint satisfaction solving, the CSAA framework. In this framework, requests are done using standard swarm algorithm techniques: artificial pheromones. Our illustration shows the opportunities that dynamic adaptation of the environment layout offers and how existing mechanisms can be used to implement this into the context of a decentralized multiagent system.

Not all problems are equally suited for the adaptive enhancements. When solving highly connected problems, there is no efficiency gain. The reason for this is the lack of structure in the problem description: the adaptations to the environment layout try to group parts of the environment that are highly related, but when all elements of the environment are equally related, these attempts do not succeed and they do not result in any efficiency gain.

However, a fully connected graph is an artificial problem: most practical problems do have some structure in them. It is not always easy for a human to determine which parts of the problem belong together, so a manual decomposition is not feasible. When using an dynamic environment, this task can be done by the system itself. The results of solving partially connected graphs – an improvement in efficiency of more than 30% – prove that the efficiency of the system can be enhanced by this approach.

Finally, while we demonstrated the use of an dynamic environment for solving constraint problems, other application domains could also benefit from it. The efficiency of all applications where some distributed coordination or computation takes place, benefits from a reduced use of the networking infrastructure and could be enhanced by a dynamic environment.

Acknowledgements

This work has been funded by the Institute for the Promotion of Innovation through Science and Technology in Flanders (IWT-Vlaanderen).

References

1. Ferber, J.: Multi-Agent System: An Introduction to Distributed Artificial Intelligence. Harlow: Addison Wesley Longman (1999)
2. Parunak, H.V.D., Brueckner, S., Fleischer, M., Odell, J.: Co-x: Defining what agents do together. In: Proceedings of the AAMAS 2002 Workshop on Teamwork and Coalition Formation. (2002) 62–69
3. Chialvo, D.R., Millonas, M.M.: How Swarms Build Cognitive Maps. In Steels, L., ed.: The Biology and Technology of Intelligent Autonomous Agents. Volume 144. Nato ASI Series (1995) 439–450
4. Huhns, M.N., Stephens, L.M.: Multiagent systems and societies of agents. In Weiss, G., ed.: Multiagent Systems: A Modern Approach to Distributed Artificial Intelligence. The MIT Press, Cambridge, MA, USA (1999) 79–120
5. Omicini, A.: Soda: societies and infrastructures in the analysis and design of agent-based systems. In: First international workshop, AOSE 2000 on Agent-oriented software engineering, Secaucus, NJ, USA, Springer-Verlag New York, Inc. (2001) 185–193
6. Parunak, H.V.D., Brueckner, S., Sauter, J., Matthews, R.S.: Distinguishing environmental and agent dynamics: A case study in abstraction and alternate modeling technologies. Lecture Notes in Computer Science **1972** (2001) 19–33
7. Weyns, D., Parunak, H.V.D., Michel, F., Holvoet, T., Ferber, J.: Environments for multiagent systems, state-of-the-art and research challenges. Lecture Notes in Artificial Intelligence **3374** (2005)
8. Larman, C.: Applying UML and Patterns: An Introduction to Object-Oriented Analysis and Design and the Unified Process. Prentice Hall PTR, Upper Saddle River, NJ, USA (2001)
9. Stützle, T., Dorigo, M.: ACO Algorithms for the Traveling Salesman Problem. In Miettinen, K., Makela, M., Neittaanmaki, P., Periaux, J., eds.: Evolutionary Algorithms in Engineering and Computer Science. Wiley (1999) 163–183
10. Ferber, J., Müller, J.P.: Influences and Reaction: A Model of Situated Multiagent Systems. In: Proceedings of the Second International Conference on Multi-agent Systems, AAAI Press (1996) 72–79
11. Weyns, D., Holvoet, T.: Formal Model for Situated Multi-Agent Systems. Formal Approaches for Multi-agent Systems. Special Issue of Fundamenta Informaticae **63** (2004) 125–158
12. Dorigo, M., Di Caro, G.: The Ant Colony Optimization Meta-Heuristic. In Corne, D., Dorigo, M., Glover, F., eds.: New Ideas in Optimization. McGraw-Hill, London (1999) 11–32
13. Mertens, K., Holvoet, T.: CSAA; a Constraint Satisfaction Ant Algorithm Framework. In: Proceedings of the Sixth International Conference on Adaptive Computing in Design and Manufacture (ACDM'04), Springer-Verlag (2004) 285–294
14. Mertens, K., Holvoet, T.: CSAA; a Distributed Ant Algorithm Framework for Constraint Satisfaction. In: Proceedings of the 17th International FLAIRS Conference, AAAI Press (2004) 764–769
15. Grasse, P.: La reconstruction du nid et les coordinations inter-individuelles chez bellicostermes natalensis et cubitermes sp. la theorie de la stigmergie: Essai d'interpretation des termites constructeurs. Insect Societies **6** (1959) 41–83
16. Ross, K.W., Yao, D.D.: Optimal load balancing and scheduling in a distributed computer system. J. ACM **38** (1991) 676–689
17. SETI@Home: http://setiathome.ssl.berkeley.edu/ (1996-1999)
18. Cao, J., Spooner, D.P., Jarvis, S.A., Nudd, G.R.: Grid load balancing using intelligent agents. Future Generation Computer Systems, Special Issue on Intelligent Grid Environment: Principles and Applications (2005) 135–149

19. Schoonderwoerd, R., Holland, O., Bruten, J.: Ant-like agents for load balancing in telecommunications networks. In: AGENTS '97: Proceedings of the first international conference on Autonomous agents, New York, NY, USA, ACM Press (1997) 209–216
20. Montresor, A., Meling, H., Babaoğlu, Ö.: Messor: Load-Balancing through a Swarm of Autonomous Agents. In: Proceedings of the International Workshop on Agents and Peer-to-Peer Computing in conjunction with AAMAS 2002, Bologna, Italy (2002)
21. Cao, J.: Self-organizing agents for grid load balancing. In: GRID '04: Proceedings of the Fifth IEEE/ACM International Workshop on Grid Computing (GRID'04), Washington, DC, USA, IEEE Computer Society (2004) 388–395
22. Fonlupt, C., Marquet, P., Dekeyser, J.L.: Analysis of synchronous dynamic load balancing algorithms. In D'Hollander, E.H., Joubert, G.R., Peters, F.J., Trystram, D., eds.: Parallel Computing: State-of-the-Art and Perspectives, Proceedings of the Conference ParCo'95, 19-22 September 1995, Ghent, Belgium. Volume 11., Amsterdam, Elsevier, North-Holland (1996) 455–462
23. Robben, B.: Language Technology and Metalevel Architectures for Distributed Objects. Phd, Department of Computer Science, K.U.Leuven, Leuven, Belgium (1999)
24. Maes, P.: Concepts and experiments in computational reflection. In: Proceedings of OOPSLA'87. Volume 22. (1987) 147–155

Self-organizing Approaches for Large-Scale Spray Multiagent Systems

Marco Mamei and Franco Zambonelli

Dipartimento di Scienze e Metodi dell'Ingegneria,
Università di Modena e Reggio Emilia, Italy
{mamei.marco, franco.zambonelli}@unimo.it

Abstract. Large-scale multiagent systems will be the key software technology driving several future application scenarios. We envision a future in which clouds of microcomputers can be sprayed in an environment to provide, by spontaneously networking with each other, an endlessly range of futuristic applications. Beside this vision, similar kind of large-scale "spray" multiagent systems will be employed in several other scenarios ranging from ad-hoc networks of embedded and mobile devices to worldwide distributed computing. All of these scenarios present strong commonalities from the application development point of view, and new approaches and methodologies will be likely to apply, to some extent, to all of them. In particular, we argue that the issues related to the design and development of such spray multiagent systems call for novel approaches exploiting self-organization as first-class tools. With this regard, we survey a number of research projects around the world trying to apply self-organization to large-scale multiagent systems. Finally, we attempt at defining a rough research agenda that – in the long run – should integrate these ideas to develop a general and more assessed methodology for large-scale spray multiagent systems crosscutting several application domains.

1 Introduction

Large-scale multiagent systems will be the key software technology driving next generation distributed computing systems. As the size and dynamism of computer networks grow, autonomous and decentralized approaches (i.e. multiagent systems) to develop applications will be the only viable solutions to handle the arising complexity.

Today, the size and the dynamism of distributed service- and data-oriented activities on the Internet, to be sustainable, requires peer-to-peer multiagent approaches to interaction and data exchange [28, 31], as well as decentralized and autonomous approaches to system management and configuration [15].

In the near future, computer-based systems will be embedded in all our everyday objects and in our everyday environments. These systems will be typically communication enabled, and capable of coordinating with each other in the context of complex mobile distributed applications [17, 25, 27]. Also in this case, large-scale multiagent systems will be fundamental to handle the dynamism of the scenario.

A. Garcia et al. (Eds.): SELMAS 2005, LNCS 3914, pp. 53–70, 2006.

Looking a bit further, it is not hard to envision a future in which network of micro computers will be literally sold as spray cans, to be sprayed in an environment or on specific artifacts to enrich them with functionalities that, as of today, may appear futuristic and visionary [20, 36]. The number of potential applications of the scenario is endless, ranging from smart and invisible clothes, intelligent interactive environments, self-assembly materials and self-repairing artifacts.

Besides the different physical scale of the components involved and of their interactions (from micro-computers interacting within networks extending across a few meters, to Internet hosts interacting at a world-wide scale), all of these types of spray multiagent system networks raise similar challenges as far as development and deployment of applications is involved, calling for radically novel approaches to distributed systems development and management.

On the one hand, to avoid the unaffordable efforts related to the placement, configuration, and maintenance of such systems, there is the need of approaches enabling of deploying components without any a priori layout effort, and letting components to self-organize their application activities and self-retune their overall behavior depending on specific contingencies (e.g., localized faults and environmental changes) [15]. On the other hand, the autonomous and decentralized nature of the activities in such scenarios, together with the possibly unpredictable dynamics of the operating environments, is likely to make those systems exhibit unexpected, "emergent" behaviors - as recent observations in several types of decentralized networks (i.e., the Internet, the Web, as well as Gnutella) suggest. Therefore, there is also need for methodologies to predict and control the emergence of such behaviors and, when possible, offensively exploit them for the achievement of complex distributed tasks [4, 24, 37].

This paper aims at exploring the above issues and will be organized as follow: Section 2 details our vision about spray multiagent systems, starting from the micro-scale (i.e., literally spray-able computers), to the medium scale (smart artifacts and MANETs), up to the macro-scale (wide-area networks), and presents the key challenges to program such systems. From Section 3 to Section 6, we present four distinct approaches relying on self-organization to deal with such challenges. In particular, Section 3 will present a direct engineering approach to self-organization. Section 4 will present a reverse engineering approach. Section 5 will present a mixed approach in which directly engineered mechanism try to control reverse engineered behaviors (direct over reverse engineering). Section 6 presents another mixed approach in which reverse engineered mechanism combine directly engineered behaviors (reverse over direct engineering). Finally, Section 7 concludes the paper by attempting to define a roadmap of activities in the area of spray multiagent systems.

2 Spray Multiagent Systems and Application

The concept of spray multiagent systems will soon pervade the ICT scenarios at every scale and at every level. In the following we will briefly survey our idea of future computer-based systems from the micro-scale (literally spray computer systems), to the medium-scale (handheld and wearable computers) to the global scale (Internet and Web computing). Moreover we introduce key challenges in programming spray multiagent systems application.

2.1 Application Scenarios

The Micro Scale. As proved in the context of the Smart Dust project at Berkeley [3], it is already possible to produce fully-fledged computer-based systems of a few cm³, and even much smaller ones will be produced in the next few years. Such computers, which can be enriched with communication capabilities (radio or optical), local sensing (e.g., optical, thermal, or inertial) and local effecting (e.g., optical and mechanical) capabilities, are the basic ingredients of our spray multiagent systems vision. Spray computers systems, as we imagine them, are clouds of sub-millimeter-scale microcomputers, to be deployed in an environment or onto specific artifacts via a spraying or a painting process. Once deployed, such components will spontaneously network with each other and will coordinate their actions (i.e., local sensing and effecting) to provide specific "smart" functionalities. We imagine it will be possible, say in 2020, to go to the local store and there buy, for a few euros, a "pipe repairing" spray, made up of a cloud of MEMS microcomputers capable of navigating in a pipeline, recognizing the presence of holes, and self-assembling with each other so as perfectly repair the pipe. Similarly, we could imagine a spray to transform our everyday desk into an active one, capable of recognizing the positions and characteristics of objects placed on it and letting them meaningfully interact.

Another peculiar application we envision is the "spray of invisibility" (described in [36]): a spray of micro devices capable of receiving and re-transmitting light emissions in a directional way, and capable of interacting with each other via short-range wireless communications. When an object is covered by a layer of such spray, the emissions of the devices make external observers perceive exactly the same light configurations that they would have perceived if there were nothing in between. In fact sensors on the rear side of the object can receive such configurations and, via distributed coordination, can communicate them to emitters on the observer's side to be retransmitted. Other types of application one could envision include any type of self-assembly artifact [20, 34], there included thing like Terminator T-1000, the nano-swarms of Michael Crichton's novel "Prey" [9], and MEMS-based artificial immune systems and drugs [10].

Whatever the applications one envision, the key characteristics that will distinguish spray multiagent systems applications from traditional distributed computing systems are not – as one could at first think – the scale at which processes take place. After all the fact that an agent is executed on a micro device rather than on a high-end computer does not change it basic nature. Instead, what we think strongly distinguish spray multiagent systems are the facts that:

- Agent activities take place in a network whose structure derives from an almost random deployment process (as a spraying process is), and that is likely to change over time with unpredictable dynamics (due to environmental contingencies, failure of components, or simply mobility);
- The number of (hardware and, consequently, software) agents involved in a distributed application is dramatically high and hardly controllable. It is neither possible to enforce a strict configuration of software components nor to control their behavior during execution at a fine-grained level.

Both the above characteristics compulsory call for execution models in which applications are made capable of self-configuring and self-tuning their activities in a spontaneous and unsupervised way, adapting to whatever network structure and surviving network dynamics.

The Medium Scale. On a different scale, spray multiagent systems well apply to the emerging scenarios of ubiquitous and pervasive computing, as enabled by handheld, wearable, and embedded, networked computing systems. We already typically carry on two or three computers (i.e., a cell phone, a laptop, and possibly a PDA). Also, our houses are already populated by a variety of microprocessor based furniture (e.g. TVs, phones, etc.). However, at the moment, the networking capabilities of these computer-based systems are under-exploited. On the contrary, very soon, the world around us will be densely populated by personal-area networks (e.g., the ensemble of Bluetooth enabled interacting computer-based devices we could carry on or we could find in our cars), local ad-hoc networks of handheld computers (e.g., networks of interacting PDAs carried by a team that have to directly interact and coordinate with each other in an open space), and furniture networks (e.g., Web-enabled fridges and ovens able to interact with each other and effectively support our cooking activities in a coordinated way).

What we want to emphasize here is that the above types of networks, although being formed by different types of computer-based devices (let's say, medium-end computers) and at different physical scales than literally spray multiagent systems, shares with them the same issues as far as the development and management of distributed multiagent applications is concerned. In fact:

- Most of these networks will be wireless, with structures dynamically varying depending on the relatives positions of devices, all of which intrinsically mobile (the persons in an ad-hoc network can move around in an environment and the position of home furniture can changed on needs) and characterized by the dynamic arrival dismissing of nodes (a PDA running out of power or a new home furniture being bought).
- Even if technically possible, it is simply not commercially and economically viable to consider deploying applications that would require explicit configuration and explicit tuning to meet the amorphous and dynamic nature of the networks in which applications will be expected to operate.

Also in these cases, new approaches are needed to develop applications in such open and dynamic scenarios.

The Global Scale. Also in the case of macro-scale networks made up of high-end computer systems, i.e., the Internet and the Web, the dramatic growth of these networks and of the information and traffic to be managed, together with the increasing request for ubiquitous connectivity and the peculiar structures exhibited by such networks [1, 29], have recently raised researchers' attention to the need of novel approaches to distributed systems management. From our perspective, these scenarios are in fact the first actually deployed systems that can be assimilated to a spray multiagent system.

Traditional approaches to management, requiring human configuration efforts and supervision, fall short when the number of nodes in the network (or the number of interrelated services and links in the Web) grows in a fully decentralized way, and when the presence of the nodes in a network is of an intrinsically ephemeral nature, as it is the case of laptops and, with regard to the Web, of several non-commercial data and services.

In a number of application scenarios, the need to access data and services according to a variety of patterns and independently of the availability/location of specific servers and of the dynamics of the network have suggested the adoption of P2P approaches [28, 29]. In P2P computing, instead of promoting a strict control over the execution of software components and of their interactions (an almost impossible task given the dynamism of the scenario), the idea is to promote and support adaptive self-organization and maintenance of a structured network of logical relationships among components (i.e., an overlay network), to abstract from the physical "sprayed" nature of the actual network and survive events such the arrival of new nodes or the dismissing of some nodes.

Overlay networks are currently the most widely investigated approach to distributed application development and management in worldwide computing, and are leveraging a variety of useful applications facilitating access to (and coordination over) a variety of world-wide distributed data and services. Although self-organizing overlay networks – as they are studied today – are not necessarily the only and best approach, the attention towards them is the body of evidence of the need – also in this scenario – for new self-organizing approaches to distributed application development.

As a final note, we emphasize that, although the micro, medium, and global scale currently represent almost separated worlds, this will not be the case in the near future. All the above systems will probably be in the near future part of a mega decentralized network, including traditional Internet nodes, smart computer-enriched objects and furniture, networks of embedded and dispersed micro-sensors. For instance, the IPv6 addressing scheme will make it possibly to assign an Internet address to every cubic millimeter in the earth surface [12], thus opening the possibility for each and every computer-based component to become part of a single worldwide network.

2.2 Programming Spray Multiagent Systems

Programming a spray multiagent system means to engineer a coherent and useful behavior from the cooperation of an immense number of unreliable parts interconnected in unknown, irregular, and time-varying ways. This translates in devising algorithms and control methodologies to let the sprayed computing devices self-organize their interaction patterns and their activities: devices have to start working together without the presence of any a-priori global supervisor or centralized controller.

The basic low-level mechanisms upon which to rely to enable self-organization appear quite well-understood and are basically the same whatever the scale, whether that of sensor networks or that of wide-area P2P computing. Among the others: dynamic discovery of potential communication partners and of available services via broadcasting; localization and navigation in some sorts of spatial environment, whether physical (as in sensor networks) or computational (as in P2P systems).

What is still missing is an assessed understanding of how to design, develop, and manage, self-organizing applications for these kinds of systems, leading to some general purpose methodologies and programming environments. The main conceptual difficulty being that, while standard programming enables a direct-engineered control only on agents' local activities, a variety of diverse application goals have to be achieved at a global scale. Identifying some general and abstract solution to enable the design and development – via a proper programming of self-organizing activities – of specific global application goals, would have a dramatic impact in all sketched scenarios (micro, medium and global scale). In this paper, without having solutions at hand, we survey a number of research efforts in this direction and try to identify some key directions to investigate. In the following sections, we are going to classify the self-organizing mechanisms being studied in the following way:

In **section 3**, we will present direct engineering approaches to self-organization. These approaches aim at designing for scratch the activities of each agent, so that the whole multiagent system behaves as desired. This is the most conservative approach, and it can be reduced to some extend to "standard" decentralized application development (e.g. peer-to-peer software).

In **section 4**, we will present reverse engineering approaches to self-organization. Here, the idea is to take a system (e.g. biological) that already exhibit some global behavior similar to the one we want to achieve. Then, try to reverse engineering its behavior and apply the result to a computation problem. This is basically the approach promoted by the swarm intelligence research community [5].

In **section 5**, we present a mixed approach (direct over reverse engineering) in which directly engineered mechanism try to control reverse engineered behaviors. The idea is to encourage the rise of only those behaviors that are useful to the application at hand.

In **section 6,** we present the complementary mixed approach (reverse over direct engineering) in which reverse engineered mechanism try to combine directly engineered behaviors for the sake of realizing the whole application.

In each section, we will first present a general overview of the approach. Then we survey a number of research projects trying to apply such ideas. Finally, we discuss the merits and shortcomings of the approach.

3 Direct Engineering of Self Organization

3.1 Overview

Direct engineering approaches to self-organization basically aims at defining distributed algorithms that, starting from a few basic mechanisms (e.g., broadcast and localization), and exploiting local interactions and local computations, can provably lead a system to a final coherent global state. Unlike traditional distributed algorithms, self-organizing algorithms disregard micro-level issues such as ordering of events, process synchronization, and structure of the underlying networks (issues for which no possibility of control is assumed). Rather, they focus on the fact that the algorithm will eventually converge despite micro-level contingencies and that it will keep the system in the stable state despite perturbations (e.g., changes in the network structure).

3.2 Research Projects

Micro Scale. Most of the researches in the area of micro-scale spray multiagent systems are performed in the context of the "sensor networks" research community [10]. There, the key issues being investigated relate to the identification of effective algorithms and tools to perform distributed monitoring activities by a cloud of distributed sensors in a physical environment (tracing the position and movement of an object, determining the occurrence of specific conditions, reporting sensed data back in an efficient way). These researches are indeed providing good insights on the theme of self-organization and are leading to some very interesting results. Techniques for self-localization, self-synchronization of activities, adaptive data distribution, all of which of primary importance for any type of spray multiagent systems, have been widely investigated [10, 21].

A typical example of a direct engineering approach to self-organization is distributed self-localization [21]. There, a number of randomly distributed particles can determine their geographical position starting from a few "beacon" particles (possibly self-determined via leader election and acting as reference frame) and recursively applying a local triangulation mechanism to determine their position with regard to close particles, until a global coherent positioning of all particles in the reference frame is reached. This is a good example for our idea of direct-engineered self-organization. The system self-organizes in that the agents act autonomously without the supervision of any external monitor or controller. However, the algorithm they follow is directly engineered so that they can achieve a final stable configuration.

Medium Scale Direct. Coming to the medium scale, as far as we can see most of the researches are focusing either on routing algorithms for mobile ad-hoc networks [7] or on the definition of effective user-level ubiquitous environments [30]. Researches on routing algorithms for mobile networks share several common issues with researches on algorithms for data distribution on sensor networks. Routing in mobile ad-hoc networks, can be considered as a multiagent application where agents need to coordinate with each other to forward each other packets, so as to enable long range, multi-hop communication. Again, in our opinion, these algorithms can be considered as self-organizing, in that agents act autonomously without any central director.

Researches on ubiquitous computing environments mostly focus on achieving dynamic interoperability of existing application-level components and of smart-artifact and pervasive computing devices. For instance, the Gaia system developed at PARC [30], defines an architecture based on "active" interaction spaces, as a reification of a specific real-world environment (e.g., a meeting room), where pre-existing (and pre-programmed) devices and user-level software components can dynamically enter, leave and autonomously interoperate with each other according to specific patterns specified as part of the active environment.

Global Scale Direct Engineering. As far as the global scale is involved, most research on adaptive and unsupervised computing focus on the key idea of self-organizing overlay networks for P2P computing, which can be considered as a typical example of a direct engineering approach to self-organization.

In P2P computing, an overlay network of peers is built over the physical network and, in that networks, peers act cooperatively to search specific data and services. In first generation P2P systems (e.g., Gnutella [29]), the overlay network is totally unstructured, being built by having peers randomly connect to a limited number of other peers. Therefore, in these networks, the only effective way to search for information is message flooding. More recent proposals [28, 31] suggest structuring the network of acquaintances into specific regular "spatial shapes", e.g., a ring or an N-dimensional torus. When a peer connects to the networks, it occupies a portion of that spatial space, and connects with those other peers that are neighbors accordingly to the occupied position of space. Then, data and services are allocated in specific positions in the network (i.e., by those peers occupying that position) depending on their content/description (as can be provided by a function hashing the content into specific coordinates). In this way, by knowing the shape of the network and the content/description of what data/services one is looking for, it is possible to effectively navigate in the network to reach the required data/services.

3.3 Pro and Cons

Direct engineering approaches to self-organization have the great advantage of enabling engineers to achieve "by design" a specific robust self-organized behavior. Engineers, following standard methodologies, can design distributed algorithms to control distributed components to let them behave as specified by the application.

Unfortunately, such approaches are effective only for a limited number of application needs. In fact, when the applications to be realized become more articulated, the complexity of the distributed algorithms involved may become overwhelming.

For instance, extending P2P overlay-algorithms to highly mobile networks that can be partitioned (because of node mobility), merged and whose topology is likely to change quickly can become an overwhelming task from a direct engineering perspective.

4 Reverse Engineering of Self-organized Behaviors

4.1 Overview

Reverse engineering approaches to self-organization aims at achieving complex coordinated behaviors by recreating in spray multiagent systems (and by adapting to specific application needs) the conditions to make some complex coordinated behaviors observed in other systems and in nature emerge in the computational spray multiagent system. In these cases, due to the complexity of the phenomena involved, engineers have no direct control on the evolution of the system, nor they can somehow prove that the system will behave as needed. Simply, they can be reasonably (i.e., probabilistically) confident that the global evolution of the system will eventually lead to the desired globally coordinated behavior.

Simulations will be the workhorse of reverse engineering approaches. Simulations of spray multiagent systems will not only provide a framework on which to test the functionalities of a systems once developed, but they will be an integral part of the design and development process. Since the behavior of the components and of their interactions can hardly be modeled and predicted "on paper", simulations appear to be the only tool with which to have feedback on how a system will actually work. In other words, in reverse engineering approaches, the modeling phase consists in verifying via simulations the correctness of an idealized model suitable, but not necessarily close, to the target scenario (this model can be for example a biological or social model), then to refine the model and the simulations (that also realize a prototype implementation of the model) to rend both enough similar to the actual scenario to be taken in consideration as a candidate solution.

In the past few years, several approaches to self-organization relying on the reverse engineering of diverse natural phenomena have been proposed in different areas and have shown their effectiveness in achieving difficult global coordination tasks. For instance, the phenomena of ant foraging [2, 18] and gossiping [6] turn out to be useful to discover path to information and diffuse information in networks of spray multiagent systems.

4.2 Research Projects

Micro Scale. Some recent works on pattern formation for cooperative mobile robots [26, 35] try to reverse engineer natural phenomena such as chemical diffusion and embryogenesis activities to drive the movements of a swarm of tiny mobile robots (particles). In these works mobile robots connect with each other in an ad-hoc network to coordinate their movements. The main reversed abstractions, being researched, are those of chemical-gradients diffusion and local density estimation. These abstractions can be used by the robots to coordinate their movements. In particular, gradients can drive robots to reach specific locations [26, 35]. Density can be used to create diffusion-like processes, where robots tend to stay as far as possible from each other [35]. Both these two abstractions can be reverse-engineered in terms of distributed data structures (e.g., field-like hop-increasing structures and gradients of density pressures) over the ad-hoc network defined by robot themselves. Despite some promising results, up to now, the cited works focused on very simple motion strategies and computational particles – not much different from cellular automata cells.

Medium Scale. In [23] a reverse-engineered pheromone-based approach to co-ordinate Unmanned Airspace Vehicles (UAVs) has been proposed. UAVs coordinate with each other by accessing a shared data space and leaving there pheromone-based data structures. In more detail, the shared data-space resembles the environment where UAVs are operating (it provides a digital representation of the battlefield). UAVs access the data-space on the basis of their physical-location that is mapped into a specific position in the data-space. On the basis of this mechanism, UAVs are able to spread and access digital pheromones in the data-space that mirrors their physical environment.

This enables UAVs to coordinate on the basis of stigmergy [5]. In particular, by reverse engineering social insects behavior (that use pheromones to coordinate), UAV are able to perform sophisticated motion coordination task ranging from moving in formation, surround a target and avoid tracked enemies. This approach has been concretely implemented in a real-world scenario with great result. However, the techniques employed are very special purpose and it is difficult to extrapolate general lessons to be widely applied outside the motion coordination domain.

Global Scale. Several recent works in the area of Internet routing and distributed interactions are rooted on reverse engineering ideas coming from biology – i.e. ant foraging [2, 5, 6], or physics – i.e. potential fields [17]. As an example of this class of approaches (based on artificial ants), Anthill [2] support the design and development of adaptive peer-to-peer applications by relying on distributed mobile components ("ants") that can travel and can indirectly interact and cooperate with each other by leaving and retrieving bunches of information (to act as synthetic pheromones) in the visited hosts. The key objective of anthill is to build robust and adaptive networks of peer-to-peer services by exploiting the capabilities of ants to re-organize their activity patterns accordingly to the changes in the network structure. These works are very promising, but a general methodology to let such reverse-abstractions widely applicable in the general context of Internet-based application, is still far from close.

4.3 Pro and Cons

Reverse engineering approaches to self-organization have several advantages. First, it is possible to rely on results from other disciplines to explore a variety of complex coordination phenomena to be exploited in spray multiagent systems systems. Second, once the basic mechanisms underlying a self-organized behavior are understood and properly reproduced via simulation, programming an actual system to exhibit such behavior is dramatically simple, and it reduces to programming typically simple local rules and local interactions. In addition, the resulting system is intrinsically robust and adaptive, the result is typically robust and adaptive.

Unfortunately, reverse-engineering approaches incur in two main potential drawbacks.

First, generally speaking, reverse engineering approaches represent *solutions looking for a problem*[1]. Such approaches, in fact, start by reverse engineering a natural or social phenomenon (e.g. ants foraging) to devise a suitable spray-computer algorithm. Then, they look for problems (e.g. network routing) that can be solved by adopting the discovered algorithm. Although for a lot of algorithms it is rather easy to find suitable application domains, it can be difficult to find an already existing solution to the problem at hand.

Second, the complex evolution of the system may cause several potential final states to be reached by a system, each of which potentially stable, without the possibility of predicting which ones will be actually reached after the self-organization process. In some cases, all of these states may be equivalent from the application viewpoint (e.g., in ant foraging, what matters is that a reasonably short path to food/information is reached, no matter what the path actually is). Also, in these cases, the presence of multi stable states may be also advantageous, because this ensure that the system, even if strongly perturbed (e.g., due to network or environmental dynamics), will be able to soon re-organize its activity into another stable state. However, in several other cases, the designer may wish that its system self-organizes to a specific global states, not to any one.

---

[1] It is rather ironic that "*solution looking for a problem*" often sounds as a synonym for useless approach, in the research community. In fact, it is actually rather common as a business model. A company that finds a clever way to do something, then looks for problems (i.e. a market share) to sell that solution.

Both these two problems could be solved by mixing together direct and reverse engineering approaches. The introduction of direct engineered control could enable to better design the activity of the system so as to better encode a specified application task. Moreover, when the evolution of a system can lead to several final global states, and only a limited set of these are useful to the specific application purposes, the problem arise on how to control/direct the evolution of the system so as to ensure that it will self-organize as desired.

Realizing such kind of mixed approach presents a number of challenges. On the one hand, introducing some sorts of direct engineered control should be done without undermining the basic advantages of the reverse engineering approach, i.e., its capability to promote the spontaneous formation of complex and robust patterns of activity with little design and coding efforts. On the other hand, for such a mixed approach to be possible, it is necessary that both direct algorithms and reversed self-organizing mechanism are modeled and coded with the same set of basic abstractions. In the next two sections we are going to survey some recent researches that aim to that direction.

5   The Control of Self-organizing Behaviors (Direct over Reverse Engineering)

5.1   Overview

The main idea of this approach is the use of *direct engineered* mechanisms to control *reverse engineered* self-organizing behaviors. Specifically, it is based on these two key points:

- Use *reverse engineering* approaches to find low-level mechanism and interaction primitives that are robust and flexible
- Use *direct engineering* to weave together several low-level mechanisms to achieve a desired application.

The core idea of this proposal is to compensate the lack of control typical of reverse approaches by superimposing a directly engineered control layer. At the same time, the lack of flexibility and scalability of most direct engineered solutions is compensated by the low level reverse engineered mechanisms that tend to be robust and flexible.

5.2   Research Projects

Micro Scale. The Amorphous Computing project at MIT focuses on the problem of identifying suitable models for programming applications over amorphous networks of computational particles [20]. The particles constituting an amorphous computer have the capabilities of locally propagating sorts of computational fields in the network, and to locally sense and react to such fields (the field abstraction has been reverse-engineered from the biological concept of morphogen gradients). By having particles sense and re-propagate these fields, coordinated patterns of activities emerge in the system independently of the structure of the network. Moreover, the Amorphous computing project has defined a simple yet effective language for programming particles on the basis of computational fields. On this base, it has been shown how it is possible to exploit such a language to let the particles (directly) self-organize a coordinate systems and self-determine their position in it, and to have a variety of global patterns getting (directly) organized in a system from local interactions. What the project has still not addressed are the problems related to mobile and ephemeral particles: the network is considered static, and the relative position of particles is considered fixed. In addition, the project focused only on the formation of spatial patterns, completely disregarding other application scenarios.

Other sources of examples, come from recent proposals to control the motion of a modular robot. A modular robot is a collection of simple autonomous actuators with few degrees of freedom connected with each other. A distributed control algorithm is executed by all the actuators that coordinate to let the robot assume a global coherent shape or a global coherent motion pattern (i.e. gait). In [32] a mixed (direct-reverse) approach like the one discussed in this section has been proposed. At the bottom-level, reverse engineering has been applied to find a flexible and robust communication mechanism to let the robots interact. Such mechanism has been reverse-engineered form the biological concept of hormones. In abstract terms, a hormone is a message that triggers different actions at different subsystems and yet leaves the execution and coordination of these actions to the local subsystems. For example, when a human experiences sudden fear, a hormone released by the brain causes different actions, e.g., the mouth opens and the legs jump. Reverse engineering a hormone consists in modeling it by means of a type of message with specific properties [32]. At the top-level, direct engineering has been applied to combine several hormones together with robots reactions to actually implement gait control mechanisms.

Medium Scale. The reverse-engineered idea of fields (or morphogen gradients) have been applied to medium-scale pervasive-computing scenario in the context of the TOTA (Tuples On The Air) middleware [16]. TOTA relies on spatially distributed tuples, implementing the concept of field, for both supporting adaptive and uncoupled interactions between agents, and context-awareness. Agents can inject these tuples in the network, to make available some kind of contextual information and to interact with other agents. Tuples are propagated by the middleware, on the basis of application specific patterns, defining sorts of "computational fields", and their intended shape is maintained despite network dynamics, such as topological reconfigurations. Agents can locally "sense" these fields and can rely on them for both acquiring contextual information and carrying on distributed self-organizing coordination activities. The TOTA programming model enable to specify and control (via direct engineering) the behavior of tuples and agents.
The TOTA model is effective in realizing applications centered on "spatial" coordination, where the goal is to coordinate the activities of components in the space – either physical or network-based (e.g. motion coordination, self-assembly, network routing, etc.). However, the generality of this approach in supporting the design and development of a variety of applications and their power in supporting very large-scale applications for highly dynamic networks is still to be proved.

Global Scale. To the best of our knowledge, very few works tries to control self-organizing behaviors in global-scale computing. Swarm-Linda [18] is an ant-inspired system to realize distributed tuple spaces over the Internet. At the low-level a reverse-engineered swarm of ant-agents performs a foraging-kind of algorithm to create routes to quickly access tuples in the distributed tuple space. At the top-level, tuples are accessed by means of the directly engineered Linda operations. Like in other ant-foraging-inspired systems, the basic drawback of this approach is in the fact that it is very special purpose. Bridging the gap between these (successful) examples and a methodology is far from simple.

5.3 Pro and Cons

This kind of approach has a number of advantages. In particular it allows to actually *design* a distributed application and eventually prove its correctness. At the same time, the application can be grounded on reverse-engineered abstractions that can deal with most of the low-level complexity assuring flexibility and robustness. For example, the hormone-based control mechanism described above is *designed* to achieve a specific motion gait. It is flexible and robust, since the hormones on which it is grounded can tolerate local malfunctions, propagation delays, etc. [32].

The main drawback of this approach is that general-purpose methodologies to weave together low-level reverse-engineered behaviors to create an application are still unknown. Up to know only few and special purpose approaches have been proposed.

6 Self-composition of Designed Tasks (Reverse over Direct Engineering)

6.1 Overview

This kind of mixed approach is complementary to the previous one. It uses reverse engineered self-organizing behaviors to weave together direct-engineered primitive applications. This is the realm of genetic-algorithms and learning-kind of approaches: direct-engineered primitive applications are combined by means of a genetic or learning based mechanism to achieve complex applications [13, 14].

Specifically, this approach is based on these two key points:

- Use *direct engineering* approaches to find low-level mechanisms and primitive solutions to the problem at hand.
- Use *reverse engineering* approaches like genetic-algorithms and learning to combine, evolve and optimize directly engineered mechanism so as obtain a complete solution with good performance.

Complementary to the previous approach, this proposal tries to adopt, well defined, directly engineered mechanism to deal with to deal with the application fundamental tasks. Then it uses reverse engineering approaches to overcome the complexity required by the application.

6.2 Research Projects

Micro Scale. One of the major problems in sensor networks is how to make sense of low-level sensor readings to infer some property on the environment being monitored.

Usually, sensors periodically transmit collected data to a central processing unit, that collects and elaborate all the data, and tries to infer what is happening in the environment. This kind of centralized architecture has several drawbacks (single-point-of-failure, high-cost in transmitting data to the central processing unit, scalability, etc.). New ideas are arising to make such computations distributed across the whole sensor network. In particular, some recent works [8, 33] are combining directly engineered approaches to data collection and data fusion, with reverse-engineered approaches to learning and data-clustering (neural networks, etc.). More in detail, low-level directly-engineered mechanism are combined together by means of high-level reverse-engineering mechanism that enable the network to learn and classify autonomously what is happening. These works achieved very significant result, by greatly reducing the programming effort to manage a sensor network. However, they mainly focused on very simple learning behaviors, and complex applications have still to be tackled.

Medium Scale. In [25] a peculiar system to tack people movements is presented. The system is based on a PDA coupled with a GPS device carried on by a user. The PDA on the basis of GPS reading is able to track the user and to infer if the user is moving by foot or it is in a vehicle (using inferred speed measure). At the low-level, this system uses directly-engineered mechanism to store and average GPS readings over time. At the high-level, it uses a reverse-engineered learning approach to let the system infer from low-level GSP reading high-level information (location and vehicle).

The same approach has been applied in other works [27] to track and infer more general user activities.

This system, although simple and special purpose, shows how reverse-engineered approaches at the top-level can greatly save programming effort. However, it is not easy to generalize it let is suitable to general application domains.

Global Scale. One of the best examples of this class of approaches is represented by Internet search (meta)engines based on genetic algorithms [19, 22]. These are applications that allow a user to find information over the Web in a more efficient way. The key idea is to let the application build a personalized user profile so as to better discriminate between relevant and irrelevant documents. These kind of systems are basically build in two main parts [19, 22]: direct engineering is applied at the low-level to encode information retrieval agents on the basis of the user profile. Here direct algorithms for text processing and ranking are applied. Reverse engineering is applied in terms of a genetic algorithm at the top-level to create new information retrieval agents. In particular, such agents are created by replicating (with genetic operations – such as mutation and crossover) top-performing existing agents, so as to iteratively increase the system performances.

Other examples come from some works related to the ADELFE methodology [11]. The ADELFE methodology proposes to design directly (with standard tools like UML) low-level agent behaviors. Top-level agent coordination patterns are instead autonomously derived from reverse-engineered evolutionary techniques. Such methodology has been applied to a number of scenarios. In [11] it has been applied to a global-computing scenario where agents are in charge of managing a work-flow application. In these context, low-level processes are modeled in terms of directly engineered agents, that have been explicitly programmed with the underlying business logic. Top-level workflow is instead processed by means of a reversed evolutionary computing mechanism. Again, the main drawback of this approach is that it is very difficult to extend and apply the evolutionary-based algorithm to complex problems.

6.3 Pro and Cons

The main advantage of this approach is that it greatly reduce the programming effort. Once the basic mechanisms to realize the application have been found, the reverse-engineering part (e.g. genetic algorithms) handles the rest finding a suitable solution. However, with this regard, it is of course fundamental that the reverse engineered recombination does not disrupt the direct algorithms.

The main drawback of this approach is that it leads to something like a black-box solution: eventual problems in the final outcome are difficult to be traced out and slight customizations in the final application are likely to need a complete rework.

Besides these examples, the general problem of combining self-organizing behaviors and engineering approaches in a complex self-organizing system – which, to the authors' opinions, will represent one of the key challenges for the whole research area of multiagent systems – is still open and widely uninvestigated.

The urge for appropriate control models and for a uniform approach to direct and reverse engineering of self-organization appears even more compulsory when considering another factor: in several cases, even simple systems engineered with a direct approach may – due to simplifications in their modeling – exhibit unexpected self-organizing behaviors. Although sometimes such unexpected behaviors may be irrelevant or even useful for them to be offensively exploited (consider, e.g., the emergence of scaling in complex networks, and the advantages it carries to the robustness of the network [1]), sometimes they may be damaging and introduce the need to defend from them by proper forms of control.

7 Concluding Remarks and Research Agenda

In the paper we presented four distinct approaches to take advantage of self-organization to deal with the challenges posed by large-scale multiagent systems. In our opinion, each of the presented approaches has merits and drawbacks and much further work will be required to develop a general framework that combines all of them meaningfully.

To conclude, we sketch a rough research agenda for what we believe are the key challenges to be faced in the area of self-organization for the design, development, and control, of spray multiagent system applications.

First, we think that researches should rely on a deeper understanding of the global behavior of spatially distributed systems of autonomous and interacting components, in any area. This could be used to exploit self-organization principles both offensively (i.e., to use them so as to achieve in a simple way globally coordinated behaviors) and defensively (i.e., to prevent the potential emergence of possibly dangerous self-organizing behaviors). Both cases may require the study of mechanisms and tools to somehow direct and engineering such systems in a decentralized way, so as to enforce some sorts of control over these systems despite the impossibility of controlling them in their full. As previously anticipated, some recent approaches already take inspiration from phenomena of self-organization in real-world systems to defines adaptive and reliable solutions to specific contingent problems (e.g., ant-inspired algorithms and coordination based on computational fields). Currently underestimated phenomena occurring in other types of spatially distributed systems of autonomous components (e.g., macro-ecology patterns of population distribution and biodiversity, physics of granular media, emergence of synchronization, morphogenesis) are worth to be explored too. Also, more simulation work to possibly predict what types of behaviors the emergent scenarios of spray multiagent systems will exhibit will be compulsory.

Once the above understanding will be quite assessed, we think there will be need to define a general purpose programming model for designing and deploying applications in such dynamic networks of spray multiagent systems, together with the development of associated middleware infrastructure and tools. One very ambitious objective could be for such a model to enable people to program, deploy, and control self-organizing and adaptive distributed applications (exploiting both direct and reverse engineering approaches) with a minimal background knowledge – the same as a undergraduate students can currently develop excellent distributed Web-based Java applications – and independently of the specific application scenario, sensor networks rather than wide-area distributed applications – the same as an undergraduate student can easily and with minimal efforts adapt its applications for execution on both a Linux workstation and a Cellular phone. The definition of such a model will clearly require the identification of a minimal set of abstractions enabling the modeling of salient characteristics of spray multiagent systems and their operational environments. In our opinion, approaches based on computational fields [16, 35] are very promising to this purpose, by enabling to uniformly model a wide variety of distributed self-organizing behaviors (both with direct and reverse engineering) and to effectively model also ant-inspired approaches [18]. However, this opinion is still to be verified.

Eventually, all the above researches will definitely increase our understanding on the potentials of spray multiagent systems at any scale, and will likely cause a range of new application areas to come to the fore. For instance, systems such as worldwide file sharing and artifacts like the cloak of invisibility could have simply never been conceived a few years ago. The new software and hardware technology will call also for visionary application-oriented thinkers, to unfold in full the newly achieved application potentials.

References

[1] R. Albert, H. Jeong, A. Barabasi, "Error and Attack Tolerance of Complex Networks", Nature, 406:378-382, 2000.

[2] O. Babaoglu, H. Meling, A. Montresor, "Anthill: A Framework for the Development of Agent-Based Peer-to-Peer Systems", International Conference on Distributed Computing Systems, Vienna (A), 2002.

[3] A. A. Berlin, K. J. Gabriel, "Distributed MEMS: New Challenges for Computation", IEEE Computing in Science and Engineering, 4(1):12-16, 1997.

[4] C. Bernon, M.P. Gleizes, S. Peyruqueou, G. Picard, "ADELFE: a Methodology for Adaptive Multi-Agent Systems Engineering", 3rd International Workshop Engineering Societies in the Agents World, LNAI No. 2577, 2002.

[5] E. Bonabeau, M. Dorigo, G. Theraulaz, "Swarm Intelligence", Oxford University Press, 1999.

[6] D. Braginsky, D. Estrin, "Rumor Routing Algorithm For Sensor Networks", 1ST Workshop on Sensor Networks and Applications (WSNA), 2002.

[7] J. Broch, D. Maltz, D. Johnson, Y. Hu, J. Jetcheva, "A Perfomance Comparison of Multi-Hop Wireless Ad Hoc Network Routing Protocols", ACM/IEEE Conference on Mobile Computing and Networking, ACM Press, Dallas (TX), 1998.

[8] E. Catterall, K. Van Laerhoven, M. Strohbach, "Self-Organization in Ad-Hoc Sensor Networks: An Empirical Study". In Proc. Of Artificial Life VIII, Sydney, Australia. MIT Press, 2002.

[9] M. Crichton, "Prey: a Novel", HarperCollins, 2002.

[10] D. Estrin, D. Culler, K. Pister, G. Sukjatme, "Connecting the Physical World with Pervasive Networks", IEEE Pervasive Computing, 1(1):59-69, 2002.

[11] George J.P., Edmonds B. Glize P., Making self-organizing adaptive multi-agent systems work. To appear in Methodologies and Software Engineering for Agent Systems, Kluwer, 2004.

[12] T. Imielinski, S. Goel, "Dataspace - querying and monitoring deeply networked collections in physical space", IEEE Personal Communications Magazine, pp. 4-9 2000.

[13] C. Jacob, "Illustrating Evolutionary Computation with Mathematica", Morgan Kauffman Publisher, San Francisco, 2001.

[14] J. Kennedy, R. Eberhart, "Swarm Intelligence", Morgan Kauffman Publisher, San Francisco, 2001.

[15] J. Kephart, D. M. Chess, "The Vision of Autonomic Computing", IEEE Computer, 36(1):41-50, 2003.

[16] M. Mamei, F. Zambonelli, "Programming Pervasive and Mobile Computing Applications with the TOTA Middleware", 2nd IEEE Conference on Pervasive Computing and Communications, Orlando (FL), 2004.

[17] M. Mamei, F. Zambonelli, L. Leonardi, "Co-Fields: a Physically Inspired Approach to Distributed Motion Coordination". IEEE Pervasive Computing, 3(2):52-60.

[18] R. Menezes, R. Tolksdorf, "SwarmLinda: a New Approach to Scalable Linda Systems based on Swarms", 16th ACM Symposium on Applied Computing, Melbourne (FL), 2003.

[19] A. Moukas, P. Maes, "Amalthaea: An Evolving Multi-Agent Information Filtering and Discovery System for the WWW", Journal of Autonomous Agents and Multi-Agent Systems", 1(1):59-88, 1998.

[20] R. Nagpal, A. Kondacs, C. Chang, "Programming Methodology for Biologically-Inspired Self-Assembling Systems", AAAI Spring Symposium on Computational Synthesis, 2003.

[21] R. Nagpal, H. Shrobe, J. Bachrach, "Organizing a Global Coordinate System from Local Information on an Ad Hoc Sensor Network", in Information Processing in Sensor Networks, LNCS No. 2643, Springer Verlag, 2003.

[22] Z. Nick, P. Themis, "Web Search Using a Genetic Algorithm", IEEE Internet Computing, 5(3):18-26, 2001.

[23] V. Parunak, S. Brueckner, J. Sauter, "Digital Pheromones for Coordination of Unmanned Vehicles", Workshop on Environments for Multi-agent Systems (E4MAS), LNAI 3374, Springer Verlag, 2004.

[24] V. Parunak, S. Bruekner, J. Sauter, "ERIM's Approach to Fine-Grained Agents", NASA/JPL Workshop on Radical Agent Concepts, Greenbelt (MD), Jan. 2002.

[25] D. Patterson, L. Liao, D. Fox, H. Kautz, "Inferring high-level behavior from low-level sensors",UBICOMP, Seattle, Washington, USA, 2003.

[26] D. Payton, M. Daily, R. Estowski, M. Howard, C. Lee, "Pheromone Robotics", Autonoumous Robots, Kluwer Academic Publishers, 11(3):319-324, 2001.

[27] M. Philipose, K. Fishkin, M. Perkowitz, D. Patterson, D. Fox, H. Kautz, D. Hahnel, "Inferring Activities from Interactions with Objects", IEEE Pervasive Computing, 3(4):50-57, 2004

[28] S. Ratsanamy,, P. Francis, M. Handley, R. Karp, "A Scalable Content-Addressable Network", ACM SIGCOMM Conference 2001, 2001.

[29] M. Ripeani, A. Iamnitchi, I. Foster, "Mapping the Gnutella Network", IEEE Internet Computing, 6(1):50-57, 2002.

[30] M. Roman et al., " Gaia : A Middleware Infrastructure for Active Spaces", IEEE Pervasive Computing, 1(4):74-83, 2002.

[31] A. Rowstron, P. Druschel, "Pastry: Scalable, Decentralized Object Location and Routing for Large-Scale Peer-to-Peer Systems", 18th ACM Conference on Middleware, Heidelberg (D), 2001.

[32] W. Shen, B. Salemi, P. Will, "Hormone-Inspired Adaptive Communication for Self-Reconfigurable Robots", IEEE Transaction on Robotics and Automation, 18(5):1-12, 2002.

[33] S. Simic, "A Learning-Theory Approach to Sensor Network", IEEE Pervasive Computing 2(4):44-49, 2003.

[34] K. Stoy, R. Nagpal, "Self-Reconfiguration Using Directed Growth", 7th International Symposium on Distributed Autonomous Robotic Systems, Toulouse (F), 2004.

[35] M. Vasirani, M. Mamei, F. Zambonelli, "Morphogenesis of Cooperative Mobile Robots with Minimal Capabilities", presented at the 1st European Workshop on Multiagent Systems, Oxford (UK), 2003.

[36] F. Zambonelli, M. Mamei, "The Cloak of Invisibility: Challenges and Applications", IEEE Pervasive Computing, 1(4):62-70, 2002.

[37] F. Zambonelli, M. Mamei, A. Roli, "What Can Cellular Automata Tell Us About the Behaviour of Large Multi-Agent Systems?", in Software Engineering for Large Scale Agent Systems, LNCS No. 2603, April 2003.

Coordination Artifacts as First-Class Abstractions for MAS Engineering: State of the Research

Andrea Omicini, Alessandro Ricci, and Mirko Viroli

DEIS, Alma Mater Studiorum – Università di Bologna a Cesena
via Venezia 52, 47023 Cesena, Italy
{andrea.omicini, a.ricci, mirko.viroli}@unibo.it

Abstract. According to social / psychological theories like Activity Theory (AT), *artifacts* plays a fundamental role in the context of human organisations for supporting cooperative work and, more generally, complex collaboration activities. Artifacts are either physical or cognitive tools that are shared and exploited by the collectivity of individuals for achieving individual as well as global objectives. The conceptual framework of *artifacts for MAS* is meant to bring the same sort of approach to multiagent systems (MAS).

In particular, *coordination artifacts* are the entities used to shape the agent environment so as to fruitfully enable, promote and govern cooperative and social activities of agent ensembles. Thus, coordination artifacts also capture and extend the notion of coordination medium as coming from the distributed system and DAI fields, by generalising over abstractions like blackboards, tuple spaces and channels.

In this paper we account for the current state of the research on coordination artifacts. First we discuss the background from AT to artifact for MAS, then we summarise the model for the coordination artifact abstraction, and the state-of-the-art of the research on models, methods and technologies currently available for engineering MAS application with coordination artifacts.

1 Introduction

The need to achieve a coherent systemic behaviour in MASs and agent societies has led to more articulated approaches than those based on direct interaction and explicit communication. Environment-based coordination and, more generally, mediated interaction frameworks and infrastructures based on forms of coordination / cooperation without direct communication (see [1] for a recent survey) are among the most promising lines of research in the MAS field. Even outside MAS and CS, mediated interaction and environment-based coordination are highly debated issues in those research fields where collaborative and cooperative activities are studied in complex social contexts. Notable examples are CSCW and HCI [2], which recently focused on cognitive and social theories explicitly taking into account the role of environment in coordination— such as Distributed Cognition [3] and Activity Theory (AT) [4]. There, one of the most relevant issues is to understand what makes a good place for actors to work together out of an environment: re-formulated in MAS terms, the question is how to design the agent environment to suitably support social activities of a (possibly open) agent society.

A. Garcia et al. (Eds.): SELMAS 2005, LNCS 3914, pp. 71–90, 2006.

Adopting AT as a conceptual framework for MAS social activities has led to the recognition that agents are not the only abstractions to build MASs. *Artifacts* are also necessary to enable and constrain agent actions, to mediate their interactions with other agents and with the environment, and more generally to improve their ability to achieve their individual and social goals [5]. More specifically, *coordination artifacts* are social artifacts shared by agents in a MAS, which are meant to enable and govern the interaction among agents, and between agents and their environment. Along this line, coordination artifacts represent a straightfroward generalisation of the notion of coordination medium as coming from fields like coordination models and languages and distributed AI—including abstractions like tuple spaces, channels, blackboards and the alike.

In this paper, we try to summarise the many results of our research on coordination artifacts and their role in the engineering of MASs (multiagent systems), and provide a comprehensive view of its many aspects and consequences, from MAS technologies and infrastructure to agent-oriented software engineering (AOSE) methodologies.

2   Artifacts: The Theoretical Background

2.1   Activity Theory as a Conceptual Frameworks

Activity Theory (AT), also defined Cultural-Historical Activity Theory (CHAT), is a social psychological theory born in the context of Soviet Psychology from the work of Lev Vygotsky (1926–62), rooted in the dialectic materialism of Marx and Engels [6]. Originated as a part of the attempt to produce a Marxist Psychology, AT has been developed and evolved in the Soviet Union by Vygotsky's students—Alexey Leontiev in particular—for the first half of the 20th century. Then, in the second half it spread also outside Soviet Union, first in Scandinavia and in Germany and then—at the end of the 1990s—in the United States. Nowadays it is widely applied also in the context of computer science related fields, such as Computer Supported Cooperative Work (CSCW) and Human Computer Interaction (HCI) (see [4] for a survey).

Broadly speaking, AT is a very general framework for conceptualising human activities—how people learn, how society evolves—based on the concept of human *activity* as the fundamental unit of analysis. The approach was developed in contrast to the purely-cognitive approaches that were dominating the first years of the 20th century: according to them, human individual and social activities could be analysed and understood by merely focussing on the internal (mentalistic) representation of the individuals—in other words, based only on the individual information-processing capabilities. By contrast, the basic inspiration principle of AT is the *principle of unity and inseparability of consciousness (human mind) and activity*: human mind comes to exist, develops, and can only be understood within the context of a meaningful, goal-oriented, and socially determined interaction between human beings and their material environment. Interesting enough, this more or less sounds like the human-organisational version of the notion of situated intelligence by Brooks [7], where intelligence cannot be thought and conceived out of context, and interaction with the environment is proposed as the main source for intelligent behaviour of artificial systems.

In fact, a fundamental aspect for AT is the *interaction* between the individuals and the *environment* where they live, in other words their *context*. After an initial focus on the activity of the individuals, AT research evolved toward the study of human collective work and social activities, then faced issues such as coordination and organisation of activities in human society. In the context of MASs, the investigation of AT is of particular relevance because it remarks the fundamental role of the environment in the development of complex systems, and suggests how to shape the environment to make it favourable to the development of collaborative activities.

According to AT, any activity carried on by one or more components of a systems— individually or cooperatively—cannot be conceived or understood without considering the tools or *artifacts* mediating the actions and interactions of the components. Artifacts on the one side mediate the interaction between individual components and their environment (including the other components), on the other side embody the part of the environment that can be designed and controlled to support components' activities. Moreover, as an observable part of the environment, artifacts can be monitored along with the development of the activities to evaluate overall system performance and keep track of system history. In other words, mediating artifacts become first-class entities for both the analysis and synthesis of individual as well as cooperative working activities inside complex systems. Such a vision can be found also as a main aspect in Distributed Cognition [3], a branch of cognitive science which proposes that human cognition and knowledge representations, rather than being soley confined to the boundaries of an individual, is distributed across individuals, tools and artifacts in the environment.

The complexity of activities of the social systems accounted for by AT and Distributed Cognition can be found nowadays in MASs. This is why we consider such conceptual frameworks as fundamental for the analysis and synthesis of social activities inside MAS, and in particular of the artifacts mediating such activities [8]. Examples range from coordination abstractions such as tuple centres [9], to pheromone infrastructure [10] in the context of stigmergy coordination, to the Institution abstraction in electronic-institution approaches [11], to cite some.

2.2 Goals of Agents and Use of Artifacts

Other contributions to the artifact theoretical background come from cognitive sciences. In fact, by considering the conceptual framework described in [12], agents can be generally conceived as *goal-governed* or *goal-oriented* system. Goal-governed systems refer to the strong notion of agency, i.e. agents with some forms of cognitive capabilities, which make it possible to explicitly represent their goals, driving the selection of agent actions. Goal-oriented systems refer to the weak notion of agency, i.e. agents whose behaviour is directly designed and programmed to achieve some goal, which is not explicitly represented. In both goal-governed and goal-oriented systems, goals are *internal*. *External goals* instead refer to goals which typically belong of the social context or environment where the agents are situated. External goals are sorts of regulatory states which condition agent behaviour: a goal-governed system follows external goals by adjusting internal ones.

This basic picture is then completed by systems or parts of a system which are not goal-oriented, but *function-oriented*, i.e. explicitly designed to provide some kind of functionality and that can be suitably exploited or *used* by goal-oriented systems to support their activities. Keeping the same nomenclature as appears in human science theories—Activity Theory and Distributed Cognition in particular—we refer such entities as *artifacts*. We define the artifact abstraction in MAS as a computational device populating agents' environment, designed to provide some kind of function or service, to be used by agents —either individually or collectively— to perform their activities. Contrary to agents, artifacts are not characterised by internal goals or by an autonomous behaviour, but in terms of a *function*[1], and its exploitation by agents through artifact *use*. If agents are often characterised by the *intentional stance*, artifacts are characterised by the *design stance*. It's worth noting that the concept of *destination* is related but not identical the concept of function: it is an external goal which can be attached to an object or an artifact by users, in the act of using it. Then an artifact can be used according to a destination which is different from its function.

Artifacts can represent either the resources or objects that are directly the objective of agent activities, or the *tools* that are used as a medium to achieve such objectives. An example for the first case is a database or a knowledge repository in general, used to store and retrieve information. A simple example for the second case is given by a blackboard, used by agents as a tool to communicate and coordinate. Actually, this is an example of *coordination artifact*, focus of next sections.

As remarked for artifacts in human societies [12], an interesting distinction holds between *use* and *use value*, which concerns agents / artifacts relationships: there, use value corresponds to the evaluation of artifact characteristics and function, in order to *select* it for a (future) use. The distinction corresponds to two different kinds of external goals attached to an artifact: *(i)* the use-value goal, according to which the artifact should allow user agents to achieve their objective—such an external goal drives the agent selection of the artifact; *(ii)* the use goal, which directly corresponds to the agent internal goal, which guides the actual usage of the artifact. From the agent viewpoint, when an artifact is selected and used it has then a use-value goal which somehow matches its internal goal.

By extending the above considerations, the classical tool-using / tool-making distinction from anthropology [13] can be articulated along three main distinct aspects, which characterise the relationship between agents and artifacts:

– use
– selection
– construction and manipulation

While the first two aspects are clearly related to use and use value, respectively, the third is the obvious rational consequence of a failure in the artifact selection process, or in the use of a selected artifact. Then, a new, different artifact should be constructed, or obtained by manipulation of an existing one.

---

[1] The term "function" here refers to a functionality embodied by an artifact, and should not be confused with the same term as used e.g. in mathematics or in programming languages.

2.3   Cognitive Use of Artifacts

Artifacts are available for agent use. So when intelligent agents are concerned, artifacts should be available for cognitive use.

The strict relationship between intelligence and use of tools and artifacts is largely debated by anthropologists, psychologists and cognitive scientists in general [14]. In the field of robotics, this has led to the proposal of a "Tooling Test for Intelligence", aimed at evaluating intelligence in terms of the ability to exploit tools [15]. In the MAS field, the same sorts of considerations have inspired the *Agens Faber* approach, based on the idea that agent intelligence should not be considered as separated by the agent ability to perceive and affect the environment—and so, that agent intelligence is strictly related to the artifacts that enable, mediate and govern any agent (intelligent) activity [16].

One of the key issues here and in the Agens Faber approach is how artifacts can be effectively exploited to improve agents' ability to achieve individual as well as social goals. The main questions to be answered are then: How should agents reason to use artifacts in the best way, making their life simpler and their action more effective? How can agents reason to select artifacts to use? How can agents reason to construct or adapt artifact behaviour in order to fit their goals?

On the one hand, the simplest case concerns agents directly programmed to use specific artifacts, with usage protocols directly defined by the programmer either as part of the procedural knowledge / plans of the agent for goal-governed systems, or as part of agent behaviour in goal-oriented system. In spite of its simplicity, this case can bring several advantages for MAS engineers, exploiting separation of concerns for programming simpler agents, by charging some burden upon specifically-designed artifacts. On the other hand, the intuition is that in the case of fully-open systems, the capability of the artifact to describe itself, its function, interface, structure and behaviour could be the key for building open MASs where intelligent agents dynamically look for and select artifacts to use, and then exploit them for their own goals.

At a first glance, it seems possible to frame the agent ability to use artifacts in a hierarchy, according to five different cognitive levels at which the agent can use an artifact:

unaware use — at this level, both agents and agent designers exploit artifacts without being aware of it: the artifact is used implicitly, since it is not denoted explicitly. In other words, the representation of agent actions never refers explicitly to the execution of operation on some kind of artifacts.

embedded / programmed use — at this level, agents use some artifacts according to what has been explicitly programmed by the designer: so, the artifact selection is explicitly made by the designer, and the knowledge about its use is implicitly encoded by the designer in the agent. In the case of cognitive agents, for instance, agent designers can specify usage protocols directly as part of the agent plan. From the agent viewpoint, there is no need to understand explicitly artifact operating instructions or function: the only requirement is that the agent model adopted could be expressive enough to model in some way the execution of external actions and the perception of external events.

cognitive use — at this level, the agent designer directly embeds in the agent knowledge about what artifacts to use, but how to exploit the artifacts is dynamically discovered by the agent, reading the operating instructions. Artifact selection is still a designer affair, while how to use it is delegated to the agent rational capabilities. So, generally speaking the agent must be able to discover the artifact function, and the way to use it and to make it fit the agent goals. An obvious way to enable agent discovery is to make artifact explicitly represent their function, interface, structure and behaviour.

cognitive selection and use — at this level, agents autonomously select artifacts to use, understand how to make them work, and then use them: as a result, both artifact selection and use are in the hands of the agents. It is worth noting that such a selection process could also concern sets of cooperative agents, for instance interested in using a coordination artifact for their social activities.

construction and manipulation — at this level, agents are lifted up to the role of designers of artifacts. Here, agents are supposed to understand how artifacts work, and how to adapt their behaviour (or to build new ones from scratch) in order to devise out a better course of actions toward the agent goals. For its complexity, this level more often concerns humans: however, not-so-complex agents can be adopted to change artifact behaviour according to some schema explicitly pre-defined by the agent designers.

To enable such scenarios, proper models, theories and then supporting frameworks and infrastructures are needed, making artifacts first-class entities from design to runtime.

2.4   A Basic Model of Artifacts in MAS

By focussing on the essence and purposes of the artifact abstraction in MAS, a basic abstract model has been identified [17], useful in particular to enable its rational exploitation by intelligent agents [18]. According to such a model, an artifact for MAS possibly exposes *(i)* a *usage interface*, *(ii)* *operating instructions*, and *(iii)* a *function description*. On the one hand, this view of artifacts provides us with a powerful key for the interpretation of the properties and features of existing non-agent MAS abstractions, which can be then catalogued and compared based on some common criteria. On the other hand, it is also meant to foster the conceptual grounding for a principled methodology for the engineering of MAS environment, where artifacts play the role of the core abstractions.

Usage Interface — One of the core differences between artifacts and agents, as computational entities populating a MAS, lays in the concept of *operation*, which is the means by which an artifact provides for a service or function. An agent executes an action over an artifact by invoking an artifact operation. Execution possibly terminates with an *operation completion*, typically representing the outcome of the invocation, which the agent comes to be aware of in terms of perception. The set of operations provided by an artifact defines what is called its *usage interface*, which (intentionally) resembles interfaces of services, components or objects—in the object-oriented acceptation of the term.

In MASs, this interaction schema is peculiar to artifacts, and makes them intrinsically different from agents. While an agent has no interface, acts and senses the environment, encapsulates its control, and brings about its goals proactively and autonomously, an artifact has instead a usage interface, is used by agents (and never the opposite), is driven by their control, and automatises a specific service in a predictable way without the blessing of autonomy. Hence, owning an interface strongly clearly differentiates agents and artifacts, and is therefore to be used by the MAS engineer as a basic discriminative property between them.

Operating Instructions — Coupled with a usage interface, an artifact could provide agents with *operating instructions*. Operating instructions are a description of the procedure an agent has to follow to meaningfully interact with an artifact over time. In other words, they are a description of the possible *usage protocols*, i.e. sequences of operations that can be invoked on the artifact, in order to exploit its function. Besides a syntactic information, they can embed also some kind of semantic information that rational agents can eventually understand and exploit in their reasoning processes, to enable and promote the cognitive use of the artifact.

So artifacts being conceptually similar to devices used by humans, operation instructions play a role similar to a manual, which a human reads to know how to use the device on a step-by-step basis, and depending on the expected outcomes he/she needs to achieve. For instance, a digital camera provides buttons and panels (representing its usage interface), and therefore comes with a manual describing how to use them—e.g. which sequence of buttons are to be pushed to suitably configure the camera resolution.

Function Description — Finally, an artifact could be characterised by a *function description* (or service description). This is a description of the functionality provided by the artifact, which agents can use essentially for artifact selection. In fact, differently from operating instructions, which describes *how* to exploit an artifact, function description describes *what* to obtain from an artifact. Clearly, function description is an abstraction over the actual implementation of the artifact: it hides inessential details over the implementation of the service while highlighting key functional (input/output) aspects of it, to be used by agents for artifact selection. For instance, when modelling a sensor wrapper as an artifact, we may easily think of the operations for sensor activation and inspection as described via usage interface and operations instructions, while the information about the sensory function itself being conveyed through function description of the sensor wrapper.

Defining a suitable formal description of function description and operating instructions is the first step toward the definition of formal theories about the rational selection and use of artifacts by intelligent agents, impacting on their reasoning (deliberation, planning) activities. First investigations about this aspect—focussing in particular on operating instructions—can be found in [18].

3 Coordination Artifacts

Coordination artifacts are artifacts designed to provide some kind of coordination functionalities, and so exhibiting a coordinating behaviour. As a special case of artifacts for MAS, coordination artifacts are of particular interest in the context of agent societies, where they are usually exploited to achieve or maintain a global behaviour which is coherent with the society's social goal [17,19]. As such, a coordination artifact is an essential abstraction for building social activities, in that it is crucial both for enabling and mediating agent interaction, and for governing the social activities by ruling the space of agent interaction. Examples range from artifacts for concurrency management—such as semaphores, synchronisers, barriers, etc.—, to artifacts for communication management—such as blackboards, event services—, up to artifacts with articulated behaviours, such as workflow engines or auction engines.

So, coordination artifacts generalise the common notion of coordination medium as coming from the field of coordination models and languages [20]: simply put, coordination artifacts are the artifacts for MAS encapsulating the activity of MAS coordination. As such, they are the main tool for engineering the space of agent interaction, taking care of issues like concurrency, synchronisation, sharing of resources, and the like.

3.1 Basic Properties of Coordination Artifacts

Among the specific properties characterising coordination artifacts as artifacts with specific coordination functionality, we can list the following:

Focus on interaction management — Coordination artifacts are specialised in automating coordination activities. For this purpose, they typically adopt a computational model suitable for effective and efficient interaction management, whose semantics can be easily expressed with concurrency frameworks, such as process algebras or Petri nets.

Encapsulating coordination — Coordination artifacts encapsulate a coordination service, allowing user agents to abstract from how the service is implemented [21]. As such, a coordination artifact is perceived as an individual entity, but it can be actually distributed on different nodes of the MAS infrastructure, depending on its specific model and implementation. Encapsulation is the key to achieve reuse of coordination. MAS engineers can create and exploit handbooks or catalogues of coordination artifacts, embodying the solutions to general coordination problems in organisations, analogously to an handbook of organisation / coordination processes [22]. Finally, a coordination artifact provides a certain *quality of coordination*, in particular in terms of the scalability with respect to the dimensions identified by Durfee in [23], which are related to performance, robustness, reliability, and so on. The description of such dimensions is important to identify the range of applicability of the artifact in the engineering of agent societies.

Changing coordination activities at run-time — Coordination artifacts are meant to support coordination in open agent systems, characterised by unpredictable events and dynamism. For this purpose, they have to support a specific form of artifact malleability: they should allow their coordinating behaviour to be adapted and changed dynamically. Changes of the coordination activities can in principle be made either *(i)* by engineers (humans) willing to sustain the MAS behaviour, or *(ii)* by agents responsible of managing the coordination artifact, with the goal of flexibly facing possible coordination breakdowns or improving the coordination service provided.

Observing and controlling the coordination activities — A coordination artifact typically supports different level of artifact inspectability: *(i)* inspectability of its operating instructions and coordinating behaviour specification, aimed at letting user agents to be aware of how to use it or what coordination service it provides; *(ii)* inspectability of its dynamic state and coordinating behaviour, aimed at supporting the testing and diagnosing (debugging) stages for the engineers and agents responsible of its management. Controllability is also fundamental for runtime management of a coordination artifact, by making it possible to freeze its working cycle, to trace it supporting step-by-step execution while watching its state, to restart it, and so on. So, from an operational viewpoint, a coordination artifact can be understood as a sort of *virtual machine of coordination*, executing some form of coordination specification, fully inspectable and controllable by artifact administrators [9].

Summing up, coordination artifacts are conceived to be engineering abstractions used for designing, building and supporting at runtime coordination in agent societies, suitably instrumenting their dynamic working environment. Also, they can be useful to support forms of scientific investigation of collective behaviours, since they encapsulate, enforce and possibly make inspectable and modifiable the(coordination) laws regulating the behaviour of agent societies. As mediating entities, coordination artifacts typically reify and manage agent communication events; accordingly, they can be used to trace and log the overall interaction behaviour of the agent societies exploiting them. Thus, they can also act as kinds of *social memory*, which can then be inspected for possible scientific analysis about global behaviours.

3.2 Engineering Social Activities with Coordination Artifacts

The introduction of coordination artifacts impacts on the methodology adopted for engineering social activities in agent societies. Taking inspiration from Activity Theory, we can identify three different stages characterising any social activities supported by coordination artifact (see Fig. 1):

Co-construction — In this stage, society engineers understand and reason about the social objectives of the society, and define a model of the social tasks required to achieve them. This implies understanding the shape of the agent interaction space, by also identifying the dependencies that need to be managed (dependency detection is a fundamental aspect of coordination, according to the theory of coordination [24] and to cognitive theories of agent societies [25]).

Co-operation — In this stage, society engineers—and possibly intelligent agents— design and build the coordination artifacts according to the objective identified in the previous stage (co-construction). This implies understanding how to manage the dependencies previously identified, and defining a coordinating behaviour useful for that purpose. A model of coordination artifact must be chosen, according to its ability of embedding and enacting such a coordinating behaviour.

Co-ordination — In this stage, coordination artifacts are exploited, supporting the execution of the social activity. Here, the focus is on the efficient execution and automation of the coordination activities.

A parallel can be drawn between the three collaborative stages listed above (and depicted in Fig. 1) and the engineering stages as typically found in (agent-oriented) software engineering methodologies, i.e., analysis, design, development and deployment / runtime. Generally speaking, individual and social tasks are identified and described

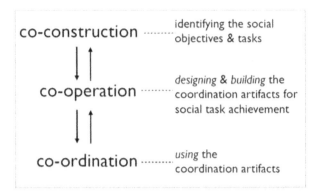

Fig. 1. Levels of a social activities

in the analysis and design stages of such methodologies. Each individual task is typically associated with one specific competence of the system. Each agent in the system is assigned to one or more individual tasks, and assumes full responsibility for their correct and timely completion. From an organisational perspective, this corresponds to assigning each agent a specific role in the organisation. Conversely, social tasks represent the global responsibilities of the agent system. In order to carry out such tasks, several possibly heterogeneous competences usually need to be combined. The design of social tasks leads to the identification of global *social laws* that have to be respected / enforced by the society of agents, to enable the society itself to function properly and in accordance with the expected global behaviour.

Given this picture, it is possible to identify a correspondence between the analysis stage (where individual and social tasks are identified) and the co-construction level, where the social objectives of the activities are shaped. Then, the identification of the social laws required to achieve the social tasks can be seen as a first step in the co-operation level. This level roughly corresponds to the design and development stages of the engineering process: coordination artifacts are the abstractions making it possible to design and develop social tasks. At the co-operation level such artifacts are designed and developed to embody and enact—as governing abstractions provided by the infrastructure—the social laws and norms previously identified. Finally, the deployment and execution stages correspond to the co-ordination level, when the coordination artifacts are instantiated and exploited.

The dynamism among the levels, compared here to the engineering stages of a system, promote a new approach to the engineering of MASs that has been called *online engineering*: coordination artifacts can be analysed, tested, debugged, manipulated, adapted, and re-designed dynamically at runtime—and whole MASs along with them. In order to support online-engineering methodologies, at least two aspects are essential: first, working with abstractions featuring suitable properties such as inspectability, controllability and malleability, which are necessary for their online analysis and synthesis; second, designing and building infrastructures that support services enabling, access and exploitation (co-ordination stage), and tools for their inspection, control, adaptation (co-operation stage).

4   Infrastructures as Providers of Coordination Artifacts

4.1   Keeping Abstractions Alive: The Role of Infrastructures

As virtual machines of coordination, coordination artifacts are more typically provided at the MAS infrastructure level rather than at the MAS application level. According to that, infrastructures should provide MAS with suitable artifacts, but also with the services for their access and use, effectively supporting the co-operation and co-ordination levels and the reflection / reification transitions (see Fig. 1). Services may range from artifacts creation and discovery to inspection and dynamic forgeability of their state and coordinating behaviour.

Given their role of rulers of agent interaction, coordination artifacts can be seen as fundamental abstractions for *governing* infrastructures [26], i.e. infrastructure providing flexible and robust abstractions to model and shape the agent interaction space, in accordance with the social and normative objectives of systems. As illustrated for instance by the SODA methodology [27], coordination abstractions provided by a MAS infrastructure should represent the runtime embodiment of the same analysis / design abstractions used since the early stages of the MAS engineering process. Keeping abstractions alive along the whole engineering process is in fact essential to support advanced practices like online engineering: there is no viable way to evolve a system online when the design abstractions are no longer in place in the runtime. Here, then, infrastructures play a key role: they should provide MAS engineers with the same coordination artifact abstractions used in the analysis / design phases, as well as the tools to for their off-line / online development, deployment, monitoring and debugging.

Infrastructures also represent an effective approach to the general issue of formalisability of complex systems, which may come from either pragmatical or theoretical problems. By their very nature, infrastructures intrinsically encapsulate key portions of systems—often in charge of the critical system behaviour. In the context of MASs, governing infrastructure encapsulate agent interaction and coordination through coordination artifacts. As a result, providing well-specified infrastructures, and in particular formally-defined coordination artifacts, promotes the discovery and proof of critical system properties. Most notably, a system property can be assessed at design-time through the formal definition of some design abstraction. Then, by ensuring compliance of the corresponding run-time abstraction provided by the infrastructure, such a property can be enforced at execution time and be automatically verified for any system based on the infrastructure.

4.2   The TuCSoN Coordination Infrastructure

As a concrete example of a model / infrastructure bringing some of the main principles that characterise the coordination artifact framework, here we consider the TuCSoN coordination infrastructure for MASs [28][2]. TuCSoN enables agent interaction and coordination by means of *tuple centres*, working as a sort of coordination artifacts. Technically, TuCSoN tuple centres are *programmable tuple spaces*—reactive,

---

[2] The TuCSoN technology can be downloaded at TuCSoN website http://tucson.sourceforge.net

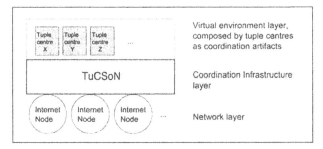

Fig. 2. A logical view of TuCSoN infrastructure

logic-based blackboards that agents associatively access by writing, reading, and consuming *logic tuples* (ordered collections of heterogeneous information chunks represented as first-order logic atoms) via simple communication operations (*out, rd, in, inp, rdp*) [9]. While the behaviour of a tuple space in response to communication events is fixed, the behaviour of a tuple centre can be tailored to the application needs by defining a set of *specification tuples* expressed in the ReSpecT language, which define how a tuple centre should react to incoming / outgoing communication events. So, unlike tuple spaces, tuple centres can be programmed with reactions so as to encapsulate coordination laws directly in the coordination media. From the topology point of view, tuple centres are collected in infrastructure nodes, distributed over the network, organised into articulated domains (see Fig. 2 for a logical view).

So, tuple centres can be conceived as general-purpose coordination artifacts, which can be dynamically inspected and forged (programmed, tuned) to entail a specific coordinating behaviour. Generally speaking, tuple centres exhibit the properties that characterise coordination artifacts: they provide different levels of inspectability—both the communication and the coordination state can be inspected at runtime—, different levels of malleability and controllability—both by changing dynamically their coordinating behaviour and by controlling its execution by means of suitable infrastructure tools [29]. Also, we can identify the basic elements that characterise the abstract model of coordination artifacts: the usage interface is composed by the basic coordination primitives plus the primitives to inspect and change tuple centre behaviour. The coordinating behaviour specification is given by the ReSpecT specification. The notion of operating instructions is not directly supported in tuple centres, even if the ReSpecT specification tuples implicitly contain a description of how to exploit the tuple centre in order to obtain the coordinating service.

4.3   Examples of Coordination Artifacts in TuCSoN

Coordination artifacts can be considered as units of reuse for engineering cooperative working environments: as agents encapsulate skills and competences concerning the execution of some task, the achievement of some goal or the solution of some problem, coordination artifacts encapsulate strategies, knowledge and experiences for constructing and ruling social activities.

In the following we describe some types of coordination artifacts commonly used in the engineering of systems, implemented on top of **TuCSoN**. The properties of inspectability, controllability and malleability of tuple centres should be considered in the background of all the examples: they are the key to conceive scenarios where the cooperative working environment can be analysed and improved at runtime, by inspecting and adapting the coordinating behaviour of its coordination artifacts.

Coordination artifacts for communication. A common form of coordination artifacts is used to provide communication services, enabling the exchange of information among agents in open and dynamic contexts which require a certain level of uncoupling among the participants. In particular, coordination artifacts can be adopted to support communication even if participants do know each other (identity uncoplying), if they are not simultaneously taking part to the interaction (temporal uncoupling), if they do not belong to the same spatial context or they ignore their mutual position (spatial uncoupling).

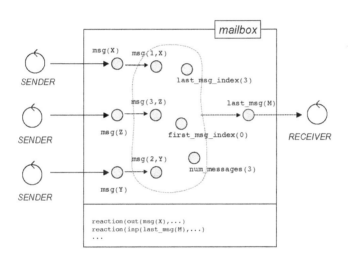

```
reaction(out(msg(M)),(
  in_r(msg(M)),
  in_r(num_messages(N)), N1 is N + 1, out_r(num_messages(N1)),
  in_r(last_msg_index(I)), I1 is I + 1, out_r(last_msg_index(I1)),
  out_r(msg(I1,M)) )).

reaction(inp(last_msg(M)),( pre,
  in_r(first_msg_index(I)), rd_r(last_msg_index(N)), I < N,
  I1 is I + 1, out_r(first_msg_index(I1)),
  in_r(msg(I1,M)), out_r(last_msg(M)) )).

reaction(inp(last_msg(M)),( post, success,
  in_r(num_messages(N)),N1 is N - 1,out_r(num_messages(N1)) )).
```

Fig. 3. Mailbox tuple centre *(Top)* and its coordinating behaviour in ReSpecT *(Bottom)*

A *mailbox* for instance can be adopted as an artifact supporting temporal and spatial uncoupling among multiple senders and typically a single receiver, with some kind of policy – e.g. FIFO – for storing and accessing the messages. Fig. 3 shows a tuple centre – called mailbox – instrumented to provide the services of a mailbox. The usage interface accounts for an operation to insert new messages (by inserting a msg tuple), to retrieve last message (by retrieving the tuple last_msg), and to read the number of messages available (by reading the tuple num_messages). The tuple centre is programmed so as to realise a FIFO policy for managing messages: the ReSpecT specification defining tuple centre behaviour (shown in Fig. 3) basically indexes the messages as soon as they are inserted in the mailbox, keeping track of the index of the first and last message, and then using it to get last one on request. This policy could be adapted dynamically according to the need, for instance adopting a strategy based on priorities or establishing a maximum number of messages which can be stored in the mailbox.

Blackboards are another kind of well-known coordination artifacts, as shared spaces of evolving knowledge where participants insert and access / retrieve information associatively. With respect to the original model developed in the context of DAI [30], here control is distributed and encapsulated within agents, while the blackboard can be programmed to have a reactive behaviour to manipulate knowledge according to social rules shared and acknowledged by the agents. Tuple centres directly map the notion of blackboard: the coordination primitives are meta-predicates to insert, inspect and retrieve knowledge in terms of logic tuples, forming a theory of communication. ReSpecT specification tuples represent the reactive rules which manipulate the theory of communication as a theory of coordination.

Coordination artifacts for knowledge mediation. Coordination artifacts can be exploited to entail automated forms of knowledge mediation for managing heterogeneity in open environments. As an example, we consider a tuple centre mediating the interaction between agents providing some services or information, and agents looking for such services or related. As an abstract case, we suppose that an agent A needs to know information pq(X,Y). According to some social knowledge – which is unknown to agent A – the information can be constructed by aggregating knowledge represented by tuple p(X) and q(Y), provided by other agents working as knowledge sources. The tuple centre can be suitably programmed then to act as knowledge mediator, applying the rules to construct the information pq from p and q:

```
reaction(rdp(pq(X,Y)), (
    pre, rd_r(p(X)), rd_r(q(Y)), out_r(pq(X,Y)) )).

reaction(rdp(pq(X,Y)), (
    post, in_r(pq(X,Y)) )).
```

Whenever a request for reading information pq is executed, the information is constructed dynamically by reading the content of the tuples p and q and inserted as a new pq tuple in the tuple set to satisfy the request. The request fails if the information cannot be constructed, because of the absence of p or q.

Coordination artifacts for resource sharing. Resource and task sharing are among the most common coordination problems in distributed and concurrent systems. A working environment can be instrumented with coordination artifacts (tuple centres) designed and programmed to provide some form of access policy in task or resource access, embodying mechanisms and synchronisation strategies well-known in concurrent systems, such as semaphores, synchronisation barries, monitors, etc.

As a simple example, we consider here a tuple centre used to act as a semaphore. The P operation provided by a semaphore used to request and obtain access to the resource can be realised by means on an in(sem) operation, i.e. retrieving a tuple sem from the tuple centre; dually, the V operation used to manifest the release of the resource can be realised by inserting back the tuple in the tuple set, by means of an out(sem). To obtain the coordinating behaviour of a semaphore it is not necessary to program the tuple centre, since the basic form of synchronisation directly provided by the *in* and *out* coordination primitives is sufficient for the purpose. Programming the tuple centre would instead be needed to obtain a more articulated and robust solution, for instance allowing multiple agents to acquire the semaphore simultaneously.

Coordination artifacts for workflow management. Workflow management concerns the automated integration and coordination of heterogeneous and independent activities involved in the same global business process. Among the others it includes activity scheduling and synchronisation, information and control flow management, exception management, and so on. Currently, in the context of service-oriented architectures – in particular Web Services – workflow management is also called *orchestration* [31].

Typically, special purpose languages – XPDL, BPEL are examples – can be used to define the workflow specification; their specification is executed by the *workflow engine*, the core component of Workflow Management Systems. A workflow engine – also called orchestration engine – can be framed here as a general purpose coordination

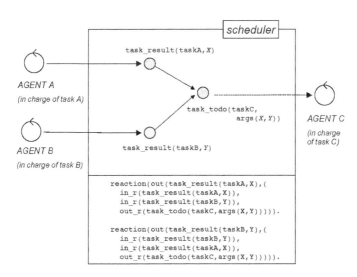

Fig. 4. Scheduler tuple centre

artifact, which is dynamically programmed to enact a coordinating behaviour according to the workflow specification.

In the context of MASs, a tuple centre then can be programmed to provide the services from a simple task scheduler up to a full-fledged general purpose workflow engine. As an example, here we consider the realisation of a simple scheduler of three activities – A, B and C – coordinated according a join pattern: task C can only start when both tasks A and B have been completed. Tasks are executed by independent agents, typically unaware of the global workflow and focussed on the achievement of their specific job. The tuple centre `scheduler` shown in Fig. 4 is an example of a coordination artifact providing such a scheduling service. The operation of the usage interface can be:

- `in(task_todo(+TaskName, -TaskInfo))`, for taking in charge the execution of a task. The presence of a tuple `task_todo` manifests the fact that a specific task has to be done, according to current workflow.
- `out(task_result(+TaskName, +TaskResult))`, for communicating the result of the execution of a task, signaling its completion.

In the example, *TaskName* can be `taskA`, `taskB` or `taskC`. The operating instructions of this coordination artifact to be followed by agents in charge of task execution would consist first in getting information about task, then in providing the result. Fig. 4 shows also the **ReSpecT** specification realising the scheduling behaviour: basically, a suitable `task_todo` tuple is automatically generated in the tuple set as soon as the results of the execution of both tasks A and B are available.

In [32] the architecture of a workflow management system based on **TuCSoN** is described, with tuple centres used as general purpose workflow engines.

5   Related Work

The coordination artifact framework discussed in this paper has been mostly inspired on the one side directly by Activity Theory studies, and on the other side by the research work developed in the context of coordination models, languages and architectures, developed mainly in the field of concurrent systems [20]. In particular the notion of coordination artifact is strictly related to the *programmable coordination medium* abstraction defined in [33], on which the tuple centre model is based. According to the frequently adopted meta-model described in [34], a coordination model can be described by identifying the *coordinables*—the entities participating to coordination activities—, and the *coordination media*—the entities enabling and managing agent communication according to some coordination laws defining the semantics of the coordination activities. Programmable coordination media extend the basic notion of coordination medium by making its behaviour programmable with some specific language, so as to flexibly specify the coordination rules according to the need. So, programmable coordination media share some properties which characterise coordination artifacts, such as encapsulation of coordination and malleability of the behaviour. Instead, differently from programmable coordination media and coordination media in general, coordination artifacts do not manage necessarily communication among agents, but—more generally—interactions caused by the execution of operations provided by the usage interface. Also, the coordination artifact framework introduces some structural properties—such as operating instructions—which are new with respect to the classic coordination meta-model, and which are indeed important in the context of open agent societies.

The design and exploitation of cooperative working environment and related infrastructures for supporting coordination activities are central themes in the context of CSCW [2]. Here, the expressiveness and effectiveness of coordination through mechanisms mediating human interaction have been clearly remarked, and related models, languages and infrastructures have been developed [35,36]. Coordination artifacts feature some of the basic properties of *coordinative artifacts* defined in such contexts [2]—in particular the properties concerning malleability and linkability—, contextualising and extending them for the MAS context. Operating instructions, for instance, are part of the extension.

Finally, the coordination artifact framework can be exploited as an analytical tool for describing existing coordination approaches based on some form of mediated interaction and environment-based coordination. For instance, the environment provided by the pheromone infrastructure in [10] supporting stigmergy coordination can be interpreted as a coordination artifact exploited by ants to coordinate: as such, it provides operations for depositing and sensing pheromones, and the coordinating behaviour is given by the environmental laws ruling the diffusion, aggregation and evaporation of pheromones. Also some coordination and organisation approaches developed in the context of intelligent / cognitive agents can be framed in terms of artifacts. A main example is is given by electronic institutions ([11] is an example), where agent societies live upon an infrastructure (middleware) which governs agent interaction according to the norms established for the specific organisation, representing both organisation and coordination rules. The institution then can be framed as a kind of shared artifact, characterised by an interface with operations that agents use to communicate, and providing a normative function on the overall set of agents.

6   Conclusion and Future Work

Along with agents, artifacts constitute the basic building blocks both for MAS analysis and modelling, and for MAS development and actual construction—i.e., real first-class abstractions available to engineers throughout MAS design and development process, down to run-time. Artifacts are objects explicitly designed to provide some function, which guides their use. Typically, artifacts take the form of objects or tools that agents share and use to support their activities, and to achieve their (individual and social) objectives. By adopting a cognitive perspective over systems [37], agents are the entities of a system that are characterised by some goals to be pursued, whereas artifacts are the entities that are not intrinsically characterised by a goal (they are not goal-oriented). Instead, artifacts are characterised by the concept of *use*, where an agent using an artifact for its own goals implicitly (and temporarily) associates an external goal to the artifact itself. So, agents and artifacts can be assumed as the two fundamental abstractions required to model and shape the structure of MASs: a MAS is made by agents *speaking* with other agents and *using* artifacts in order to achieve their goals.

Coordination artifacts are a case of particular interest in the context of agent societies, where they are usually exploited to achieve or maintain a global behaviour which is coherent with the society's social goal [17,19]. As such, a coordination artifact is an essential abstraction for building social activities, in that it is crucial both for enabling and mediating agent interaction, and for governing the social activities by ruling the space of agent interaction.

In this paper, we summarised the main lines of the research about coordination artifacts, by trying to provide the reader with a coherent perspective of a number of different views and related results. Many developments still lay before us: to list just some, the full formalisation of the artifact model, the complete definition of an AOSE (agent-oriented software engineering) methodology exploiting the artifact abstraction —first investigations about this point can be found in [38]—, the construction of a well-structured and comprehensive taxonomy working both as a criterion for artifact classification and as a foundation for a well-principled methodology, the precise characterisation of the specific notion and role of coordination artifact, the development of an infrastructure fully exploiting the power of coordination artifacts. Along these lines, we expect MAS models and technologies to progress to a great extent in the next years.

References

1. Weyns, D., Parunak, H.V.D., Michel, F., eds.: Environments for MultiAgent Systems. Volume 3374 of LNAI. Springer-Verlag (2005) 1st International Workshop (E4MAS 2004), New York, NY, USA, 19 July 2004. Revised Selected Papers.
2. Schmidt, K., Simone, C.: Coordination mechanisms: Towards a conceptual foundation of CSCW systems design. International Journal of Computer Supported Cooperative Work (CSCW) **5** (1996) 155–200
3. Kirsh, D.: Distributed cognition, coordination and environment design. In: European conference on Cognitive Science. (1999) 1–11
4. Nardi, B.A., ed.: Context and Consciousness: Activity Theory and Human-Computer Interaction. MIT Press (1996)
5. Ricci, A., Viroli, M., Omicini, A.: Programming MAS with artifacts. In Bordini, R.P., Dastani, M., Dix, J., El Fallah Seghrouchni, A., eds.: 3rd International Workshop "Programming Multi-Agent Systems" (PROMAS 2005), AAMAS 2005, Utrecht, The Netherlands (2005) 163–178
6. Vygotsky, L.S.: Mind and Society. Harvard University Press (1978)
7. Brooks, R.A.: Intelligence without representation. Artificial Intelligence **47** (1991) 139–159
8. Ricci, A., Omicini, A., Denti, E.: Activity Theory as a framework for MAS coordination. In Petta, P., Tolksdorf, R., Zambonelli, F., eds.: Engineering Societies in the Agents World III. Volume 2577 of LNCS. Springer-Verlag (2003) 96–110 3rd International Workshop (ESAW 2002), Madrid, Spain, 16–17 September 2002. Revised Papers.
9. Omicini, A., Denti, E.: From tuple spaces to tuple centres. Science of Computer Programming **41** (2001) 277–294
10. Parunak, H.V.D., Brueckner, S., Sauter, J.: Digital pheromone mechanisms for coordination of unmanned vehicles. In: 1st International Joint Conference on Autonomous Agents and Multiagent Systems AAMAS'02, ACM Press (2002) 449–450
11. Esteva, M., Rosell, B., Rodríguez-Aguilar, J.A., Arcos, J.L.: Ameli: An agent-based middleware for electronic institutions. In Jennings, N.R., Sierra, C., Sonenberg, L., Tambe, M., eds.: 3rd international Joint Conference on Autonomous Agents and Multiagent Systems (AAMAS 2004). Volume 1. New York, USA, ACM (2004) 236–243

12. Conte, R., Castelfranchi, C., eds.: Cognitive and Social Action. University College London (1995)
13. Gibson, K.R., Ingold, T., eds.: Tools, Language & Cognition in Human Evolution. Cambridge University Press (1993)
14. Hewes, G.W.: A history of speculation on the relation between tools and languages. [13] 20–31
15. Wood, A.B., Horton, T.E., Amant, R.S.: Effective tool use in a habile agent. In Bass, E.J., ed.: 2005 IEEE Systems and Information Engineering Design Symposium (SEADS 2005), Charlottesville, VA, USA, IEEE (2005) 75–81
16. Omicini, A., Ricci, A., Viroli, M.: *Agens Faber.* Toward a theory of artifacts for MAS. Electronic Notes in Theoretical Computer Sciences (2005) 1st International Workshop "Coordination and Organization" (CoOrg 2005), COORDINATION 2005, Namur, Belgium, 22 April 2005. Proceedings.
17. Omicini, A., Ricci, A., Viroli, M., Castelfranchi, C., Tummolini, L.: Coordination artifacts: Environment-based coordination for intelligent agents. In Jennings, N.R., Sierra, C., Sonenberg, L., Tambe, M., eds.: 3rd international Joint Conference on Autonomous Agents and Multiagent Systems (AAMAS 2004). Volume 1. New York, NY, USA, ACM (2004) 286–293
18. Viroli, M., Ricci, A.: Instructions-based semantics of agent mediated interaction. In Jennings, N.R., Sierra, C., Sonenberg, L., Tambe, M., eds.: 3rd International Joint Conference on Autonomous Agents and Multiagent Systems (AAMAS 2004). Volume 1. New York, USA, ACM (2004) 286–293
19. Ricci, A., Viroli, M., Omicini, A.: Environment-based coordination through coordination artifacts. In Weyns, D., Parunak, H.V.D., Michel, F., eds.: Environments for Multi-Agent Systems. Volume 3374 of LNAI. Springer (2005) 190–214 1st International Workshop (E4MAS 2004), New York, NY, USA, July 2004, Revised Selected Papers.
20. Papadopoulos, G.A., Arbab, F.: Coordination models and languages. Advances in Computers **46** (1998) 329–400
21. Viroli, M., Omicini, A.: Coordination as a service: Ontological and formal foundation. Electronic Notes in Theoretical Computer Science **68** (2003) 457–482 1st International Workshop "Foundations of Coordination Languages and Software Architecture" (FOCLASA 2002), Brno, Czech Republic, 24 August 2002. Proceedings.
22. Malone, T.W., Crowston, K., Lee, J., Pentland, B., Dellarocas, C., Wyner, G., Quimby, J., Osborn, C.S., Bernstein, A., Herman, G., Klein, M., O'Donnell, E.: Tools for inventing organizations: Toward a handbook of organizational processes. Management Science **45** (1999) 425–443
23. Durfee, E.H.: Scaling up agent coordination strategies. IEEE Computer **34** (2001)
24. Malone, T., Crowston, K.: The interdisciplinary study of coordination. ACM Computing Surveys **26** (1994) 87–119
25. Conte, R., Castelfranchi, C.: Cognitive and Social Action. University College London (1995)
26. Omicini, A., Ossowski, S.: Objective versus subjective coordination in the engineering of agent systems. In Klusch, M., Bergamaschi, S., Edwards, P., Petta, P., eds.: Intelligent Information Agents: An AgentLink Perspective. Volume 2586 of LNAI: State-of-the-Art Survey. Springer (2003) 179–202
27. Omicini, A.: SODA: Societies and infrastructures in the analysis and design of agent-based systems. In Ciancarini, P., Wooldridge, M.J., eds.: Agent-Oriented Software Engineering. Volume 1957 of LNCS., Springer (2001) 185–193
28. Omicini, A., Zambonelli, F.: Coordination for Internet application development. Autonomous Agents and Multi-Agent Systems **2** (1999) 251–269

29. Denti, E., Omicini, A., Ricci, A.: Coordination tools for MAS development and deployment. Applied Artificial Intelligence **16** (2002) 721–752 Special Issue: Engineering Agent Systems – Best of "From Agent Theory to Agent Implementation (AT2AI-3)".

30. Corkill, D.D.: Blackboard systems. Journal of AI Expert **9** (1991) 40–47

31. Peltz, C.: Web services orchestration and choreography. IEEE Computer **36** (2003) 46–52

32. Ricci, A., Omicini, A., Denti, E.: Virtual enterprises and workflow management as agent coordination issues. International Journal of Cooperative Information Systems **11** (2002) 355–380 Cooperative Information Agents: Best Papers of CIA 2001.

33. Denti, E., Natali, A., Omicini, A.: Programmable coordination media. In Garlan, D., Le Métayer, D., eds.: Coordination Languages and Models – Proceedings of the 2nd International Conference (COORDINATION'97). Volume 1282 of LNCS. Berlin (D), Springer-Verlag (1997) 274–288

34. Ciancarini, P.: Coordination models and languages as software integrators. ACM Computing Surveys **28** (1996) 300–302

35. Cortes, M.: A coordination language for building collaborative applications. International Journal of Computer Supported Cooperative Work (CSCW) **9** (2000) 5–31

36. Agostini, A., De Michelis, G., Grasso, M.A.: Rethinking CSCW systems: The architecture of MILANO. In Hughes, J.A., Prinz, W., Rodden, T., Schmidt, K., eds.: 5th European Conference on Computer Supported Cooperative Work (ECSCW'97), Kluwer Academic Publishers (1997) 33–48

37. Conte, R., Castelfranchi, C.: Cognitive and Social Action. UCL Press Limited, University College London, Gower Street, London, UK (1995)

38. Molesini, A., Omicini, A., Ricci, A., Denti, E.: Zooming multi-agent systems. In: 6th International Workshop on Agent-Oriented Software Engineering (AOSE 2005), AAMAS 2005, Utrecht, The Netherlands (2005)

Analysis and Design of Physical and Social Contexts in Multi-agent Systems*

Florian Klein** and Holger Giese

Software Engineering Group, University of Paderborn,
Warburger Str. 100, D-33098 Paderborn, Germany
fklein@upb.de, hg@upb.de

Abstract. The multi-agent paradigm promises to provide systems with the ability to adapt to changing external contexts. In this paper, we propose an approach for the model-driven design of context-aware multi-agent systems. We provide a classification for differentiating between different aspects of context and present a specification technique for modeling these aspects. We finally discuss the difficult transition from general requirements to implemented solution and propose some techniques.

1 Introduction

As embedded systems and the programs running on them become more and more ubiquitous, the multi-agent paradigm is steadily gaining importance as a powerful approach to designing flexible solutions for real-world problems. Multi-agent systems (MAS) shift the primary focus from solving sophisticated, highly structured problems to less structured problems in complex environments, i.e. are oriented towards a more practical kind of intelligence. Interaction between agents and between agents and their surroundings, rather than the agents' internal processes, is what predominantly drives multi-agent system analysis or design. Hence derives one of the major promises of the multi-agent paradigm, the ability to adapt to changing external conditions and interface with a wide variety of agents in open and highly heterogeneous systems. On the flip side, this means that properly handling context – in a nutshell, with whom and in which way to interact – is one of the most important challenges in engineering multi-agent systems facing developers today.

Context is often equated with location, especially in the mobile computing field. Consequently, many approaches are concerned with providing location transparency and/or ad hoc interaction with other agents or devices that are physically close to an agent [1]. This is often achieved by means of some sort of middleware providing an abstraction from the physical environment and location-transparent services, e.g., a shared tuple space [2] or some more sophisticated form of synchronized virtual environment

* This work was developed in the course of the Special Research Initiative 614 - Self-optimizing Concepts and Structures in Mechanical Engineering - University of Paderborn, and was published on its behalf and funded by the Deutsche Forschungsgemeinschaft.

** Supported by the International Graduate School of Dynamic Intelligent Systems.

A. Garcia et al. (Eds.): SELMAS 2005, LNCS 3914, pp. 91–108, 2006.

[3]. The focus is generally on practical and implementation-level problems, as location as a concept seems fairly straight-forward.

However, context in a broader sense is a more complex concept, as it can cover anything that affects the scope, shape and meaning of an agent's interactions. Schmidt et al. stress that context 'is more than location' [4] and propose human factors (user, social environment, task) and physical environment (conditions, infrastructure, location) as relevant aspects. We conjecture that dealing with such aspects conceptually, i.e., properly differentiating them and explicitly representing them when modeling a system, is essential for the development of complex embedded multi-agent systems. We therefore propose a meta model that captures various aspects of context and their relationships, which provides us with a unifying framework for analysing and modeling these aspects and exploiting the relationships between them. The elements of this meta model are presented in the following section, drawing on a number of real-world examples for illustration and motivation.

A recent survey classifying and comparing approaches to context modeling [5] evaluates them with respect to formality and their ability to deal with distribution, ambiguity, perturbations, and existing environments. The survey identifies the ontology-based and the object-oriented categories as the most suitable. For specifying multi-agent systems based on our meta-model, we use a UML-based, i.e. fundamentally object-oriented, notation with proprietary extensions that allows us to model both structural and behavioral aspects. What differentiates our specification technique from other approaches [6,7,8,9] is that all diagrams have operational semantics that allow their interpreted execution and enable code generation, whereas many of the conceptual diagrams used for expressing social dependencies and types of sequence diagrams used for protocol specifications by those approaches require human intervention for interpretation and disambiguation when implementing the specification. Section 3 presents the specification technique in more detail.

A fundamental problem when dealing with context is the gap between the specification of desirable properties of a system, which are often expressed from a global, objective perspective, and the specification of agent behavior, which is necessarily connected to the agent's subjective context. In Section 4, we discuss this transition from analysis (problem domain, requirements) to design (agent specification). We argue how the semantics of our specification facilitate this transition and, being operational, allow us to generate and validate prototypes of (even early) designs. We also present concrete approaches to handling different types of context and strategies for their distributed realization in Section 5.

We close with an outlook on future work.

2   Classifying Context

Formalizations of the concept of context have long been studied in AI research. [10] compares the two dominant formal theories of context, Propositional Logic of Context [11] and Local Models Semantics [12]. While these provide important insights on the epistemological aspects and theoretical limitations of context, they have gained, as [13] notes, little practical relevance for the design of multi-agent systems. In the vein of [4], various more pragmatic context classification schemas have been proposed (see [14] for a survey), often geared towards a specific aspect like human interaction or tied to a particular middleware or implementation technique.

We see the added value of our meta model in the ability to pragmatically describe context at various levels in a consistent way, with operational semantics. Our model is characterized by the fundamental distinction between Physical and Conceptual entities. Whereas the former exist in their own right and may be observed by agents, the latter are derived by convention, based on observations. This grounding differentiates our metamodel from others that distinguish between physical/metaphysical contexts, e.g. [15]. Ultimately, we are primarily interested in enabling a layered approach to modeling, the Conceptual Layer being the place to deal with knowledge or social level [16] characterizations.

While this is intuitive for embedded systems with physical components, it does not appear to be applicable to software in a meaningful way, as software is, in itself, completely based on conventions. This, however, depends on the selected level of abstraction: from an agent's perspective, sensors and effectors operate in a direct fashion, and objects, files, messages, or other agents are observable entities in their own right. We believe the distinction to be helpful as it provides a way to define complex social constructs grounded in concrete entities. Our complete model covers many aspects of multi-agent systems, though we restrict our presentation to those parts that are directly relevant for understanding and handling contexts.

2.1   The Physical Layer

On the Physical Layer, context is concrete. We differentiate between a general notion, describing the agent's surroundings, and the specific instance situation facing an agent within those surroundings.

Environment. An agent's Environment is the system inside which it exists, and with which it interacts using its Sensors and Effectors. Setting system boundaries is a somewhat arbitrary modeling decision depending on the desired level of abstraction. The size of the Environment should be minimally sufficient for modeling all of an agent's interactions and observations. For a software agent, the agent platform it runs on would be a good starting point. An intrinsic feature of Environments is that they are themselves embedded in and usually connected to other Environments. For a mobile information agent migrating to a different agent platform, the respective operating systems and the network infrastructure become relevant Environments, if only in transit. Likewise, when analyzing possible faults in an agent system, the Environment hierarchy should probably be extended to include the hardware it runs on. Even in the physical world, the exact boundaries remain arbitrary - a Mars rover's most relevant Environment is (part of) the surface of planet Mars, but when communications with ground control are considered, one might want to include large parts of the solar system, if only at a very abstract level of detail.

While the environment used to be seen as a kind of passive backdrop for the agents' behavior, its importance for agent coordination, e.g., through stygmergy or by providing distributed services, is currently gaining attention (cf. [17]). This makes explicitly modeling them essential, even more so if agents are not specific to a particular Environment but expected to migrate between and perform well in different Environments.

Even though the requirements regarding environment models are very heterogeneous, we therefore propose three aspects that we consider essential in any description technique for specifying Environments: modeling Entities, Processes and Services.

Entities represent the elements of the Environment that agents can perceive and influence. An Agent is thus a special kind of Entity. Entities and their relationships can be modeled by any kind of domain model or ontology description. The first step towards context-awareness on this level is to provide a model that an agent can understand or at least implicitly use. While for embedded systems the outside world can potentially serve as its own model, pure software agents need to be explicitly compatible with the target platform's concepts or at least be able to map them to corresponding internal representations. E.g. [13] calls attention to this problem and proposes an algorithm that allows agents to acquire knowledge about their environment using fuzzy learning techniques. [18] discusses the transformation of terminological context expressed by formal ontologies.

Processes basically describe change not caused by Agents, especially the rules and laws governing the Environment's behavior. Examples include gravity on Earth or Mars and an agent platform scheduling execution, retrieving an Agent from persistent storage, or crashing. Processes can also be used to model the mechanical behavior of Entities that are no Agents. While these behavioral aspects could be subsumed under the ontology concept, consistently communicating them between heterogeneous agents is notoriously difficult.

This leads to Services, which could be seen as a sort of low level abstraction placed on top of Entities and Processes. Services are provided through Processes or Entities (called Facilities) by the Environment. They may include generation (creation / retrieval) of agents, execution (scheduling / resources), life cycle management, discovery (directory services), communication infrastructure (message transport, (virtual) shared spaces), persistence, migration, security (authentication / integrity) and interfaces to other environments. Services are the domain of standards, be it de facto standards like Java or dedicated efforts like the FIPA.

While homogenization is a pragmatic approach to this problem, the ultimate goal of ubiquitous, networked agent systems seems to require heterogeneous systems offering standardized service descriptions, e.g. extending techniques already used in conjunction with web services. Artifacts [19,20] could be seen as a generic approach to the conceptual modeling and description of Facilities. For the developer, context-awareness at this level basically comes down to understanding the nature and structure of one's surroundings and ensuring technical interoperability.

Interactional Context. The Agent's Interactional Context is what is at the heart of 'context-aware' behavior. It consists of the Perceptive Context, the set of Entities the Agent can currently sense with its Sensors, and the Effective Context, the set of Entities it can directly affect with its Effectors. The relationship established by the Interactional Context is clearly neither symmetric nor transitive. We do not elaborate on the inverse relationship, i.e. who can sense or affect an Agent, as it is less relevant and difficult to operationalize (while an avatar in a shooter game has a vital interest both in knowing whom it can see and shoot and who can see and shoot it, the latter question is impossible to answer conclusively). The Interactional Context is determined by an Agent's

Sensors and Effectors and the Environment: In a physical setting, the Environment acts on the Sensors' and Effectors' effectiveness and thus implicitly sets the context; in a software system, the Interactional Context is explicitly created by publishing information, providing interfaces and setting permissions.

An Agent's Interactional Context represents a collection of the partitions on an Environment's Entities for the different Sensors and Effectors. Here, context-awareness corresponds to situation-awareness, i.e. the ability to grasp and reason about specific instance situations, which probably comes closest to the common understanding of 'context'. The Interactional Context is very important for an agent's behavioral decisions because, on the one hand, it defines which interactions are at all possible, e.g. which communication partners or resources are available, and, on the other hand, it often suggests which actions might be required. Intelligent behavior in a real world scenario is closely connected to adapting to the current Interactional Context, reacting appropriately or even proactively anticipating it. Using a cooperative adaptive automotive lighting system that achieves optimal illumination while avoiding headlight glare, two oncoming cars enter each others Interactional Context as soon as they come in range of their wireless link. Informing each other of their presence, they can prepare to shade the appropriate area of their adaptive headlights as soon as the other car enters the effective context of the headlights, i.e. its driver could be blinded by the glare. Obviously, being able to focus on 'local' interactions can also greatly simplify designing and verifying agent behavior. This is not limited to agents in the physical world: The Interactional Context introduces a generalized concept of locality into a system's description that is helpful when trying to structure and modularize the design.

2.2   The Conceptual Layer

On the Conceptual Layer, we again distinguish a general notion of social structures existing in a system and an agent's specific membership in these structures.

Social Environment. The social environment is primarily concerned with organizational structure [21]. In [22,23], we introduced Communities as a flexible way to describe such structures by means of groups of agents sharing a common set of rules, possibly in a quite informal or ad-hoc fashion. Communities define Roles, prohibit, allow, or require certain behaviors and introduce conventions for interpreting observable behavior. This last aspect, the idea of Norms for deriving Conceptual from Physical entities, is central for dealing with the higher level aspects of MAS. The Conceptual Layer is an abstraction created to structure complex interactions and allow a more intuitive understanding – it is not concerned with the way these concepts are ultimately implemented, nor does the use of social metaphors imply any assumptions with respect to the agents' cognitive capabilities. We therefore do not model an agent's beliefs or intentions – which would presume a specific type of implementation – but merely its Professed Intentions (or Beliefs), i.e., what other agents can imply about an agent's 'state of mind' from their observations, based on said Norms.

Languages are Norms for interpreting specific observations, i.e. ascribing Professed Intentions to messages. Meaningful communication is thus only possible within the same Community, i.e., between agents sharing the same frame of reference. The types of Communities that exist in an Environment thus limit the possible interactions and exchanges.

An Agent's Social Environment is therefore defined by the composition of Community Types that exist in its current Environment – in fact, we have proposed using Communities as architectural views for modeling non-orthogonal concerns [22]. An Agent moving to an auction platform would e.g. encounter a Community Type specifying the rules of conduct and a single persistent Community containing all trading agents, and a type for ad hoc Communities containing the participants of individual auctions. Once again, a central problem is interoperability: support for the relevant rule sets needs to be designed into the agents, or there needs to be a generic mechanism for communicating a standardized description to agents migrating into the environment.

Social Context. Social Context provides a very powerful notion of context, dealing with dynamic social dependencies. It is, first of all, set by the Communities of which an agent is a member, and the Roles it plays in them. Based on the Norms of these Communities, Agents can then enter into a web of relationships with other agents by performing actions that are associated with Professed Intentions. An Agent may send a message or make a change in the Environment that is interpreted as a promise to follow a certain course of action (commissive), a command issued to another agent (directive), a permission to perform a certain action (permissive) or the simple profession that the agent holds a certain fact to be true (assertive). These Professed Intentions can then be used in rules to control the behavior of the Agent itself or other Agents, e.g., that an agent may only use a controlled resource if the controller agent has issued a permission, or that the debtor's commitment to pay the winning bid in an auction is only fulfilled once the creditor has asserted receipt of the payment. In short, Social Context is about what an agent may expect of others and what others expect of it.

The ability to dynamically assume Roles, as proposed by [24], or even dynamically join and quit Communities provides an important abstraction for modeling adaptive agent behavior. It is realized using the same mechanism based on Norms as above, e.g., two agents reaching the same intersection might form a 'right-of-way'-community, decide who gets to first based on its rules, pass the intersection, and break up the community again. Likewise, an Agent could commit to a Role in reaction to certain perceptions, which would correspond to the concept of situated commitment [25].

The Social Context is thus shaped by observations, which in turn depend on the Interactional Context, i.e. what an Agent can actually sense. However, an Agent's Social Context is not limited to the confines of its current Interactional Context. As opposed to the Physical Layer, conceptual relationships often are transitive, which allows Agents to leverage their Social Context in order to extend their Interactional Context. For example, robotic vehicles in a warehouse could only possess sensors for accurately detecting their own position, i.e. each position sensor's Interactional Context only contain the vehicle itself. For locating other vehicles, they rely on the community of agents in the same warehouse. By committing to the execution of a publication pattern that mandates sending continuous updates about the agent's position over a wireless link, the agents can suddenly 'sense' all other members of the community (if only with a certain latency).

Nonetheless, one should never forget that Social Context is grounded in and thus dependent on the Physical Layer. In the above example, if the position sensor or the sensor/effector pair implementing the wireless link break, the transportation agent *will* break its commitment, a contingency that needs to be anticipated and handled by the community. There are therefore two challenges with respect to Social Context: One is analyzing it at runtime and exploiting its potential, an application-specific problem that allows for any amount of creativity on the part of the designer; the other one is properly operationalizing it at the implementation (Physical) level, a more clearly defined problem that can be tackled by suitable design techniques as discussed below.

3   Specifying Context

We now present the notation we use for specifying the various types of context described above. We use the control of autonomous (robotic) agents (see Figure 1) cooperatively handling the storing and shipping of goods in a warehouse as our example. Inside warehouses on a pier, cargo is stored on shelves. *Forklifts* can load *Cargo* into *Shelves* and onto *Carriers*, which move it into and out of the warehouses. *Virtual Shipment Manager* agents that can move between servers in the warehouses are responsible for accomplishing tasks, which consist of storing or retrieving a certain set of cargo items. Agents within the same warehouse can communicate using a wireless LAN.

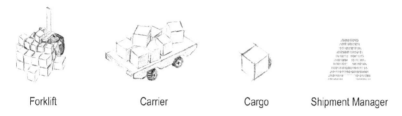

| Forklift | Carrier | Cargo | Shipment Manager |

Fig. 1. The Agents of the application example and a cargo item

Our notation is based on standard UML 2.0. Note that we employ the UML as a formal specification language with precise semantics: Prominently using story patterns [26], an extended type of UML collaboration diagram that allows specifying pre- and postconditions expressed as instance graphs, the open source UML CASE tool Fujaba[1] is able to generate executable programs from graphical specifications. By adding a UML profile introducing the appropriate stereotypes, we strive to provide a precise but accessible description of a multi-agent system's physical and social structure that is grounded in established modeling techniques from the software engineering domain.

Our use of the UML parallels the application of notations that offer themselves for specific modeling purposes by several other approaches (see [6] for a survey), e.g. in the use of class diagrams for ontology modeling, object diagrams to describe system states and state charts for control structures [7], or a component-based model of agent interactions [8].

3.1   Physical Layer

Environment. The key element for the description of the Environment is the Entity model, which we describe using UML class diagrams. This model serves as the

---

[1] www.fujaba.de

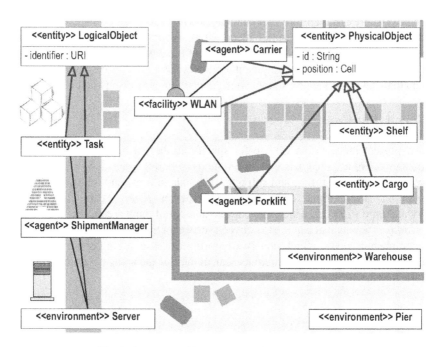

Fig. 2. Overview of key elements of the environment

foundation for the discussion of further concepts such as events or behaviors. Figure 2 gives an impression of the key elements of the system and their basic properties by means of a partial class diagram containing only selected associations. The pier is logically divided into a grid of discrete cells in order to simplify reasoning about positions.[2]

Based on this model, the Environment's Processes can be defined by means of story patterns. Inertial movement of physical objects is implemented as a Process; agents only have Effectors for de- and accelerating. Figure 3 (a) shows a carrier moving from one cell to another.

It also illustrates how story patterns specify graph transformations. The transformation rule consists of two instance graphs, the left-hand side (LHS), which is the precondition, and the right-hand side (RHS), which is the postcondition. The LHS is matched against the system's instance graph at runtime. If an occurrence is identified, it is transformed to correspond to the RHS by creating, modifying and removing the appropriate elements. To achieve a more compact syntax, the LHS and the RHS are collapsed into a single graph: unmarked elements are unaffected by the transformation and are part of both the LHS and RHS. Elements marked with ≪destroy≫ are part of the LHS, but not anymore present in the RHS. Elements marked with ≪create≫ do not exist in the LHS and are created when applying the pattern.

---

[2] Sparse, graph-like UML rules and difference equations provide a limited way of describing a system's mechanics that is, however, sufficient for many applications. Differential equations and the underlying more complex numerics that are required for more accurate physical modeling can be included, but require specific approaches.

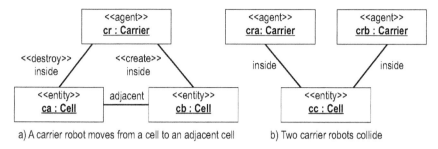

a) A carrier robot moves from a cell to an adjacent cell   b) Two carrier robots collide

Fig. 3. Processes and conditions can be defined by story patterns

The Entity model also allows reasoning about relevant system properties. Instance situations that correspond to hazardous events we would like to preclude, e.g. collisions, can be specified using story patterns without side effects. As each logical cell can only accommodate one carrier at a time, two carriers that occupy the same cell have collided. This is expressed by the diagram in Figure 3 (b).

We also need to model the Services offered by the Environment, i.e., the Entities (Facilities) through which they are provided and the Processes describing their functionality. The corresponding classes and story patterns can be reused between systems with similar infrastructure.

In our example, the most important service is the wireless network provided through an access point that serves as the corresponding Facility. Besides, there are higher level services that e.g. provide the robots with knowledge about the warehouse layout or mobility to the Shipment Management agents. As the example system is closed and homogeneous, we can use the environment specification to design support for this particular Environment directly into the agents and do not need to provide mechanisms for communicating it at runtime, a problem in its own right.

Interactional Context. We also need to describe the agents' potential interactions with their environment. [27] models contexts by selecting specific subsets of a class structure. We proceed in a similar fashion, but use subsets induced by the agents' Sensors and Effectors. These agent-specific views on the Entity model are described using the stereotype ≪context≫. Figure 4 defines how a carrier agent can sense other physical objects by means of sonar if they are in range. The story pattern adds a concrete *PhysicalObject* to the *Carrier*'s Perceptive Context. Accessible attributes are marked read. Read marks can be annotated with the accuracy and delay of the measurements and the update frequency the corresponding Sensor provides. For example, agents can get a much more precise reading on their own position than on other agents, using sonar. Similar annotations specify valid ranges and limitations on changes to modifiable attributes made by Effectors.

Fig. 4. Definition of a Sensor's Perceptive Context

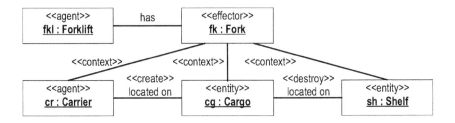

Fig. 5. Applying an Effector to Entities in the Effective Context

Story patterns that describe the actual application of an Effector (or Sensor) can than explicitly reference the ≪context≫ relation between the Effector and an Entity, as the Effector is of course restricted to interacting with Entities from its Effective Context. Figure 5 defines how a *Forklift* moves a *Cargo* item from a *Shelf* onto a *Carrier* using its *Fork*-Effector. In this case, the (previously specified) ≪context≫ relation implies that *Forklift*, *Carrier*, and *Cargo* are in adjacent cells.

3.2 Conceptual Layer

Social Environment. In the Conceptual Layer, we consider the purpose of the system, i.e. transporting tasks, and other functional (e.g. avoiding collisions) and non-functional (e.g. efficiency, reliability, and fault tolerance) requirements.

Depending on the nature of the requirements, we use different techniques to specify Community Types dealing with them. Safety-critical aspects like collision avoidance are handled by specialized Community Types expressed using an extended real-time variant of UML 2.0. They are modeled as *coordination patterns* that enable a scalable compositional technique for the automated verification of safety properties.[3] The approach supports modeling complex behaviors through adding layers of refining patterns to a verified design. Aspects that are rather concerned with efficiency, such as the allocation of transportation tasks, are modeled with rules expressed as story patterns to allow for greater flexibility. The Social Environment of the warehousing system prominently features two types of Communities: the safety-critical *LocalCoordination* Community Type for coordinating robot movements and the *Task Execution* Community Type for allocating and carrying out tasks.

Collision avoidance implemented in the Physical Layer would leave the vehicles without a way of reliably predicting behavior and entirely dependent on what limited information they can obtain from their Interactional Context. Even barring sensor failure, the limited perception of the Agents makes intelligently anticipating and avoiding hazards difficult. By designing a solution in the Conceptual Layer, we can partially overcome these limitations. Using a Community Type that requires the shuttles to commit to the continuous publication of their position and using cooperative and proactive collision avoidance strategies, we enable much more intelligent movement patterns. As the

---

[3] A detailed description of our verification technique and an extensive review of related work concerning the modeling of real-time systems and compositional verification can be found in [28].

wireless network's range is limited to the respective warehouse, one persistent Community exists per warehouse and wireless base station. This is actually a desirable situation, as a centralized solution would not scale well in terms of bandwidth and memory consumption, important factors for embedded systems.

The *Task Execution* Community Type simply specifies rules of conduct for agreeing to take on and completing a task. A temporary Community implementing it is dynamically created whenever a Shipement Manager starts working on a new task. We provide more details in conjunction with the discussion of Social Context.

Social Context. The specified Communities and Community Types shape the Social Environment. To compute the actual Social Context, we need to be able to specify rules for membership, assuming roles and professing intentions, each of which are expressed as story patterns in terms of Entities.

Each access point is the defining member of a *LocalCoordination* Community. When a *carrier* enters the range of the access point, it becomes a member of the corresponding Community (see Figure 6 (a)). Besides the ≪member≫ relation, joining the Community implicitly adds a Commitment to adhere to its Community Type to the agent's Professed Intentions.

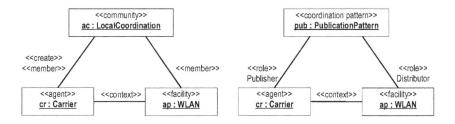

Fig. 6. Membership and required behavior in a Community

The Community Type specifies structural invariants in the form of compulsory roles triggered by sets of associated preconditions. In the example, every vehicle agent is required to act as a *Publisher* in the *Publication* pattern that ensures that all participants are kept informed about each other's position. Using the information guaranteed by the *Publication* pattern as a bootstrap, it is then possible to implement complex routing and collision avoidance schemes by means of additional patterns that make use of the information about vehicle positions guaranteed to be available. The instantiation of the pattern is again triggered by a story pattern describing instance situations at the Entity level, provided in Figure 6 (b). A maximum acceptable delay for the instantiation of the pattern can also be supplied.

For the non-critical task allocation, we use rule-based behavioral specifications. In Figure 7, we specify how a *Carrier* – that is cooperating with a *ShipmentManager* in order to complete a *Task* and is therefore member of the corresponding ad-hoc Community – announces its schedule and thus makes an implied commitment to it. The story pattern in the *ScheduledTransport* Commitment explicitly describes an observable instance situation at the Entity level that the agent will strive to bring about.

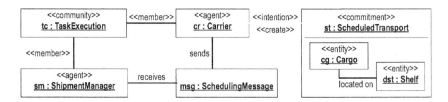

Fig. 7. An agent commits to the execution of a schedule

Fig. 8. An agent professing conflicting commitments

In analogy to the hazardous events we specified in the Physical Layer, we can also specify undesirable constellations in the Conceptual Layer using the same techniques. The story pattern in Figure 8 describes a conflict caused by concurrent Commitments to two different schedules.

4   Analysing and Designing Context

4.1   Analysis

The layered nature of our approach suggests beginning analysis in the Physical Layer. Especially when designing embedded systems, the hardware already determines much of the Physical Layer, whereas the Conceptual Layer is less constrained and leaves more room for creativity. Thus, (the object-oriented) analysis starts with the Entity model and then moves on to Processes and whichever Services may already be offered by the system. We also identify potential Agents, their Sensors and Effectors. As, in an embedded system, the Agents' capabilities and Interactional Contexts are already fixed by the laws of physics, modeling these aspects correctly is essential.

As the second step of the analysis phase, we turn to modeling system requirements, from a global perspective. Even though we focus on modeling the operational goals and dependencies here, it seems feasible to carry out the initial analysis using a notation incorporating soft goals and dependencies (e.g. [9]). For requirements that need to be formally verified, it is, however, desirable to express them as story patterns in terms of the elements of the analysis model.

During analysis, the proposed categories, on the one hand, provide a structured way of looking at the system and, on the other hand, encourage thinking in terms of observable behavior, which will make implementing and especially validating the system later easier.

4.2   Iterative Design

In order to decompose and operationalize the requirements, the first design step is to identify Community Types providing separate architectural views and charge each of them with fulfilling specific requirements [22]. Depending on the nature of these requirements, we then specify a solution using the appropriate formalism, as discussed above. As the Community Types break down and structure the requirements, it should often be possible to reuse a solution for a similar problem. In the literature, specific answers for certain types of systems and contexts have been proposed. In the context of social laws [29], much work has been done to identify behavioral restrictions that are both effective and feasible. Law-governed interaction [30] is an approach that is based on designing social laws into the middleware that agents have to use to interact with a system. In this way, the Interactional Context is restricted to socially acceptable actions. Other approaches (e.g. [31]) introduce an authority that penalizes undesired behavior, thereby making social behavior the rational choice. [32] use model checking to verify the effectiveness of social laws. In [33], they tackle the question whether an agent's knowledge is sufficient to fulfill its commitments by extending their model to include epistemological aspects.

As our specification technique builds on existing software engineering techniques, we can apply our existing model checking techniques to a solution. We can formally verify whether the rules of an individual Community Type are sufficient for ensuring certain formal requirements, e.g. safety properties. We have formally verified several examples using this approach, among them an intersection management scheme and control structures for autonomous tracked vehicles.

At this stage, it is also possible to generate prototypes from the specification. Simulating the Physical Environment based on the analysis model, we can execute a prototypical implementation of the specification of the Community Types. Using our unrestricted access to the simulated environment, we explicitly keep track of instantiated Communities, compute Interactional Contexts, determine membership in Communities, and assign Professed Intentions to behavior. The agents themselves, which are not specified yet at this time, are emulated by randomly picking from the required or, if no Community currently requires specific behavior, enabled behaviors for the agent. Here, the principle of grounding abstract concepts in implemented, observable entities and observable agent behavior allows us to test our specification at this early stage. Obviously, nondeterministic execution is not sufficient to decide whether an implementation fulfilling the specification exists, but it can already establish that a sufficiently narrow specification, e.g. a set of concrete traffic laws, can guarantee its requirements even for adversarial implementations. We have used this technique on a system containing 60 agents to validate the rules that controlled their movements.

5   Realization

A correct realization of an agent needs to commit to all required behavioral invariants and respect all constraints imposed by the agent's current Social Context. Locally, each Community correctly implements a subset of the system's requirements, while the structure of the Social Environment should ensure a proper composition. As the Community Type specifications are expressed in terms of observable agent behavior, the transition from the social to the agent level is basically straight-forward. However, as the different aspects do not need to be orthogonal, the rules of different Cultures might be in conflict, depending on the specific Social Context. It is the agents' responsibility to resolve such conflicts and consistently manage their Social Context.

Also, the assumptions about the Agents' Interactional Context need to hold at the implementation level, i.e. they need to be able to perceive and achieve what the specification requires of them. This may make adding Sensors and Effectors or, preferably, infrastructure (by means of Services) necessary. We will discuss some strategies below.

5.1 Centralized Realization

As discussed above, the operational semantics of our model and our specifications facilitate the realization of prototypes. As many aspects of the specification are expressed as story patterns, it is possible to directly implement these aspects by running graph matching algorithms that try to match the specification against the instance graph representing the system state at runtime. In this manner, required behavior or forbidden instance situations can be identified by a generic mechanism. If the Physical Layer is virtual, i.e. simulated, we run an Process for each agent that determines its Interactional Context. Another Process manages Community instantiation and decides membership. Each Community is explicitly represented in the system and monitors its own constraints.

The transparency that such an explicit instantiation of the analysis and design model offers is very appealing when designing the agents' internal structures, as it gives the developer direct insights into the agents' contexts and reactions. However, a centralized implementation is in contradiction to the very nature of multi-agent systems and may not scale well to large systems.

Still, it is an attractive idea is to keep a centralized prototype of the Community Type specifications around while designing a distributed solution on the agent level. Running both versions in parallel – on top of the simulated environment – not only enables the detection of observable behavior that violates the requirements, but also allows the identification of the discrepancies between the actual context and an agent's perception of it that have caused the violation. This is similar to the debugging support presented in [34], where the agents' behavior is validated against Petri Net specifications, but additionally factors in an agent's context and perception of the system.

5.2 Distributed Realization

The actual embedded systems force a transition to a distributed realization, as no simulated environment providing a global perspective exists. Generally, an agent can only be expected to react to events that are – directly or through social mediation – within its Interactional Context. A distributed model for realizing the specified interactions will have to take this into account, both with respect to physical and social contexts. Obviously, the idealized assumptions that the agents have direct access to an explicit representation of their physical and social environment and that pattern roles are triggered instantaneously and simultaneously for all involved agents have to be dropped. Below, we suggest strategies for compensating this.

Strategies for Context Access. At the most basic level, agents require access to elementary knowledge that allows them to understand their Environment and interact with it. The Environment needs to provide Services to this respect that are established on top of known infrastructure, e.g. look-up services [35] that enable clients to search a network for a specific service. In the example, the instantiation rules for *LocalCoordination* Communities depend on knowledge about the vehicles current position.

Once agents have access to all relevant parts of the physical environment, we need to create an internal representation of the agents' resulting knowledge about its physical context. By mirroring the Entity model, we obtain an object structure for matching the membership rule of the *LocalCoordination* Communities.

This Explicit Context Model strategy suffers from the overhead required to represent the whole known physical environment as specified by the Entity model. Often, a stripped down model of the agent's context that uses a simplified structure and represents only elements that are relevant for the agent's decisions is sufficient. We refer to this strategy as the Specialized Context Model strategy. In our example, many patterns concerning physical location, membership and pattern instantiation can be interpreted using the same reduced context model.

As mentioned above, the routing mechanism depends on the publication pattern, which extends the context information available to an agent with the other agents' position and velocity data. The publication pattern in turn only depends on data that is locally available to an agent and some implied knowledge about the system's topology. Such bootstrapping allows us to realize instantiation rules for patterns or communities which require additional information which is not directly available in the Interactional Context of the agents. We call extending the physical context model of an agent in this manner the Context Bootstrapping strategy.

Strategies for Role Instantiation. To ensure that the local and concurrent instantiation of the pattern roles in each agent works, we have to extend the initialization phase of the pattern. The protocols employed within the patterns have to be able to compensate time differences introduced by delayed instantiation within bounds of the specified time frame (e.g. 0-40 ms for the *Publication* pattern). Notably in case of bootstrapping via other patterns, this time frame will often be reduced by the time spent gathering all required information. We refer to this step as the Asynchronous Instantiation strategy.

Moreover, the pattern behavior must take into account that the instantiation of other pattern roles or opening a communication channel might fail. This is achieved by either the Fail-Safe Role Instantiation or Fail-Operational Role Instantiation strategy. If the *Publication* pattern fails for any reason, all vehicles in the affected warehouse could be required to simply stop in order to reach a fail-safe state. A fail-operational strategy would be to switch to a different sensor, i.e. sonar (which is used outside the range of the wireless network anyway), and keep working a lower speeds until the pattern is successfully established.

6   Conclusion and Future Work

We have presented both a pragmatic classification of different types of context in multi-agent systems and techniques for analysis and design using this classification. The operational semantics of our model facilitate the generation of centralized prototypes, which can then be used for validating distributed implementations.

Building a framework for the prototyping of large multi-agent systems is currently the objective of a large student project. We have already begun to extensively use and evaluate different techniques for the explicit and distributed handling of context and hope to develop additional realization strategies to compile a more comprehensive catalogue. The small examples we have implemented and verified already suggest that the meta model is indeed of practical value in designing and understanding a system, which we hope to fully evaluate by implementing the above warehouse scenario on a large scale.

We also intend to continue working on the questions raised in Section 4. We believe there to be great potential for automated synthesis and formal verification of correct individual implementations of a social level specification.

References

1. Sen, R., Roman, G.C.: Context-sensitive binding - flexible programming using transparent context management. Technical Report WUCSE-03-72, Washington University, Department of Computer Science, St. Louis, Missouri (2005) To appear in the journal Synthese.
2. Julien, C., Payton, J., Roman, G.C.: Adaptive access control in coordination-based mobile agent systems. In Choren, R., Garcia, A., Lucena, C., Romanovsky, A., eds.: Software Engineering for Multi-Agent Systems III. Volume 3390 of Lecture Notes in Computer Science (LNCS)., Springer Verlag (2005) 254–271
3. Schelfthout, K., Holvoet, T.: Objectplaces: An environment for situated multi-agent systems. In: 3rd International Joint Conference on Autonomous Agents and Multiagent Systems (AAMAS), New York, NY, USA, ACM Press (2004) 1500–1501
4. Schmidt, A., Beigl, M., Gellersen, H.W.: There is more to context than location. Computers & Graphics **23** (1999) 893–901
5. Linnhoff-Popien, C., Strang, T.: A context modeling survey. In: Workshop on Advanced Context Modelling, Reasoning and Management (UbiComp 2004), Nottingham, England. (2004)
6. Bauer, B., Mller, J.P.: Using uml in the context of agent-oriented software engineering: State of the art. In: Agent-Oriented Software Engineering IV. Volume 2935 of Lecture Notes in Computer Science (LNCS). Springer Verlag (2003) 1–24
7. Kinny, D., Georgeff, M.: Modelling and Design of Multi-Agent Systems. In: Proceedings of Agent Theories, Architectures, and Languages (ATAL) 96. (1996)
8. Bauer, B., Odell, J.: Uml 2.0 and agents: how to build agent-based systems with the new uml standard. Engineering Applications of Artificial Intelligence **18** (2005) 141–157
9. Bresciani, P., Giorgini, P., Giunchiglia, F., Mylopoulos, J., Perini, A.: TROPOS: An Agent-Oriented Software Development Methodology. Journal of Autonomous Agents and Multiagent Systems (2003)
10. Serafini, L., Bouquet, P.: Comparing formal theories of context in AI. AI **155** (2004) 41–67
11. Buvač, S., Buvač, V., Mason, I.: Metamathematics of contexts. Fundamenta Mathematicae **23** (1995) Available from http://www-formal.stanford.edu/buvac.
12. Ghidini, C., Giunchiglia, F.: Local models semantics, or contextual reasoning = locality + compatibility. Artificial Intelligence **127** (2001) 221–259
13. Edmonds, B.: Learning and exploiting context in agents. In: Proceedings of the first international joint conference on Autonomous agents and multiagent systems, ACM Press (2002) 1231–1238
14. Kaenampornpan, M., O'Neill, E.: Modelling context: An activity theory approach. In: Proc. of the Second European Symposium on Ambient Intelligence (EUSAI 2004). Volume 3295 of Lecture Notes in Computer Science (LNCS)., Eindhoven, The Netherlands, November 8-11, 2004, Springer Verlag (2004) 367–375

15. Benerecetti, M., Bouquet, P., Bonifacio, M.: Distributed context-aware systems. Human-Computer Interaction **16** (2001) 213–228

16. Jennings, N.R.: On agent-based software engineering. Artificial Intelligence **117** (2000) 277–296

17. Weyns, D., Parunak, H.V.D., Michel, F., Holvoet, T., Ferber, J.: Environments for multiagent systems state-of-the-art and research challenges. In Weyns, D., Parunak, H.V.D., Michel, F., eds.: Environment for multi-agent systems: first international workshop, 2004, New York, NY. Volume 3374 of Lecture Notes in Computer Science. (2004) 1–47

18. Wache, H., Stuckenschmidt, H.: Practical context transformation for information system interoperability. In Akman, V., Bouquet, P., Thomason, R., Young, R., eds.: Modeling and Using Context: CONTEXT 2001, Dundee, UK. Volume 2116 of Lecture Notes in Computer Science (LNCS)., Springer Verlag (2001) 367–380

19. Viroli, M., Omicini, A., Ricci, A.: Engineering MAS Environment with Artifacts. In Weyns, D., Parunak, V., Michel, F., eds.: Proceedings of the Second International Workshop on Environments for MAS at AAMAS 2005, Utrecht, The Netherlands. (2005)

20. Omicini, A., Ricci, A., Viroli, M., Castelfranchi, C., Tummolini, L.: Coordination Artifacts: Environment-based coordination for intelligent agents. In Jennings, N., Sierra, C., Sonenberg, L., Tambe, M., eds.: 3rd International Joint Conference on Autonomous Agents and Multiagent Systems (AAMAS), New York, NY, USA, ACM Press (2004) 286–293

21. Ferber, J., Gutknecht, O.: A meta-model for the analysis and design of organizations in multi-agent systems. In: Proceedings of the 3rd International Conference on Multi Agent Systems (ICMAS98), Paris , France. (1998) 128–135

22. Klein, F., Giese, H.: Separation of concerns for mechatronic multi-agent systems through dynamic communities. In Choren, R., Garcia, A., Lucena, C., Romanovsky, A., eds.: Software Engineering for Multi-Agent Systems III. Volume 3390 of Lecture Notes in Computer Science (LNCS). Springer Verlag (2005) 272–289

23. Giese, H., Burmester, S., Klein, F., Schilling, D., Tichy, M.: Multi-Agent System Design for Safety-Critical Self-Optimizing Mechatronic Systems with UML. In: OOPSLA 2003 - Second Workshop on Agent-Oriented Methodologies, Anaheim, CA, USA. (2003)

24. Kendall, E.A.: Role models – patterns of agent system analysis and design. BT Technology Journal **17** (1999) 46 – 57

25. Weyns, D., Steegmans, E., Holvoet, T.: Integrating free-flow architectures with role models based on statecharts. In: Software Engineering for Multi-Agent Systems III: Research Issues and Practical Applications. Volume 3390 of Lecture Notes in Computer Science (LNCS)., Springer Verlag (2005) 104–120

26. Fischer, T., Niere, J., Torunski, L., Zündorf, A.: Story Diagrams: A new Graph Rewrite Language based on the Unified Modeling Language. In Engels, G., Rozenberg, G., eds.: Proc. of the 6th International Workshop on Theory and Application of Graph Transformation (TAGT), Paderborn, Germany. LNCS 1764, Springer (1998)

27. Felfernig, A., Jannach, D., Zanker, M.: Contextual diagrams as structuring mechanisms for designing configuration knowledge bases in uml. In Evans, A., Kent, S., Selic, B., eds.: UML'2000 - The Third International Conference on The Unified Modeling Language, York, UK. Volume 1939 of Lecture Notes in Computer Science., Springer Verlag (2000) 240ff

28. Giese, H., Tichy, M., Burmester, S., Schäfer, W., Flake, S.: Towards the compositional verification of real-time uml designs. In: Proc. of the European Software Engineering Conference (ESEC/FSE), Helsinki, Finland, ACM Press (2003)

29. Shoham, Y., Tennenholtz, M.: On the synthesis of useful social laws for artificial agent societies. In: Proceedings of the Tenth National Conference on Artificial Intelligence (AAAI-92), San Diego, CA. (1992)

30. Minsky, N.H., Ungureanu, V.: Law-governed interaction: a coordination and control mechanism for heterogeneous distributed systems. ACM Transactions on Software Engineering and Methodology (TOSEM) (2000)
31. Boella, G., Torre, L.V.D.: Enforceable Social Laws. In Dignum, F., Dignum, V., Koenig, S., Kraus, S., Singh, M.P., Wooldridge, M., eds.: Proceedings of the Fourth International Joint Conference on Autonomous Agents and Multiagent Systems (AAMAS), Utrecht, The Netherlands, ACM Press (2005) 682–689
32. van der Hoek, W., Roberts, M., Wooldridge, M.: Social laws in alternating time: Effectiveness, feasibility, and synthesis. Technical Report Technical Report ULCS-04-017, University of Liverpool (2005) To appear in the journal Synthese.
33. van der Hoek, W., Roberts, M., Wooldridge, M.: Knowledge and Social Laws. In Dignum, F., Dignum, V., Koenig, S., Kraus, S., Singh, M.P., Wooldridge, M., eds.: Proceedings of the Fourth International Joint Conference on Autonomous Agents and Multiagent Systems (AAMAS), Utrecht, The Netherlands, ACM Press (2005) 674–681
34. Padgham, L., Winikoff, M., Poutakidis, D.: Adding debugging support to the prometheus methodology. Engineering Applications of Artificial Intelligence 18 (2005) 173–190
35. Waldo, J.: The Jini architecture for network-centric computing. Communications of the ACM 42 (1999) 76–82

Engineering Organization-Based Multiagent Systems

Scott A. DeLoach

Multiagent and Cooperative Robotics Laboratory,
Department of Computing and Information Sciences, Kansas State University,
234 Nichols Hall, Manhattan, Kansas 66506, USA
sdeloach@cis.ksu.edu
http://www.cis.ksu.edu/~sdeloach/

Abstract. In this paper, we examine the Multiagent Systems Engineering (MaSE) methodology and its applicability to developing organization-based multiagent systems, which are especially relevant to context aware systems. We discuss the inherent shortcomings of MaSE and then present our approach to modeling the concepts required for organizations including goals, roles, agents, capabilities, and the assignment of agents to roles. Finally, we extend MaSE to allow it to overcome its inherent shortcomings and capture the organizational concepts defined in our organization metamodel.

1 Introduction

Recent trends in multiagent systems are toward the explicit design and use of organizations, which allow heterogeneous agents to work together within well-defined roles to achieve individual and system level goals [8], [19]. When focusing on team goals, organizations allow agents to work together by using individual agents to perform the tasks for which they are best suited. When emphasizing an individual agent's goals, organizations provide the structure and rules that allow agents to find and carry out collaborative tasks with other, previously unknown agents, to the mutual benefit of each agent.

In situations where the nature of the application environment makes teams susceptible to individual failures, these failures can significantly reduce the ability of the team to accomplish its goal. Unfortunately, most multiagent teams are designed to work within a limited set of configurations. Even when the team possesses the ability to accomplish its goal, it may be constrained by its own knowledge of team member's capabilities. In most multiagent methodologies, the system designer analyzes the possible organizational structure and then designs one organization that will suffice for most anticipated scenarios. Unfortunately, in dynamic applications where the environment as well as the agents may change, a designer can rarely account for, or even consider, all possible situations. To overcome these problems, we are investigating techniques that allow multiagent teams to design their own organization at runtime [7]. In essence, we propose to provide the team with the organizational knowledge and let the team define its own organization based on its current context, goals and team capabilities.

In this paper, we present a proposal to extend the Multiagent Systems Engineering (MaSE) methodology toward the analysis and design of multiagent organizations. While

A. Garcia et al. (Eds.): SELMAS 2005, LNCS 3914, pp. 109–125, 2006.

MaSE already incorporates many of the required organizational concepts such as goals, roles, laws, and the relations between these entities, it cannot currently be used to completely define a multiagent organization. Most importantly, we must extend MaSE with the notion of capabilities, upon which the definition of roles is based. We also add some specific relationships between these capabilities and existing MaSE concepts.

The remainder of this paper is organized as follows. First, we present a review of relevant background research, including a short description of MaSE and its current weaknesses. Next, we give an overview of our metamodel that describes the elements in multiagent organizations. Finally, we discuss our extensions to MaSE that support the development of multiagent organizations and overcome some of its recognized problems.

2 Background

A recent advance in agent-oriented software engineering has had a significant impact on multiagent development approaches such as MaSE [6], Gaia [18], and MESSAGE [12]. This advancement concerns the separation of the agents from the system framework, or organization [19]. Agents play roles within an organization; however, they are not the organization. The organization defines the social setting in which the agent must exist. An organization includes a structure as well as rules, which constrain valid agent behavior and interaction within the organization.

While these advances are recent, there have been some discussions on how to incorporate them into existing multiagent systems methodologies. For instance, there is a proposal to extend the Gaia to incorporate social laws [19] and organizational concepts [18], while others have proposed implementing the organization as a separate institutional agent [17]. We have even proposed extending MaSE with rules and environmental entities [4], [5].

More recently, new methodologies and approaches have been proposed for building highly adaptive multiagent systems including Adelfe, which follows the AMAS theory [1, 14]. The goal of methods such as Adelfe is to allow designers to build systems that will produce some unknown functionality. This varies from the approach presented here as we are attempting to give the system the ability to adapt while still producing a know function and within certain limitations.

2.1 Multiagent Systems Engineering

MaSE was originally designed to develop general-purpose multiagent systems and has been used to design systems ranging from computer virus immune systems to cooperative robotics systems [6], [7]. Each phase is presented below.

Analysis Phase. The goal of the MaSE analysis phase is to define a set of roles that can be used to achieve the system level goals. This process is captured in three steps: capturing goals, applying use cases, and refining roles.

- Capturing Goals. The first step is to capture the system goals by extracting them from the requirements, which is done by Identifying Goals and Structuring Goals. The purpose of the Identifying Goals is to derive the overall system goal and its subgoals. This is done by extracting scenarios from the requirements and then identifying scenarios goals. After the goals have been identified, the second step, Structuring Goals, categorizes and structures the goals into a goal tree, which results in a Goal Hierarchy Diagram that represents goals and goal/subgoal relationships.

- Applying Use Cases. In this step, goals are translated into use cases, which capture the previously identified scenarios with a detailed description and set of sequence diagrams. These use cases represent desired system behaviors and event sequences.
- Refining Roles. Refining Roles organizes roles into a Role Model, which describes the roles in the system and the communications between them. Each role is decomposed into a set of tasks, which are designed to achieve the goals for which the role is responsible. These tasks are documented using finite state automata-base Concurrent Task Diagrams. Concurrent tasks consist of a set of states and transitions that represent internal agent reasoning and communications.

Design Phase. The purpose of the design phase is to take roles and tasks and to convert them into a form more amenable to implementation, namely agents and conversations. The MaSE design phase consists of four steps: designing agent classes, developing conversation, assembling agents and deploying the agents.

- Construction of Agent Classes. The first step in the design phase identifies agent classes and their conversations and then documents them in Agent Class Diagrams. The Agent Class Diagram that results from this step is similar to object-oriented class diagrams with two differences: (1) agent classes are defined by the roles instead of attributes and methods and (2) relations between agent classes are conversations.
- Constructing Conversations. Once the agent classes and the conversations are identified, the detailed conversation design is undertaken. Conversations model communications between two agent classes using a pair of finite state automata similar in form and function to concurrent tasks. Each task usually generates multiple conversations, as they require communication with more than one agent class.
- Assembling Agent Classes. Assembling Agent Classes involves defining the agents' internal architecture. MaSE does not assume any particular agent architecture and allows a wide variety of existing and new architectures to be used. The architecture is defined using components similar to those defined in UML.
- Deployment Design. The final design step is to choose the actual configuration of the system, which consists of the number and types of agents in the system and the platforms on which they should be deployed. These decisions are documented in a Deployment Diagram, which is similar to a UML Deployment Diagram.

2.2 MaSE Weaknesses

While MaSE provides many advantages for building multiagent systems, it is not perfect. It is based on a strong top-down software engineering mindset, which makes it difficult to use in some application areas.

1. MaSE fails to provide a mechanism for modeling multiagent system interactions with the environment. While we examined this topic in [5], it has never been fully integrated into MaSE.

2. MaSE also tends to produce multiagent systems with a fixed organization. Agents developed in MaSE tend to play a limited number of roles and have a limited ability to change those roles, regardless of their individual capabilities. As discussed above, a multiagent team should be able to design its own organization at runtime. While MaSE already incorporates many of the required organizational concepts such as goals, roles and the relations between these entities, it cannot currently be used to define a true multiagent organization.
3. MaSE also does not allow the integration of sub-teams into a multiagent system. MaSE multiagent systems are assumed to have only a single layer to which all agents belong. Adding the notion of sub-teams would allow the decomposition of multiagent systems and provide for greater levels of abstraction.
4. The MaSE notion of conversations can also be somewhat bothersome, as it tends to decompose the protocols defined in the analysis phase into small, often extremely simple pieces. When the original protocol involves more than two agents, it often results in conversations with only a single message. This makes comprehending how the individual conversations fit together more difficult.

3 Organization Metamodel

To allow teams of agents to adapt to their environment by determining their own organization at runtime, we have developed a metamodel that describes the knowledge required to define an organization [7], [11]. Given this knowledge, we hypothesize that multiagent teams will be able to organize (and reorganize) themselves to adapt to their dynamic environments.

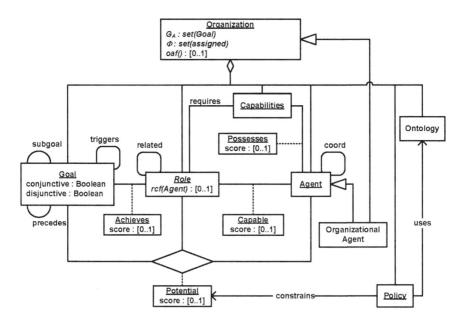

Fig. 1. Artificial Organization Metamodel

From the early days of organization research, organizations have typically been defined as including the concepts of agents who play roles within a structure that defines the relationships between the various roles [2]. We thus begin the foundation for our metamodel by defining what is meant by goals (G), roles (R), and agents (A). We also add four additional entities to our metamodel: capabilities (C), assignments (Φ), policies (P), and an ontology (Σ). Capabilities are central to the process of determining which agents can play which roles and how well they can play them, while policies constrain the assignment of agents to roles thus controlling the allowable states of the organization. The organization ontology supports agent communication and policy definition. A UML-based depiction of our organization metamodel is shown in Fig. 1.

3.1 Goals

Every artificial organization is designed with a specific purpose, which defines the overall function, or goal of the organization. Within our metamodel, each organization has a set of goals, G, that it seeks to achieve in support of a single top-level goal g_o. We define a goal in its normal way as some desired end state. G is derived by decomposing g_o into a tree of subgoals that describe how g_o can be achieved. Following the KAOS goal based requirements modeling approach [16], we allow goals to be decomposed into a set of non-cyclic subgoals using either AND-refinement or OR-refinement, which are denoted via conjunctive and disjunctive predicates. Eventually, g_o is refined into a set of leaf nodes, denoted by G_L, that may be achieved in order to achieve g_o. The active goal set, G_A (where $G_A \subseteq G_L$), is the set of goals that an organization is trying to achieve at the current time.

Goal g_1 *precedes* goal g_2 if g_1 must be achieved before g_2 can be achieved. Essentially, goal precedence allows the organization to work on one part of the goal tree at a time, thus reducing the size of G_A. The *triggers* relation is similar to precedes in that it also restricts goals from being inserted in G_A. However, instead of requiring goal achievement, the triggers relation allows new goals to be inserted into G_A when a specified event occurs.

$$\text{precedes: } G, G \rightarrow \text{Boolean}$$
$$\text{triggers: } G_L, G \rightarrow \text{Boolean}$$

All goals are unachieved when the organization is initialized. Therefore, the initial active goal set, G_{A0}, consists of all goals that have no predecessor goals or that do not require a trigger. However, as goals are achieved or events occur triggering new goal instances, G_A, changes. Essentially, achieved goals are removed from the active goal set and new goals to be achieved are inserted. New goals must be *startable* (all their predecessor goals have been achieved) and, if they are triggered, they must have been triggered by an active goal. We denote a sequence of active goal sets G_A' as $G_A' = [G_{A1}, G_{A2}, \ldots G_{An}]$.

3.2 Roles

Each organization has a set of roles R that it can use to achieve its goals. A role defines an entity that is able to achieve a set of goals within the organization. Each role is responsible for achieving, or helping to achieve or maintain specific system goals.

The *achieves* function describes how well (in a range of 0 to 1) a particular role achieves a specific goal.

$$\text{achieves: } R, G_L \rightarrow 0 .. 1$$

In order to perform a particular role, agents must have a sufficient set of capabilities (which are simply defined as atomic, named entities in our model). Agents possess capabilities, which may include physical capabilities (sensors or actuators) or computational capabilities (data access, knowledge, algorithmic, etc.), and roles require a certain set of capabilities. The set of capabilities required by a particular role is captured using the *requires* predicate.

$$\text{requires: } R, C \rightarrow \text{Boolean}$$

Many times, instead of requiring agents to inherently posses all the required capabilities for a role, we would like to *bestow* the required capabilities on agents to allow them to play that role. While this does not generally work well with hardware agents (robots), with software agents, we are often free to download new algorithms, etc. Our approach to capabilities does not deny this type of role bestowal; it just requires care in defining the capabilities types in the model. Thus if an agent has the appropriate physical capabilities (computational power, communication access, etc.) we can download the specific algorithms and/or knowledge necessary to carry out a role. In many of our current multiagent systems, the algorithm is packaged with the role, not in the individual agents themselves.

To carry out their responsibilities, roles may have to work with other roles within the organization. We capture the basic notion of two roles being related using a *related* predicate, which provides a means of identifying the allowable structure of a given organization.

3.3 Agents

Our metamodel also includes a set of heterogeneous agents, A, within each organization. For our purposes, agents are computational system instances that inhabit a complex dynamic environment, sense and act autonomously in this environment, and by doing so realize a set of goals. Agents are assigned specific roles in order to achieve organizational goals. The current set of potential assignments of agents to a role is captured by the *potential* function. The range of the potential function indicates how well an agent can play a role and how well that role can achieve the goal, based on the achieves and capable scores.

$$\text{potential: } A, R, G_L \rightarrow 0 .. 1$$

However, the potential function does not indicate that the actual assignment of agent a to role r to achieve goal g, has been made within the organization. It simply defines a set of possible assignments. To capture the notion of the actual assignments, we define an *assignment set*, Φ, which consists of agent-role-goal tuples, $<a,r,g>$. If $<a,r,g> \in \Phi$, then agent a has been assigned by the organization to play role r in order to achieve goal g. As discussed above, however, only agents with the right set of capabilities may be assigned to a specific role. To capture a given agent's capabilities, we define a *possesses* function, which returns a value in the range of 0 to 1 indicating no (0) capability or excellent (1) capability, which may change with time. Using the capabilities required by a role and capabilities possessed by an agent, we can compute the ability of an agent to play a give role, which we capture in the capable function. Finally, we capture the notion of agents coordinating, to achieve their goals using the *coord* predicate.

$$\text{possesses: } A, C \rightarrow 0 .. 1$$
$$\text{capable: } A, R \rightarrow 0 .. 1$$
$$\text{coord: } A, A \rightarrow \text{Boolean}$$

Organizational agents (OA) are organizations that function as agents within another organization. Thus, organizational agents possess capabilities, may coordinate with other agents, and may be assigned to play roles. They represent an extension to the traditional Agent-Group-Role (AGR) model developed by Ferber [9] and the meta-model proposed by Odell [13]. Organizational agents allow the definition of a hierarchy of organizations, which provides both flexibility and scalability.

3.4 Capabilities

Capabilities are key in determining exactly which agents can be assigned to what roles in the organization. *Capabilities* are atomic entities used to define the abilities of agents in relation to roles. Capabilities can capture *soft* abilities such as the ability to access resources, communicate, migrate, or computational algorithms. They also capture *hard* capabilities such as those of hardware agents such as robots, which include sensors and effectors.

3.5 Policies

Organization *policies* are formally specified rules that describe how an organization may/may not behave in specific situations. In our metamodel, we distinguish between two specific types of policies: *assignment* policies (P_Φ) and *behavioral* policies (P_{beh}). Assignment policies deal with constraints that the assignment set, Φ must satisfy such as "an agent may play one role at a time" or "agents may work on a single goal at a time". Behavioral policies define how agents should behave in solving the problem at hand.

3.6 Ontology

The organization ontology defines the entities within the application domain and their relationships. From these definitions, we extract a set of data types and relationships that allow agents to communicate about application specific information. These domain entities and relationships are also used to help in defining application specific organization policies. We currently use static UML diagrams to define ontological concepts similar to the approach in [3].

3.7 Organization Example

An example of a multiagent team developed using our organization metamodel is shown in Fig. 2. The boxes at the top of the diagram represent goals (*A ... G*), the circles represent roles (*R1* … *R5*), the pentagons represent capabilities (*C1* … *C5*), and the rounded rectangles are agents (*A1* … *A4*). The arcs on subgoal links denote conjunctive subgoals, whereas undecorated links denote disjunctive subgoals. The arrows between the entities represent the *achieves*, *requires*, and *possesses* functions/relations as defined above. The numbers beside the arrows represent the function value (e.g., possesses(*A1,C1*) = 0.5). These *achieves* values are generally assigned at design time and do not change. The *possesses* values, on the other hand, are computed by the individual agents based on their own internal assessment of their capabilities. We also assume we have assignment policies that (1) we only assign a single agent to each goal and (2) only one of the disjunctive goals F or G can be active at any time.

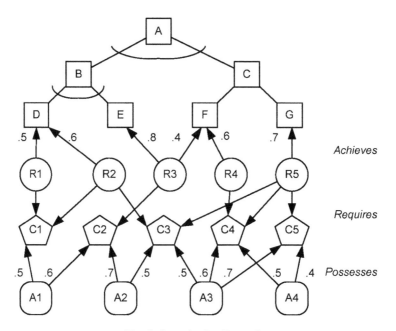

Fig. 2. Organization Example

Therefore, in this example the top-level goal, A, can be achieved by achieving both subgoals B and C, which can be achieved by achieving D and E in addition to either F or G. The *achieves* relation shows that either of the roles R1 or R2 can be used to achieve goal D while only role R3 can be used to achieve goal E. However, role R3 can also be used to achieve goal F, which can also be achieved by role R4. The only role capable of achieving goal G is role R5. The aim is for the organization to assign agents that can play the appropriate roles to achieve specific goals. Because of the disjunctive nature of goal C and the ability to use different roles in achieving individual goals, there is some assignment flexibility built into the system.

Determining which agents should be assigned specific roles in order to achieve particular goals is based on the capabilities the agents currently possess. For instance,

Table 1. Capability Function

	R1	R2	R3	R4	R5
A1	0.5	0	0.6	0	0
A2	0	0	0.7	0	0
A3	0	0	0	0.6	0.6
A4	0	0	0	0.5	0

role R1 requires only capability C1 while R3 requires only capability C2. Therefore, since agent A1 possesses both capabilities C1 and C2, it could be assigned to either role R1 or R3 in order to achieve goals D, E, or F.

In this example, we thus compute the *capable* function value for each agent-role pair as shown in Table 1. For simplicities sake, we average the individual capability score required for each role. Combining the *capable* scores with the *achieves* score, we can easily compute the organizational capability score, Os, for any set of assignments that might be made. Based on these computations (keeping in mind our assignment policies), we can see that the maximum organizational capability score, and thus the optimal assignments are as follows:

$$potential(A1,R1,D) = 0.25$$
$$potential(A2,R3,E) = 0.56$$
$$potential(A3,R5,G) = 0.42$$
$$Os = 1.23$$

3.8 Exemplar Implementation

Although there is not a single "correct" way to implement our organizational meta-model, we suggest an example to help cement the concepts. Fig. 3 shows the implementation approach used in our current projects. Each *agent* is composed of two components: an Organizational Reasoning component and an Application Reasoning

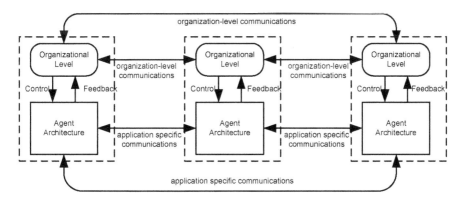

Fig. 3. Example Implementation

component. The Organizational Reasoning component is concerned with computing the current assignment set ϕ based on the active goal set G_A and the feedback received from the Application Reasoning component in regards to goal achievement, goal failure, or the occurrence of triggering events.

The Application Reasoning component accepts its assignment and carries out the tasks necessary to play its assigned roles in pursuit of its assigned goals. The Organizational Reasoning component interacts with the other agent's Organizational Reasoning components to ensure system coherence. Exactly how the coordination is carried out can vary. We have implemented a variety of centralized and distributed approaches to this coordination process; the best approach to this coordination process is domain and application specific. Part of the goal of the architecture presented in Fig. 3 is to be able to provide "plug-and-play" Organizational Reasoning components that can be selected based on application criteria.

4   O-MaSE

To avoid designing static multiagent systems, we have extended MaSE to allow designers to design a multiagent organization, which provides a structure within which the multiagent system may adapt. This extended version of MaSE is called Organization-based MaSE (O-MaSE). A preliminary proposal for the O-MaSE methodology is described below. In general, many of the diagrams used in O-MaSE are variants of the UML class diagrams and use keywords to denote the difference between goals, roles, capabilities, agent classes, etc.

Throughout this section, an Information Flow Monitoring System (IFMS) is used as an example of an organization-based multiagent system. The overall goal of the IFMS is to keep track of the information producers and consumers along with the actual flow of information through a dynamically reconfigurable enterprise information system. The information producers and consumers use a publish/subscribe mechanism that allows consumers to find and subscribe to appropriate information producers. Therefore, the IFMS must keep track of the various information paths between the producers and consumers as well as monitor the actual data flowing along those paths. The IFMS provides data in the form of current paths and information flow statistics to enterprise system operators who monitor the system for problems.

4.1   Requirements

Requirements are translated into system level goals, which are documented in the form of an AND/OR goal tree. Fig. 4 shows the goal tree for the IFMS described above. Given goal precedence relations, it is possible to design goal structures that cannot be achieved, thus we would like to provide the assurance that the top-level goal can be achieved. We have replaced the non-specific MaSE goal tree with a tree with specific AND/OR decompositions to match the organization metamodel.

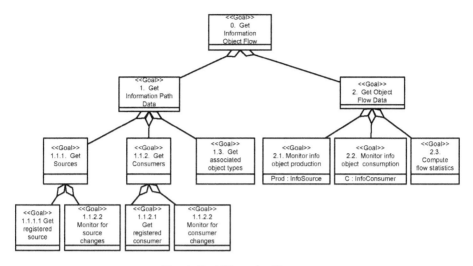

Fig. 4. Goal Hierarchy Diagram

The syntax has also changed in the O-MaSE goal model. We use standard UML class notation with the keyword «Goal». Each goal may be parameterized, with parameters annotated as attributes of the goal class. When goals are instantiated, they are given specific values for these attributes. The aggregation notation is used to denote AND refined goals whereas the generalization notation is used to denote OR refined goals. This notation is somewhat intuitive as AND refined goals require a composition of its subgoals to be achieved. Subgoals of an OR refined parent goal can be thought of as alternative ways to achieve the parent goal, or that they can be substituted in place of the parent goal.

4.2 Analysis

Analysis begins by creating the Organization Model, which defines the organization's interactions with external actors. Generally, there is one organization at the top level (denoted by the «Organization» keyword) and that organization becomes responsible for the top goal in the goal tree. Each organization can achieve goals and provide services, which are further refined via activity diagrams (similar to UML activity diagrams, not included in this paper). The designer can also use sequence diagrams for describing use cases at the system level, similar to the original version of MaSE. Each organization may also include sub-organizations to allow for abstraction during the design process.

While we allow the use of *services* in O-MaSE to help define the activities that agents carry out while performing roles, they do not map directly to the organization metamodel as presented earlier. For the purposes of this paper, we only mention them for completeness, but do not elaborate on them, as their use in defining organizations is not required.

An example of an Organization Model is shown in Fig. 5, where there are three actors making up the system's environment: the *ClientAPI*, the *ServerAPI*, and the *Admin*. The arrows connecting the organization to the actors denote protocols that

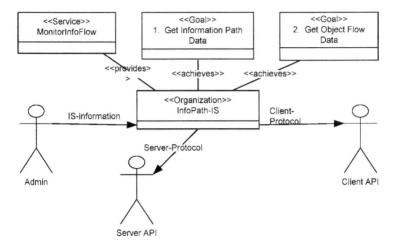

Fig. 5. Organization Model

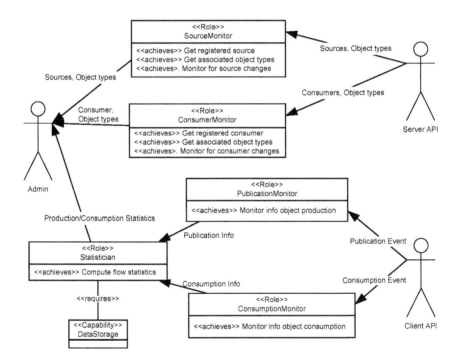

Fig. 6. Role Model

define the agent class's interactions with the environment (these protocols are defined in detail in the high-level design stage). The relations between the organization and the goal and service classes (classes denoted by «Goal» and «Service» keywords) are fixed relation types. An organization provides services while achieving goals. These relations may be shown via explicit relations between organizations and goals; however, the relations may also be embedded in a class as shown in Fig. 6 (where «achieves» relations are shown embedded within roles).

Next, the organization model is refined into a role model (Fig. 6) that defines the roles in the organization, the services they provide, and the capabilities required to play them. Each role is designed to achieve specific goals from the Goal Model and provide specific activities refined from top-level services in the Organization Model. Again, the arrows between actors and roles and between two roles indicate protocols that are fully defined later in the design stage. The Role Model may also include capabilities (denoted by the «Capability» keyword), which are attached to the roles that require them by the «requires» keyword.

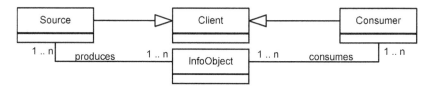

Fig. 7. Domain Model

At this point, O-MaSE differs from MaSE in that O-MaSE does not require the analyst to create concurrent task diagrams to describe the behavior of each role. This task is more appropriately carried out at the low-level design stage. The use of activities, which are refined via activity diagrams, allow the analyst to specify high-level behavior without resorting to low-level details required by concurrent task diagrams.

Throughout the analysis phase, the analyst should also capture and document the ontology that will be used within the system as part of the Domain Model. We have explored the integration of domain models into MaSE in [4]. The Domain Model allows the analyst to model domain entities, their attributes, and their relationships. Fig. 7 shows a simple example of a domain model using standard UML notation to show the relationships between two types of Clients: Source and Consumer. Sources produce *InfoObjects* while Consumers consume *InfoObjects*.

4.3 High-Level Design

The first step in the high-level design is for the designer to use the Role Model and service activity diagrams to define the Agent Class Model as shown in Fig. 8. In the Agent Class Model, agents classes and lower-level organizations are defined by the roles played (which determines the goals they can achieve), capabilities possessed (which determines the roles they can play), or services provided. Fig. 8 shows the use of both explicit and embedded relations. The «plays» and «provides» keywords in the agent classes (denoted by the «Agent» keyword) define which roles instances of the agent class can play as well as the services it can provide. The «possesses» relation between agent classes and capabilities (denoted by the «Capability» keyword) indicates the capabilities possessed by instances of that class of agent.

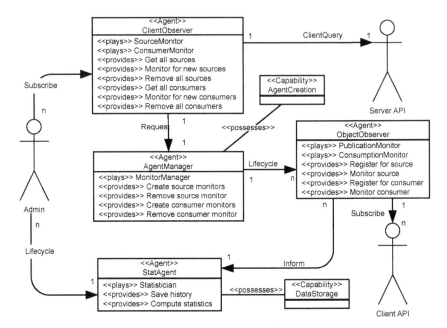

Fig. 8. Agent Class Model

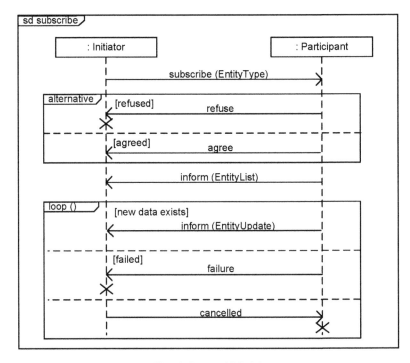

Fig. 9. Protocol Model

One the Agent Class Model is complete, Protocol Models (Fig. 9) are used to define the message-passing protocols between agent classes. These Protocol Models follow the currently proposed AUML protocol diagrams [10], which allow the ability to show alternative and repetitive message structures.

Fig. 9 captures a subscription protocol where the initiator wants to subscribe to information published periodically by the participant. After the initial subscribe message, the participant may either refuse or agree. If the participant refuses, the protocol terminates, which is denoted by the **X** symbol. Assuming the participant agrees, the participant sends an inform message with the current subscription information. The protocol then enters a loop where, typically, the participant sends an inform message with new information. However, the participant may send a failure message or the initiator a cancelled message, both of which end the protocol.

4.4 Low-Level Design

In low-level design, we define agent behavior using an Agent State Model, which is based on finite state automata (Fig. 10). The Agent State Model is similar to the

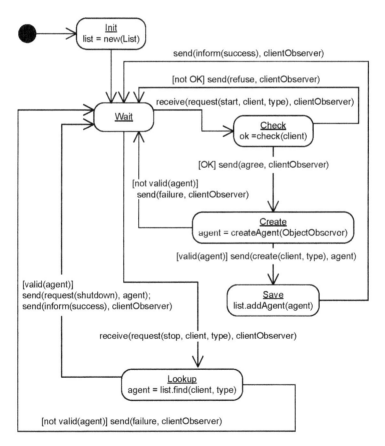

Fig. 10. Agent State Model for AgentManager

original MaSE concurrent task diagrams, as it captures internal behavior and message passing between multiple agents. They feature an explicit send and receive actions to denote sending and receiving messages. The remainder of the syntax and semantics is defined in [6].

5 Conclusions

In this paper, we have discussed the current version of MaSE and some of its short-comings. With the extension of MaSE to O-MaSE we have dealt with each of these problems. Specifically, we have provided a mechanism for defining the multiagent systems interactions with the environment by adding external actors and defining the interactions protocols between the system and the actors.

Second, we have extended MaSE to capture the organizational concepts identified in our organization metamodel. New concepts include AND/OR refinement of goals, integration of capabilities and the ability to model sub-teams, or sub-organizations. This feature allows designers greater levels of abstractions and directly complements the notion of organizational agents in our organization metamodel.

Finally, we took the notion of concurrent tasks out of the analysis phase and integrated concurrent tasks with conversations into Agent State Models in the low-level design phase. We are currently using O-MaSE and our organization metamodel in several projects including an adaptive Battlefield Information System [7], cooperative robotic teams [11] and a system to monitor and control a large-scale information system.

We are continuing to evolve O-MaSE to provide a flexible methodology that can be used to develop both traditional and organization-based systems. A long term goal is to provide a tailorable methodology that is fully supported by automated tools. We are currently building a new version of agentTool (aT^3) within the Eclipse IDE to support O-MaSE[1]. Future plans include code generation for various platforms as well as integration with the Bogor model checking tool [15] to provide model validation and performance prediction metrics.

References

1. Bernon, C., Camps, V., Gleizes M.P., Picard G. Engineering Adaptive Multi-Agent Systems: the ADELFE Methodology. In B. Henderson-Sellers and P. Giorgini (Eds.), Agent-Oriented Methodologies. Idea Group Pub, June 2005, pp.172-202.
2. Blau, P.M. & Scott, W.R., Formal Organizations, Chandler, San Francisco, CA, 1962, 194-221.
3. Cranefield, S. & Pruvis, M. UML as an Ontology Modelling Language. Proc of the Workshop on Intelligent Information Integration, 1999.
4. DeLoach, S. A. Modeling Organizational Rules in the Multiagent Systems Engineering Methodology. Proc of the 15th Canadian Conference on Artificial Intelligence. 2002.
5. DeLoach, S. A. Analysis and Design of Multiagent Systems Using Hybrid Coordination Media. Proceedings of Software Engineering in Multiagent Systems (SEMAS 2002). 2002.

---

[1] The current status of O-MaSE and the aT^3 project can be found at the Multiagent and Cooperative Robotics Laboratory web site (http://macr.cis.ksu.edu/).

6. DeLoach, S. A., Wood, M. F. and Sparkman, C. H., "Multiagent Systems Engineering". The International Journal of Software Engineering and Knowledge Engineering, 11(3), pp. 231-258, June 2001.

7. DeLoach, S.A., & Matson, E. An Organizational Model for Designing Adaptive Multi-agent Systems. The AAAI-04 Workshop on Agent Organizations: Theory and Practice (AOTP 2004). 2004.

8. Dignum, V. A Model for Organizational Interaction: Based on Agents, Founded in Logic. PhD thesis, Utrecht University, 2004.

9. Ferber, J., and Gutknecht, O. A meta-model for the analysis and design of organizations in multi-agent systems. In Proceedings of Third International Conference on MultiAgent Systems (ICMAS'98), pages 128-135, IEEE Computer Society, 1998.

10. Huget, M.P., Bauer, B., Odell, J., Levy, R., Turci, P., Cervenka, R., and Zhu, H. http://www.auml.org/. FIPA Modeling: Interaction Diagrams, Working Draft. 2002.

11. Matson, E., DeLoach, S. Capability in Organization Based Multi-agent Systems, Proceedings of the Intelligent and Computer Systems (IS '03) Conference, 2003.

12. MESSAGE: Methodology for Engineering Systems of Software Agents. Deliverable 1. Initial Methodology. July 2000. EURESCOM Project P907-GI.

13. Odell, J., Nodine, M., Levy, R. A Metamodel for Agents, Roles, and Groups. Agent-Oriented Software Engineering V, 5th International Workshop, AOSE 2004. 2004.

14. Picard, G. and Gleizes, M.-P. The ADELFE Methodology – Designing Adaptive Cooperative Multi-Agent Systems. In Bergenti, F. and Gleizes, M-P. and Zambonelli, F., editor, Methodologies and Software Engineering for Agent Systems. Kluwer Publishing, 2004.

15. Robby, Dwyer, M.B., & Hatcliff, J. Bogor: An Extensible and Highly-Modular Model Checking Framework, Proceedings of the Fourth Joint Meeting of the European Software Engineering Conference and ACM SIGSOFT Symposium on the Foundations of Software Engineering (ESEC/FSE 2003).

16. van Lamsweerde, A., Darimont, R., Letier, E. Managing conflicts in goal-driven requirements engineering. IEEE Transactions on Software Engineering. 24(11), pp 908-926, 1998.

17. Wagner, G. Agent-Oriented Analysis and Design of Organizational Information Systems. Proceedings of the 4th IEEE International Baltic Workshop on Databases and Information Systems, May 2000.

18. Zambonelli, F., Jennings, N.R., and Wooldridge, M.J. Developing Multiagent Systems: The Gaia Methodology. In AMC Transactions on Software Engineering Methodology 12(3), 317-370, 2003.

19. Zambonelli, F., Jennings, N.R., and Wooldridge, M.J. Organisational Rules as an Abstraction for the Analysis and Design of Multi-Agent Systems. IJSEKE. 11(3) pp. 303-328, June 2001.

Developing and Evaluating a Generic Metamodel for MAS Work Products

Ghassan Beydoun[1,2], César Gonzalez-Perez[1,2], Brian Henderson-Sellers[2], and G. Low[1]

[1] School of Information Systems, Technology and Management,
University of New South Wales, Sydney, Australia
{g.beydoun, g.low}@unsw.edu.au
[2] Faculty of Information Technology, University of Technology of Sydney, Sydney, Australia
{brian, cesargon}@it.uts.edu.au

Abstract. MAS development requires an appropriate methodology. Rather than seek a single, ideal methodology, we investigate the applicability of method engineering, which focuses on project-specific methodology construction from existing method fragments and provides an appealing approach to organize, appropriately access and effectively harness the software engineering knowledge of MAS methodologies. In this context, we introduce a generic metamodel to serve as a representational infrastructure to unify the work product component of MAS methodologies. The resultant metamodel does not focus on any class of MAS, nor does it impose any restrictions on the format of the system requirements; rather, it is an abstraction of how the work product elements in any MAS are structured and behave both at design time and run-time. Furthermore, in this paper we validate this representational infrastructure by analysing two well-known existing MAS metamodels. We sketch how they can be seen as subtypes of our generic metamodel, providing early evidence to support the use of our metamodel towards the construction of situated MAS methodologies.

1 Introduction

There is an increasing software engineering interest in the use of multi-agent systems (MAS), a new class of distributed parallel software applications, that have already proved effective in the core tasks of automating management of information within businesses (e.g. computer network management applications [23]), building computational models of human societies to study emergent behaviour [14, 17, 34] and building cooperative distributed problem solving [22, 24]. The building blocks of a MAS are intelligent, autonomous and situated software entities: agents. The agent, the concept of agency and the full range of MAS abstractions offer the promise of making software systems easier to embed within our daily lives as suggested in [10].

In order to develop a MAS, some appropriate methodological approach is needed. Indeed, a significant number of such MAS methodologies already exist [20]. Notable examples are Gaia [36], Adelfe [2], Prometheus [28], PASSI [8]. However, since it is generally agreed [7, 18] that no single methodology is sufficient, regardless as to how well thought out it might be, any one of these individual methodologies will, by definition, have limited applicability e.g. to a specific domain or a specific type of software application.

A. Garcia et al. (Eds.): SELMAS 2005, LNCS 3914, pp. 126–142, 2006.

We argue in this paper that attempting to simply combine existing methodologies into one large, high quality methodology, as suggested in e.g. [1] will prove to be impossible, because the sets of assumptions underlying each methodology are likely to be inconsistent and irreconcilable. We propose instead using *method*[1] *engineering* [5, 26] to empower software developers to create methodologies from existing (method) fragments (i.e. self-contained components). Method engineering approaches have been successful in object-oriented development due to widely accepted modelling languages and constructs of OO software systems and development processes [19, 21, 30]. For method engineering to be equally successful in the context of MASs, a suitable representation of any potential agent-oriented methodology is required. The goal of such representation is to capture knowledge about methodologies. This includes concepts (plus their properties) related to products of the software development process, as well as concepts and their properties related to the software development process itself. These collections of concepts are often known respectively as *product metamodel* and *process metamodel* [30].

In this paper, we present a generic *product* metamodel[2] for any MAS methodology. In this context, "product metamodel" is synonymous with "modelling language specification". Our generic metamodel comprises the abstract syntax and semantics of such a modelling language. It does not make any assumptions about the kinds of MAS that it describes. It only makes assumptions about what are the essential properties of an *agent*. Our metamodel is the first to focus on conceptual and ontological underpinnings rather than being constrained for use in a single methodological approach. Moreover, in this paper, we reinforce our case for method engineering in the context of MAS development by validating our generic metamodel against two well known and applied MAS metamodels: TAO [32] and Islander[3] [13]. We sketch how our metamodel can generate both of them. This constitutes early evidence that our method engineering proposal for MAS development is plausible.

The rest of this paper is organised as follows: In Section 2, we justify our method engineering endeavour and describe our metamodel and its synthesis. In Section 3, we present a comparative analysis of this metamodel and two prominent (although not explicit) metamodels: those of Islander [13] and TAO [32]. We indicate that these two metamodels can be viewed as particular refinements of our metamodel. In Section 4, we conclude with a description of future work.

2   Generic MAS Metamodelling

Edmonds et al. [10] rightly point out that we do not currently know all possible features of any MAS. They compare the science of MAS to the science of zoology, where we have a lot to discover about how the internals of a MAS change dynamically, and how this alters the overall behaviour of the system. They use this to formulate a theoretical argument against the possibility of having a one-size-fits-all methodology. In this section, we point to other current limitations in pursuing an

---

[1] Both terms, *method* and *methodology* are considered synonymous in this paper.

[2] Henceforth, we use the term "metamodel" and "product metamodel" interchangeably.

[3] Islander is a specification language. We compare our metamodel to its underlying model.

all-encompassing methodology, advocating the alternative context-dependent method engineering approach.

Methodologists often do not make it explicit (for instance, in terms of a meta-model or an ontology) what their assumptions are about the software development process, developers' behaviour and the intended software products – assumptions that may even be contradictory between pairs of methodologies. Quite the opposite, they mostly remain implicit in the intermediate products, process steps and relationships between constructs of the methodology. Indeed, the methodology may be intended as a set of steps to be followed rigorously. Furthermore, a methodology remains constrained by its inherent process and modelling assumptions as to what kinds of MAS can be developed. For instance, a methodology that assumes agents to be cooperative (for adaptive systems) e.g. Adelfe [2] cannot be readily combined with any methodology that assumes agents to be competitive, as is the case in many market simulation applications [17] or negotiating agents in an e-market [11]. Thus, combining methodologies as they are turns out to be very difficult in the absence of explicit metamodels.

In [1], combining metamodels of three methodologies led to a cumbersomely large model with little overlap. This suggests a missing intermediate layer of representation that unifies the different concepts from the three metamodels. Instead of attempting to combine metamodels, we propose factoring out common constructs for any MAS into a unifying metamodel of all methodologies (here just focussing on the work product aspects). Such a metamodel will clearly be more generic than any particular, methodology-specific metamodel. Its creation is presented in the next section.

2.1 Procedure to Create a Generic, Work Product Metamodel for MAS

We start with a high level representation of what MASs look like and, from this, represent their generic common features. If strong assumptions are required to develop a MAS feature (e.g. mediation policies between negotiating agents), then such a feature is methodology-specific and therefore its representation is left to the methodology itself. Our metamodel is a consensual picture of what a MAS looks like. It is developed by surveying a range of methodologies as well as systems. We identify common concepts that developers often use and methodologists agree upon. Since our resultant metamodel is intended to be widely applicable, without any constraining prerequisites, it will be able to generate most methodologies (we anticipate).

Our metamodel creation starts with what an agent is, and we extend this to how a MAS is distinguished from other software systems. At the system level, we do not make any assumptions about agents beyond their essential properties: *autonomy, situatedness* and *interactivity*. Any other non-definitional agent characteristic, visible at the system level, suggests a methodology-specific feature. For instance, *adaptivity, sociability and proactivity* are non-definitional properties of agents; some agents do not have them. For example, Adelfe's [2] adaptive system design requires learning agents, hence some concepts in Adelfe's metamodel are too specific to be included in our generic metamodel. At the same time, in developing our metamodel, we aim to cover as many features of a MAS as possible. We consider a wide range of MASs and we focus on what behavioural characteristics agents exhibit in this varying range. With regard to internal agent design, we ensure that any agent behaviour and internals can be described by our metamodel. Thus, any methodology (e.g. Adelfe which assumes *adaptive* agents) can be successfully generated using this metamodel.

In formulating this new metamodel, we ensure consistency, at the same time aiming to maximise coverage (including as many MAS concepts as possible) and generality (wide acceptance and familiarity to methodologists). To ensure consistency, coverage and generality are occasionally sacrificed. In some cases, coverage and generality are opposing and trade-off decisions are made. To construct our generic metamodel, we first decide on the set of concepts to be used, describing entities in any MAS and the relationships amongst them. Towards this, four initial steps are taken (iteratively):

Step 1: We decide on the set of general concepts relevant to any MAS and its model. Some problem-specific concepts are omitted. For example, terms specific to robots (e.g. actuators) or to single-agent systems are not included. Literature from the following areas are all relevant: agent software engineering e.g. [4, 8, 27, 33], AI e.g. [25, 31, 35], distributed AI [9, 14] and cognitive science e.g. [29].

Step 2: We decide on definitions worth considering. Choice of a definition from a particular source depends on how explicit the source is in providing the definition. In addition, wide acceptance of the definition is taken into account. This way, the set of adopted concepts is grounded in what other people in the agent community think.

Step 3: We reconcile differences between definitions where possible, giving hybrid definitions. Otherwise, choices are made based on consistency with earlier choices, i.e. where contradictory use of concepts between two or more sources occurs, we opt for the more coherent usage with the rest of the set of chosen concepts. For example, 'Task' is defined as set of *behaviours* by [29], and as '*behaviour* but with the significance of atomic part of the overall *agent behaviour*' in [15]. Our suggested definition is "specification of a piece of behaviour that the MAS can perform".

Step 4: We designate chosen concepts into two sets: run-time concepts and design-time concepts. Each set has two scopes: system-related or agent internals related scope. This makes it easier to identify relationships between the chosen concepts according to its set and its scope.

The results of our efforts in steps 1 to 4 are shown in Tables 1 and 2. It should be noted that the concept of *environment statement* is both a design-time and run-time concept. It is a unit of environment description, which is used by system designers. Environment statements may also be used by the agents themselves at run-time.

Steps 1 to 4 above do not depend on any single software development methodology. The metamodel is not expected to be large enough to express a method to the same level of detail as the method itself. Rather, this proposed new metamodel, named FAML (FAME[4] Agent-oriented Modelling Language) provides a complete set of concepts that describe all models to be included in any methodology, but not necessarily providing all required details for every methodology; some details being left to each individual methodology.

The FAML metamodel is expected to be complete as far as describing internal structure of single agents is concerned (according to our three definitional properties of agents). However, not all concepts in the metamodel have to be used by a given

---

[4] FAME is the project name under which FAML has been developed.

Table 1. Design-time concepts and their definitions

Term	Definition
Action Specification	Specification of an action, including any preconditions and postconditions.
Agent Definition	Specification of the initial state of an agent just after it is created.
Convention	Rule that specifies an arrangement of events expected to occur in a given environment.
Environment Statement	A statement about the environment.
Facet Action Specification	Specification of a facet action in terms of the facet definition it will change and the new value it will write to the facet.
Facet Definition	Specification of the structure of a given facet, including its name, data type and access mode.
Functional Requirement	Requirement that provides added value to the users of the system.
Message Action Specification	Specification of a message action in terms of the message schema and parameters to use.
Message Schema	Specification of the structure and semantics of a given kind of messages that can occur within the system.
Non-Functional Requirement	Requirement about any limits, constraints or impositions on the system to be built.
Ontology	Structural model of the application domain of a given system.
Ontology Aggregation	Whole/part relationship between two ontology concepts.
Ontology Concept	Concept included in a given ontology.
Ontology Relationship	Relationship between ontology concepts.
Ontology Specialisation	Supertype/subtype relationship between two or more ontology concepts.
Performance Measure	Mechanism to measure how successful the system is at any point in time.
Plan Specification	An organised collection of action specifications.
Requirement	Feature that a system must implement.
Role	Specification of a behavioural pattern expected from some agents in a given system.
System	Final product of a software development project.
Task	Specification of a piece of behaviour that the system can perform.

methodology. For example, if a given methodology is geared towards a simulation MAS composed of reactive agents, then concepts such Intention and Plan would not be needed. Such an omission for a specific situational method is well supported by the optional (0..1) cardinalities seen in the metamodel diagrams below.

In connecting all filtered and synthesized concepts into one coherent metamodel, we omit all relations that are specific to some kinds of agents e.g. we do not include

Table 2. Run-time concepts and their definitions

Term	Definition
Action	Fundamental unit of agent behaviour.
Agent	A highly autonomous, situated, directed and rational entity.
Belief	An environment statement held by an agent and deemed as true in a certain timeframe.
Desire	An environment statement held by an agent, which represents a state deemed as good in a certain timeframe.
Environment	The world in which an agent is situated.
Environment History	The sequence of events that have occurred between the environment start-up and the present instant.
Environment Statement	A statement about the environment.
Event	Occurrence of something that changes the environment history.
Facet	Scalar property of the environment that is expected by the agents contained in it.
Facet Action	Action that results in the change of a given facet.
Facet Event	Event that happens when the value of a facet changes.
Goal	Ultimate desire.
Intention	A committed desire.
Message	Unit of communication between agents, which conforms to a specific message schema.
Message Action	Action that results in a message being sent.
Message Event	Event that happens when a message is sent.
Obligation	Behaviour expected from an agent at some future time.
Plan	An organised collection of actions.

learning features of adaptive agents. We also ensure that the set of terms is self-contained, that is, concepts may only depend on each other in this set. We include only relations and concepts that apply to a general kind of agents (autonomous, situated and interactive). Some issues are left to the methodology or the developers, e.g. how plans are generated and discarded, how beliefs are updated and maintained/shared, verification and validation of the system.

2.2 The Proposed Generic Metamodel

The FAML metamodel has two layers: design-time and runtime layers. Each layer may have two scopes: a system-related or agent-related scope. We present the metamodel in four different diagrams (Figure 1-4) to clearly group classes into four areas of concern: design-time system-related, runtime system-related (environment), design time agent-internals and run-time agent-internals classes.

Figure 1 shows the classes of the metamodel that are directly related to the description of a MAS, i.e. design-time system-related classes.

Design-time system-related classes (Figure 1) are concerned with features that can only be perceived by looking at the whole system at design time:

- Roles, relationships between roles, relationship with message schemata.
- Tasks, and their relationships with roles.

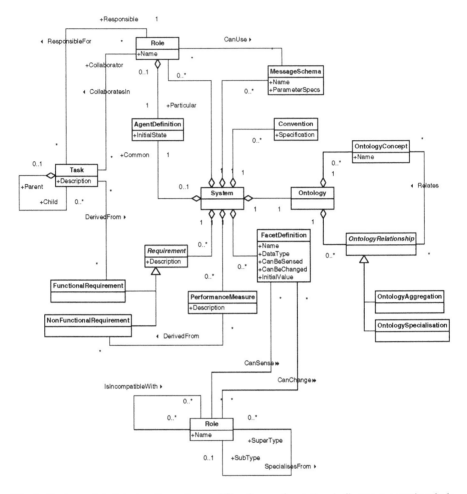

Fig. 1. System-related design-time classes. [The diamond notation indicates a generic whole-part relationship].

- Agent definitions and relationships with roles.
- Use of ontologies to define domain application semantics.
- Environment access points and relationship with roles.

Figure 2 shows the classes related to the environment in which agents "live", that is, run-time environment-related classes. Run-time environment-related classes are concerned with MAS features that exist only at runtime in the environment:

- Environment history of totally ordered instantaneous events, showing the message log and the events.
- Events of different kinds.
- System access points and relationships with events.
- Relationships amongst agent definitions and the above constructs.

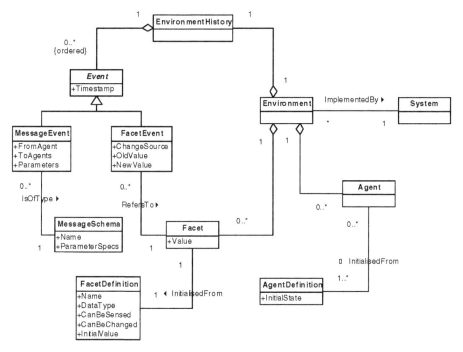

Fig. 2. Run-time, environment-related classes

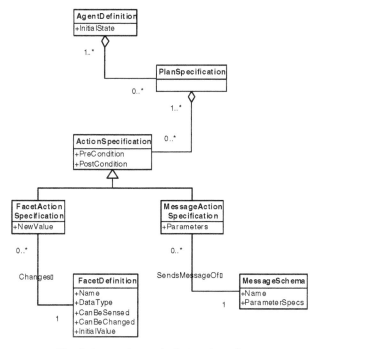

Fig. 3. Agen+t-internals design-time classes

Figure 3 shows the classes related to the agent internals at design time. These include:

- Plan specification (if any).
- Action specification which can be a facet action or a message action specification.
- How action specification relates to facet definitions and message schemata.

Finally, Figure 4 shows the classes related to agent internals at run-time. These classes can only be perceived by considering the internals of agents at run-time:

- Plans and actions.
- Relationships between actions, messages and message schemata.
- Desires and beliefs.
- Intentions.
- Relationships between each of the above and the environment.

In the next section, we compare and contrast each of the above classes of our meta-model with the metamodels of two well known MAS descriptors: Islander [12, 13] and TAO [32, 33]. We will argue that all modelling components of TAO and Islander can indeed be seen as particular subtypes refining some classes in FAML.

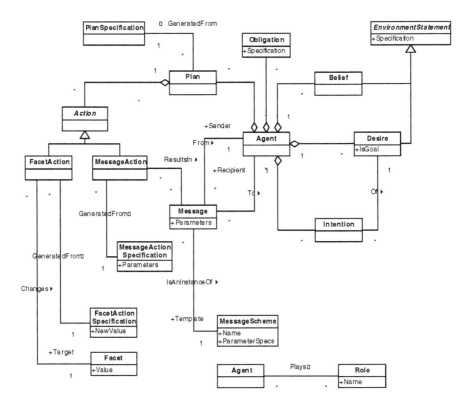

Fig. 4. Agent-internals run-time classes

3   Comparative Study of Our Metamodel

Multi Agent Systems modelling languages e.g. [6, 13, 32] allow software analysts to specify the structure and key features of the behaviour of the target system. Metamodels underlying such languages are product metamodels with similar scope to FAML. They do not include process-oriented concepts – in contrast to many AO methodologies, such as Gaia and Tropos, which focus on the process aspects at the expense of any product metamodel. MAS-ML [32] and Islander [11] are MAS modelling languages. In this section, we have chosen the TAO metamodel (underlying MAS-ML) and the metamodel underlying Islander as benchmarks to assess completeness of the FAML metamodel. Both metamodels are well documented and explained in [32, 33] and [12, 13] respectively. In addition, they both have been successfully applied in designing and building actual MASs. We compare the coverage of our generic metamodel with each. In the case of any clear overlap, we assess the rigour of the description in the given metamodel with the FAML metamodel.

3.1   Refinement of Islander from the FAML Metamodel

Islander is a specification language targeting a particular class of MASs: electronic institutions. Hence, its underlying metamodel focuses on MASs with a large number of external agents that enter the system with their own plans and desires. Interactions amongst external agents are assumed to be mediated by internal agents that follow institutional policies rather than plans of their own. In other words, internal agents in Islander are reactive. In the case when plans (and internal constructs such as beliefs, learning mechanisms, intentions) are required, programming outside the specification of Islander would be required. Hence, classes related to agent internals in our metamodel are not refined at all in Islander. Using Islander, a MAS is described as a formal specification consisting of three components: a dialogical framework, which describes the set of roles and the format of messages exchanged (i.e. the communication language between agents within the institution); a set of scenes, which describe possible states of different activities taken by groups of agents; and a performative structure, which establishes how different activities (scenes) relate to each other in the broader context of the institution [12, 13]. An example of a high level specification of an e-market MAS, negotiation_space, modelling mediated negotiation between buyers and sellers, looks as follows in Islander:

```
define-institution negotiation_space as
dialogic-framework = negotiation_space_df
performative-structure = negotiation_scenes
norms = ()
```

At the system level, Islander refines our notions of roles and their relationships, IsIcompatibleWith and SpecialisesFrom (Figure 1), in its dialogical framework. However, it does not have our notion of Facet that specifies what things an agent can change in the environment, nor actions associated with the change. Islander assumes that the only action an agent can execute is sending a message to another agent. It implicitly associates messages with roles, within the intra-scene specification (task specification).

Islander's notion of Scene refines our notion of Task. It describes an activity in an e-institution that may involve a number of agents. Islander also refines our hierarchical decomposition of tasks and the associated child-parent relation between tasks (see Figure 1): intra-scene activities are decomposed into scene states. Transition between states is conditioned by messages exchanged and by scene constraints. This detailed refinement is beyond the scope of our metamodel and is an Islander-specific feature i.e. an example of a methodology-specific extension that the method engineer is responsible for. At our level of abstraction, a coarse Islander refinement of our task decomposition would only include identifying scenes and their states, together with all relevant roles.

In Islander, some inter- and intra-scene activities are conditioned by institutional norms and constraints. These refine our notion of Convention, which explicitly describes static restrictions on agent behaviour. However, we do not anticipate a high level refinement to distinguish between task-specific constraints and institutional constraints (norms) as Islander does. We again view these as Islander-specific. Given the scope of Islander, specifying electronic institutions, this is not unexpected.

Table 3. Islander refinement of FAML

FAML Construct	Corresponding Islander Refinement
Message	Message
Roles	Roles
Task	Scene
Task hierarchy	Scene states
Convention	Norms, Constraints
Ontology (domain structure)	Ontology (messages structures)
Non-functional requirements	#agent per scene, synchronization of agents
Obligation	Obligations (of activities within a scene).
Environment History	Stacks of messages (a stack of messages exists for each scene).
Environment	Implicit in the collection of interactions available to all agents within the system, and determined by external agents leaving or entering scenes.
Agent definition	Implicit in: sub-task allocation to agents, message specification assignment and constraints, and association between messages and roles within scenes.
Facet Event	External agents entering or exiting a scene

Using Islander assumptions, the only activities taken by agents are receiving and sending messages. Indeed, the lowest level description of all activities generated within an institution can be expressed as a sequence of messages. The ontology specification in Islander describes the structures of messages exchanged about a domain. This view of ontology is a refinement of our more general view, where an ontology describes domain constructs and their relationships. Islander's view again highlights its assumptions about what kind of a MAS it models: electronic institutions revolving around controlled communication between agents. Agents do not have the power to change the institution, they only exchange messages.

Islander specifies the number of agents in each scene, and the synchronisation of agents as they move between scenes. These are the only instances of non-functional requirements we find in Islander. In our metamodel, we leave all details of non-functional requirements to the refining method.

Our notion of an explicit Agent Definition is not directly refined in Islander. Instead, Islander focuses on restricting the behaviour of external agents to the sending and receiving of messages applicable to the task and context in which the agent is interacting. The specification in Islander is a description of messages exchanged between agents, and constraints regarding which agent sends which message and when, all according to the role of the agent and their state in the e-Institution. This indirectly defines what agents can do and is a substitute of a refinement of our notion of Agent Definition. That is, Agent Definition is indirectly available through detailed specification of each scene, through allocation of sub-tasks (or scene states) within a scene.

Our notion of Convention is also indirectly refined in Islander in dispersed details of the specification of sub-tasks within a scene (a transition between two states in a scene is restricted by conventions and message schemata).

Finally, with respect our run-time concepts: Islander refines our notion of Obligation, Islander obligations are generated as a result of activities within a scene. Our notion of Environment is indirectly refined through the collection of interactions available to all agents within the system. In particular, the interactions environment in Islander is determined by external agents that may leave or enter the system at any time. This refines our notion of Facet Event. Our notion of Environment History is refined in Islander through a collection of stacks of messages. One stack of messages exists for each scene (task) being executed by the system.

3.2   Refinement of TAO from the FAML Metamodel

TAO (Taming Agents and Objects) [33] is the metamodel underlying an extension to UML, to accommodate agent-oriented development, called MAS-ML (figure 5). The TAO metamodel retains object-oriented design concepts. In the following analysis, we are concerned only with the agent-oriented features of TAO. We analyse TAO metamodel units to show how they refine our metamodel. We choose TAO since it is another product metamodel. It focuses on structural aspects of MASs [33].

TAO's refinement of our Functional Requirement centres on the notion of Organisation. Every TAO organisation is tightly coupled with an owner agent which has an *ownership* relation with the organisation (see Figure 5). Large goals are decomposed and allocated to agent roles controlled by the owner agent. Thus the notion of organisation is a container of refinements of our three notions of Task, Role and Agent Definition. These three notions are respectively refined within TAO organisations as follows: Responsibility, Role and its Owning Agent. TAO refines hierarchical relations between tasks as hierarchical relations between organisations. This, in turn, introduces hierarchical associations between roles. This is a TAO-specific refinement that is a direct consequence of the tight coupling of tasks, roles and agent definitions.

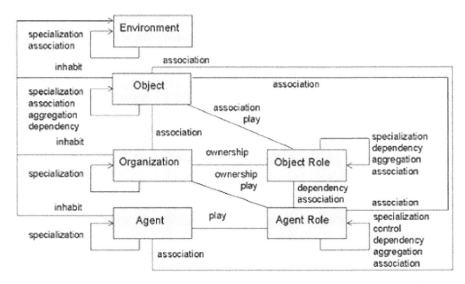

Fig. 5. TAO metamodel showing MAS-ML abstractions and relationships[5]

TAO's notion of Organisation is more specific than Task Analysis, in that it assumes that organizing agents into cooperative and hierarchical groups is inherent to any MAS. Whilst cooperation between agents is a very useful and a common assumption, it is not a generic and inherent feature of all MASs. For example, it renders TAO impractical to competitive agents in many market simulation MASs. To maintain genericity of our metamodel, we do not assume that agent grouping is a methodology-dependent feature. It is unclear to us whether or not identifying agent groups in the early stages of system analysis would assist in moving to the next architectural phase more effectively

For every modelled system in TAO, there is a Main Organisation. This is an instance of our System construct (Figure 1). TAO bridges modelling the internals of agents to the functional requirements through the definition of the owner agent coupled with each organisation, which includes beliefs and plans that can be used to allocate roles and to control the entities involved in the goal of the organisation (Task). The owner agent may allocate some of these to agents that assume roles that are part of the organisation. Organisations have axioms that must be followed. This refines our notion of Convention.

TAO has three notions to specify agent behaviour: Rights, Duties and Protocols. These respectively refine the following three notions from our metamodel: Action, Obligation and Message Schema. TAO's protocols distinguish between sent and received messages for each role. TAO does not represent how plans are generated or dumped (this is left to the developers).

TAO's Environment notion refines the FAML Environment construct. It provides the habitat for executing agents. However, TAO is not explicit in making a distinction between messages exchanged between agents and agents changing certain features of

---

[5] http://www.les.inf.puc-rio.br/mastools/masml_masmltool.html

the environment. This seems to be taken care of by the object-oriented features of the environment (in TAO, objects as well as agents may inhabit an environment (see Figure 5)). For instance, in the example of the online bookstore [32], objects are used to describe books being bought and sold (and the trading environment is changed consequently).

4 Discussion, Summary and Future Work

We have argued that it is possible to refine our metamodel to obtain both the metamodel underlying Islander and TAO. To strengthen our argument, in this section, we compare the two refinements of our metamodel. We highlight key features of each of TAO and Islander and sketch possible extensions to both; then we conclude with an overview of future work.

4.1 Discussion on Our Comparative Study

Our metamodel is explicit in some notions, whereas both Islander and TAO are implicit. Examples are Facet, Facet Event and Convention. Both emphasise task analysis and allocation of sub-tasks to agent roles. Islander does this with Scenes. TAO uses Organisations to represent the allocation of a task to a group of agents. TAO Organisation internals make it explicit which agent roles are responsible for which sub-tasks. This is dispersed in Islander's state description of scenes.

TAO is more comprehensive (in coverage) than Islander's metamodel. Hence, there are more concepts of our metamodel that are not refined in Islander in comparison with those not refined in TAO. Particularly, this is the case for specifying internals of planning agents.

Islander-specific features include a detailed modelling framework for specifying tasks. They are called scenes, decomposed into states, with transition between these states being conditioned by agent messages. Islander is richer than TAO in runtime concepts: it specifies synchronisation requirements between scenes and it also refines our Environment History. Neither feature exists in TAO. The later version of TAO [33] includes new dynamic features but Environment History is not one of them.

Changing the structure of the system dynamically, that is system evolution, is not explicitly accommodated in our metamodel, neither for TAO nor Islander. However, we see the importance of this for future systems. Towards this, our current metamodel would entail new (dynamic) relationships amongst roles and between roles, as well as dynamic constructs such as Environment History.

A way to evolve roles, involving monitoring message flows and using the Environment History, is described in [3]. Both TAO and Islander need enhancing to accommodate such an evolutionary MAS. In TAO, monitoring of messages and corresponding roles is easier because it has centralized associations between messages and roles. However, TAO needs the addition of Environment History, which Islander already possesses. Islander could benefit from a centralized association between roles and message schemata. TAO can use conditional boundaries of the organisation to implement evolutionary changes, combined with loosened authority of the organisation over roles of their agents. Islander could also include an ontology revision mechanism for its message specification.

4.2 Summary and Future Work

In this paper, we have provided a first step towards context-dependent method engineering for MAS development: a process-independent metamodel for an agent-oriented modelling language to describe software components of any MAS. It captures problem-independent concepts and attributes involved in MAS requirement description and system design at various levels of details.

The focus on the capturing of MAS features led us to a generic metamodel that is methodology independent. At the system level it can capture any problem independent concept, to a high level of abstraction. At the same time, our generic FAML metamodel is highly useable. It describes detailed product knowledge at the agent level and is enriched with constructs to represent the *behaviour* of agents within any MAS. It can represent properties of any type of agent.

This paper provides, as well, preliminary evidence for the expressive power of our language constructed as a formalised synthesis of the implicit modelling approaches found in a number of existing agent-oriented methodologies. We have shown how the FAML metamodel can be refined to express metamodels underlying known MAS descriptors: MAS-ML (representing TAO) and Islander. The current work shown in this paper does not, however, totally validate our metamodel for its use towards MAS method engineering. Towards this, we plan to validate it against underlying metamodels of a number of other prominent methodologies, including Gaia [36] and Tropos [16]. We also plan to further identify and exemplify its individual elements in the analysis of an actual P2P retrieval MAS application.

Beyond the metamodel validation, the next step of our work is to create a complementary generic *process* metamodel and to situate the presented agent-oriented modelling language within a full method engineering framework. The FAML modelling language will be stored in a repository as a collection of method fragments, which will be subsequently linked to other method fragments describing potential activities, tasks, techniques (i.e. process aspects), teams and roles (i.e. people aspects). Thus, a complete methodological framework will be provided, able to support the generation of complete, custom-made agent-oriented methodologies using the tenets of method engineering.

Acknowledgement

This is contribution number 05/12 of the Centre for Object Technology Applications and Research. The work is supported by the Australian Research Council under Discovery grant number: DP0451213.

References

1. C. Bernon, M. Cossentino, M. Gleizes, .P. Turci and F. Zambonelli: A Study of some Multi-Agent Meta-Models, in *AOSE04*. 2004. New York.
2. C. Bernon, M.-P. Gleizes, S. Peyruqueou and G. Picard: ADELFE, a Methodology for Adaptive Multi-Agent Systems Engineering, in *Engineering Societies in the Agents World*. 2002. Spain.

3. G. Beydoun, J. Debenham and A. Hoffmann: Using Messaging Structure to Evolve Agents Roles, in *Intelligent Agents and Multi-Agent Systems VII*, M. Barley and N. Kasabov, Editors. 2005, Springer: Australia. p. 18-30.
4. P. Bresciani, A. Perini, P. Giorgini, F. Giunchiglia and J. Mylopoulos: A Knowledge Level Software Engineering Methodology for Agent Oriented Programming, in *Agents2001*. 2001. Montreal: ACM.
5. S. Brinkkemper: Method Engineering: Engineering of Information Systems Development Methods and Tools. *Information and Software Technology*, 1996. **38**(4): p. 275-280.
6. R. Choren and C. Lucena: Modeling multi-agent systems with ANote. *Software and Systems Modelling*, 2005. **4**: p. 199-208, doi 10.1007/s10271-004-0065-y.
7. A. Cockburn: Selecting a project's methodology. *IEEE Software*, 2000. **17**(4): p. 64-71.
8. M. Cossentino and C. Potts: A CASE tool supported methodology for the design of multi-agent systems, in *International Conference on Software Engineering Research and Practice (SERP'02)*. 2002. Las Vegas (NV), USA.
9. E. Durfee and V. Lesser: Negotiating task decomposition and allocation using partial global planning., in *Distributed Artificial Intelligence*, L. Gasser and M. Huhns, Editors. 1989, Morgan Kaufmann: San Francisco. p. 229-244.
10. B. Edmonds and J. Bryson: The Insufficiency of Formal Design Methods - the necessity of an experimental approach, in *AAMAS04*. 2004. New York: ACM.
11. M. Esteva: Electronic Institutions: From Specification To Development, in *AI Research Insitute*. 2003, UAB - Universitat Autonòma de Barcelona: Barcelona.
12. M. Esteva: Electronic Institutions: From Specification To Development (PhD thesis), in *AI Research Insitute*. 2003, UAB - Universitat Autonòma de Barcelona.
13. M. Esteva, D.d.l. Cruz and C. Sierra: ISLANDER: an electronic institutions editor, in *International Conference on Autonomous Agents & Multiagent Systems (AAMAS02)*. 2002. Italy: ACM.
14. J. Ferber and A. Drogoul: Using Reactive Multi-Agent Systems in Simulation and Problem Solving, in *Distributed AI: Theory and Praxis*, L. Avouris, Editor. 1992, Kluwer: Brussels.
15. FIPA: Methodology Glossary - FIPAMG. 2003.
16. F. Giunchiglia, J. Mylopoulos and A. Perini: The Tropos Software Development Methodology: Processes, Models and Diagrams, in *Agent-Oriented Software Engineering III: Third International Workshop, AOSE 2002*, F. Giunchiglia, J. Odell, and G. Weiß, Editors. 2003, Springer. p. 162-173.
17. Z. Guessoum, L. Rejeb and R. Durand: Using Adaptive Multi-Agent Systems to Simulate Economic Models, in *AAMAS04*. 2004. New York: ACM.
18. B. Henderson-Sellers: Method engineering for OO systems development. *Comm. ACM*, 2003. **46**(10): p. 73-78.
19. B. Henderson-Sellers, J. Bohling and T. Rout: Creating the OOSPICE Model Architecture - a Case of Reuse. *Software Process Improvement and Practice*, 2004. **8**(1): p. 41-49.
20. B. Henderson-Sellers and P. Giorgini, eds.: *Agent-Oriented Methodologies*. 2005, Idea Group: Hershey, USA.
21. B. Henderson-Sellers, A. Simons and H. Younessi: *The OPEN Toolbox of Techniques*. The OPEN Series. 1998, Harlow (Essex), UK: Addison-Wesley Longman.
22. T. Hogg and C. Williams: Solving the Really Hard Problems with Cooperative Search, in *11th National Conference on Artificial Intelligence*. 1993. Washington, DC, USA: MIT Press.
23. E. Horlait: *Mobile Agents for Telecommunication Applications (Innovative Technology Series: Information Systems and Networks)*. 2004, Portland: Kogan Page.

24. L. Hunsberger and B.J. Grosz: A combinatorial auction for collaborative planning, in *4th International Conference on Multi-Agent Systems (ICMAS-00)*. 2000.

25. G.F. Luger: *AI: Structures and Strategies for Complex Problem Solving*. 2002: Addison Wesley.

26. J. Martin and J. Odell: *Object-Oriented Methods: A Foundation*. 1995, Englewood Cliffs, NJ: Prentice-Hall.

27. J. Odell, M. Nodine and R. Levy: A Metamodel for Agents, Roles, and Groups, in *AOSE 2004*, J. Odell and e. al., Editors. 2005, Springer: Berlin. p. 78-92.

28. L. Padgham and M. Winikoff: *Developing Intelligent Agent Systems. A Practical Guide*. Vol. 1. 2004, Chichester: J. Wiley & Sons. 225.

29. R. Pfeifer and C. Sheier: *Understanding Intelligence*. 2001: MIT Press.

30. J. Ralyté and C. Rolland: An Assembly Process Model for Method Engineering, in *13th Conference on Advanced Information Systems Engineering (CAiSE)*. 2001. Berlin: Springer.

31. S. Russell and P. Norvig: *Artificial Intelligence, A modern Approach, the intelligent agent book*. 2003: Prentice Hall.

32. V. Silva, R. Choren and C. Lucena: Using the MAS-ML to Model a Multi-Agent System, in *Software Engineering for Multi-Agent Systems (SELMAS2003)*. 2003. Springer.

33. V. Silva and C. Lucena: From a Conceptual Framework for Agents and Objects to a Multi-Agent System Modeling Language. *Autonomous Agents and Multi-Agent Systems*, 2004. **8**: p. 1-45.

34. G. Tidhar, C. Heinze, S. Goss, G. Murray, D. Appla and I. Lloyd: Using Intelligent Agents in Military Simulation or " Using Agents Intelligently", in *11th Conference on Innovative Applications of AI.*. 1999. Orlando,Florida: MIT Press.

35. M. Wooldridge: *Reasoning About Rational Agents*. 2000: MIT Press.

36. M. Wooldridge, N.R. Jennings and D. Kinny: The Gaia Methodology for Agent-Oriented Analysis and Design, in *Autonomous Agents and Multi-Agent Systems*. 2000. The Netherlands: Kluwer Academic Publishers.

Agent Roles, Qua Individuals and *the Counting Problem*

Giancarlo Guizzardi

Laboratory for Applied Ontology (ISTC-CNR), Trento, Italy
guizzardi@loa-cnr.it

Abstract. Despite the relevance of the concept of *role* for conceptual modeling and agent-orientation, there is still in the literature a lack of consensus on the meaning of this notion and how it should be incorporated in existing conceptual modeling languages and frameworks. In this paper, we offer a contribution to this problem by employing a well-founded reference ontology (UFO) to analyze and reconcile two competing notions of role existing in the conceptual modeling literature. Moreover, a modeling solution based on this ontology is proposed, which incorporates the benefit of the two approaches analyzed.

1 Introduction

Roles represent a fundamental notion for our conceptualization of reality. This notion has received much attention both in philosophical investigation [20,32] and in the conceptual modeling literature [2,31,34]. In particular, in the sub-area of conceptual modeling concerned with *agent-oriented conceptual modeling*, the concept of role is considered of fundamental relevance [5,25,26].

In a comprehensive study on this topic, Friedrich Steimman [31] defends that the role concept naturally complements those of *object* and *relationship*, standing on the same level of importance. However, Steimann also recognizes that *"the role concept, although equally fundamental, has long not received the widespread attention it deserved"*, and that *"although there appears to be a general awareness that roles are an important modelling concept, until now no consensus has been reached as to how roles should be represented or integrated into the established modeling frameworks"* [ibid., p.84]. The last statement can be verified by inspecting the diversity and incompatibility of the several conceptualizations of roles currently co-existing in the literature [2,18,31,34].

Recently, not only has the interest in roles grown continuously, but also has the interest in finding a common ground on which the different notions of role can be judged and reconciled [20,22]. In this paper, we employ the *foundational ontology* developed in [11,12] to provide real-world semantics, and to harmonize two competing notions of role present in the conceptual modeling literature.

In section 2 we present the theoretical background of the work presented here, i.e., the foundational ontology which is employed in the rest of the paper. A discussion on the categories of this ontology is continued in section 3, in which we formally define the notion of *role* that is adopted in our ontological framework. In section 4, we discuss a second notion of role that deviates from most of the proposals in the literature. This second notion of role has been initially proposed in [34] to address a philosophical

A. Garcia et al. (Eds.): SELMAS 2005, LNCS 3914, pp. 143–160, 2006.

problem known as *The Counting Problem* but it has been later adopted by other modeling approaches. In section 5, by using the foundational ontology presented in section 2, we manage to provide an ontological interpretation for both notions of role discussed. Moreover, we propose a conceptual modeling solution based on this ontology that is able to harmonize these two competing notions of role while maintaining the benefits of the two approaches. Section 6 concludes the article by presenting some final considerations.

2   Background: The Unified Foundational Ontology (UFO-A)

In this section, we present a fragment of a philosophically and cognitively well-founded reference ontology (foundational ontology) that has been developed in [11,12]. In particular, in [12], this ontology is named UFO (Unified Foundational Ontology) and is presented in three compliance sets. Here, we focus on the first of these sets (UFO-A), which is an *ontology of endurants*. As demonstrated in [12], this ontology comprise a number of core ontological categories that can be extended to provide a foundation for *Agent Modeling Concepts* (UFO-C). In the sequel, we restrict ourselves to a fragment of UFO-A, depicted in Figure 1 (see aforementioned references for details).

In what follows, we offer a formal characterization of some of the notions discussed by using a language of quantified modal logics with identity. The domain of quantification adopted is that of *possibilia*, which includes all possible entities independent of their actual existence. Therefore we shall quantify over a constant domain in all possible worlds. Moreover, all worlds are equally accessible. As a result we have the simplest language of quantified modal logics (QS5) with identity [9]. Finally, all formulas described are assumed to hold necessarily.

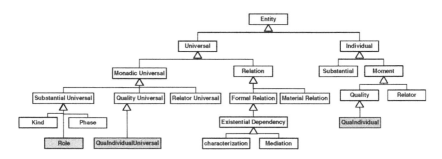

Fig. 1. Excerpt of the Foundational ontology UFO-A

A fundamental distinction in this ontology is between the categories of ***Individual*** and ***Universal***. Individuals are entities that exist in reality possessing a unique identity. Universals, conversely, are space-time independent pattern of features, which can be realized in a number of different individuals. The core of this ontology exemplifies the so-called *Aristotelian ontological square* comprising the category pairs ***Substantial-Substantial Universal***, ***Moment-Moment Universal***. From a metaphysical point of view, this choice allows for the construction of a parsimonious ontology, based on the primitive and formally defined notion of *existential dependence* [11]:

Definition 1 (existential dependence). Let the predicate ε denote existence. We have that an individual *x* is *existentially dependent* on another individual *y* (symbolized as *ed(x,y)*) iff, as a matter of necessity, *y* must exist whenever *x* exists, or formally **(1)**. **ed(x,y) =$_{def}$ □(ε(x) → ε(y)).**   ■

2.1 Moments

The word *Moment* is derived from the german *Momente* in the writings of E. Husserl and it denotes, in general terms, what is sometimes named *trope, abstract particular, individual accident*, or *property instance* [21]. In the scope of this work, the term bears no relation to the notion of time instant in ordinary parlance. The origin of the notion of moment lies in the theory of individual accidents developed by Aristotle. According to him, an accident is an individualized property, event or process that is not a part of the essence of a thing. We here use the term "moment" in a more general sense and do not distinguish *a priori* between essential and inessential moments.

As pointed out by [28], there is solid evidence for moments in the literature. On one hand, in the analysis of the content of perception, moments are the immediate objects of everyday perception. On the other hand, the idea of moments as *truthmakers* underlies a standard event-based approach to natural language semantics.

The notion of moment employed here comprises: (a) *Intrinsic Moments* or **Qualities**: an individualized (objectified) color, temperature, or weight, a symptom, a skill, a belief, an intention, an electric charge; (b) *Relational Moments* or **Relators**: a kiss, a handshake, a covalent bond, a medical treatment, but also *social objects* such as a flight connection, a purchase order and a commitment or claim [12].

An important feature that characterizes all *moments* is that they can only exist in other individuals (in the way in which, for example, electrical charge can exist only in some conductor). To put it more technically, we say that moments are *existentially dependent* on other individuals. Existential dependence can also be used to differentiate intrinsic and relational moments: qualities are dependent of one single individual; relators depend on a plurality of individuals.

A special type of existential dependence relation that holds between a moment *x* and the individual *y* of which *x* depends is the relation of **inherence** (*i*). Thus, for an individual *x* to be a moment of another individual *y*, the relation *i(x,y)* must hold between the two. For example, inherence glues your smile to your face, or the charge in a specific conductor to the conductor itself. We formally characterize a moment as an individual that inheres in (and, hence, is existentially dependent upon) another individual:

Definition 2 (Moment). (2). Moment(x) =$_{def}$ Individual(x) ∧ ∃y i(x,y)   •

In our framework, we adopt the so-called *non-migration* (or *non-transferability*) *principle*. This means that it is not possible for a moment *m* to inhere in two different individuals *a* and *b*: **(3). ∀x,y,z (Moment(x) ∧ i(x,y) ∧ i(x,z) → y = z)**

This characteristic of moments seems at first counterintuitive. For example, if we have two particulars *a* (a red apple) and *b* (a red car), and two moments r_1 (particular redness of *a*) and r_2 (particular redness of *b)*, we consider r_1 and r_2 to be different individuals, although perhaps qualitatively indistinguishable. What does it mean then to say that *a* and *b* have the *same* color? Due to (3), sameness here cannot refer to strict (numerical) identity, but only to a qualitative one (i.e., equivalence in a certain respect). In conformance with DOLCE [21], we distinguish between the color of a particular apple (its quality) and its 'value' (e.g., a particular shade of red). The latter is named *quale*, and describes a projection of an individual quality into a certain *conceptual space* [11].

The unique individual *y* that a moment *x* inheres in is termed the *bearer* of *x* and is defined as follows:

Definition 3 (Bearer of a Moment)[1]: (4). $\beta(x) =_{def} \iota y\, i(x,y)$ •

Finally, the bearer of a moment can itself be another moment. An example of moment inhering in another moment is the individualized time extension, or the graveness of a particular symptom. The infinite regress in the inherence chain is prevented by the fact that there are individuals that cannot inhere in other individuals, namely, *substantials*.

2.2 Substantial

Substantials are individuals that posses (direct) spatial-temporal qualities and that are founded on matter. Examples of Substances include ordinary objects of everyday experience such as an individual person, a dog, a house, a hammer, a car, Alan Turing and The Rolling Stones but also the so-called *Fiat Objects* such as the North-Sea and its proper-parts, postal districts and a non-smoking area of a restaurant. In contrast with moments, substantials do not inhere in anything and, as a consequence, they enjoy a higher degree of independence. We define the category of substantials as follows:

Definition 4 (Substantial). A substantial is an individual that does not *inhere in* another individual, i.e., which is not a moment. Formally, **(5). $\text{Substantial}(x) =_{def} \text{Individual}(x) \wedge \neg\text{Moment}(x)$** ■

As we have previously stated, substantials enjoy a higher degree of independence when compared to moments. Can we make a stronger statement? Can we say that substantials are existentially independent from all other individuals? If we take the notion of existential dependence that we have given in definition 1, the answer is no. Since, there are certainly pairs *(x,y)* where *x* is a substantial that satisfy *ed(x,y)*. For example, if *y* is any of the essential moments of *x* (the particular DNA of a person). Moreover, even if both *x* and *y* are substantials, *ed(x,y)* can be satisfied. Take for example a substantial and any of its *essential parts* (e.g., a car and its chassis as an essential part). Or, alternatively, a substantial *x* and another object *y* of which *x* is an *inseparable part* (e.g., a brain and person of which this brain is an inseparable part). The notions of essential and inseparable parts are discussed in depth in [11].

---

[1] The iota operator (ι) used in a formula such as ιxφ was defined by B. Russel and implies both the existence and the uniqueness of an individual *x* satisfying predicate φ.

However, suppose that x and y are two substantials that are *disjoint* from each other, i.e., they are neither part of each other nor they share a common part. The symbols $\int$ and $<$ below represent disjointness and *proper parthood²*, respectively:

(6). $(x \int y) =_{def} \neg(x < y) \wedge \neg(y < x) \wedge \neg(\exists z\ (z < x) \wedge (z < y)).$

Then, in this case, we can say that x and y are necessarily *independent* from each other (symbolized as *indep*):

(7). indep(x,y) $=_{def} \neg$**ed(x,y)** $\wedge \neg$**ed(y,x)**
(8). $\forall$**x,y Substantial(x)** $\wedge$ **Substantial(y)** $\wedge$ **(x** $\int$ **y)** $\rightarrow$ **indep(x,y)**

For example, a person depends on her brain, and a car depends on its chassis. However, a person (car) does not dependent on any other substantial that is disjoint from her (it). Notice that formula (8) also excludes the case of mutual existential dependence between substantials that share a common essential part (e.g., two rooms that share a wall as a mutual essential part).

2.3 Relations, Relators and Qua Individuals

Relations are entities that glue together other entities. In the philosophical literature, two broad categories of relations are typically considered, namely, *material* and *formal* relations [14,29]. Formal relations hold between two or more entities directly, without any further intervening individual. Examples of formal relations include existential dependence (*ed*), inherence (*i*), *part-of* (<), *subset-of, instantiation,* among many others not discussed here [11,21].

Material relations, conversely, have material structure on their own and include examples such as *working at, being enrolled at,* and *being connected to.* Whilst a formal relation such as the one between Paul and his knowledge x of Greek holds directly and as soon as Paul and x exist, for a material relation of *being treated in* between Paul and the medical unit MU_1 to exist, another entity must exist which *mediates* Paul and MU_1. We name these entities *relators.* Relators are individuals with the power of connecting entities. For example, a medical treatment connects a patient with a medical unit; an enrollment connects a student with an educational institution; a covalent bond connects two atoms. The notion of relator (relational moment) is supported by several works in the philosophical literature [14,28,29] and, the position advocated here is that they play an important role in answering questions of the sort: what does it mean to say that John is married to Mary? Why is it true to say that Bill works for Company X but not for Company Y?

An important notion for the characterization of relators (and, hence, for the characterization of material relations) is the notion of *foundation.* Foundation can be seen as a type of *historical dependence* [8], in the way that, for instance, an instance of *being kissed* is founded on an individual *kiss,* or an instance of *being punched by* is founded on an individual *punch,* an instance of *being connected to* between airports is founded on a particular flight connection.

---

² Formally, an individual x is a proper part of an individual y iff x is part of y and x is not identical to y, i.e., $(x < y) =_{def} (x \leq y) \wedge \neg(x = y).$

Suppose that John *is married to* Mary. In this case, we can assume that there is an individual relator (relational moment) m_1 of type *marriage* that mediates John and Mary. The foundation of this relator can be, for instance, a wedding event or the signing of a social contract between the involved parties. In other words, for instance, a certain event e_1 in which John and Mary participate can create an individual marriage m_1 which existentially depends on John and Mary and which mediates them. The event e_1 in this case is the foundation of relator m_1 and, m_1 is the so-called truthmaker of the propositions "John is married to Mary".

Now, let us elaborate on the nature of the relator m_1. There are many qualities that John acquires by virtue of being married to Mary. For example, imagine all the legal responsibilities that John has in the context of this relation. These newly acquired properties are intrinsic moments of John which, therefore, inhere and are existentially dependent on him. However, these moments also depend on the existence of Mary. We name this type of qualities *externally dependent qualities*, i.e., externally dependent qualities are intrinsic moments that inhere in a single individual but that are existentially dependent on (possibly a multitude of) other individuals.

Definition 5 (Externally Dependent Quality). A quality x is externally dependent iff it is existentially dependent of an individual which is independent of its bearer. Fornally, **(9). ExtDepQuality(x) =$_{def}$ Quality(x) $\land$ $\exists$y indep(y,β(x)) $\land$ ed(x,y).**   ■

In the case of a material externally dependent moment x there is always an individual *external* to its bearer (i.e., which is not one of its parts or intrinsic moments), which is the foundation of x. Again, in the given example, we can think of a certain event e_1 (wedding event or signing of social contract) in which both John and Mary participate and which founds the existence of these externally dependent moments inhering in John. Now, we can define an individual that bears all externally dependent qualities of John that share the same external dependencies and the same foundation. We term this particular a *qua individual* [22]. Qua individuals are, thus, treated here as a special type of *complex externally dependent qualities*. In this case, the complex quality inhering in John that bears all responsibilities that John acquires by virtue of a given wedding event can be named *John-qua-husband*.

To continue with the same example, we can think about another qua individual *Mary-qua-wife* which is a complex moment bearing all responsibilities that Mary acquires by virtue of the same foundation and that albeit inhering in Mary are also existentially dependent on John. The qua individuals *John-qua-husband* and *Mary-qua-wife* are existentially dependent on each other. Now, we can define an aggregate m_1 composed of these two qua individuals that share the same foundation, i.e., (*John-qua-husband* < m_1) and (*Mary-qua-wife* < m_1). In this example, m_1 is exactly the instance of the relational property *marriage* that mediates John and Mary and that makes true propositions such as "John is married to Mary", "Mary is married to John", "John is the husband of Mary", and "Mary is the wife of John".

In this example, a particular instance of the relational property marriage (i.e., a particular marriage relator) is the sum of all instantiated responsibilities that the involved parties acquire by virtue of a common foundation. In general, a relator can be defined as the aggregation of a number of qua individuals that share the same foundation. A relator is said to mediate (or connect) the relata of a material relation. Formally we have that: let x, y and z be three distinct individuals such that (a) x is a relator; (b) z is a qua individual and z is part of x; (c) z inheres in y. In this case, we say that x *mediates* y, symbolized by $m(x,y)$, and the following holds:

(10). $\forall x,y \; m(x,y) \rightarrow$ relator(x) $\wedge$ Individual(y)
(11). $\forall x$ Relator(x) $\rightarrow \forall y \; (m(x,y) \leftrightarrow (\exists z \; \text{quaIndividual}(z) \wedge (z < x) \wedge i(z,y)))$

Additionally, we require that a relator mediates at least two distinct individuals, i.e.,

(12). $\forall x$ Relator(x) $\rightarrow \exists y,w \; (y \neq w \wedge m(x,y) \wedge m(x,w))$.

Again, using the example above, we say that the particular relator marriage m_1 mediates the substantials John and Mary and, for this reason, we can say that John and Mary are married to each other.

Finally, in the theory present here, qua individuals are always *inessential* moments. In other words, if a qua individual q inheres in a substantial x then it does so *contingently*, i.e., only in certain situations. To see that this must be the case, suppose the contrary. By definition 5, a qua individual q that inheres in x is also existentially dependent on a individual y which is independent from x, i.e., $ed(q,y)$ and $\neg ed(x,y)$. However, if q is a essential to x then we have that $ed(x,q)$. Now, since existential dependency is a transitive relation, with $ed(x,q)$ and $ed(q,y)$ we have that $ed(x,y)$, which is a contradiction. Hence, we have that qua individuals cannot inhere in its bearer necessarily.

2.4 Universals

A **Substantial Universal** is a universal whose instances are substances (e.g., the universal Person or the universal Apple). A **Quality Universal** is a universal whose instances are individual qualities (e.g., the objectified color of this apple is an instance of the universal color, a particular headache is an instance of the universal Symptom), and a **Relator Universal** is one whose instances are individual relational moments (e.g., the particular enrollment connecting John and a certain University is an instance of the universal Enrollment). Both quality and relator universals are moment universals.

In general, conceptual specifications (such as UML class diagrams and ER specifications) represent conceptualizations only at the type level, i.e., only universals and relations among universals are typically represented. Thus, we define the formal relations of **Characterization** and **Mediation** as the counterparts at the type level of the relations *inheres in* and *mediates*, respectively. In these definitions, the symbol :: represents the formal relation of instantiation.

Definition 6 (Characterization). A universal U is characterized by a moment universal M iff every instance of U bears an instance of M. Formally, **(13). charac(U,M) $=_{\text{def}}$ Universal(U) $\wedge$ MomentUniversal(M) $\wedge \forall x \; (x{::}U \rightarrow \exists y \; y{::}M \wedge i(y,x))$** ∎

Definition 7 (Mediation). The mediation relation holds between a universal U and a relator universal U_R iff every instance of U is *mediated by* (m) an instance of U_R. Formally, **(14). mediation(U,U_R) $=_{\text{def}}$ Universal(U) $\wedge$ RelatorUniversal(U_R) $\wedge \forall x \; (x{::}U \rightarrow \exists r \; r{::}U_R \wedge m(r,x))$** ∎

Figure 2 below exemplifies the ontological categories discussed in this section. It depicts the *substantial universals* Person, Patient and Medical Unit, the *quality universal* Symptom, the *relator universal* Treatment. Moreover, it represents the *quality universal* Duration which characterizes the quality universal Symptom, and the corresponding *formal relations* connecting these entities. As argued in [11], a complex quality universal such as Symptom in figure 2 is the ontological counterpart of the concept of *Weak entity types* in EER diagrams.

In this figure and in the remainder of this article we use a UML class *stereotype* «quality» and «relator» to represent quality and relator universals. Additionally, we use the UML association stereotypes «characterization» and «mediation» to represent the respective formal relations. The classes stereotyped as «kind» and «role» represent substantial universals and will be discussed in the next section. These stereotyped constructs belong to an ontologically well-founded UML profile defined in [11] for the purpose of conceptual modeling and ontology representation. For UML extension mechanisms and, in particular, stereotypes, we refer to [24].

In the conceptual models represented in this article, we only represent as UML associations the stereotyped existential dependence formal relations discussed above, i.e., *characterization* and *mediation*. Material relations are represented by explicitly representing their founding relators. As discussed in depth in [11], this approach introduces many benefits to conceptual modeling when compared to the traditional modeling of relational properties as *associations*.

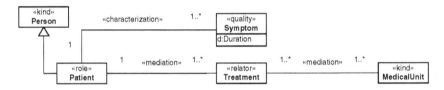

Fig. 2. Conceptual model exemplifying some of the ontological categories discussed

3   Roles as Substantial Universals

In [23], cognitive psychologist John Macnamara investigates the role of *substantial universals* in cognition and provides a comprehensive theory for explaining the process that a child undergoes when learning proper names and common nouns. He proposes the following example: suppose a little boy (Tom), who is about to learn the meaning of a proper name for his puppy. When presented to the word "Spot", Tom has to decide what it refers to. A demonstrative such as "that" will not suffice to determinate the bearer of the proper name. How to decide that "that", which changes all its perceptual properties is still *Spot*? In other words, which changes can Spot suffer and still be *the same*? As Macnamara (among others) shows, answers to these questions are only possible if *Spot* is taken to be a *proper name* for an individual that instantiates a special type of substantial universal, namely, one that supplies a principle through which we can judge whether two individuals are *the same*, i.e., a *principle of identity*. The principles of identity supplied by these universals are essential to judge the validity of all identity statements. For example, if for an instance of the universal

Statue loosing a piece will not alter the identity of the object, the same does not hold for an instance of *Lump of Clay*.

Let us take another example. Consider a statement such as *"Exactly five X were in the kitchen last night"*. This statement is only determinate (i.e., has a determinate truth value) if X stands for a universal that supplies a principle through which we can individuate and, thus, count individuals, i.e., a *principle of individuation*. To verify this, we can substitute X in the sentence above by the universals *Thing*, *Object* or *Red*. A request to "count the red in this room" cannot receive a definite answer: Should a red shirt be counted as one or should the shirt, the two sleeves, and two pockets be counted separately so that we have five reds? The problem in this case is not that one would not know how to finish the counting but that one would not know how to start, since arbitrarily many *subparts of a red thing are still red*.

In summary, a sentence such as *"The X which is the same as Y"* is only be determinate if X and Y can supply a principle of identity for its instances, and a sentence such as *"Exactly five X"* is only determinate if X can supply a principle of individuation and counting. Substantial Universals such as Person, Car, Dog, Student that carry a principle of identity, individuation and counting for its instances are named *Sortal Universals*. In contrast, universals such as Thing, Red, Tall, Heavy are named *Characterizing Universals*, since they only attribute properties to (characterize) individuals which have already being individuated by sortal-supplied principles. The distinction between sortal and characterizing universals is reflected in natural language in the distinction between common nouns and other general terms (e.g., adjectives, verbs), respectively. Notice that only the substitution of X and Y in the sentences above by common nouns will render sentences which are grammatical. For a fuller formal theory of substantial universals that propose further distinction among both sortal and characterizing universals one should refer to [10,11].

The statement that the identity of an individual can only be traced in connection with a Sortal Universal, which provides a *principle of individuation* and *identity* to the particulars it collects amounts to one of the best-supported theories in the philosophy of language [13,19,23,32]. The position advocated in this article affirms an equivalent stance for a theory of conceptual modeling. We defend that every substantial individual in a conceptual model of the domain must be an instance of a conceptual modeling type representing a sortal universal.

As argued by Kripke [16], a proper name such as Spot or Mick Jagger are rigid designators, i.e. they refer to the same individual in all possible situations, factual or counterfactual. For instance, the proper name Mick Jagger refers to the same individual both now (when he is the lead singer of Rolling Stones and a sexagenarian) and in the past (when he was the boy Mike Philip living in Kent, England). Moreover, it refers to the same individual in counterfactual situations such as the one in which he decided to continue in the London School of Economics and has never pursued a musical career. For this reason, a proper name must be typed by a sortal that applies to its instances *necessarily*, i.e., in all possible situations. In this case, the sortal Person is the sortal that defines the validity of the claim that Mick Jagger is *the same* as Mike Philip or, in other words, that Mike Philip persists through changes in height, weight, age, appearance, etc., as the same individual.

Once more, person can only be the sortal that supports the proper name Mick Jagger in all possible situations because it applies *necessarily* to the individual referred by the proper name, i.e., instances of Person cannot cease to be so without ceasing to exist. This meta-property of universals is named *Modal Constancy* [13] or *rigidity* [10] and can be formally characterized as in the *formula schema* below:

Definition 9 (Rigidity). A universal U is rigid if for every instance x of U, x is necessarily (in the modal sense) an instance of U. In other words, if x instantiates U in a given world w, then x must instantiate U in every possible world w': **(15).** $\square(\forall x \; x::U \rightarrow \square(x::U))$. ∎

In summary, since principles of identity apply to individuals in all possible situations, we have that only *rigid sortals* can supply principles of identities for their instances. A rigid sortal universal that supplies a principle of identity for its instances is named here a ***Kind***. Examples of sortal universals that apply to their instances only *contingently* (i.e., possibly only in certain situations) include universals such as *Boy* and *Adult Man*, but also *Student, Employee, Caterpillar* and *Butterfly, Philosopher, Writer, Alive* and *Deceased*. Sortals that possibly apply to an individual only during a certain phase of its existence are named *phased-sortals*. Contrary to kinds, phased-sortals are *anti-rigid* universals:

Definition 10 (Anti-rigidity). A universal U is anti-rigid if for every instance x of U, x is *possibly* (in the modal sense) not an instance of U. In other words, if x instantiates U in a given world w, then there is a possible world w' in which x does not instantiate U: **(16).** $\square(\forall x \; x::U \rightarrow \Diamond(\neg x::U))$. ∎

Being anti-rigid, phased-sortals cannot *supply* a principle of identity for their instances. However, since they are sortals, they must *carry* a principle of identity, which they inherit from a Kind. Therefore, we have that every phase-sortal PS must be a *subtype* of Kind such that PS inherits the principle of identity supplied by K. In other words, every instance of PS is necessarily a K and, thus, obeys the principle of identity supplied by K. For example, for an individual John instance of Student, we can easily imagine John moving in and out of the Student type, while being the same individual, i.e. without loosing his identity. This is because the principle of identity that applies to instances of Student and, in particular, that can be applied to John, is the one which is supplied by kind Person of which the phase-sortal Student is a subtype.

If PS is a phased-sortal and K is the substance sortal specialized by PS, there is a *specialization condition* φ such that x is an instance of PS iff x is an instance of K that satisfies φ [32]. A further clarification on the different types of specialization conditions allows us to distinguish between two different types of phased-sortals which are of great importance to the practice of conceptual modeling, namely, *phases* and *roles*.

Phases (also named *states* in [2]) constitute possible stages in the history of a substance sortal. Examples include: (a) Alive and Deceased: as possible stages of a Person; (b) Catterpillar and Butterfly of a Lepidopteran; (c) Town and Metropolis of a City; (d) Boy, Male Teenager and Adult Male of a Male Person. *Universals representing phases constitute a partition of the kind they specialize.* For example, if ‹Alive, Deceased› is a *phase-partition* of the kind Person then for every world w, every Person x is either an instance of Alive or of Deceased but not of both. Moreover, if x is an instance of Alive in world w then there is a world w' such that x is not an instance of Alive in w', which then implies that x is an instance of Deceased in w'.

Contrary to phases, **Roles** do not necessarily form a partition of kinds. Moreover, they differ from phases with respect to the specialization condition φ. For a phase Ph, φ represents a condition that depends solely on intrinsic properties of Ph. For instance, one might say that if Mick Jagger is a Living Person then he is a Person who has the property of being alive or, if Spot is a Puppy then it is a Dog who has the property of being less than one year old. For a role Rl, conversely, φ depends on extrinsic (relational) properties of Rl. For example, one might say that if John is a Student then John is a Person who is enrolled in some educational institution, if Peter is a Customer then Peter is a Person who buys a Product x from a Supplier y, or if Mary is a Patient than she is a Person who is treated in a certain medical unit. In other words, an entity plays a role in a certain context, demarcated by its relation with other entities. This meta-property of Roles is named *Relational Dependence* and can be formally characterized as follows [10,11]:

Definition 11 (Relational Dependence). A universal U is relationally dependent on another universal W via relation R iff for every instance x of U there is an instance y of W such that x and y are related via R: **(17).** $\Box(\forall x\ x::U \rightarrow \exists y\ y::W \land R(x,y)).$ ■

In figure 1 we show the refinements in the category of substantial universals proposed in this section. Thus, the material **Roles** employed both in conceptual modeling and natural language (e.g., Student, Customer, Supplier, Husband, Patient) are defined here as *anti-rigid* and *relationally dependent substantial sortals*.

4   Roles as Qua Individual Universals

In [34], Wieringa and colleagues discuss the need for elaborating on the distinctions among the types of universals used in conceptual modeling and propose three type categories: *static classes*, *dynamic classes* and *roles*. The first two of these correspond to our categories of *kinds* and *phases*, respectively. However, differently from our proposal, in their approach a role universal is not a phased-sortal. Conversely, their roles are *rigid* universals whose instances are said to be *played by* instances of ordinary (static and dynamic) types. The *played by* relation (also termed *inheritance by delegation* by the authors) between a role r and an object o implies that r is *existentially dependent* on o. This means that r can only be played by o, and that r can only exist when played by o. However, in contrast, o can possibly be associated via the *play by* relation to many instances of the role class (and to many different role classes). Moreover, role universals are responsible for supplying a principle of identity for its instances, which is different from the one supplied by the universals instantiated by their players. Figure 3 depicts an example of an ordinary and a role universal according to Wieringa et al.

Fig. 3. Example of Role and Role Player Universals

An inspection of the role literature shows, however, that most authors conceive role universals in a way which is akin to the notion proposed in section 3, i.e., as substantial universals. This includes authors both in philosophy [32] and in conceptual modeling in computer science [2,7,15,31]. Moreover, several authors share the view sponsored in section 3 that the identity of a role instance is supplied by a (kind) universal subsuming the role type that it instantiates [1,17,27]. Finally, there are authors that explicitly share both views [10,31]. In fact, in an extensive study about the topic of roles in the conceptual modeling literature, Steimann [31] deems the approach of Wieringa and colleagues to be a singular case in which the identity of role instances is not supplied by a universal subsuming the role type they instantiate.

The motivation for such a view proposed by Wieringa and colleagues lies in a philosophical problem known as *The Counting Problem* [13]. Consider the following argument:

> KLM served four thousand passengers in 2004
> Every passenger is a person
> Ergo, KLM served four thousand persons in 2004

Thus, as Wieringa et al. write [34]: *"if we count persons, we may count 1000, but if we count passengers, we may count 4000. The reason for this difference is that if we count things we must identify those things, so that we can say which things are the same and which are different. But in order to identify them, we must classify them."* In other words, the counting problem is that, by following the premises in the argument above, one can derive a mistaken conclusion.

Although, we appreciate and share the view of connecting *counting with identity* and *identity with classification*, we do not agree with the conclusion the authors draw from this example, namely, that since person and passenger do not share a principle of counting then they must not share a principle of identity either. Since, a principle of identity can only be supplied by a rigid universal, this must be the foundation of the authors' conclusion that a role universal therefore must be a rigid universal.

Why do we think the conclusions made by the authors are not warranted? To start with, in line with [32], we defend that the counting problem is actually a fallacy. Take the argument posed by its defenders: "The person that boarded flight KL124 on April 22nd, 2004 is a different passenger from the person who boarded flight KL256 on November 19th, 2004, but the two passengers are the same person". We do not agree that it can be correctly said that *the two passengers are the same person*, or, alternatively, that a single *person is distinct passengers* (at different times), if we are truthful to our commonsense use of the *common noun* passenger. However, let us suppose that this is the case, i.e., that person and passenger obey different principles of identity. In this situation, the second premise of the argument is no longer valid, i.e., one cannot say anymore that *every passenger is a person* in a reading in which the copula "is" is interpreted as a relation of identity. This is because, due to the so-called *Leibniz Rule of Identity* [32], the identity relation holds necessarily if it holds at all. Moreover, since identity is an equivalence relation, we would have that

"passenger x on flight KL124" is (necessarily) identical to person y
"passenger z on flight KL256" is (necessarily) identical to person y
Ergo, "passenger x on flight KL124" is (necessarily) identical to "passenger z on flight KL256"

This conclusion contradicts the initial premise that the two passengers were different. Therefore, if we have the second premise interpreted in the strong reading, one must conclude that passenger carries the same principle of identity as person and, hence, that "passenger x on flight KL124" and "passenger z on flight KL256" are indeed numerically the same. In this case, though, the first premise ceases to be true, i.e., one can no longer say that "KLM served four thousand passengers in 2004". We must conclude then that the second premise should have a weaker reading in which the copula does no represent a relation of identity but one of *coincidence* [21]. But, if this interpretation is taken the whole argument is clearly invalid, since the conclusion cannot be expected to follow from the premises.

In summary, the conclusion that different principles of identity must be supplied by role types and the types instantiated by their players cannot follow from this argument. However, despite disagreeing with the conclusions, we think there is an important truth highlighted by the argument of Wieringa and colleagues. If not instances of passengers, what does one count when stating that "KLM served four thousand passengers in 2004"? Let us analyze the concept of role proposed by Wieringa et al [34]:

1. a role universal is a rigid classifier;
2. role instances are (one-sidely) existentially dependent of a unique object, which is said to *play* the role;
3. objects *play* these roles only contingently, i.e., the *play* relation is only a contingent relation for the player. As a consequence, ceasing to play the role does not alter the identity of the player object.

A recent work that has a concept of role similar to the one of Wieringa et al [34] is the one of Frank Loebe [18]. However, Loebe's roles are not only *existentially dependent* on their players, but they also depend on the existence of another entity (distinct from their players), in the way, for instance, that *being a student* depends on the existence of an education institution, or *being a husband* depends on the existence of a wife, *being an employee* depends on the existence of an employer, etc. This feature of roles is recognized in our analysis in section 3. In fact, it is generally accepted in the literature that roles only exist in a certain context, or in the scope of a certain relation [2,4,6,10,20,30,31]. Thus, Loebe's notion of role agrees with that of Wieringa et al. in the points (1), (2) and (3) above, but it also characterizes role instances as existentially dependent on each other.

It should be clear by now that the concept of role in Wieringa et al [34] and Loebe is equivalent to our notion of *qua individual* discussed in section 3. We can interpret their *play by* relation as a sort of inherence. Both relations represent a one-side monadic existential dependence relation. Thus we can say that, like their notion of role, our qua individuals are: instances of a rigid classifier (1); one-side existentially dependent on objects, which are related to their "players" via a contingent sort of existential dependence relation (2)(3). Furthermore, a qua individual is a complex of externally dependent qualities (e.g., in figure 3, *student id*, *average grade*[3]), which, by definition, depends also on the existence of another object extrinsic to its bearer

---

[3] To see that, for example, having a particular *student id* is an externally dependent moment, the reader should imagine a person that is registered in different departments of a university, having a different student id for each department.

(player). Thus, as in Loebe's concept of role, asides from the inherence (play) relationship with its bearer (player), our *qua individuals* stand in parthood relationship with a unique relator in the scope of a material relation. Since relators consist of at least two distinct qua individuals (formula 12), we conclude that the qua individuals composing a relator are existentially dependent on each other.

5 Harmonizing the Two Notions

Now, how can we relate the notion of role as a qua individual discussed in section 4 with the one proposed in section 3? Let us revisit the example depicted in figure 3 above. To start with, a point that can be argued against this model is the representation of optional cardinality constraints. In fact, since no restriction is defined for the kind subsuming a role classifier, optional cardinalities must be represented in both Wieringa's and Loebe's approaches. As argued, for instance, in [33], from an ontological standpoint, there is no such a thing as an optional property and, hence, the representation of optional cardinality leads to unsound models, with undesirable consequences in terms of clarity. Moreover, as empirically demonstrated in [3], conceptual models without optional properties lead to better performance in problem-solving tasks that require a deeper-level understanding of the represented domain. To put it simply, not all persons bear a student moment, but only those persons that, for example, are enrolled in an educational institution. We can then define a restriction of the universal Person, whose instances are exactly those individuals that bear a student *moment*, i.e., that are enrolled in an educational institution (see figure 4).

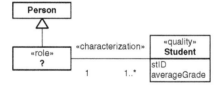

Fig. 4. A Role universal, its subsuming kind and an exemplification relation to a qua individual universal

Now, the universal stereotyped as «role» in figure 4 is exactly what we mean by a role in section 3 and it is the one idea of role that accurately corresponds to the common-sense use of roles in ordinary language. For this reason, we propose to use the role name for the role universal and to create a new name for the *qua individual* universal (see figure 5). Notice that the general term Student (Passenger, Employee, etc.) in natural language belongs to the grammatical category of *count nouns* as it is usually the case of substantial sortals, not to the category of *adjectives*[4] as it is usually the

---

[4] Etymologically the English word *noun* comes from the latin word *substantivus*, meaning expressing *substance*. The original form is still preserved in latin languages such as Portuguese (substantivo) and Italian (sostantivo), as well as in the English word *substantive*, which is a less familiar synonym for noun. Conversely, one of the meanings of *adjective* in English is "not standing by itself, dependent" (see, for example, www.m-w.com).

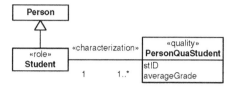

Fig. 5. A Role universal, its subsuming kind and an exemplification relation to a qua individual universal (revised version)

case with substantial characterizing universals corresponding to *determinate* moment universals (Red, Tall, Heavy).

Although an improvement of figure 4, figure 5 is still incomplete in the sense that it does not express the additional dependence relation that a *qua individual* has with other objects external to its bearer. This problem is solved in figure 6, in which relators (as aggregates of qua individuals) are represented explicitly and in which the externally dependent moments of a qua individual are represented as *resultant moments*[5] of the relator. In this figure, the associations between Student and Enrolment and between Education Institution and Enrolment stand for formal relations of mediation.

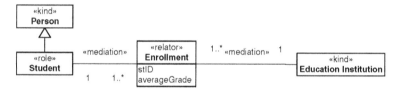

Fig. 6. A Role universal, its subsuming kind and an associated Relator universal

Now, let us return to the "counting problem" previously discussed:

500 students graduated from the University of Twente in 2004
Every student is a person
Ergo, 500 persons graduated from the University of Twente in 2004

In this argument, if the first premise is true than the word *student* refers to the mode *Person qua student*. The counting of these entities in a given situation is equal to the cardinality of the extension of the PersonQuaStudent universal in figure 5 (i.e., #*ext*(PersonQuaStudent)) or the cardinality of the extension of the Enrollment universal in figure 6 (i.e., #*ext*(Enrollment)), since there is always a 1-1 correspondence between relators and their composing qua individuals. However, if this interpretation for student is assumed, the second premise is simply false, since the relation between a student and a person would be one of inherence, not one of identity. Alternatively, if the word student is interpreted (in the more natural way) as in figure 5, then the counting of students is equal to the cardinality of the extension of the Student universal in this figure (i.e., #*ext*(Student)). Though, in this case, premise one is not necessarily true.

---

[5] Resultant properties of an object are properties that a whole inherits from one of its parts.

In both cases, the alleged "counting problem" disappears. Nonetheless, with the model of figure 6 we are still able to represent for both kinds of entities (roles and qua individuals) and their respective counting in an unambiguous manner. Additionally, this solution is able to make explicit and harmonize the two diverse senses of Role which have been used in the conceptual modeling literature.

Finally, we can refine the characteristic or *relational dependence* defined for roles in section 3 by explicitly relating the two notions of role discussed in this article. Roles, as substance sortals, are always defined in the context of material relations [11]. Thus, the relation R in definition 11 can be further analyzed as being derived from a certain relator universal U_R [11]. Consequently, we can state that a role universal as a substantial sortal (in the first sense of section 3) is always characterized by a qua individual universal (role in the second sense of section 4):

(18). ∀x Role(x) → ∃y QuaIndividualUniversal(y) ∧ charac(x,y)

Or alternatively, we can state that a role universal (as a substantial sortal) bears always a mediation relation to a relator universal.

(19). ∀x Role(x) → ∃y RelatorUniversal(y) ∧ mediation(x,y)

As a consequence of formula (19), we have that, in the UML profile employed in figures 2 and 6, a UML class stereotyped as «role» must always be connected to an association end of a «mediation» relation [11].

6 Final Considerations

The development of a philosophically well-founded upper level ontology is an important step towards the definition of real-world semantics for conceptual modeling and agent-oriented concepts. In this article, we focus on the concept of *Role*. Despite its fundamental relevance to conceptual modeling and, in particular, to agent-orientation, there is still a lack of consensus on the meaning of this category and on how it should be incorporated in the metamodels of existing conceptual modeling languages.

In this paper, we use a fragment of the Unified Foundation Ontology (UFO) proposed in [11,12] to analyze two competing notions of role existing in the conceptual modeling literature. In particular, we consider the notion of role offered by Wieringa et al. in [34], which proposes the complete separation of roles and kind taxonomies, therefore, deviating from most of the approaches in the literature.

The proposal of Wieringa et al. is motivated by a philosophical problem known as *The Counting Problem*. As we demonstrate in this article, this problem is actually fallacious and, thus, the separation of role and kind taxonomies cannot be argued for on this basis. Nonetheless, there is an important truth highlighted by their argument which is generally neglected in most conceptual modeling approaches, namely, that in different situations one might want to count "role instances" in different senses.

By relying of the ontological category of *qua individual* discussed in this article, we manage to provide an ontological interpretation for the notion of roles proposed by Wieringa and colleagues. Moreover, we manage to harmonize it with the more common view of roles taken in the literature, and the one which more naturally represents the commonsense use of roles in ordinary language, namely, the conception of roles as *relationally dependent and anti-rigid substantial universals.*

Finally, by explicitly representing roles as both substantial universals and *qua individual* universals, we can account in an unambiguous way for the alternative senses of counting "role instances" previously mentioned.

Acknowledgements. The author would like to thank Gerd Wagner, Luis Ferreira Pires, Marten van Sinderen, Nicola Guarino, Renata Guizzardi and Roberta Ferrario for fruitful discussions and for providing valuable input to the issues of this article.

References

1. Albano, A.; Bergamini, R.; Ghelli, G.; Orsini, R. (1993): *An object data model with roles*, in: R. Agrawal, S. Baker, D. Bell (Eds.), Proceedings of the 19th International Conference on Very Large Databases, Morgan Kaufmann, Dublin, pp. 39-51.
2. Bock, C.; Odell, J. (1998): *A More Complete Model of Relations and their Implementation: Roles.* Journal of OO Programming, May, 1998, 51–54.
3. Bodart, F., Patel, A., Sim, M., Weber, R. (2001): *Should Optional Properties Be Used in Conceptual Modelling? A Theory and Three Empirical Tests*, Information Systems Research, Vol.12, No. 4, December, pp.384-405.
4. Chu, W.W.; Zhang, G. (1997): *Associations and roles in object-oriented modeling*, in: D.W. Embley, R.C. Goldstein (Eds.), Proceedings of the 16th International Conference on Conceptual Modeling: ER'97, Springer, Berlin, pp. 257-270.
5. Dignum, V. (2003): *A model for organizational interaction: based on agents, founded in logic*, PhD Thesis, University of Utrecht, The Netherlands.
6. Elmasri, R; Weeldreyer, J.A.; Hevner, A.R. (1985): *The Category Concept: An Extension to the Entity-Relationship Model*, International Journal on Data and Knowledge Engineering, 1(1):75-116.
7. Essink, L.J.B.; Erhart, W.J. (1991): *Object modelling and system dynamics in the conceptualization stages of information systems development*, in: F. van Assche, B. Moulin, C. Rolland (Eds.), Proceedings of the IFIP TC8/WG8.1. Working Conference on the Object Oriented Approach in Information Systems, North-Holland, Amsterdam, pp. 89-116.
8. Ferrario, R.; Oltramari, A. (2004): *Towards a Computational Ontology of the Mind*, Proceedings of the 3rd International Conference on Formal Ontology in Information Systems (FOIS), Torino, Italy.
9. Fitting, M., Mendelsohn, R.L. (1998): *First-Order Modal Logic*, Synthese Library Studies in Epistemology Logic, Methodology, and Philosophy of Science, Volume 277, Kluwer Academic Publishers.
10. Guarino, N.; Welty, C. (2004): *An Overview of OntoClean*, in S. Staab, R. Studer (eds.), Handbook on Ontologies, Springer Verlag, pp. 151-159.
11. Guizzardi, G. (2005): *Ontological Foundations for Structural Conceptual Models*, PhD Thesis, University of Twente, The Netherlands.
12. Guizzardi, G.; Wagner, G. (2005): *Towards Ontological Foundations for Agent Modeling Concepts using UFO*, Lecture Notes on Artificial Intelligence (LNAI) 3508, Springer-Verlag.
13. Gupta, A. (1980): *The Logic of Common Nouns: an investigation in quantified modal logic*, Yale University Press, New Haven, 1980.

14. Heller, B., Herre, H. (2004): *Ontological Categories in GOL*. Axiomathes 14: 71-90, Kluwer Academic Publishers.
15. Jungclaus, R.; Saake, G.; Hartmann, T.; Sernadas, C. (1991): *Object-Oriented Specification of Information Systems: The TROLL Language*, Informatik Berichte 91-04 TU Braunschweig, Braunschweig.
16. Kripke, S. (1982): *Naming and Necessity*, Harvard University Press.
17. Kristensen, B.B. (1995): *Object-oriented modeling with roles*, in: J. Murphy, B. Stone (Eds.), OOIS '95: Proceedings of the International Conference on Object-Oriented Information Systems, Dublin, Springer, 1996, pp. 57-71.
18. Loebe, F. (2003): *An Analysis of Roles*, Master thesis in Computer Science, University of Leipzig, Germany.
19. Lowe, E.J. (2001): *The possibility of Metaphysics: Substance, Identity and Time*, Oxford University Press.
20. Masolo, C., Vieu, L., Bottazzi, E., Catenacci, C., Ferrario, R., Gangemi, A., Guarino, N. (2004): *Social Roles and their Descriptions*, in D. Dubois, C. Welty, M.A. Williams (eds.), 9th Intl. Conf. on the Principles of Knowledge Representation and Reasoning, Whistler, Canada.
21. Masolo, C.; Borgo, S.; Gangemi, A.; Guarino, N.; Oltramari, A. (2003): *Ontology Library*, WonderWeb Deliverable D18.
22. Masolo, C.; Guizzardi, G.; Vieu, L.; Bottazzi, E.; Ferrario, R. (2005): *Relational Roles and Qua Individuals*, AAAI Fall Symposium on Roles, an Interdisciplinary Perspective, Virginia, USA.
23. McNamara, J. (1994): *Logic and Cognition*. In McNamara, J.; Reyes, G. (eds.), The Logical Foundations of Cognition, Vancouver Studies in Cognitive Science, Vol. 4.
24. Object Management Group, (2003): *UML 2.0 Infrastructure Specification*, Doc.# ptc/03-09-15, Sep.
25. Odell, J.; Nodine, M.; Levy, R. (2005): *A Metamodel for Agents, Roles, and Groups*, Agent-Oriented Software Engineering (AOSE) IV, James Odell, P. Giorgini, Jörg Müller, eds., Lecture Notes on Computer Science volume (forthcoming), Springer, Berlin.
26. Odell, J.; Parunak, H.V.D; Fleischer, M. (2003): *The Role of Roles in Designing Effective Agent Organizations*, Software Engineering for Large-Scale Multi-Agent Systems, Garcia, A.; Lucena, C.; Zambonelli, F.; Omicini, A.; Castro, J. (eds.), LNCS 2603, Springer, Berlin, pp 27-28.
27. Richardson, J.; Schwartz, P. (1991): *Aspects: Extending objects to support multiple, independent roles*, in: J. Cli.ord, R. King (Eds.), Proceedings of the 1991 ACM SIGMOD International Conference on Management of Data, SIGMOD Record ACM Press, vol. 20, no. 2, pp. 298-307.
28. Schneider, L. (2002): *Formalised Elementary Formal Ontology*, ISIB-CNR Technical Report 03/2002, [online: http://www.loa-cnr.it/Publications.html].
29. Smith, B.; Mulligan, K (1986): *A Relational Theory of the Act*, Topoi (5/2), 115-30.
30. Sowa, J.F. (1984): *Conceptual Structures: Information Processing in Mind and Machine*, Addison-Wesley, New York.
31. Steimann, F. (2000): *On the representation of roles in object-oriented and conceptual modeling*. Data & Knowledge Engineering 35:1, 83–106.
32. van Leeuwen, J. (1991): *Individuals and sortal concepts : an essay in logical descriptive metaphysics*, PhD Thesis, Univ. of Amsterdam.
33. Weber, R. (1997): *Ontological Foundations of Information Systems*, Coopers & Lybrand, Melbourne, Australia.
34. Wieringa, R.J. de Jonge, W., Spruit, P.A. (1995): *Using dynamic classes and role classes to model object migration*. Theory & Practice of Object Systems, 1(1), 61-83.

A Product-Line Approach to Promote Asset Reuse in Multi-agent Systems

Josh Dehlinger[1] and Robyn R. Lutz[1,2]

[1] Department of Computer Science, Iowa State University, 226 Atanasoff Hall,
Ames, Iowa 50011, USA
dehlinge@cs.iastate.edu
http://www.cs.iastate.edu/~dehlinge
[2] Jet Propulsion Laboratory / Caltech
rlutz@cs.iastate.edu
http://www.cs.iastate.edu/~rlutz

Abstract. Software reuse technologies have been a driving force in significantly reducing both the time and cost of software specification, development, maintenance and evolution. However, the dynamic nature of highly autonomous agents in distributed systems is difficult to specify with existing requirements analysis and specification techniques. This paper offers an approach for open, agent-based distributed software systems to capture requirements specifications in such a way that they can be easily reused during the initial requirements phase as well as later if the software needs to be updated. The contribution of this paper is to provide a reusable requirements specification pattern to capture the dynamically changing design configurations of agents and reuse them for future similar systems. This is achieved by adopting a product-line approach for agent-based software engineering. We motivate and illustrate this work through a specific application, a phased deployment of an agent-based, distributed microsatellite constellation.

1 Introduction

Software reuse technologies have been a driving force in significantly reducing both the time and cost of software requirements specification, development, maintenance and evolution. Industry's continuous demand for shorter software development cycles and lower software costs encourages software development methodologies to exploit software reuse principles whenever possible.

Agent-oriented, software-based approaches have provided powerful and natural high-level abstractions in which software developers can understand, model and develop complex, distributed systems [5]. Yet, the realization of agent-oriented software development partially depends upon whether agent-based software systems can achieve reductions in development time and cost similar to other reuse-conscious software development methods such as object-oriented design, service-oriented architectures and component based systems.

In recent years, several agent-oriented software engineering (AOSE) methodologies have been proposed for various agent-based application domains. The Gaia methodology [28], in particular, offers a comprehensive analysis and design

A. Garcia et al. (Eds.): SELMAS 2005, LNCS 3914, pp. 161 – 178, 2006.

framework based on organizational abstractions by supplying schemas, models and diagrams to capture the requirements of an agent-based software system.

However, Gaia has two limitations. First, although Gaia provides a mechanism to allow the role of an agent to change dynamically, it is unclear how to document agent requirements specifications during the analysis and design phases when an agent must be updated to include new functionality. Second, the Gaia methodology fails to provide a mechanism by which the requirements specification templates developed during the analysis phase can be reused to be incorporated into the current system or to build a new, similar but slightly different system.

This paper offers an approach for open, agent-based distributed software systems to capture requirements specifications that can be easily reused during the initial requirements phase as well as later if the software needs to be updated. Our approach uses a product-line perspective to promote reuse in agent-based, software systems early in the development lifecycle so that software assets can be reused in the development lifecycle and during system evolution. We define a *product-line asset* as a software engineering output (including, but not limited to, architecture, reusable software components, domain models, requirements statements, documentation and specifications, and test cases) that forms, along with other product-line assets, the core for the development of a software product line [8]. We define *system evolution* as either the updating of an existing agent(s) in a deployed system or the inclusion of additional agents in the system.

The contribution of this paper is to provide a requirements specification pattern to capture the dynamically changing design configurations of agents and reuse the requirement specifications for future similar systems. This is achieved by adopting a product-line approach into AOSE. Requirements specifications reuse is the ability to easily use previously defined requirements specifications from an earlier system and apply them to a new, slightly different system.

The integration of product-line concepts into AOSE expands the techniques and tools available to developers of multi-agent systems. For example, software safety analysis tools [10, 18] and techniques [10, 12, 16] have been developed by the authors to assure developers that the reuse of requirements specifications is safe and will not compromise the system via incompatible features interacting in such a way as to cause unsafe conditions. We motivate and illustrate this work through a specific application, a phased deployment of an agent-based, distributed microsatellite constellation [19, 22]. A constellation is a group of semi- or fully autonomous satellites working together to fulfill complex mission objectives such as monitoring ocean levels or the spread of wildfires.

The remainder of the paper is organized as follows. Section 2 reviews related research in AOSE, product-line software engineering and a microsatellite application. Section 3 presents our approach to define the requirements specification of an agent-based, distributed system using the case study. Section 4 provides step-by-step guidance for documenting the requirements specifications of a distributed, multi-agent-based system using the requirements specification pattern presented in this work in a product-line-like way. Section 5 describes how to use the requirements specification detailed in Section 4 for reuse during system changes and updates. Finally, Section 6 provides concluding remarks and future research directions.

2   Related Work

This work is based on two different areas of software engineering: agent-oriented software engineering (AOSE) and software product-line engineering. This section discusses background information and related work in each of these areas as well as the application we use to illustrate our approach in this work.

2.1   Agent-Oriented Software Engineering

Agent-oriented software engineering (AOSE) [26] methodologies surfaced in the late-90's to provide tools and techniques for abstracting, modeling, analyzing and designing agent-based software systems early in the development lifecycle [21]. Different methodologies, such as Gaia [4, 27, 28], Tropos [2] and MaSE [11] for example, use different abstractions and models for agent-oriented software development. Although Tropos and MaSE are not the focus of this paper, an investigation of integrating a product-line approach into these AOSE methodologies is planned future work.

From its onset, one of the goals of AOSE has been to provide methodologies for reusing and maintaining agent-based software systems [23]. In spite of this goal, AOSE methodologies have failed to adequately capture the reuse potential, since many of the developed methodologies center on the development of specific software applications [13]. A few attempts, including [13] and [14], have been proposed for reuse in an agent-oriented development environment. However, in each case, reuse is positioned in the later stages of design and development. In [13], the Multi-Agent Application Engineering (MaAE) work exploits reuse during the design phase of a multi-agent software system. Likewise, [14] utilizes reuse principles from component-based development to reuse components from a previously developed agent-based component repository. The work described here differs from previous work in that we present an approach to capture the reuse potential of distributed, agent-based software systems in the requirements analysis and specification stage.

As in Gaia, our approach follows an early requirements engineering phase that focuses on analyzing the "characteristics to be exhibited and the goals to be achieved by the system-to-be" [27]. Our approach utilizes the output produced from the requirements-engineering phase which may include goals and sub-goals, detailed requirements and partial requirements specifications [24].

2.2   Product-Line Engineering

We follow Northrop et al. in defining a software product line as a set of software-intensive systems sharing a common, managed set of features that satisfy the specific needs of a particular market segment or mission [17]. The common, managed set of features shared by all members of a product line is called its commonalities. For example, a commonality of a planner role for a microsatellite would be that it should be able to know (i.e., read) its current position. The members of a particular product line may differ from each other via a set of allowed variabilities. In our application, an important variability is the *level of intelligence* of the agent or member. For example, a particular intelligence level of a planner role for a microsatellite would be that it has the ability to command other microsatellites to move to another position. Additional examples of commonalities and variabilities are given in Figure 2. The benefits of the product-line approach come from the reuse of the commonalities in developing a new product-line member [20]. We define a member as a single instance or system of the product line. In the application used in this work, a member is a single microsatellite within the constellation.

Weiss and Lai defined the Family-Oriented Abstraction, Specification and Translation (FAST) software engineering model to analyze and design software product lines [25]. This model employs a two-phase software engineering approach: the domain engineering phase and the application engineering phase. The *domain engineering* phase defines the product line requirements specifications and design. The second phase, the *application engineering* phase, reuses these product-line assets (i.e., the product line requirement specifications and design) to develop the requirements and design of new product-line members.

Product-line requirements are often specified through a Commonality and Variability Analysis (CVA) [1, 25]. The CVA, developed during the domain engineering phase of FAST, provides a comprehensive definition of the product line requirements including the commonalities (i.e., requirements of the entire product line) and the variabilities (i.e., specific features not contained in every member of the product line) of the product line.

In this paper we use product-line techniques to transfer agent roles in the Gaia methodology into reusable assets. We demonstrate how requirements detailed in a CVA can be easily mapped into the Role Schema and the Role Variation Point Schema of the Gaia analysis phase using a product-line approach. Doing so helps link the requirements specification patterns for defining roles within the Gaia methodology to earlier requirements engineering assets. Our approach maintains consistency with the widely published Gaia methodology [28] of AOSE as well as the FAST methodology [25] of software product-line engineering.

2.3 Application

We illustrate how our approach can be used by applying it to portions of an agent-based implementation of a constellation, loosely based on the requirements for the TechSat21 (Technology Satellite of the 21st Century) [19]. TechSat21 was a proposed mission, originally scheduled to launch in January 2006 but cancelled in late 2003 with much of the software reused on a subsequent mission [6]. It was designed to explore the benefits of a distributed, cooperative approach to satellites employing agents [7, 22]. TechSat21 is a constellation (i.e., cluster) of context-aware microsatellites (weighing less than 100 kilograms). New microsatellites will be deployed to the constellation in multiple, planned phases with the new microsatellites potentially having additional capabilities not found in previously deployed microsatellites while sacrificing functionality found in other microsatellites [7, 22]. For example, after the initial cluster of microsatellites is deployed, some additional microsatellites may be deployed with extra functionality for the Cluster Allocation Planner role that the initially deployed microsatellites will lack.

Within the constellation, each microsatellite must know its context in order to meet certain functional or non-functional requirements placed upon the constellation. For example, a context-based, functional requirement placed upon the constellation is to perform earth science (i.e., taking sensor readings, photographs, etc.). Thus, each microsatellite needs to know its context in relation to Earth. A context-based, non-functional requirement placed upon TechSat21 microsatellites is that each microsatellite must know its position in relation to others to avoid collisions. Similarly, microsatellites within the constellation must cooperate to meet mission requirements.

Schetter, Campbell and Surka have investigated several possible agent-based, organizational architectures for the TechSat21 constellation. They evaluated each agent-based, organizational architecture through a simulation tool to derive a multi-agent architecture that would offer good support for fault tolerance and upgradeability [19]. Separately, Chien et al. have similarly proposed a high degree of agent autonomy for a constellation of satellites. In their work, they demonstrate how continuous planning, model-based mode identification and reconfiguration and other artificial intelligence technologies can be used in a hybrid, multi-layer control architecture to facilitate a virtual spacecraft agent [7]. We partially use the agent specifications for the TechSat21 microsatellite constellation detailed in [7] and [19] for the requirements specification presented here as well as the notion of an agent possibly having different levels of intelligence described in [19].

3 Approach

To illustrate the adaptation of a product-line approach to multi-agent system development, we use the agent-based implementation of the microsatellite constellation (i.e., distributed system) detailed in [19]. Like them, we define an *agent* as a major onboard subsystem of a microsatellite or the microsatellite itself [9, 19].

3.1 Adopting Product-Line Concepts into the Gaia Methodology

The work presented here ties some of the analysis steps performed in Gaia to earlier requirements engineering outputs. Gaia, however, does not explicitly handle the requirements capturing and modeling of early requirements engineering. To address this, we link the Commonality and Variability Analysis (CVA) [1], performed within the domain engineering phase of the Family-Oriented Abstraction, Specification and Translation (FAST) product-line methodology (detailed in Section 2.2) [25] to the analysis and design of roles in a distributed, multi-agent system. Doing so, we are able to use a product-line-like approach to specify the requirements of a distributed, multi-agent system where differing intelligence is a design consideration. Note that the use of a CVA is not necessary. Developers may utilize other requirements modeling techniques such as goal-oriented [3] or feature-oriented [15] approaches. We discuss the advantages of using a CVA over these approaches in Section 4.1.

We first give an overview of how we integrate product-line concepts into multi-agent system development in order to build reusable patterns. Our approach, shown in Figure 1, partially encompasses three phases of multi-agent system development. Figure 1 illustrates how we incorporate elements of our approach into pieces of the Gaia methodology. The requirements collection and documentation phase, a part of FAST's domain engineering phase [25], partitions the requirements for the proposed

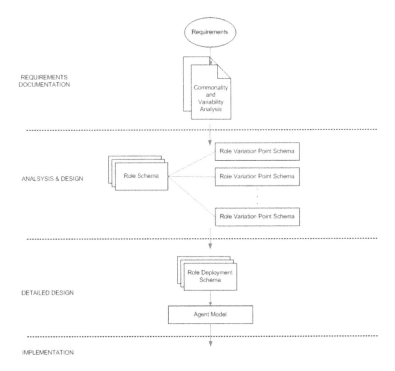

Fig. 1. An overview of the software engineering assets used in our Gaia-based product-line approach during requirements documentation, analysis and design and detailed design phases

system into commonalities and variabilities in the CVA. The analysis and design phase, equivalent to FAST's domain engineering phase [28] and loosely corresponding to Gaia's Preliminary Role Model and Role Model steps [30], entails documenting a role's requirements specifications within both the Role Schema and the Role Variation Point Schema. The Role Schema provides a description of the role and defines the variation points possible, described below, for the role. For each variation point, a Role Variation Point Schema details the requirement specifications for a role at a specific intelligence level.

We claim that the Role Schema and Role Variation Point Schema fall into the analysis and design phase, rather than solely the analysis phase, since the determination of variation points may influence, or be influenced by, the organizational architecture chosen (a product of the design phase in Gaia) for the multi-agent system being developed. For example, the decision to use an active/passive or master/slave type of variation point indicates that the architecture will display a top-down or a central coordination scheme. On the other hand, the intelligence-based design described below allows for a distributed or fully distributed coordination scheme. This process is described in Section 4.

In the detailed design phase of our approach, we first instantiate a role for a specific member of the distributed, multi-agent system by selecting the variation points (i.e., intelligence levels) it is capable in the Role Deployment Schema. It is in this phase that we are able to take advantage of the reuse principles inherent in the

FAST product-line methodology's application engineering phase [25]. Secondly, we define an agent using an Agent Model by declaring which roles, along with their variation points, it is responsible for fulfilling. We provide a full description of how the product-line concepts utilized in the analysis and design phase are taken advantage of to exploit the reuse potential in the detailed design phase in Section 5.

As in the Gaia methodology [27], we define the requirements specification of an agent's role, documented in the Role Variation Point Schema, in terms of the following characteristics: protocols, activities, permissions and responsibilities. *Protocols* define the way agents interact. *Activities* are the computations associated with the role that can be executed without interacting with other agents. *Permissions* are the information resource rights a role has to read, change and generate resources. *Responsibilities* define the functionality of a role and are divided into liveness properties and safety properties. Liveness properties refer to the "state of affairs that an agent must bring about, given certain environmental conditions" [27]. Safety properties refer to that subset of the non-functional requirements that the agent must maintain throughout the duration of the agent's life to prevent and handle hazards.

3.2   Using Variation Points in Multi-agent Systems

Product-line engineering uses *variation points* to capture the allowed differences amongst members belonging to the same family. We define the variation points for a specific role as the differing protocols, activities, permissions and responsibilities available to that role. Variation points typically stem from the grouping of the variabilities defined in the Commonality and Variability Analysis (CVA) documented as part of the output of the requirements engineering phase.

An important way to classify variation points for a satellite constellation is intelligence levels. In this work, we focus on these variation points. Here, we adopt the notion of variation points to model a multi-agent system as a product line. The variation point notion is important because it aids in capturing the different arrangements of agents and promotes reuse. For example, TechSat21 roles [19], ordered in terms of increasing intelligence levels, I4 through I1, display the following variation points:

- I4: receive/execute commands
- I3: local planning and receive/execute commands
- I2: local planning, interaction, partial cluster-knowledge and receive/execute commands
- I1: cluster-level planning, interaction, full cluster-knowledge and receive/execute commands

Thus, as a role is promoted to a higher intelligence level (from I3 to I2, for example) the configuration of the agent dynamically changes by incorporating additional protocols, activities, permissions and/or responsibilities. The reverse occurs when a role is demoted from a higher intelligence level to a lower intelligence level (from I2 to I3, for example). Using this construct, our notion of *an agent has one or more roles where each role may have one or more variation points*.

The variation points will initially be fixed upon deployment based upon the software and hardware facilities available as well as the role's goal. At deployment a default intelligence level for each role is set. During execution, a role may change its variation point (i.e., intelligence level) based upon its internal state, commands from external sources or the environment. Alternatively, within a distributed, agent-based system, it is not likely that the same set of intelligence levels will be included in any given role throughout the entire distributed system [19]. Thus, from a product-line engineering perspective, we can view the set of roles containing different role/variation point combinations as a product line. The set of roles and dynamic variation points an agent contains is its *configuration*.

The variation points in the constellation will not be universal to all agent-based, distributed systems. Variation points are particular to each application and, indeed, particular to each role. For example, other variation points could include active, passive; hot-spare, cold-spare; etc. For every variation point identified, we associate a *binding time* which defines the time at which the variation point could be assumed by a role. Potential binding times include specification-time, configuration-time and run-time. In the case of the constellation, the binding time for all the variation points described here is at run-time. The actual decision as to which features to group together and how to classify each variation point (e.g., I1, I2, etc., versus hot-spare, warm-spare, cold-spare) is likely domain and/or application specific and is not covered in this work. Rather, we assume that domain experts group the variabilities listed into variation points so that they can be used during the analysis phase of Gaia.

Variation points are added with the Gaia characteristics of a role [27]. This allows us to leverage a product-line-like perspective to maximize reuse among software products that share a great many similarities amongst each other and differ by only a few variations. For example, it might be the case that all the microsatellites in a constellation responsible for monitoring volcano eruptions will be very similar while other microsatellites in the same constellation responsible for capturing Earth atmosphere pictures will greatly differ from the previously mentioned microsatellites but will be similar amongst each other.

Identifying the variation points to which a role may dynamically switch allows us to classify at which variation points the protocols, activities, permissions and/or responsibilities are introduced to the role. Partitioning the requirements specifications (i.e., the protocols, activities, permissions and responsibilities) of an agent in this manner will allow us to reuse the requirement specifications for future systems. Thus, future agents within a domain such as Earth-orbiting microsatellites can more readily utilize assets that have been specified in such a way. These future systems employ roles comprising some of the variation points previously defined as well as new capabilities not found in any of the previous systems. Section 5 gives a more complete description of how requirements specifications can be reused.

Lastly, we here introduce identification numbers to all schemas for traceability, organization and management purposes. The schemas serve as a requirements specification pattern in which requirements can be defined and documented.

4   Documenting the Requirements Specifications Using a Product-Line Approach

This section describes the documentation of requirements, analysis and design, and the detailed design phases, illustrated in Figure 1, incorporating a product-line approach into multi-agent system development. For each phase, we describe the documentation process and how each document will later contribute to the ease of reuse, discussed in Section 5.

4.1 Requirements Documentation Phase

In the development of a software product line, requirements are collected and then documented in a Commonality and Variability Analysis (CVA) [1, 25]. Using the CVA, requirements can be further refined and detailed requirements can be derived during the analysis and design phases so that requirements specifications can be documented. An excerpt of a CVA detailing the commonality and variability requirements for the constellation is shown in Figure 2.

A developed and documented CVA during the requirements collection phase may give developers an insight into what roles might be appropriate for the multi-agent system to be developed. In terms of multi-agent system development, a CVA may assist in the identification of possible roles since it partitions those requirements that will be found in every future instantiation of a particular role from those requirements that will only be found in some instantiations of a particular role. That is, only the commonality should be investigated for potential agent roles since the variability can be thought of as features that will not be found in every role.

Commonalities

C_1. An agent capable of performing cluster allocation planning shall be able to receive/execute commands from other known members of the constellation at all times (i.e., during times of degraded system functionality).

C_2. An agent capable of performing cluster allocation planning shall be able to know its current position and velocity increment.

C_3. An agent capable of performing cluster allocation planning shall be able to change its current position and velocity increment.

C_4. An agent capable of performing cluster allocation planning shall be able to move to a new position.

Variabilities

V_1. An agent capable of performing cluster allocation planning may be able to have partial cluster knowledge.

V_2. An agent capable of performing cluster allocation planning may be able to have full cluster knowledge.

V_3. An agent capable of performing cluster allocation planning may be able to receive and accept change in velocity bids from other members during cluster reconfiguration.

V_4. An agent capable of performing cluster allocation planning may be able to issue a request to members of the cluster for change in velocity bids.

V_5. An agent capable of performing cluster allocation planning may be able to issue a move to new position message to members of the cluster during cluster reconfiguration.

V_6. An agent capable of performing cluster allocation planning may be able to receive a velocity increment calculation from other members of the cluster.

V_7. An agent capable of performing cluster allocation planning may be responsible to optimize the fuel use of all members of the cluster.

Fig. 2. A sample Commonality and Variability Analysis of the requirements for the Cluster Allocation Planner role

The actual identification of appropriate roles for a multi-agent system is not discussed here. Gaia proposes to identify roles through an inspection of the problem (via the division of a system into organizations and sub-organizations) [28]. Rather, we only claim that documenting a multi-agent system's requirements in a CVA may aid in confirming the role definition and help in the preliminary role model(s).

The variabilities of the CVA will help define the variation points of the product-line, multi-agent system. Partitioning the variabilities into similar groups (e.g., by similar required intelligence level) provides the initial requirements for the variation points of a system. For example, from Figure 2 we can assign variabilities V_1, V_3 and V_4 as belonging to intelligence level I2 since each indicates that it would at least require the intelligence level of I2 to occur.

Alternative approaches to the CVA in documenting product-line requirements and performing variability analysis include the goal-oriented [3] or the feature-oriented [15] approach. Alternatively, the use of domain or application expertise may also suffice in this process. This work exclusively used the CVA as the medium for variability documentation and analysis because of our use of the FAST methodology (in which a CVA is exclusively utilized to document and analyze variabilities). In terms of reuse, CVA is superior to either goal-oriented or feature-oriented approaches since it clearly defines those requirements that will be found in every member of a product line (i.e., commonalities) and those requirements that will only be found in a subset of the members of a product line (i.e., variabilities).

4.2   Analysis and Design Phase

Requirements specifications are documented in two schemas. The Role Schema, shown in Figure 3, defines a role and the variation points that the role can assume during its lifetime (e.g., whether it only implements the assignments it receives or it can also assign positions). The Role Variation Point Schema, shown in Figure 4, captures the requirements of a role variation point's capabilities. Both schemas are slightly modified adaptations of Gaia's Role Schema [28]. The Role Schema and the Role Variation Point Schema are both needed to capture the different levels of intelligence possible in a role throughout a large, distributed, multi-agent system.

Role Schema: Cluster Allocation Planner	**Schema ID:** F32
Description: Assigns a new cluster configuration by assigning new microsatellite positions within the cluster. This is done to equalize fuel use across the cluster.	

Variation Points:
    I4: receive/execute commands [F32-I4]
    I3: local planning and receive/execute commands [F32-I3]
    I2: local planning, interaction, partial cluster-knowledge and receive / execute commands [F32-I2]
    I1: cluster-level planning, interaction, full cluster-knowledge and receive/execute commands [F32-I1]	

Binding Times: All binding time for the variation points are at run-time.	

Fig. 3. Sample Role Schema for the Cluster Allocation Planner role of TechSat21

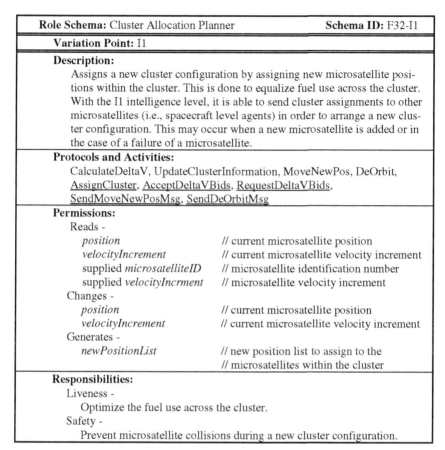

Role Schema: Cluster Allocation Planner	**Schema ID:** F32-I1
Variation Point: I1	
Description: Assigns a new cluster configuration by assigning new microsatellite positions within the cluster. This is done to equalize fuel use across the cluster. With the I1 intelligence level, it is able to send cluster assignments to other microsatellites (i.e., spacecraft level agents) in order to arrange a new cluster configuration. This may occur when a new microsatellite is added or in the case of a failure of a microsatellite.	
Protocols and Activities: CalculateDeltaV, UpdateClusterInformation, MoveNewPos, DeOrbit, AssignCluster, AcceptDeltaVBids, RequestDeltaVBids, SendMoveNewPosMsg, SendDeOrbitMsg	

Permissions:
  Reads -
    position   // current microsatellite position
    velocityIncrement // current microsatellite velocity increment
    supplied *microsatelliteID* // microsatellite identification number
    supplied *velocityIncrment* // microsatellite velocity increment
  Changes -
    position // current microsatellite position
    velocityIncrement // current microsatellite velocity increment
  Generates -
    newPositionList // new position list to assign to the
        // microsatellites within the cluster	

Responsibilities:
  Liveness -
    Optimize the fuel use across the cluster.
  Safety -
    Prevent microsatellite collisions during a new cluster configuration.	

Fig. 4. Sample Role Variation Point Schema for the I1 variation point of the Cluster Allocation Planner role of the Cluster Configuration

During the initial development of a distributed system (the product-line domain engineering phase of the Family-Oriented Abstraction, Specification and Translation (FAST) product-line methodology [25]), the focus must be primarily on identifying the overall requirement specifications of the system. It is later (during the product-line application engineering phase of FAST) that actual members of the distributed system can be instantiated with some or all of the requirements established earlier. We consider those initial requirement specifications in the Role Schema and the Role Variation Point Schema.

To capture the requirement specifications and document them in the two schemas, we use the following procedure:

1. Identify the roles within the system. Each role will constitute a new Role Schema to be created.
2. For each role, provide the role's name, a unique identification and a brief description of the role in the appropriate fields of the Role Schema. We partly follow the naming and numbering scheme from [19] for the Cluster Allocation Planner role depicted in Figure 3.

3. For each role, identify and define the differing intelligence levels that the role can adopt during all envisioned execution scenarios of the system. These differing intelligence levels will represent the variation points that the role can adopt. For each variation point, fill in the Variation Points section of the Role Schema by including the name, a brief description of the variation point and a reference identification number to the Role Variation Point Schema that gives the detailed requirements of the variation point (see Step 4a).
4. For each identified variation point (Step 3), create a new Role Variation Point Schema. For each Role Variation Point Schema:
   a. Document the name of the role to which the variation point corresponds as well as the name of the variation points in the appropriate sections of the Role Variation Point Schema. Indicate the variation point identification tag (corresponding to the variation point identification in Step 3) in the appropriate field in the Role Variation Point Schema.
   b. Identify the protocols, activities, permissions and responsibilities that are particular to only that variation point. That is, define the protocols, activities, permissions and responsibilities that are not found in any of the lower intelligence level variation points.
   c. Document and define the identified protocols, activities, permissions and responsibilities in the appropriate sections of the Role Variation Point. (Note, in accordance with the Gaia conventions, activities are distinguished from protocols by being underlined).

These steps result in a set of Role Schemas that have an associated set of Role Variation Point Schemas. Additionally, these steps conform to the domain engineering phase of product-line development [25]. Figure 3 illustrates a Role Schema example, and Figure 4 gives an example of a Role Variation Point Schema, both derived from the TechSat21 agent specifications given in [19].

4.3 Detailed Design Phase

Upon completion of the initial requirements analysis and development of an agent-based, distributed system, it will be necessary to utilize the derived requirements specifications to instantiate a number of members of the distributed system. During this initial deployment of distributed members, it is not necessary that all members be equipped with equal capabilities, intelligence or functionality. Since the prior steps have specified all the possible variation points of the roles in the schemas, we instantiate a new member (i.e., agent) to be added to the distributed system by specifying each new member to be deployed in the Role Deployment Schema. An example is shown in Figure 5.

Thus, the process is as follows:

1. Identify the roles that will constitute the member to be deployed.
2. For each role identified, create a new Role Deployment Schema and:
   a. Provide the role's name, unique system(s) identification and a brief description of the role specific to this deployment in the appropriate fields of the Role Deployment Schema. The system(s) unique identification, to be placed in the

System ID field, identifies the specific member(s) of the distributed system to be deployed that has the role configuration described in the particular Role Deployment Schema. For example, if members 2,3, 8-10 are to employ the Cluster Allocation Planning Agent in which only variation points I3 and I4 are possible, we denote this in the System(s) ID field of the Role Deployment Schema, shown in Figure 5, as 2,3, 8-10. This avoids repetitive manual overhead when designing new members to be deployed in the distributed system.

  b. Identify all possible variation points that the role can assume during its lifetime. The set of possible variation points was previously established when the original Role Schema was developed for the particular role.

  c. Identify the variation points in which the role will be deployed and specify it in the Role Deployment Schema. This variation point represents the default intelligence level at which the agent will most commonly operate during normal operations.

These steps produce a (set of) completed Role Deployment Schemas describing how different members of the distributed system to be deployed are instantiated.

Role Deployment Schema: Cluster Allocation Planner   **System(s) ID:** 2,3, 8-10
Description: A microsatellite member of the TechSat21 constellation that lacks the intelligence to globally assign new positions to other microsatellites within the cluster during a reconfiguration caused by a new microsatellite joining the cluster or a failure in one of the microsatellites. The sacrifice of this capability was chosen in favor of accommodating additional science instrumentation and software not found in microsatellites that allow I1 and I2 Cluster Allocation Planning Agent intelligence levels.

Variation Points:
 	
  I4: receive/execute commands [F32-I4]
  I3: local planning and receive/execute commands [F32-I3]

Fig. 5. Sample Role Deployment Schema for the Cluster Allocation Planner role of the Cluster Configuration agent of a member of TechSat21

Fig. 6. A sample Agent Model for the Cluster Configuration Agent for a member of TechSat21

We illustrate how an Agent Model, expanded from the Agent Model of Gaia [4], can be derived in Figure 6. The Agent Model graphically illustrates the assignment of roles to agents as well as variation points to roles. The cardinality relationship between agent and role is indicated and all possible variation points are listed for each role. At runtime, the designer annotates the actual cardinality and the specific possible variation points of an agent instance.

These steps conform to the application engineering phase of FAST [25] and produce the documentation shown in the detailed design phase shown in Figure 1. Documenting the requirements specifications in such a way allows easy reuse when instantiating actual systems. We detail how the documentation created in this section can easily be reused during both initial development and system evolution in the next section.

5   Multi-agent Requirements Specification Reuse

Requirements specification reuse is using previously defined requirements specifications from an earlier system and applying them to a new, slightly different system. Increasing the amount of requirements specification reuse for any given product will reduce the production time and cost of the software system [8].

Requirements specification reuse for agent-based, distributed systems is simplified in our approach by our use of variation points to handle the variabilities in similar software systems. Our approach takes advantage of how the requirement specifications for an agent's role were partitioned and documented in the Role Schema and Role Variation Point Schema based on their variation points. This section describes how the requirements specifications documentation detailed in Section 4 can be reused during the initial deployment of a distributed system as well as during system evolution. We define *system evolution* as the updating of an existing member(s) of a deployed system or the addition of new members to the system.

5.1   Requirements Specification Reuse During Initial Development

The members of a distributed system often will be heterogeneous in their functional capabilities yet mostly similar in structure. For example, some microsatellites of the constellation may have additional scientific imaging software while others may have additional cluster planning and reconfiguration software. Heterogeneity may also arise when resources (such as weight limits, memory size, etc.) are limited and different members of a distributed system must assume different roles. In the case of agent-based, distributed systems, members also may be heterogeneous in terms of their intelligence levels. For example, depending on the level of coordination (centralized, distributed or fully distributed, for example) among agents, not all agents must support roles at the highest level of intelligence. That is, not all agents may be capable of having full cluster-knowledge and/or being capable of making cluster-level decisions. For this reason, initially deployed members of a distributed system will likely contain a role that differs amongst other members in terms of which intelligence levels (i.e., variation points) it is capable of assuming. Several members of the distributed system will have the same role but at different levels of intelligence.

Requirements specification reuse can be exploited during the initial development and deployment of the members of a distributed system using the Role Deployment Schema, illustrated in Figure 5. Rather than repeatedly defining the requirements of a role for any given agent, the Role Deployment Schema allows us to define the intelligence levels it can assume. This reuse is possible because the requirements specifications for each of the levels of intelligence were documented in the Role

Variation Point Schemas, and because the agents of a distributed system will be similar. Thus, to document a particular role for several different heterogeneous members of a distributed system we must only indicate which variation points (i.e., previously defined intelligence levels) it can assume and give the reference number(s) to the Role Variation Point Schemas. After assigning variation points to an instance of a role and a role to an instance of an agent, an Agent Model can be used to illustrate an actual instance of an agent. We provide an example Agent Model in Figure 6.

5.2 Requirements Specification Reuse During System Evolution

Change is inevitable. Hardware failures or altered mission goals in a deployed distributed system typically necessitate software updates to one or more members. For example, a satellite of the constellation may have a malfunctioning planning and control module that could motivate operators to update that particular satellite's software to erase it and replace it with updated mission planning software. Alternatively, technology or mission goals after the initial deployment of a distributed system routinely evolve in such a way that future deployments of members joining the distributed system will require additional functionality (i.e., new features requiring new requirements). In the case of the satellite constellations, designers envision that new microsatellites will be deployed in multiple, planned phases [7, 22]. The new microsatellites will likely contain additional features not found in previously deployed microsatellites. Examples of the types of evolution the constellation may undergo include improved sensors, new scientific software, new communication devices, etc.

When the system evolves, new members may include additional functionality not previously defined in the requirements specifications. The requirements specification pattern detailed in Section 4 is extensible in that it can accommodate this kind of system evolution by being able to include a new set of requirements while still reusing the previously documented requirements.

If the system evolution is an update of a member of the distributed system where the update includes functionality previously defined in the requirements specifications (Role Schema and Role Variation Point Schema), it suffices to modify the Role Deployment Schema and, possibly, the Agent Model to reflect the update.

The addition of a new role within the distributed, agent-based system was described in Section 4.2. Briefly, we create a new Role Schema and a Role Variation Point Schema just as during the initial development of a multi-agent system. Following the creation of a Role Schema and a set of Role Variation Point Schemas, the process for the detailed design phase, outlined in Section 4.3, is used to instantiate a new agent with the new role.

The addition of a new variation point to an existing role, however, requires a modification to existing Role Schema documentation as well as the creation of a new Role Variation Point Schema. For example, the need to add a fifth intelligence level to an existing role would require such modification. For a new intelligence level desired for a particular role in future deployments of members of a distributed system, the following process suffices:

1. Create a new Role Variation Point Schema for the new intelligence level (i.e., variation point) giving the role's name, variation point's name and a unique variation point identifier in the appropriate fields.

2. Document the variation point indicating how the new variation point differs from previously defined variation points in the Description section.
3. Identify the protocols, activities, permissions and responsibilities that are particular to only that variation point. That is, define the protocols, activities, permissions and responsibilities that are not found in any of the lower intelligence level variation points and that are not found in any other variation points.
4. Document and define the identified protocols, activities, permissions and responsibilities in the appropriate sections of the Role Variation Point.
5. Update the Role Schema to which the new variation point corresponds, and add the new variation point, along with a description and schema reference identification, to the Variation Points section.

These steps will produce a new variation point for a role and the accompanying Role Variation Point Schema for future versions of members of the system.

6 Concluding Remarks

This paper incorporates a product-line approach into an agent-oriented software engineering methodology to support the reuse of the derived requirements specifications of an agent-based, distributed system. The requirements specification templates are constructed in such a way that varying dynamic software configure-ations of an agent are supported. The benefit is that the agent's configurations can then be reused during initial system development and during periods of system changes and updates. This can significantly reduce the software development time and cost.

To allow for the integration of product-line concepts into the Gaia methodology, we modified some of Gaia's schemas to better suit the concepts of software product-line engineering. In this paper we describe how a Role Schema, a Role Variation Point Schema, a Role Deployment Schema and an Agent Model can be created using a product-line approach. Using this approach assists in capturing the shifting configurations of agents/roles during the requirements analysis, design, detailed design and specification phases. Specifically, we describe how requirements specifications reuse can be achieved during initial system development, during periods of system changes and updates and during the addition of new members with previously defined functionality to a deployed, heterogeneous, distributed system.

Although this work was specifically intended for use in distributed multi-agent systems, this work may also be useful for distributed systems that are not necessarily agent-based such as sensor networks, grid-computing applications and peer-to-peer applications. Planned future work includes an application of this approach to a multi-agent system under development to evaluate the scalability of this approach.

Acknowledgements

This research was supported by the National Science Foundation under grants 0204139 and 0205588, and by the Iowa Space Grant Consortium.

References

1. Ardis, M. A. and Weiss, D. M., "Defining Families: The Commonality Analysis", *Proc. 19th Int'l Conf. on Software Engineering*, pp. 649-650, 1997.
2. Bresciani, P., Giorgini, P., Guinchiglia, F. and Perini, A., "TROPOS: An Agent-Oriented Software Development Methodology", *Journal of Autonomous Agents and Multi-Agent Systems*, 8(1):203-236, 2004.
3. Castro, J., Kolp, M. and Myopoulos, J. "Towards Requirements-Driven Information Systems Engineering: The Tropos Project" *Information Systems* 27(6):365-389, 2002.
4. Cernuzzi, L., Juan, T., Sterling, L. and Zambonelli, F., "The Gaia Methodology: Basic Concepts and Extensions", *Methodologies and Software Engineering for Agent Systems.The Agent-Oriented Software Engineering Handbook Series: Multiagent Systems, Artificial Societies, and Simulated Organizations*, 11:69-88, 2004.
5. Chan, K. and Sterling, L., "Specifying Roles within Agent-Oriented Software Engineering", *Proc. 10th Asia-Pacific Software Engineering Conf.*, pp. 390-395, 2003.
6. Chien, S., Sherwood, R., Tran, D., Cichy, B., Rabideau, G., Castano, R., Davies, A., Mandl, D., Frye, S., Trout, B., D'Agostino, J., Shulman, S., Boyer, D., Hayden, S., Sweet, A. and Christina, S., "Lessons Learned from Autonomous Sciencecraft Experiment", *Proc. Autonomous Agents and Multi-Agent Systems Conf.*, 2005.
7. Chien, S., Sherwood, R., Rabideau, G., Castano, R., Davies, A., Burl, M., Knight, R., Stough, T., Roden, J., Zetocha, P., Wainwright, R., Klupar, P., Van Gaasbeck, J., Cappelaere, P. and Oswald, D., "The Techsat-21 Autonomous Space Science Agent", *Proc. 1st Int'l Conf. on Autonomous Agents*, pp. 570-577, 2002.
8. Clements, P. and Northrop, L., *Software Product Lines: Practices and Patterns*, Addison-Wesley, Reading, MA, 2002.
9. Das, S., Krikorian, R. and Truszkowski, W., "Distributed Planning and Scheduling for Enhancing Spacecraft Autonomy", *Proc. 3rd Conf. on Autonomous Agents*, pp. 422-423, 1999.
10. Dehlinger, J. and Lutz, R. R., "PLFaultCAT: A Product-Line Software Fault Tree Analysis Tool", *The Automated Software Engineering Journal*, to appear.
11. DeLoach, S. A., "The MaSE Methodology", *Methodologies and Software Engineering for Agent Systems-The Agent-Oriented Software Engineering Handbook Series: Multiagent Systems, Artificial Societies, and Simulated Organizations*, 11:107-125, 2004.
12. Feng, Q and Lutz, R. R., "Bi-Directional Safety Analysis of Product Lines", *Journal of Systems and Software*, to appear.
13. Girardi, R., "Reuse in Agent-based Application Development", *Proc. 1st Int'l Workshop on Software Engineering for Large-Scale Multi-Agent Systems*, 2002.
14. Hara, H., Fujita, S. and Sugawara, K., "Reusable Software Components Based on an Agent Model", *Proc. Workshop on Parallel and Distributed Systems*, 2000.
15. Kang, K. C., Kim, S., Lee, J. and Lee, K., "Feature-Oriented Engineering of PBX Software for Adaptability and Reusability", *Software Practice and Experience*, 29(10):167-177, 1999.
16. Lutz, R. R., "Extending the Product Family Approach to Support Safe Reuse," *Journal of Systems and Software*, 53(3):207-217, 2000.
17. Northrop, L., "A Framework for Product Line Practice", *Software Engineering Institute*, http://www.sei.cmu.edu/productlines/framework.html, (current November 2005).
18. Padmanabhan, P. and Lutz, R. R., "Tool-Supported Verification of Product Line Requirements", *The Automated Software Engineering Journal*, 12(4):447-465, 2005.
19. Schetter, T., Campbell, M. and Surka, D., "Multiple Agent-Based Autonomy for Satellite Constellations", *Proc. 2nd Int'l Symposium on Agent Systems and Applications*, 2000.
20. Sommerville, I., *Software Engineering*, Addison-Wesley, Reading, MA, 2004.

21. Sutandiyo, W., Chhetri, M. B., Krishnaswamy, S. and Loke, S. W., "Experiences with Software Engineering of Mobile Agent Applications", *Proc. 2004 Australian Software Engineering Conf.*, pp. 339-349, 2004.
22. "TechSat21 - Space Missions Using Satellite Clusters", *Space Vehicles Factsheets*, http://www.cs.afrl.af.mil/ Factsheets/techsat21.html, (current February 2005).
23. Tveit, A., "A Survey of Agent-Oriented Software Engineering", *NTNU Computer Science Graduate Student Conf.*, 2001.
24. United States Department of Defense, "Draft DoD Software Technology Strategy", Office of the Director, Defense Research & Engineering, DRAFT: December 1991.
25. Weiss, D. M. and Lai, C. T. R., *Software Product-Line Engineering*, Addison-Wesley, Reading, MA, 1999.
26. Wooldridge, M. and Jennings, N. R., "Agent Theories, Architectures and Languages: A Survey", *Workshop on Agent Theories, Architecture and Languages*, pp. 1-32, 1995.
27. Wooldridge, M., Jennings, N. R. and Kinny, D., "The Gaia Methodology for Agent-Oriented Analysis and Design", *Journal of Autonomous Agents and Multi-Agent Systems*, 3(3):285-312, 2000.
28. Zambonelli, F., Jennings, N. R. and Wooldridge, M., "Developing Multiagent Systems: The Gaia Methodology", *ACM Transactions on Software Engineering and Methodology*, 12(3):317-370, 2003.

Characterization and Evaluation of Multi-agent System Architectural Styles

Paul Davidsson, Stefan Johansson, and Mikael Svahnberg

Department of Systems and Software Engineering,
Blekinge Institute of Technology,
Soft Center, 372 25 Ronneby, Sweden
{pdv, sja, msv}@bth.se

Abstract. We argue that it is useful to study classes of Multi-Agent System (MAS) architectures, corresponding to architectural styles in addition to particular architectures. In this work we focus on a particular abstraction level where MAS architectural styles are characterized according to properties, such as, the type of control used (from fully centralized to fully distributed), and the type of co-ordination used. Different architectural styles support different quality attributes to different extent. When choosing architectural style for a given application domain, we argue that it is important to evaluate the them according to the quality attributes relevant to that application. The architectural style that provides the most appropriate balance between these attributes should then be selected. As a case study we investigate the problem of dynamic and distributed resource allocation and compare six MAS architectural styles that can be used to handle this task. We also illustrate the use of the Analytic Hierarchy Process, which is a basic approach to select the most suitable alternative from a number of alternatives evaluated with respect to several criteria, for selecting the architectural style that balance the trade-off between the relevant quality attributes in the best way.

1 Introduction

Much effort has been spent on suggesting and implementing new architectures of Multi-Agent Systems (MAS). However, less work has been done in studying how these architectures may be characterized and evaluated in a more general way. Typically, a (group of) researcher(s) invents a new architecture and applies it to a particular domain and concludes that it seems to be appropriate for this domain, without drawing any general conclusions. We believe that this area has now reached the level of maturity when it is appropriate to compare and evaluate MAS architectures on a more abstract level. In this paper, we show how the concept of *architectural styles* can be used to achieve this. We will also illustrate how to choose the proper architectural style by taking into account several quality attributes and weighting them according to the requirements of the application at hand.

Of course, there is no single MAS architectural style that is the most suitable for all applications. On the other hand, to find out whether one architecture performs better than another for a particular application is usually of limited scientific interest. (Although this information may be very useful to solve that particular problem.) Instead,

A. Garcia et al. (Eds.): SELMAS 2005, LNCS 3914, pp. 179–188, 2006.

we suggest the study of more general problem domains corresponding to sets of applications with common characteristics. In this paper we will as a case study investigate the problem of selecting a MAS architectural style for dynamic and distributed resource allocation.

The rest of the paper is structured as follows. In Section 2 we will discuss Architectural styles followed by a case study in Section 3. Section 4 discusses the method and finally in Section 5 we draw a few conclusions and suggest some future directions of research.

2   Architectural Styles

As mentioned earlier, we argue that it is useful to study classes of MAS architectures, corresponding to *architectural styles* [18] in addition to particular architectures. These may describe abstractions of software entities of varying abstraction levels such as enterprise architectures, system architectures, subsystem architectures, or the architecture within a particular component, and may involve several views of the architecture to capture all relevant aspects cf. Kruchten [13].

In this work we focus on a particular abstraction level and characterize MAS architectural styles according to two properties: the type of control used (from fully centralized via hierarchical to fully distributed), and the type of coordination (synchronous vs. asynchronous). The degree of *synchronization* is a way of characterizing the coordination in terms of how the execution of the agents interrelate with each other. We may have agents that are highly sophisticated, but who only interact at special slots in time, and thus have a high degree of synchronization. There are also systems in which the agents may interact continuously, independently of when other agents interact, which we will refer to as *asynchronous*. As well as having an intermediate level of centralization, we may study architectural styles that exhibit properties in between being fully synchronous and totally asynchronous. However, we limit this work to {synchronous, asynchronous} × {centralized, hierarchical, distributed} architectural styles.

It should be noted that the terminology varies between different sources. Shaw & Garlan [18] introduced the concept of *architectural styles*. In their work, an architectural style consists of components, connectors, and constraints, and defines a family of systems with a specific pattern of structural composition. This encompassed higher level architectural styles such as *client-server, pipes and filters, repositories/blackboard,* and *layered*, but also lower levels such as *object-oriented, dataflow,* and *event-based*. Buschmann et al [5] presents a taxonomy containing, among others, *pipes and filters, blackboard,* and *layered*, and presents these as *architectural patterns*. We can thus interpret architectural patterns to be a subset of Shaw & Garlan's architectural styles. Bosch [4] uses the term *architectural style* in the same way as Shaw & Garlan, but also uses the term *architectural pattern* to denote a lower level solution that can be merged with an architectural style, such as *concurrency, persistence, distribution,* and *graphical user interface*. In this article we use the term architectural style in the same meaning as Shaw & Garlan [18]. In other words, we see an architectural style as an abstraction over a family of systems. Thus, an architectural style is used as a starting point when creating a concrete architecture for a particular MAS system.

3   Case Study

We will now illustrate the use of our method by going through a case study, starting with a description of the domain and the chosen quality attributes. We then present the six MAS architectural styles[1] and their qualitative as well as quantitative evaluations.

3.1   Domain

Since agent technology has shown to be successful for *dynamic and distributed resource allocation*, e.g. power load management [22], cellular phone bandwidth allocation [3], and transportation systems management [9,21], we have chosen this domain for our architectural style comparison. Basically, the problem concerns allocation of resources between a number of *customers*, given a number of *providers*. Both the providers and the customers may reside at different geographical locations, hence the distributed aspect of the problem. The dynamics of the problem lie in that the needs of the customers, as well as the amount of resources made available by the providers, vary over time. The needs and available resources not only vary on an individual level, but also the total needs and available resources within the system may vary over time. We will here assume that the resources cannot be buffered, i.e., they have to be consumed immediately, and that the cost of communication (and transportation of resources) between any customer-provider pair is equal.

3.2   Quality Attributes

It is possible to evaluate MAS architectural styles with respect to several different quality attributes [7]. Some of these attributes are domain independent and some are specific for each set of applications, e.g., performance-related attributes. We have identified the following important performance-related attributes to dynamic and distributed resource allocation:

- Reactivity: *How fast are resources re-allocated when there are changes in demand?*
- Load balancing: *How evenly is the load balanced between the resource providers?*
- Fairness: *Are the customers treated equally?*
- Utilization of resources: *Are the available resources utilized as much as is possible?*
- Responsiveness: *How long does it take for the customers to get response to an individual request?*
- Communication overhead: *How much extra communication is needed for the resource allocation?*

In addition, there are a number of more general software architecture quality factors [14] that could be addressed,[2]

---

[1] {synchronous, asynchronous} × {centralized, hierarchical, distributed}.

[2] In further addition to these attributes, there are of course a number of attributes that are not mentioned here but that are of interest to include in the specific evaluation of the specific case. The method as such does of course not exclude any quality attributes. It is up to the architectural style evaluator to set the specific attributes when applying the method.

- Robustness: *How vulnerable is the system to node or link failures?*
- Modifiability: *How easy is it to change the system after it is implemented (and often deployed)?*
- Scalability: *How good is the system at handling large numbers of users (providers and customers)?*

It is impossible to find a MAS architectural style that is optimal with respect to all the attributes relevant for a certain application. Instead, there is typically a trade-off between these attributes and different architectures balance this trade-off in various ways. Different applications, on the other hand, often require different balancing of this trade-off. Thus, in order to choose the right architecture for a particular application, knowledge about relevant attributes and how different MAS architectural styles support them is essential.

3.3   Candidate MAS Architectural Styles

There are many ways of characterizing the space of possible MAS architectures, e.g., the topology of the system, the degree of mobility and dynamics of the communications, the degree of distribution of control, and the degree of synchronization of interaction. We have chosen to focus the two last properties and will discuss and compare the following six potential MAS architectural styles for dynamic and distributed resource allocation:

- centralized synchronous architectures,
- centralized asynchronous architectures,
- hierarchical synchronous architectures,
- hierarchical asynchronous architectures,
- distributed synchronous architectures, and
- distributed asynchronous architectures.

3.4   Qualitative Evaluation

We will now briefly discuss how the architectural style may influence the quality attributes identified above.

- *Reactivity* should be promoted by asynchronous architectures since there is no need to await any synchronization event before i) an agent can notify other agents about changes in demand and ii) other agents can take the appropriate actions to adapt to these changes.
- *Load balancing* should be favored, or at least not disfavored, by centralized control since it is possible to take advantage of the global view of the state of the system, e.g., the current load at the providers and the current demand of the customers.
- Similarly should *fairness* be easier to achieve for architectures with centralized control since they have information about the global state of the system.
- The ability to *utilize* the *resources* seems to be favored by centralized, asynchronous solutions which improve the fairness (and thus the utilization) in near-overload situations, and may have better reactivity (which leads to better utilization of resources in highly dynamic domains).

- Also, it is not clear from a strictly theoretical analysis if there is any correlation between *responsiveness* and the architecture properties.
- *Communication overhead* can be measured either by the number of messages sent, or by the bandwidth required for the allocation. Synchronous architectures tend to concentrate the message sending to short time intervals, and thus requiring a large bandwidth, whereas asynchronous architectures tend to be better at utilizing a given bandwidth over the time. Also, communication in distributed architectures has a tendency to be more local than in centralized architecture, using smaller parts of the network.
- In a distributed system, the reallocation may function partially even though some agents have failed, although the probability of failures in *one* of these controler nodes is higher than the probability of failure in the single node of the centralized solution. At this level of abstraction, it is hard to see that the *robustness* is clearly favored by any of the two properties.
- *The modifiability*, to add or remove a provider or customer, may be slightly better in centralized architectures since changes may only be necessary in one part of the system. However, this attribute seems to be more dependent on other architectural style properties not considered in this evaluation.
- *Scalability* seems to be better supported by distributed architectures than centralized architectures. Firstly, the computational load for the resource allocation is divided between a number of computers, and secondly, the risk for communication bottlenecks is smaller.

It is important to note that this analysis can only say something about the *potential* of a particular architectural style. Thus, there is no guarantee that an implemented instantiation of a architectural style actually realizes the potential even though some support for the claims above may be found in previous work where we simulated four instantiations of the architectural styles mentioned [10] which were later evaluated using AHP [8].

3.5   Quantitative Evaluation

Typically, an architecture constitutes a balance between different quality attributes, just as different applications may require a specific balance or trade-off between quality attributes. Hence, to select the most suitable architectural style for a particular application knowledge about relevant attributes and how different MAS architectural styles support them is essential. We will now show how the trade-off between quality attributes can be quantified.

The Analytic Hierarchy Process (AHP) [16,17] is a multi-criteria decision support method from Management Science [1] that has previously been successfully tried and used in software engineering settings similar to the use in this article (e.g. [11,12,19,20]). One of the cornerstones in AHP is to evaluate a set of alternatives based on a particular blend of criteria, i.e. considering a specific trade-off situation. The AHP can quantify subjective assessments through a process of pair-wise comparisons or use measured data e.g. from a simulation.

The following steps are identified in our method:

Table 1. Priorities of the various properties in the case of a restricted communication (P_c) and limited resources (P_u)

Property	React.	Load Bal.	Fairness	Utiliz.	Respons.	Com. OH	Robustness	Modifi.	Scala.
Priority P_c	0.10	0.05	0.10	0.05	0.10	0.30	0.10	0.10	0.10
Priority P_u	0.10	0.20	0.10	0.20	0.10	0.00	0.10	0.10	0.10

- The first step in AHP is to set up a hierarchy of the criteria that are being evaluated. This means that one criterion can be broken down into several sub-criteria, and the evaluation of the different alternatives is done by weighing in all levels of this decision support hierarchy. In our case, the top-level goal is *Most Appropriate Architectural Style*. Under this root node in the hierarchy the different evaluation criteria are listed, in our case *Reactivity, Load Balancing, Fairness, Utilization of Resources, Responsiveness, Communication Overhead, Robustness, Modifiability,* and *Scalability*. For some of these criteria a further specialization may be necessary, e.g., the expected load of the target system. In that case, sub-criteria should be added as children in the hierarchy.

- For a particular application, the criteria are then prioritized in accordance with how important they are for that application. This prioritization is done for all levels in the hierarchy, and can be done using e.g. the pair-wise comparison process provided in the AHP method or by means of any other prioritization method. For future use, we also at this stage make sure that the priorities on a particular level in the decision tree are normalized so that they sum up to one. If the quality attributes are not independent, care may be taken when setting the weights of the dependent attributes so that their interaction does not lead to unexpected effects in the evaluation.

  As an illustration, we provide two examples of priorities for the different quality attributes shown in Table 1. These two cases corresponds to one situation where the (potential) system bottleneck lies in the communication network (P_c) and one where the resources are the limiting factor (P_u). In the first situation it is important to keep communication overhead at a low level, whereas in the second situation it is not. Instead, utilization of the resources and load balancing are prioritized.

  We include the two different priorities in order to show how changes in priorities may change the results. It should be noted that these are *examples* of priorities and as such they are of course of limited interest in a general meaning. The actual priorities should be set for the specific system considered. They can be derived in a multitude of ways (for a comparison of different prioritization techniques, see e.g. [12]), including AHP, and the 100-point method.

- For each of the leaf nodes in the decision support hierarchy we compare each of the candidate architectural styles with the other candidates. This can be done by using a pair-wise comparison process or by providing tangible data. In this study, we use the subjective judgments that are presented in Table 2.

- The obtained normalized values for the candidate architectural styles are then multiplied with the normalized priorities for each level in the decision support hierarchy.

Table 2. The score of each of the properties of the six architectural styles

	Synchronous			Asynchronous		
	Centralized	Hierarchical	Distributed	Centralized	Hierarchical	Distributed
Reactivity	0.033	0.033	0.033	0.300	0.300	0.300
Load Balancing	0.300	0.150	0.050	0.300	0.150	0.050
Fairness	0.300	0.150	0.050	0.300	0.150	0.050
Util. of resources	0.167	0.167	0.167	0.167	0.167	0.167
Responsiveness	0.167	0.167	0.167	0.167	0.167	0.167
Com. overhead	0.080	0.120	0.200	0.120	0.180	0.300
Robustness	0.050	0.150	0.300	0.050	0.150	0.300
Modifiability	0.300	0.150	0.050	0.300	0.150	0.050
Scalability	0.050	0.150	0.300	0.050	0.150	0.300

– Lastly, the results of these multiplications are summed for each candidate architectural style. These sums represent the suitability of each alternative *in relation to the other alternatives*. It is not absolute numbers but a ratio compared to the other alternatives that is obtained.

Thus, using the data described above, we are now able to instrument the AHP decision support hierarchy with the evaluations of the architectural styles for each of the criteria. For each of the two cases we take the product of the priorities of the quality attributes, and multiply this with the corresponding value for each candidate architectural style. The result of this is then summed for each candidate architectural style, and presented in Table 3. As can be seen, in the first case P_c, with restricted communication abilities, the distributed asynchronous architectural style is the most suitable, followed by the other two asynchronous styles. In the second case P_u, with restricted computing resources, the centralized architectural styles seems to be the best choice and the asynchronous version the first option.

4   Discussion

Naturally, there are limitations to the suggested evaluation method.

Firstly, it only evaluates the *potential* of different architectural styles. A good implementation may achieve this potential, and a bad implementation may not reach the potential at all. When developing a software system, the potential of the chosen architecture is one important influence of the resulting system, but there are others. For example, familiarity with a particular architectural style, development organization, and coding standards may also influence the final result.

Table 3. Results of the AHP given the two priorities P_c and P_u

P_c	
Distributed asynchronous	0.218
Hierarchical asynchronous	0.177
Centralized asynchronous	0.176
Distributed synchronous	0.161
Centralized synchronous	0.137
Hierarchical synchronous	0.132

P_u	
Centralized asynchronous	0.210
Centralized synchronous	0.183
Hierarchical asynchronous	0.170
Distributed asynchronous	0.160
Hierarchical synchronous	0.143
Distributed synchronous	0.133

Secondly, which architecture candidate the evaluation framework proposes is highly dependent on the priorities of the quality attributes and the way we choose to define them. Hence, care must be taken when prioritizing the needs of the system so that the priorities are in fact truly representing the needs for the target system.

Thirdly, the quantitative suggestion that the framework produces should be seen as one input among many to the decision process. Other inputs may include e.g. previous experiences or intuition.

As the studies that can be performed on MAS architectural styles are mostly of a theoretical nature, they often need to be supplemented with empirical studies using instantiations of these styles in concrete domains. In a previous study [8], we investigated the problem of load balancing and overload control of Intelligent Networks, a dynamic and distributed resource allocation problem. Four concrete MAS architectures were instantiated corresponding to four different architectural styles (centralized synchronous, centralized asynchronous, hierarchical synchronous, and distributed asynchronous). Metrics were defined for six different quality attributes (Reactivity, Load balancing, Fairness, Utilization of resources, Responsiveness, and Communication overhead). The instantiations were studied in simulation experiments and measurements of the metrics were recorded. The measurements where then used as raw data for the AHP in a similar way as the subjective judgments were used in this article. Moreover, this work concerning architectural styles and their implementation may be seen as an early attempt to construct a domain-specific system of patterns as is discussed in Chapter 5 of Buschmann et al. [5].

It can of course be questioned if this is a purely objective method. In one way that is an important discussion, however somewhat irrelevant since the method itself does not define the quality attributes. Instead the method should be seen as a structured tool that may be used by the system designer to choose an appropriate architectural style based on his/her definitions and weights of the quality attributes. In fact, the suggested method isolates and makes explicit the subjective parts of the evaluation, i.e., the priorities and the scores, and separates them from the objective parts, i.e., the AHP calculations.

Finally, the work presented in this paper can be viewed in the perspective of a more general evaluation framework, wich can be described in terms of the following three-dimensional space:

- the set of possible applications,
- the set of possible MAS architectures, and
- the set of quality attributes.

The suggested approach is to investigate substantial parts of this space rather than just single points. We believe that this approach, besides of enabling a more systematic investigation of the space, will lead to a deeper understanding of MASs and their applications, which, in turn, will contribute to reach the long-term goal of obtaining general design principles of MASs. We argue that this work will contribute to bridge the current gap between theory and application of MAS.

5   Conclusions and Future Work

Architectural styles have received considerable attention in the software engineering community during the past 10 years (cf. ref. [2,5,4,18]) because of the way that they capture previous experiences and extract the essentials of different architectural design solutions. One important issue that is mentioned e.g. by Buschmann et al. [5] is the need for building *pattern languages*, i.e. a collection of architectural styles, for different domains in addition to identifying generic architectural styles that can be used over a number of domains. In this article we have outlined a path forward in identifying essentials of MAS architectures for different application domains, i.e. MAS architectural styles. We also described a way of evaluating such styles according multiple criteria for different applications and situations. The method was applied to the problem of dynamic and distributed resource allocation where six different MAS architectural styles were evaluated according to nine different quality attributes in two different situations (priorities between the attributes).

The results of the case study are, not very surprisingly, that different architectural styles excel in different situations. The choice of MAS architectural style for a particular application should hence be based on a trade-off between the involved quality attributes that is optimal for that application. We believe that if the systematic approach suggested here is widely adopted, such choices can be more informed than is currently the practice.

Our plans for future work include:

- Further development of the concept of architectural styles for characterizing multi-agent systems.
- Further experimental validation in dynamic distribution resource allocation domains.
- Investigate the applicability of the suggested evaluation method in other domains.
- Investigating to what extent the implementations of the individual agents influence system performance.
- Compare the approach to other methods of selecting architectural styles, e.g. Qualitative evaluation [6] and ELECTRE [15].

Acknowledgements

The authors would like to thank Blekinge Institute of Technology and the Swedish Knowledge Foundation for funding this work.

References

1. D. R. Anderson, D. J. Sweeney, and T. A. Williams. *An Introduction to Management Science: Quantitative Approaches to Decision Making*. South Western College Publishing, Cincinnati Ohio, 2000.
2. L. Bass, P. Clements, and R. Kazman. *Software Architecture in Practice*. Addison-Wesley Publishing Co., Reading MA, 1998.
3. E. Bodanese and L. Cuthbert. An intelligent channel allocation scheme for mobile networks: An application of agent technology. In *Proceedings of the 2nd International Conference on Intelligent Agent Technology*, pages 322–333. World Scientific Press, 2001.
4. J. Bosch. *Design & Use of Software Architectures - Adopting and Evolving a Product Line Approach*. Addison-Wesley, Harlow UK, 2000.
5. F. Buschmann, C. Jäkel, R. Meunier, H. Rohnert, and M. Stahl. *Pattern-Oriented Software Architecture - A System of Patterns*. John Wiley, Chichester UK, 1996.
6. L. Chung, K. Cooper, and A. Yi. Developing adaptable software architectures using design patterns: an nfr approach. *Comput. Stand. Interfaces*, 25(3):253–260, 2003.
7. P. Clements, R. Kazman, and M. Klein. *Evaluating Software Architectures*. Addison Wesley, 2002.
8. P. Davidsson, S. Johansson, and M. Svahnberg. Characterization and evaluation of multi-agent system architectural styles. In *Software Engineering for Multi-Agent Systems IV*, Lecture Notes in Computer Science. Springer Verlag, 2006. To appear.
9. J. Himoff, P. Skobelev, and M. Wooldridge. Magenta technology: Multi-agent systems for industrial logistics. In *Proceedings of Autonomous Agents and Multi Agent Systems*, volume Industry Track, pages 60–66. ACM press, 2005.
10. S. Johansson, P. Davidsson, and M. Kristell. Four architectures for dynamic resource allocation. In A. Karmouch, T. Magedanz, and J. Delgado, editors, *Mobile Agents for Telecommunication Applications*, volume 2521 of *LNAI*, pages 239–248. Springer Verlag, 2002.
11. J. Karlsson and K. Ryan. A cost-value approach for prioritizing requirements. *IEEE Software*, 14(5):67–74, 1997.
12. J. Karlsson, C. Wohlin, and B. Regnell. An evaluation of methods for prioritizing software requirements. *Information and Software Technology*, 39(14-15):938–947, 1998.
13. P. Kruchten. The 4+1 view model of architecture. *IEEE Software*, pages 42–50, July 1995.
14. J. McCall. *Encyclopedia of Software Engineering*, chapter Quality Factors, pages 959–969. John Wiley & Sons Inc., 1994.
15. J. C. McPhail and D. Deugo. Deciding on a pattern. In *IEA/AIE '01: Proceedings of the 14th International conference on Industrial and engineering applications of artificial intelligence and expert systems*, pages 901–910, London, UK, 2001. Springer-Verlag.
16. T. L. Saaty. *The Analytic Hierarchy Process*. McGraw Hill, Inc., New York NY, 1980.
17. T. L. Saaty and L. G. Vargas. *Models, Methods, Concepts & Applications of the Analytic Hierarchy Process*. Kluwer Academic Publisher, Dordrecht the Netherlands, 2001.
18. M. Shaw and D. Garlan. *Software Architecture - Perspectives on an Emergin Discipline*. Prentice Hall, Upper Saddle River NJ, 1996.
19. M. Shepperd, S. Barker, and M. Aylett. The analytic hierarchy process and almost dataless prediction. In R. J. Kuster, A. Cowderoy, F. Heemstra, and E. P. van Veenendaal, editors, *Project Control for Software Quality - Proceedings of ESCOM-SCOPE 99*, Maastricht the Netherlands, 1999. Shaker Publishing BV.
20. M. Svahnberg. An industrial study on building consensus around software architectures and quality attributes. *Journal of Information and Software Technology*, 46(12):805–818, 2004.
21. D. Weyns, K. Schelfthout, T. Holvoet, and T. Lefever. Decentralized control of E'GV transportation systems. In *Proceedings of Autonomous Agents and Multi Agent Systems*, volume Industry Track, pages 67–74. ACM press, 2005.
22. F. Ygge. *Market-Oriented Programming and its Application to Power Load Management*. PhD thesis, Lund University, Sweden, 1998.

Improving Flexibility and Robustness in Agent Interactions: Extending Prometheus with Hermes

Christopher Cheong and Michael Winikoff

RMIT University, Melbourne, Australia
{chris, winikoff}@cs.rmit.edu.au

Abstract. A crucial part of multi-agent system design is the design of agent interactions. Traditional approaches to designing agent interaction use interaction protocols, which focus on defining legal sequences of messages. Such approaches do not naturally exhibit flexibility and robustness, and are not a good match for intelligent software agents which are autonomous, proactive, flexible and robust. The *Hermes* approach to designing agent interaction uses interaction goals, actions, and a number of failure recovery mechanisms to give a design methodology which is a good fit with intelligent software agents. However, the Hermes approach only covers part of the design process. In this paper we integrate Hermes with the Prometheus methodology, thus providing a complete methodology for designing multi-agent systems where interaction design is goal-oriented, yielding flexible and robust interactions.

1   Introduction

Since intelligent agents are social entities, a crucial part of multi-agent system design is the design of interactions between agents. Typical approaches to designing agent interactions, such as AUML [1], which is used in agent-oriented design methodologies such as Prometheus [2], Gaia [3], and Tropos [4], define interactions in terms of legal message sequences. These message-centric approaches to interaction design restrict the autonomy of intelligent agents as the agents are forced to follow them mechanistically.

The agents which partake in these interactions are goal-oriented entities, in which autonomy and proactivity are key concepts. Agents are able to deliberate about their goals, that is, determine which goal to achieve and how to achieve it. As such, there is a mismatch between the agents and their interactions.

Intelligent agents are flexible and robust. Similarly, it is desirable for the interactions between agents to also be flexible and robust, and to exploit beneficial characteristics of intelligent agents. Alternative approaches to message-centric protocols, such as the goal-oriented interactions of Hermes [5,6], are required to achieve this.

The main idea behind goal-oriented interactions is that agents partake in interactions because they have certain goals in common to achieve and thus the interaction is mutually beneficial. The main inspiration of such interactions is the way intelligent agents are structured and defined (i.e. in terms of goals and the plans which achieve them). Therefore, the interaction is modelled in terms of interaction goals (IGs), temporal constraints and actions. The IGs are common goals that the interacting agents

A. Garcia et al. (Eds.): SELMAS 2005, LNCS 3914, pp. 189–206, 2006.

want to achieve, whilst the temporal constraints allow for temporal ordering and dependencies between IGs. The agents are guided through the interaction by the IGs, which are organised in a hierarchy (with temporal constraints), and actions are used to achieve the IGs.

Unlike message-centric protocols, the message sequences are neither prescribed nor are they the focus of the interaction. Rather, the sequences emerge as interacting agents decide which IGs to achieve and which actions to use to achieve these IGs. As such, the focus is on the interaction goals and the exchanged messages are by-products of the interaction. The combination of goal-oriented interactions and intelligent agents is a more natural fit than the combination of message-centric protocols and intelligent agents.

However, the Hermes approach only addresses the design of interactions. In order to obtain a complete methodology for designing agent systems we integrate Hermes with the Prometheus methodology, thus providing a complete methodology for designing multi-agent systems where interaction design is goal-oriented, yielding flexible and robust interactions. We also refine the Hermes methodology and present a more detailed process for deriving action maps than previously described [5].

Section 2 provides the required background, whilst in section 3 we explain the integrated process and provide a partial example design on a case study. Section 4 concludes our paper.

2   Background

2.1   Hermes

The Hermes methodology is a goal-oriented approach to agent interactions which covers design and implementation. In this section the design aspects are briefly covered. For a more detailed explanation of the design process refer to [5]. The implementation process is not explained in this paper (see [6] for details).

Figure 1 provides an overview of the Hermes methodology. The first two steps involve determining which agents are to participate in the interaction (i.e. which roles they will undertake) and what they have to achieve in the interaction (i.e.interaction goals). The interaction goals (IGs) are goals of the interaction that are common to the agents involved in the interaction. Once IGs have been identified, they are structured into an Interaction Goal Hierarchy (IGH), and temporal constraints are added.

Compound IGs, that is IGs that have sub-IGs, such as *Order Book* and *Retrieve Details* (refer to Figure 6), are achieved when their own sub-IGs are achieved. Atomic IGs, such as *Retrieve Credit Card Details* from Figure 6 are achieved by agents executing appropriate actions: discrete steps that single agents take towards achieving an IG. These action flows are organised into *action maps* [1]. Therefore, each atomic IG should have a corresponding action map. Once defined, the action maps are then improved iteratively.

The last two steps of the Hermes design process require identification of messages and formally defining their structures. Messages are needed between actions that occur

---

[1] Action maps dictate the flow of actions between agents involved in an interaction. More details on action maps can be found in Section 3.4.

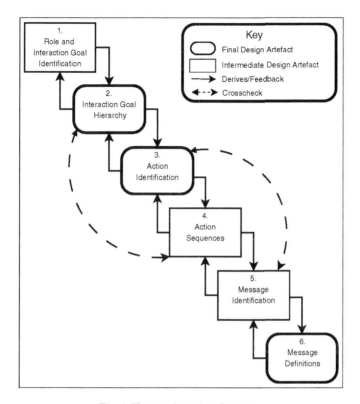

Fig. 1. Hermes Overview Diagram

in different roles that have a causality arrow in between them. For example, in Figure 7 the *Delivery Manager* will need to send a message to the *Stock Manager* after the *Log Outgoing Delivery* action to trigger the *Log Books Outgoing* action. Although Hermes provides guidelines for identifying messages, it does not provide any guidelines for developing message format. The interaction designer is free to use KQML, FIPA, SOAP or message types provided by a particular agent platform.

2.2 Prometheus

Prometheus is an agent-oriented software engineering methodology that aims to be practical and usable by software developers and undergraduate students, not only by agent researchers and postgraduate students. Its distinguishing features include that it is complete (from system specification to implementation with some work on debugging [7]), is described in considerable detail (see [2]), supports the development of agents that use goals and plans to deliver flexible behaviour, and has tool support [8].

For the purposes of this paper we do not attempt to describe the entire methodology, instead we focus on the inputs to the interaction design part of the methodology.

Prometheus' system specification phase (see Figure 2) defines system goals using a goal overview diagram that shows all of the goals and the goal-subgoal relationships. The system specification phase also uses scenarios. Each scenario is an example

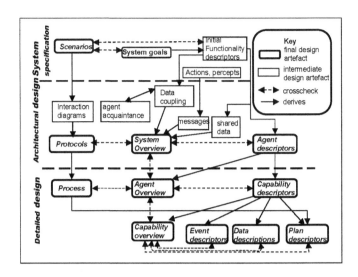

Fig. 2. Prometheus Overview Diagram

sequence of events illustrating desired system functionality. Scenarios are captured using a structured form (see Figure 5) which includes a sequence of steps. Each step is either a Goal, a Percept (incoming information from the environment), or an Action[2].

Goals are used as the basis for identifying functionalities: specific chunks of behaviour formed by grouping related goals. Based on considerations including data coupling, these functionalities are grouped to form agent types.

The interaction design part of Prometheus is fairly conventional. It begins by taking individual scenarios and creating corresponding interaction diagrams where instead of showing steps associated with functionalities, messages between agents are shown. These interaction diagrams are then generalised into interaction protocols (using AUML) which capture all possible sequences of messages.

3   Integrating Hermes and Prometheus

3.1   Overview

Since Hermes is specifically for interaction design, the obvious approach to integrating the two methodologies is to replace the typical Prometheus interaction design process with Hermes. This replacement leads to alterations to inputs needed for the interaction design process. These alterations are shown in Figure 3, which is an overview of the integrated methodology (the changed artefacts are shaded, and additional lines and arrows are shown in bold).

The major difference between Prometheus and Hermes interaction design is that the latter is *goal-oriented*. Therefore, a crucial alteration is to ensure that the design of the interaction goal hierarchy (the first Hermes artefact) is derived from both scenarios and system goals.

---

[2] Other step types are sub-scenario and "other".

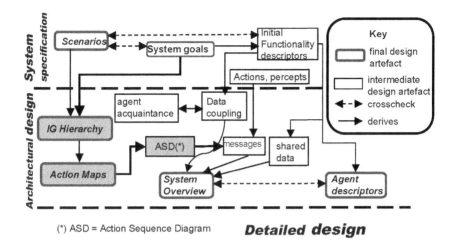

(*) ASD = Action Sequence Diagram

Fig. 3. Integrated Overview Diagram

Additionally, Hermes requires information about roles and data stores involved in the interactions[3]. Obviously, roles and data stores are integral parts of interactions as the former are necessary to determine inter-agent communication paths and the latter to determine the transmission of required data from agent to agent. From the Prometheus process, this information can be obtained from agent types, which summarises each type of agent in the system, including the functionalities and data stores they each possess. These details are used in the design of the action maps.

The end of the Hermes process results in a number of artefacts which are to be re-integrated with Prometheus. Note that the action maps are closer to process diagrams, i.e. it is easier to go from action maps to process diagrams than it is to go from AUML interaction protocols to process diagrams. This is due to the fact that process diagrams contain only internal agent processes and action maps contain both inter-agent communications and internal agent processes, whereas AUML interaction protocols only contain inter-agent communications.

3.2 The Amalgamated Design Process

Figure 4 summarises the steps involved in interaction design in the integrated methodology. The first five steps are taken directly from the usual Prometheus process. Before step 6 an assessment is made of whether it is worthwhile to use Hermes, and if not, then steps 6-11 are replaced with the existing Prometheus methodology. This decision is made based on the complexity of the interaction and likelihood of failures. For example, if it is a simple query and response scenario between two agents, it would not be worthwhile to use Hermes to design the interaction.

---

[3] Figure 3 omits links from the shared data and agent descriptors to the action maps and IG hierarchy respectively.

1. System Description
2. Develop System Goals
3. Identify Functionalities by grouping goals
4. Develop Scenarios
5. Determine agent types by grouping functionalities
6. Identify Hermes Roles and Interaction Goals
7. Develop Interaction Goal Hierarchy (section 3.3)
8. Develop Action Maps (section 3.4)
9. Develop Action Sequence Diagrams
10. Identify Messages
11. Develop System Overview Diagram (Prometheus)
12. Proceed with rest of Prometheus process

Before step 6 an assessment is made of whether it is worthwhile to use Hermes. If not, then replace steps 6-11 with the existing Prometheus methodology.

Fig. 4. Steps in Interaction Design

The identification of roles is usually straightforward as they are usually Prometheus agent types or roles that a particular Prometheus agent type assumes in an interaction. For example, in an e-commerce system, there may be two agent types, *Merchant* and *Customer*. In this case, it is quite obvious that Merchant and Customer are the roles involved in the interactions as they are aptly named after their roles. There are some designs in which agent types are not named after roles and will need to assume roles in their dealings with other agent types. For example, in an academic conference system, there may exist an agent type, *Academic Agent*, which may undertake a number of different roles, such as *Reviewer, Chairperson* and *Author*. In such circumstances, it is best to use the role as opposed to the agent type in the interactions.

The interaction goals are usually determined by analysing (i.e. grouping, abstract-ing and decomposing) the goals in the given scenario. Designing interaction goal hier-archies and action maps is detailed in sections 3.3 and 3.4 respectively.

The remainder of the goal-oriented interaction design (steps 9 and 10) follows the typical Hermes procedure. The action sequence diagrams are derived from the action maps, the action messages are derived from the action sequence diagrams and messages are described in (Prometheus) message descriptors. As these are unchanged from the original Hermes methodology, they are not discussed in this paper.

The messages obtained from the Hermes process are re-integrated into Prometheus. Hermes interactions are shown on the system overview diagram in the same way that protocols were previously represented. This simply represents that there is a goal-oriented interaction between those agents and the Hermes design artefacts can be referred to for more details. The messages produced as part of the Hermes design process are formally defined in message descriptors. Also, the IGs from the interaction goal hierarchy and the actions from the action maps are added to the agent overview diagrams[4].

---

[4] Both IGs and Hermes actions are mapped to plans: The former to *coordination plans* and the latter to *achievement plans* [6].

Name: Order Book
Description: An order is received from the WWW page interface (goal Place Order).
                 Information is obtained in order to place the order and the order is placed.
Trigger: Goal: Place Order
Steps:

Step	Type	Name	Role	Data
1	Goal	Obtain delivery options	Delivery handling	...
2	Goal	Calculate delivery time estimates	Delivery handling	...
3	Goal	Present information	Online interaction	...
4	Percept	User input	Online interaction	...
5	Goal	Obtain credit card details	Purchasing	...
6	Percept	User input	Online interaction	...
7	Action	Bank Transaction	Purchasing	...
8	Percept	Bank transaction response	Purchasing	...
9	Goal	Arrange Delivery	Delivery handling	...
10	Action	Place delivery request	Delivery handling	uses: customer order record
11	Goal	Log outgoing delivery	Delivery handling	produces: Customer Orders
12	Goal	Log books outgoing	Stock management	uses: Customer order record produces: Stock DB
13	Goal	Update customer record	Profile monitor	produces: Customer DB
14	Action	Send email	Customer contact	uses: Customer DB

Variation: Book is not currently available. Include information with delivery options.
Replace steps 7–12 with steps to add the order to an orders pending file.

Fig. 5. Order Book Scenario (From [2, p. 164])

The subsequent sections explain how the interaction goal hierarchy and its action maps are developed. In these sections we will use an example from the book store described in [2]. In particular, we will develop an interaction around ordering a book, based on the *Order book* scenario [2, p. 146] which is reproduced (in abridged form) in Figure 5. In addition to the scenario, we also need to know which agent types have been defined, and for each agent type what functionalities and data it contains. The book store example defines the following agent types:

– *Sales Assistant*: comprising the functionalities of *Book finding*, *Welcoming*, *Purchasing*, and *Online interaction*.
– *Customer Relations*: comprising the functionalities *Profile monitor* and *Customer contact* and the *Customer DB* database.
– *Delivery Manager*: comprising the functionalities *Delivery handling* and *Lost goods management* and the databases *Customer orders* and *Delivery problems*. This agent type also has access to external databases of couriers and postal areas.
– *Stock Manager*: comprising the functionalities of *Stock management*, *Competition management*, *Price setting*, and *Catalogue management*; and the databases *Pending orders*, *Books DB*, *Stock orders* and *Stock DB*.

3.3   Interaction Goal Hierarchy

To create the interaction goal hierarchy (IGH) we must first determine the overall intent of the scenario. Given the scenario in Figure 5, it is obvious that the overall intent is *order book* (as the scenario is aptly named). Thus, the top-most interaction goal (IG) is named *Order Book* and it is appropriately placed at the apex of the IGH (refer to Figure 6).

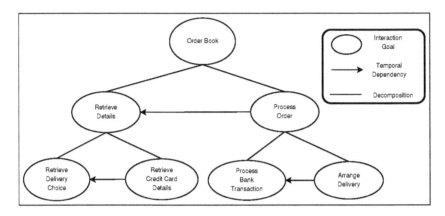

Fig. 6. Interaction Goal Hierarchy

We now further analyse the scenario to elicit other interaction goals. This can be done by abstracting or grouping related steps from the scenario, by decomposing scenario steps, or by mapping system goals.

System goals can be mapped to either interaction goals or Hermes actions; which artefact it maps to depends on the specific system goal and its properties. Typically, high-level system goals (abstract or easily decomposable into sub-goals) or those that involve more than one agent (e.g. Purchase, a goal that requires *Customer* and *Merchant* agents to achieve it) map to interaction goals. Low-level system goals (concrete or not easily decomposable into sub-goals) or system goals that involve only a single agent (e.g. *SendConfirmationEmail*) are usually mapped to Hermes actions.

In deriving IGs from scenarios it is more common to abstract or group existing steps than to decompose scenario steps. For example, from the scenario it appears that steps 1–4 are related: they gather, present and obtain information about delivery details. Thus, an IG, *Retrieve Delivery Choice* is created. Similarly, steps 5 and 6 are related; they gather, present and obtain information about credit card details. Thus, a *Retrieve Credit Card Details* IG, which represents scenario steps 5 and 6, is created.

Since the two IGs are very similar they can be further abstracted to a single IG, *Retrieve Details*. Thus, the *Retrieve Details* IG is composed of two sub-IGs, *Retrieve Delivery Choice* and *Retrieve Credit Card Details*. The scenario suggests that *Retrieve Delivery Choice* (i.e. steps 1–4) is completed before *Retrieve Credit Card Details* (i.e. steps 5 and 6). As this is a sensible suggestion (payment details are usually retrieved at the end, just before the delivery of the product), we have elected to keep this sequence. As such, we place a temporal dependency between the *Retrieve Delivery Choice* and

Retrieve Credit Card Details IGs. The *Retrieve Details* IG and its sub-IGs are added as a sub-IG to *Order Book* (refer to Figure 6) in the IGH.

Scenario steps 7 and 8 are abstracted into an IG, *Process Bank Transaction*, as they are related to performing transactions with the bank. Steps 9–14 are grouped into an IG, *Arrange Delivery*, as they deal with organising delivery of the book to the purchaser. Both *Process Bank Transaction* and *Arrange Delivery* are then grouped into an IG, *Process Order*. Again, the scenario steps suggest that *Process Bank Transaction* occurs before *Arrange Delivery* and, once more, we have chosen to retain this sequence. Thus, a temporal dependency is placed between *Process Bank Transaction* and *Arrange Delivery*. *Process Order* is then added to the IGH under the *Order Book* IG. As *Retrieve Details* should be achieved before *Process Order* is attempted (this is also implied in the scenario), we also place a temporal dependency between the two.

The resulting IGH (refer to Figure 6) is, in terms of temporal dependencies, a strongly constrained design. In order to successfully complete the *Order Book* interaction, the following atomic goals must be achieved in sequence: (1) *Retrieve Delivery Choice*, (2) *Retrieve Credit Card Details*, (3) *Process Bank Transaction*, and (4) *Arrange Delivery*.

In fact, since Prometheus scenarios are defined as a (strongly ordered) sequence of steps, any action map that takes this into account will be strongly constrained. Therefore, part of the process of moving from scenarios to interaction design, be it using the Hermes process or the existing Prometheus process, is to consider which of the temporal constraints implied by the scenario should be retained, and which temporal constraints should be weakened.

When developing the IGH it is important to consider *all* scenarios, as well as the variations of these scenarios. In some cases in order to accommodate all scenarios and scenario variations the IGH may need to be refined.

3.4 Action Maps

Action maps are used to determine how an *atomic* IG (i.e. leaf-node goal from the IGH) can be achieved. Thus, there is usually one action map per atomic IG. In a full interaction design for our case study four action maps would be created, however, due to space limitations, we only present the development of the action map for the *Arrange Delivery* IG.

The process in which action maps are designed is an iterative one. For ease of explanation, we describe the action map design as a four-step process, however, we do not intend that these four steps be followed rigidly. For example, the designer is free to skip steps if they are not deemed relevant, or to use as many iterations over these steps as are deemed necessary. The four steps, which are discussed below, are:

1. Develop initial action maps by transcribing scenario steps and assigning them to the appropriate agent
2. Add data to the action map and consider data flow issues
3. Extend action map to cover scenario variations
4. Extend action map to deal with failures

Step 1: Initial Action Maps. In this first step, the relevant steps of the scenario are transcribed onto action maps. Scenario steps that are goals correspond to goals of a single agent, and are mapped to actions in action maps. Scenario steps that are actions map (obviously) to actions. For example, step 10 of the scenario is the action *Place delivery request* which is mapped to the Hermes action of the same name. Scenario steps that are percepts also (less obviously) map to actions. In Prometheus, percepts are incoming information from the environment. When translated to Hermes, percepts are perceived as actions that somehow gain the required information in the interaction. Typically, this means that percepts are mapped to actions that either wait for incoming information (e.g. wait for an agent to send it information or for a belief to change) or retrieve the information themselves (e.g. read a file or access a database).

Designing the initial action map for the *Arrange Delivery* IG (scenario steps 9–14) involves placing five steps (10–14, 9 is omitted as it is achieved by steps 10–14) into the action map. It is best to follow the scenario steps as closely as possible. However, it is likely that some slight deviations from the scenarios will be necessary. Deviations include changing the ordering of some of the actions or creating new actions to clarify certain parts of the action maps.

The action maps have the roles placed as headings of the swim lanes, so the designer needs to ensure that actions are placed in the correct swim lane. With our case study, the roles involved in the interaction are simply the agent type identified in the earlier (Prometheus) steps of design. Determining the correct swim lane is a matter of assigning steps to the agent type that has been formed out of the corresponding functionality. For example, step 10 in the scenario, *Place delivery request*, is associated with the *Delivery handling* functionality which is part of the *Delivery Manager* agent type. Thus, this action is placed in the *Delivery Manager* swim lane.

It is also important to select the correct *action type* for each action. In some cases, the action types will need to be revised during other iterations of the design. An explanation of the different action types (*independent, caused* and *final caused*) follows.

An *independent action* is an action which can start without being triggered by another action, that is, it is not necessarily triggered by another action, but *may* be triggered by another action. Typically, independent actions are used as entry points into action maps. An independent action is denoted as a rectangle with dashed borders. For example, since *Place Delivery Request* (refer to Figure 7) is the first action to be executed, it is defined as an *independent action*.

A *caused action* is denoted by a rectangle and can only be triggered by another action. For example, *Log Outgoing Delivery* in Figure 7 only occurs after *Place Delivery Requested* is executed.

A *final caused action*, denoted by a rectangle with bold borders, is a caused action which terminates the IG for a particular role. For example, *Send Email* is the final action for the Customer Relations in Figure 7.

Once the actions have been placed, causality arrows are added between the actions to identify the flow of actions (based on, but not restricted to, the scenario sequence). After adding the causality arrows, the designer is free to make any alterations as sometimes the flow process will need to be different to the scenario.

The result of this first step is the action map in Figure 7.

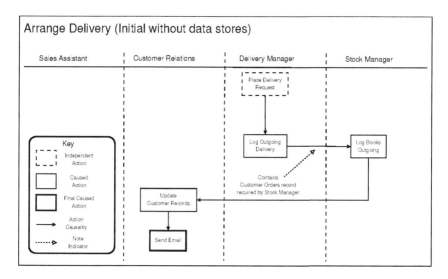

Fig. 7. Initial Action Map without Data Stores: Arrange Delivery

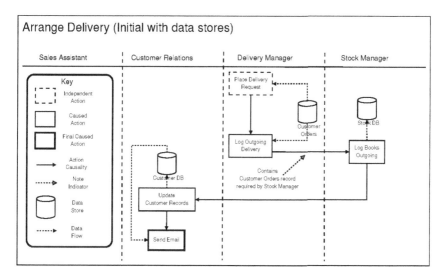

Fig. 8. Initial Action Map with Data Stores: Arrange Delivery

Step 2: Data Flow. This step focuses on incorporating data stores into the action maps and ensuring that all the data each agent requires are accessible. Firstly, we add the data stores onto the action maps. Data stores usually belong to specific agents (as defined in the agent groupings summarised earlier) and should be placed in the correct swim lanes in the action maps. It is not necessary to display every data store an agent contains, only the data stores that are used in the action map should be displayed. For example, in scenario step 10, *Place Delivery Request*, the *Delivery Handling* role requires data from *Customer Orders*. As the *Place Delivery Request* step is represented by the *Place*

Delivery Request action on the *Arrange Delivery* action map (Figure 8), the *Customer Orders* data store is added to the *Delivery Manager* agent's swim lane (since the data store belongs to that role).

Once the data stores have been added, it is necessary to ensure correct data flow between actions, which are depicted by dotted directed lines. In the case of the *Place Delivery Request* action, as it reads from the *Customer Orders* data store, the data flows from the data stores to it. If the action was writing to a data store, the data flow would be from the action to the data store, as with the *Log Books Outgoing* action and the *Stock DB* data store on on Figure 8.

It is not sufficient to simply add data stores and ensure that actions which read and write have *direct* access to the data stores. The designer must ensure that actions will have access to required data even if the data belongs to a data store in a different agent. This may mean that required data are read from a data store and passed through a number of different actions to reach a particular action that requires the data. For example, in scenario step 12, *Log Books Outgoing*, the *Stock Manager* (Prometheus) role requires data from the *Customer Orders* data store (which belongs to the *Delivery Manager* role). Thus, in the action map, the designer must ensure that the *Log Books Outgoing* action has access to the data store. In Figure 8, this is done and noted along the causality arrow that flows between the actions *Log Outgoing Delivery* and *Log Books Outgoing*.

The result of this second step is the action map in Figure 8.

Step 3: Incorporating Scenario Variations. Adding scenario variations provides alternative paths to successfully complete the interaction goal. As a result, this improves the flexibility and robustness of the interaction. There are no set guidelines for adding scenario variations into action maps as the variations will vary greatly depending on the domain, the agents involved and the actual interaction. In some cases, extending the interaction to cover scenario variations will require changes to the interaction goal hierarchy (IGH) if the variation affects more than a single IG. However, in the case of the *Order Book* scenario the variation only affects a single IG, and can be incorporated into the *Arrange Delivery* IG, and hence only the action map needs to be changed, and not the IGH.

In the case of the *Order Book* scenario, the variation states that if the book ordered is not available, replace steps 7–12 with steps to add a pending order. This can be incorporated into the action map by having two ways in which the *Arrange Delivery* IG can be achieved: (1) when the ordered book is available, the delivery order is placed and processed (as depicted in Figure 8), and (2) when the ordered book is unavailable, a pending order is created. Once the book is available, the pending order is filled and the delivery is processed.

Note that in our interaction, the availability of the ordered book is not explicitly queried; it is assumed to be part of the delivery options. In order to improve clarity we decide to make querying for book availability explicit. We do this by adding two new actions at the start of the action map: *Check Book Availability* and *Check Stock* (refer to Figure 9). These two actions are used to determine how to arrange the delivery. *Check Book Availability* is used to query *Stock Manager* about the availability of the ordered book. *Check Stock* is the action in *Stock Manager* that replies to the query. If

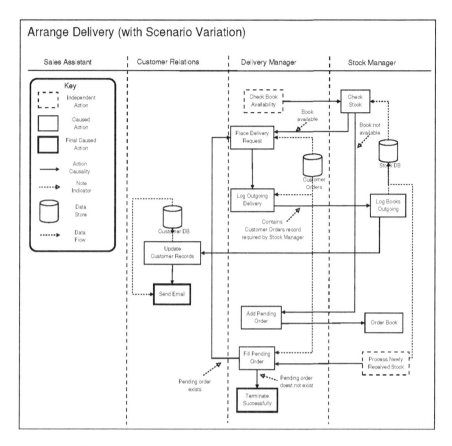

Fig. 9. Action Map: Arrange Delivery (with scenario variation)

the ordered book is available, the delivery order is placed and processed. If the ordered book is not available, the *Add Pending Order* action is used to order the book (from the publishing firm). Once the book comes in (from the publishing firm), *Process Newly Received Stock* is triggered, the pending order is filled and the delivery is processed.

The result of this third step is the action map in Figure 9.

Step 4: Adding Failure Tolerance. This step of the action maps focuses on failures in the interaction and how to handle them and is of crucial importance as failure handling is what gives the action maps, and thus Hermes, the majority of their flexibility

Table 1. Possible Failures and Remedial Actions for *Arrange Delivery*

Action	Possible Failures	Remedial Actions
Order Book	Book out of print	Suggest alternative title or edition
Place Delivery Request	Invalid address	Get details from user and validate
Send Email	Email bounces	Use different medium to contact user (e.g. send mail via post)

and robustness. This iteration has three sub-steps: *Failure Identification, Adding Action Retries* and *Adding Rollbacks.*

In the first sub-step, *Failure Identification*, action maps are analysed to determine where possible failures can occur. In general, think about each action on the action maps and determine whether it can fail or not. If it can fail then determine what different types

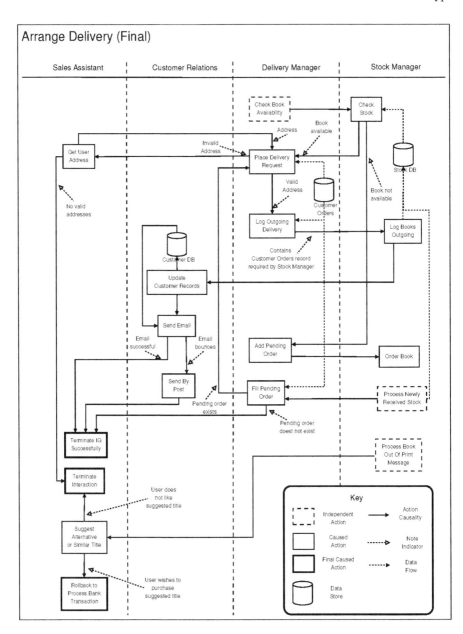

Fig. 10. Final Action Map: Arrange Delivery

of failures can result from each of the actions. Once the failures have been identified, determine ways in which they can be addressed.

For each action map we summarise in a table the possible failures and what remedial actions can be taken to recover from the failure. For example (see Table 1), the *Order Book* action can fail if the book is out of print, and in this case one, way of dealing with the failure is to suggest alternative titles or editions to the shopper.

To further enhance flexibility and robustness, the designer can also analyse each action and determine different ways in which they can succeed (i.e. alternative success paths). However, this was not carried out in this case study.

The remaining two sub-steps deal with handling the identified failures by incorporating the remedial actions into the design using respectively action retries and rollbacks.

In the *Adding Action Retries* sub-step, the action maps are updated with *action retries* to incorporate remedial actions. For example, it has been identified that the *Order Book* action could fail if a book is out of print, and the suggested remedial action for this is to suggest an alternative title. In Figure 10, this is achieved by the *Process Book Out Of Print Message* action which leads to the *Suggest Alternative or Similar Title* action.

Adding *action retries* can create loops between actions, and it is important to ensure that there are no unintended endless loops. For example, in Figure 10, there is a loop between *Place Delivery Request* and *Get User Address*. The intention is that the user is re-prompted for an address every time invalid addresses are encountered. However, an additional action, *Terminate Interaction*, has been provided in the case the user cannot or does not wish to enter an address and would like to exit the interaction at that point.

In the *Adding Rollbacks* sub-step the action map is extended with rollbacks. In this case study none of the identified remedial actions involved rolling back to a previous stage, so no changes are made in this sub-step.

The result of this fourth step is the action map in Figure 10. Although the action map appears fairly complex, it provides flexible and robust interaction, including dealing with the failure cases summarised in Table 1. The action map in Figure 10 and the IGH in Figure 6 were developed by following the sequence of steps that comprise the amalgamated methodology.

4 Conclusion

There are a number of other approaches to agent interactions which, like Hermes, focus on providing more flexible and robust interactions. These approaches include those based on social commitments [9,10,11,12], Kumar *et al.*'s Landmark-based approach [13,14], and Hutchison and Winikoff's goal-plan approach [15].

The work of Yolum and Singh [9,10] defines a social commitment as an agreement between two agents in which one agent is responsible for bringing about a certain condition. Flores and Kremer [11,12] have a slightly different definition of social commitments in that an agent is responsible for performing certain actions as opposed to bringing about certain conditions. To progress through commitment-based interactions, agents acquire, manipulate and discharge commitments. Both these approaches support complex agent interactions, however, the design aspects are not well defined. Given a particular interaction, it is difficult to determine what commitments are required for the design of the interaction.

The work of Kumar *et al.* is focused on landmarks, which can be thought of as states of affairs. Their work argue that the states of affairs are more important than the actions that bring about the states of affairs. That is, the states that are brought about by communicative acts are more important that the communicative acts themselves. In this regard, landmark-based interactions are about navigating through landmarks to reach a desired final state. This work relies heavily on expertise in modal and temporal logics.

In Hutchison and Winikoff's work [15], protocols are defined in terms of goals and plans, and can be seen as predecessor to the Hermes methodology; its design process is not detailed and it does not provide a mapping from design to implementation.

None of the aforementioned studies, which aim to provide increased flexibility and robustness in agent interactions, have been integrated with full agent system design methodologies. For such work to be practical, integration with full agent system design methodologies is important.

The authors are not aware of any such integration. The closest work to integrating more flexible and robust agent interaction design with full agent system design methodologies is in methodologies in which agent interactions are treated as first class entities. On such example is SODA [16]. However, although SODA deals with inter-agent design and regards interactions as first class entities, it has a different aim to the enhanced methodology we have presented.

There are two main differences between SODA and the integrated Hermes and Prometheus methodology. Firstly, SODA is for the analysis and design of Internet-based systems whilst the integrated Hermes and Prometheus methodology is for general purpose agent system design (i.e. not specifically for Internet-based systems). Secondly, and most importantly, the SODA interaction design appears to be message-centric as the design process is focused on resources and on information passing.

We have shown how the Prometheus methodology can be modified by replacing its current interaction design process with the Hermes methodology. We have also refined the Hermes methodology and presented a more detailed process for developing action maps than has previously been published. The enhanced methodology provides a guided iterative process for the design of agent interactions. Since the design artefacts produced are pure Hermes artefacts, they can be mapped to an implementation on goal-based agent platforms as explained in [6].

One of the main advantages of the amalgamation is the flexibility and robustness of the interactions, which is a direct result of merging Hermes with Prometheus. Furthermore, since Hermes is goal-oriented, it is more congruent with the agent paradigm. Additionally, the Hermes design process explicitly considers possible failures and how they can be recovered from, which tends to lead to more robust interactions. Preliminary results from a brief comparison of AUML and Hermes have shown that AUML, which focuses on alternative message sequences, cannot easily identify some types of failures which are easily identifiable by the Hermes process.

One disadvantage of Hermes is that it is time-consuming and, depending on the design and the particular interaction, is likely to result in a greater number of design artefacts than the AUML approach. However, the result provides for greater flexibility and robustness, and is more compatible with intelligent software agents that are proactive and autonomous. It should be noted that we do not propose that all interactions be designed using the Hermes process: as discussed in section 3.2, the decision whether to use Hermes or Prometheus to design a given interaction should be made explicitly based on the complexity of the interaction, the need for flexibility, and the extent to which failure may arise.

A key piece of future work that we have begun is an evaluation of the ease-of-use and effectiveness of the Hermes methodology. This comparison involves having a number of designers design an interaction using either the original Prometheus process (using the AUML notation) or the process presented in this paper. We will then compare the designs produced in terms of the range of interaction sequences supported (flexibility) and the types of failure that can be recovered from (robustness).

Another area of future work is tool support for the amalgamated methodology. Tool support is important for the amalgamated methodology to be practical, and as such we intend to develop such tool support. We currently have developed a prototype tool using UMLet[5] for the aforementioned evaluation. Future tool support development may involve building upon the existing Prometheus Design Tool (PDT) [8].

Acknowledgements

We would like to acknowledge the support of Agent Oriented Software Pty. Ltd. and of the Australian Research Council (ARC) under grant LP0453486.

References

1. Huget, M.P., Odell, J.: Representing agent interaction protocols with agent UML. In: Proceedings of the Fifth International Workshop on Agent Oriented Software Engineering (AOSE). (2004)
2. Padgham, L., Winikoff, M.: Developing Intelligent Agent Systems: A Practical Guide. John Wiley and Sons (2004) ISBN 0-470-86120-7.
3. Jennings, N., Kinny, D., Wooldridge, M., Zambonelli, F.: The Gaia methodology. In Bergenti, F., Gleizes, M.P., Zambonelli, F., eds.: Methodologies and Software Engineering for Agent Systems. Kluwer Academic Publishing (New York) (2004)
4. Bresciani, P., Giorgini, P., Giunchiglia, F., Mylopoulos, J., Perini, A.: Tropos: An agent-oriented software development methodology. Journal of Autonomous Agents and Multi-Agent Systems **8** (2004) 203–236
5. Cheong, C., Winikoff, M.: Hermes: Designing goal-oriented agent interactions. In: Proceedings of the 6th International Workshop on Agent-Oriented Software Engineering (AOSE-2005). (2005)
6. Cheong, C., Winikoff, M.: Hermes: Implementing goal-oriented agent interactions. In: Proceedings of the Third international Workshop on Programming Multi-Agent Systems (ProMAS). (2005)
7. Padgham, L., Winikoff, M., Poutakidis, D.: Adding debugging support to the Prometheus methodology. Engineering Applications of Artificial Intelligence **18** (2005) 173–190 Special issue on Agent-oriented Software Development.

---

[5] http://qse.ifs.tuwien.ac.at/ auer/umlet/

8. Padgham, L., Thangarajah, J., Winikoff, M.: Tool support for agent development using the Prometheus methodology. In: Proceedings of the First International Workshop on Integration of Software Engineering and Agent Technology (ISEAT). (2005)

9. Yolum, P., Singh, M.P.: Reasoning about commitments in the event calculus: An approach for specifying and executing protocols. Annals of Mathematics and Artificial Intelligence (AMAI), Special Issue on Computational Logic in Multi-Agent Systems **42** (2004) 227–253

10. Yolum, P., Singh, M.P.: Flexible protocol specification and execution: Applying event calculus planning using commitments. In: Proceedings of the 1st Joint Conference on Autonomous Agents and MultiAgent Systems (AAMAS). (2002) 527–534

11. Flores, R.A., Kremer, R.C.: A pragmatic approach to build conversation protocols using social commitments. In: Autonomous Agents and Multi-Agent Systems (AAMAS). (2004) 1242–1243

12. Flores, R.A., Kremer, R.C.: A principled modular approach to construct flexible conversation protocols. In Tawfik, A., Goodwin, S., eds.: Advances in Artificial Intelligence, Springer-Verlag, LNCS 3060 (2004) 1–15

13. Kumar, S., Huber, M.J., Cohen, P.R.: Representing and executing protocols as joint actions. In: Proceedings of the First International Joint Conference on Autonomous Agents and Multi-Agent Systems, Bologna, Italy, ACM Press (2002) 543 – 550

14. Kumar, S., Cohen, P.R., Huber, M.J.: Direct execution of team specifications in STAPLE. In: Proceedings of the First International Joint Conference on Autonomous Agents & Multi-Agent Systems (AAMAS 2002), ACM Press (2002) 567–568

15. Hutchison, J., Winikoff, M.: Flexibility and Robustness in Agent Interaction Protocols. In: Workshop on Challenges in Open Agent Systems at the First International Joint Conference on Autonomous Agents and Multi-Agents Systems. (2002)

16. Omicini, A.: SODA: Societies and infrastructures in the analysis and design of agent-based systems. In: Proceedings of the 1st International Workshop on Agent-Oriented Software Engineering (AOSE-2000). (2000) 185–193

Patterns for Modelling Agent Systems with Tropos

Haralambos Mouratidis[1] and Michael Weiss[2]

[1] School of Computing and Technology,
University of East London, England
h.mouratidis@uel.ac.uk
[2] Department of Computer Science, Carleton University,
Ottawa, Canada
weiss@scs.carleton.ca

Abstract. Tropos is an agent-oriented development methodology based on knowledge-level concepts (such as actor, goal, and the dependency between actors) with a particular focus on requirements analysis. This paper presents a pattern language for guiding developers, especially those without previous Tropos experience, through the various design challenges faced when using Tropos. The patterns format allows us to motivate the modelling constructs, justify each of the development stages, and address specific modelling problems. These patterns are inter-linked in such a way that developers can navigate from higher-level to lower-level patterns as they apply the Tropos methodology. The paper has two goals: to motivate the use of agent-oriented methodologies such as Tropos to a wider set of developers, and to provide guidance for the different development activities of the Tropos methodology. Specifically, we focus on the development stages, models, and diagrams of Tropos. The patterns in this paper cover the early and late requirements analysis stages.

1 Introduction

The design of open systems, whose architecture evolves, which need to operate robustly, and to adapt to changing computational resources in their environment has renewed the interest in agent-oriented approaches. Such systems require higher-level abstractions of software than object-oriented methodologies can provide. These are concepts at the knowledge level rather than at the software level. The construct of a knowledge-level as introduced by [12] allows software to embed notions of goal-orientedness and intentionality, and provides a bridge between the complex social, human-oriented environments in which the software operates, and objects.

Tropos has been proposed as a comprehensive methodology for all phases of agent-oriented software development [3]. It is based on intentional and social concepts such as actor, goal, and the dependency between actors, and is, therefore, particularly suitable for modelling and reasoning about the needs of multiple stakeholders. Distinguishing it from other agent-oriented modelling approaches, Tropos is characterised by three key aspects [13,5,8,1]:

A. Garcia et al. (Eds.): SELMAS 2005, LNCS 3914, pp. 207–223, 2006.
© Springer-Verlag Berlin Heidelberg 2006

1. Tropos deals with *all phases* of system development (requirements analysis, system design, and implementation), adopting a uniform and homogeneous way based on the notion of agents and all the related mentalistic notions, such as actors, goals, tasks, resources, and intentional dependencies.
2. Tropos pays particular attention to early requirements, emphasising the need to understand not only *what* organisational goals are required, but also *how* and *why* the intended system would meet these organisational goals. This allows for a more refined analysis of system dependencies, leading to a better treatment not only of the system's functional requirements, but also of its non-functional requirements such as security, reliability, and performance [13].
3. Tropos is based on the idea of building a model of the system that is incrementally refined and extended from a conceptual level to executable artefacts by means of a sequence of *transformational steps* at the goal, softgoal and actor level [1,2]. Such transformations allow developers to move towards the final complete model by progressively introducing more structure and details.

Much work has already been undertaken in the Tropos project. However, the following key challenges still need to be answered to allow the effective and widespread use of Tropos: (1) what modelling *constructs* should be used at which stage of the development process; (2) what *amount of detail* should be provided in a model; (3) how should the models be *mapped* between different stages.

We believe that patterns provide an invaluable tool to provide answers to these challenges. Patterns have been successfully used to capture and communicate established knowledge in a domain. They document solutions together with the reasons for applying them and the trade-offs made in the process. Besides architectural and design patterns, process and organizational patterns have been documented in the patterns literature. Patterns are therefore suitable for describing both process and modelling aspects of a development methodology. For example, Evitts [5] documents patterns for applying the Unified Modeling Language (UML).

Patterns have also been used in relation to the Tropos project to document domain-specific recurring solutions. Fuxman et al. [7], have proposed a set of social patterns and organizational styles. Similarly, Kolp et al [9] have proposed a set of organizational patterns for early requirements analysis using the Tropos methodology. In addition, in our own previous work [10] have defined a security pattern language that can be employed as part of a security-aware development process based on Tropos.

However, we are not aware of work that introduces the Tropos approach itself in the form of a pattern language. The existence of such a language is important for two main reasons: (1) it will provide a guideline through the various design challenges faced by developers when employing Tropos; and (2) it will motivate the use of agent-oriented methodologies such as Tropos to a wider set of developers and researchers, moving agent oriented software engineering outside the borders of the agent community. We see our work as a stepping stone towards this objective.

The goal of this paper is to present an initial pattern language to guide developers through the process of using Tropos. It is worth noting that our aim is not to provide a language for experienced users of the Tropos methodology, looking for an overview of architectural patterns; but rather to provide a language that will communicate the core modelling activities of the Tropos methodology to developers who are not familiar with it, and therefore make the methodology usable by a larger audience.

The paper focuses on the early phases of Tropos development, namely the early and late requirements analysis stages. The rest of the paper is structured as follows. Section 2 presents an overview of key Tropos concepts and development stages. The patterns themselves are described in Section 3. The section also introduces the case study used as a running example in the description of the patterns. Conclusions and venues for future work are presented in Section 4.

2 Overview of Tropos Concepts and Stages

The *Tropos* methodology is based on the *i** modelling framework [15], which uses the concepts of actor, goal, and social dependency for defining the obligations of actors (dependees) to other actors (dependers). In Tropos a multiagent system and its environment are viewed as a set of actors, which depend on other actors to help them fulfil their goals. In particular, an *actor* represents an entity that has intentionality and strategic goals within the multiagent system, or within its organisational setting. A (hard) *goal* represents a condition in the world that an actor would like to achieve.

In Tropos, the concept of a hard goal (or simply goal, hereafter) is differentiated from the concept of a softgoal. A *softgoal* is used to capture non-functional requirements of the system, and unlike a (hard) goal, it does not have clear criteria for deciding whether it is satisfied or not, and, therefore, it is subject to interpretation. Moreover, in Tropos, a *task[1]* represents, at an abstract level, a particular way of doing something, a particular course of action. A *resource* presents a physical or informational entity that one of the actors requires. A *dependency* link between two actors indicates that one actor depends on the other to achieve some goal, execute a task, or deliver a resource. The depending actor is called the *depender*, and the actor depended upon the *dependee*. The type of dependency (goal, task, resource) describes the nature of the agreement (called *dependum*) between the dependee and depender.

The Tropos methodology covers five main software development stages:

1. During *early requirements analysis*, developers are concerned with understanding a problem by studying an existing organisational setting. This involves the identification of the domain stakeholders, and modelling them as social actors. The output of this phase is an organisational model, which includes relevant actors, their goals, and their respective dependencies.
2. During *late requirements analysis*, the system-to-be is introduced as another actor, and specified within its operational environment, together with relevant functions and qualities. The output of this stage is a revised model which includes the system, any relevant actors, and their respective dependencies.
3. During *architectural design*, the system's global architecture is defined in terms of additional system actors, interconnected via data and control dependencies. The final output of this stage is a set of software agents corresponding to the actors of the system, each characterised by its specific capabilities.

---

[1] Also known in Tropos as plan [1-3].

4. During *detailed design*, each architectural component is defined in further detail in terms of inputs, outputs, control, and other aspects such as security.
5. During the *implementation*, the actual implementation of the system components takes place according to the specification produced during detailed design. It is worth mentioning that Tropos (similar to other agent-oriented methodologies) does not force the use of an agent platform as the implementation technology.

3   Tropos Pattern Language

This section describes the patterns for modelling agent systems with Tropos[2]. The actual description of the patterns is preceded by a discussion of the design considerations that affect the use of Tropos in general, and thus underlie every pattern in one way or other. This is followed by a roadmap that shows the relationships between the patterns and suggests a way of using the patterns, and by the pattern template that we will follow in our description of the patterns. Finally, we describe the running example we will use in the description of each pattern to illustrate its application.

A note on formatting: each pattern has its own heading in bold face. The pattern description follows as a table with entries according to the pattern template. The description is followed by (excerpts of) the application of the pattern to the running example. When one pattern refers to another pattern, the pattern name is italicised. Our patterns have been derived from various case studies [3,4,5,10,15,16] and modelling projects, which use the *i** framework and the Tropos methodology.

Basic forces
A set of basic forces push and pull the solutions in different directions for all patterns in the pattern language. Each pattern is a trade-off among those forces, as well as forces specific to the pattern. For example, the level of refinement is typically bounded by the amount of detail that can be processed by the developer at any given stage. A pattern will make an appropriate balance between these forces.

The basic forces underlying the use of Tropos are:

— A model is built of the system-to-be which is incrementally refined and extended from a conceptual level to executable artifacts.
— Too much detail can be confusing. This is the basic force underlying stepwise refinement, and limiting the amount of detail at each stage.
— Actors cannot achieve all of their goals on their own. This is the basic force motivating the need to model actor dependencies.
— To complete the model, all goals need to be refined to tasks, resources, or softgoals. This is the basic force underlying the analysis of actor internals.

---

[2] Since the introduction of the original *i** and Tropos concepts and modelling activities, various researchers have extended these in more than one ways. However, many of these extensions are not proven in practice and since patterns produce proven solution to a recurring problem, our language focuses on the core modelling activities of the original *i**/Tropos.

—New actors might be introduced at any point during the development process. This is the basic motivating for iterating through the development stages.

—The same concepts (actor, goal, etc.) are used to model early requirements, late requirements, as well as architectural design, and detailed design.

Pattern Roadmap

Fig. 1 shows the patterns and their relationships in a pattern roadmap. The arrows indicate the suggested order in which the patterns should be applied. The labels on the arrows summarize the rationale for consulting the next pattern, or set of patterns. For example, the link between *Define Actors* and *Refine Actor Goals* is labeled more details of actors to indicate that *Refine Actor Goals* should be applied after *Define Actors* for the purpose of adding more details to the actors. Note that repeated application of patterns, as part of an iterative process, is not shown in the roadmap.

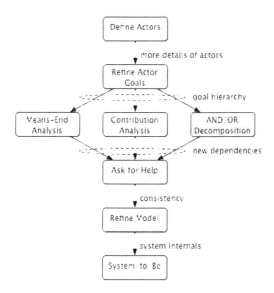

Fig. 1. Roadmap to the pattern language

As shown, modelling a system in Tropos starts with the development activities, models, and diagrams described in *Define Actors*. This pattern is concerned with modelling the system environment in terms of actors. Then the focus shifts towards individual actors in *Refine Actor Goals*. This refinement process involves three types of refinement as described in *Means-End Analysis*, *Contribution Analysis*, and *AND/OR Decomposition*. The resulting model is a goal hierarchy for each actor. During refinement, dependencies between actors will be discovered, and added as suggested by *Ask for Help*. New actors may be added to the system as a result, and to make the model consistent, existing models need to be revisited as described in *Refine Model*. Once the refinement of the environment actors is complete, the system-to-be is added as an actor on its own, as suggested by *System-to-Be*. As stated, the actual development process is iterative and will follow these patterns repeatedly, while applying the patterns in the sequence suggested by the roadmap.

Pattern Template

Although there are a number of different templates used for describing patterns, it is generally agreed that the following are mandatory parts of a pattern [14]:

Name: A good pattern name should be short and precise. But it also needs to convey the essence of the pattern so it can be remembered by that name.

Context: A description of a situation when the pattern would apply. However, in and by itself the context does not provide the only determining factor as to the situations in which the pattern should be applied. Every pattern also has a number of forces that need to be balanced before applying the pattern.

Problem: A precise statement of the problem to be solved. A good problem for a pattern is one that software engineers will ask themselves often

Forces: A description of items that influence the decision as to when to apply the pattern in a context. Forces can be thought of as pushing or pulling the problem towards different solutions, or that indicating trade-offs that may be made [Cop96].

Solution: A description of the solution in the context that balances the forces.

Consequences: A list of the consequences of applying the pattern. How does the pattern resolve the forces, and are any new problems introduced by this pattern.

Known uses: A list of known applications of the pattern, proving that the pattern does, indeed, describe a proven solution to a recurring problem.

We have extended this template by one entry:

Stages: It is very important for the applicability of our language to determine in which stages of the development the pattern is applicable.

Case Study

To better illustrate the usability and applicability of our pattern language, we use an online auction system as a running example in the description of the patterns. In particular, we assume an English auction mechanism, according to which an auctioneer seeks to find the market price of a good by proposing a price below that of the supposed market value and then gradually raising the price. Each time the price is announced, the auctioneer waits to see if any buyers will signal their willingness to pay the proposed price. As soon as one buyer signals that he agrees to a price, the auctioneer issues a new call for bids at a higher price. The auction ends when no more buyers are prepared to pay the proposed price. If the last price accepted by a buyer equals or exceeds the auctioneer's reserve price, then the item is sold to that buyer. If the last accepted price is less than the reserve price, the item is not sold.

Define Actors

Context	You are modelling the environment of the system-to-be.
Stages	Early Requirements
Problem	How to model the system environment?
Forces	— All stakeholders should be able to understand the model. — The developer should be able to define the functional as well as the social dimension of the environment.
Solution	Model the system's environment in terms of its stakeholders. Identify the stakeholders and model them as social actors. Elicit the goals of each stakeholder and make them the root goals of the corresponding actor. Use an actor diagram to graphically represent the stakeholders along with their root goals. Roles (functions) that stakeholders can play may also be modeled as actors.
Consequences	The stakeholders and their intentions are identified and represented by actors who have some root goals. This provides developers with a high-level representation of the environment in which the system-to-be will be situated. However, a more detailed description of each of the actors is required as discussed in *Refine Actor Goals*.
Known Uses	eSAP case study [10] Tropos tool [3] eCultural case study [4]

In the running example, we identify three main actors, an Auctioneer, a Buyer and a Seller. These are external actors that will be involved in the execution of the auction system. The main goal of the Auctioneer is to Facilitate Auction, the main goal of the Buyer is to Buy Item, and the main goal of the Seller is to Sell Item. Using standard Tropos notation, the actor diagram in Fig. 2 models the actors along with their root goals. Actors are represented by circles. Goals are shown as rounded rectangles. Root goals are specified by attaching them to their actors. In the text, we set off the names of model elements by putting them into a sans serif font, as we have done above.

Fig. 2. Applying *Define Actors* to the example

This pattern describes the initial step to help developers understand the context in which the system-to-be must operate. It avoids exposing developers to too much detail by focusing their attention on just stakeholders and their root goals. This helps avoid that a developer will design a system that does not reflect the goals and interests of those stakeholders. It also supports the needs of the common situation, in which developers are faced with redesigning an existing system using agents. By uncovering the root goals of the stakeholders that will use the intended system, developers can also think about new, alternative ways of achieving those goals.

Refine Actor Goals

Context	You have identified actors, and assigned high-level root goals. Each of these actors, and goals needs to be further analysed.
Stages	Early Requirements, Late Requirements
Problem	How can actors and their goals be analysed in detail?
Forces	—Too much detail can be confusing. —New goals/tasks/resources might be discovered.
Solution	Refine goals from the perspective of its respective actor. For this reason, goal diagrams are used. For each of the goals of an actor a hierarchy (consisting of new goals, softgoals, and tasks) is built. Goals lower on the hierarchy are more specific and motivated by higher-level goals in the hierarchy. Moreover, multiple alternative ways of achieving a goal can also be modelled.
Consequences	The root goal of the actor is further analysed, and new goals are identified. One of the following three patterns should be used in order to generate the goal hierarchy, and to identify new goals: *Means-End Analysis, Contribution Analysis,* or *AND/OR Decomposition.* However, if an actor cannot achieve a subgoal resulting from the refinement on its own, you need to use *Ask for Help.*
Known Uses	eCultural case study [4] eSAP case study [10] Media Shop case study [5]

Returning to our case study, let us consider the Buy Item root goal of the Buyer actor. The problem is that the current definition of the Buyer actor is at too high a level and doesn't provide developers with a realistic definition of the actor. Therefore, as it was identified in *Refine Actor Goals*, the solution to this problem is to refine the root goal from the perspective of the actor. For instance, buyers know that in order to buy an item, they should identify the item and also pay for the item. Moreover, the Buyer actor most likely wishes to buy in a fast and convenient way, and without exceeding their budget. By applying *Refine Actor Goal*, we are able to further refine the actor's root goal. But how can we represent these new goals in a hierarchy that will help developers generate even more goals, tasks, and softgoals, as well as to consider alternatives? According to the proposed pattern language, developers can use *Means-End Analysis, Contribution Analysis,* and *AND/OR Decomposition.*

This pattern provides a context for three more specific patterns describing the different refinement approaches available in Tropos. Part of the difficulty in using Tropos effectively is to understand which kind of refinement to use with what kind of intentional elements (goals, tasks, resources). Typically, one would first use *Means-End Analysis* to discover subgoals representing means to achieve the root goals of an actor. These subgoals subsequently become subject of refinement themselves, until they have been refined to a satisfactory level, typically into tasks or resources. *Contribution Analysis* can then be used to identify interdependencies between goals, and to document trade-offs between alternative means to achieve an end. Finally, *AND/OR Decomposition* allows developers to bring goal refinement to a closure, that is, to map high-level goals to particular ways (tasks, resources) of achieving them.

Means-End Analysis

Context	You need to further analyse the goals of the actor.
Stages	Early Requirements, Late Requirements
Problem	How can goals /tasks be refined in a systematic manner?
Forces	—Goals need to be refined to tasks, resources, or softgoals. Otherwise the model is incomplete. —A goal can be satisfied by a subgoal, and/or a task, and/or a resource, or a combination of several of these.
Solution	For each higher-level goal (end), identify lower-level goals, tasks, or resources as possible means for satisfying the goal.
Consequences	When all goals have been dealt with to the satisfaction of the actors that want to achieve them, refinement is complete.
Known Uses	eSAP System [10] Meeting Scheduling [15] eCultural project [4] Buyer-driven e-commerce system [16]

For instance, we identify through *Means-End Analysis* that to achieve the Buy Item goal the Buyer actor needs to Identify Item and also Pay for it, as shown in Fig. 3. In the Tropos notation, the means to achieve a goal (end) are represented by links in the direction of the end with an open arrow head. This diagram says that Identify Item and Pay for it are both means for achieving the higher-level Buy Item goal. *Means-End Analysis* may be applied recursively to the newly discovered goals. This type of analysis helps with the discovery of subgoals, which still need to be either refined into particular ways of achieving them, or delegated to other agents using *Ask for Help*.

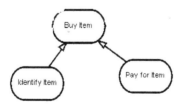

Fig. 3. Applying *Means-End Analysis* to the example

However, the application of *Refine Actor Goals* will also result in the identification of several softgoals (such as Within Budget, Fast, or Convenient). A softgoal does not have clear criteria for deciding whether it is satisfied or not and, therefore, it is subject to interpretation. For example, "fast" for one buyer might mean within two hours, whereas for someone else it could be within five hours. Such softgoals contribute to the satisfaction of a goal and represent qualities related to the goal. As a result, they cannot guarantee the goal, and they can only contribute (positively or negatively) towards its satisfaction. For this reason, a *Contribution Analysis* is employed.

Contribution Analysis

Context	You need to identify new goals to contribute to existing goals.
Stages	Early Requirements, Late Requirements
Problem	How can you identify new goals to contribute to existing goals?
Forces	—Newly identified goals may contribute either positively or negatively to existing goals. —There can be multiple, competing ways of achieving a goal, each resulting in different trade-offs.
Solution	Identify goals that can contribute positively or negatively to reach the goal being analyzed.
Consequences	Contribution analysis can be thought of as a special case of means-end analysis in which means are goals or softgoals. Goals/softgoals are identified that can contribute either positively or negatively to the achievement of the goal being analyzed.
Known uses	IP management model [16] Insurance claim modelling [15] eSAP system [10]

The application of the *Contribution Analysis* pattern to the example results in the model in Fig. 4, in which each of the softgoals contributes positively to the root goal of the Buyer actor. Fast, Convenient, Within Budget are softgoals that cannot be achieved in an absolute sense, but whose achievement is subject to interpretation. In the Tropos notation, softgoals are represented as curly shapes (clouds). Contributions are shown as arrows with labels indicating their strength (for example, + or -). It is important to understand that *Contribution Analysis* can be performed in a downwards, as well as a upwards manner. In the downward direction, contribution links capture refinements of higher-level to lower-level goals, and contributions upwards.

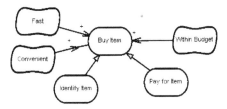

Fig. 4. Applying *Contribution Analysis* to the example

However, as the hierarchy is generated, some goals/tasks can be achieved in more than one way. In other words, there are alternative means to satisfy a task or goal. In our example, multiple application of *Means-End Analysis* results in the identification of the task Get Item Description of the Buyer actor as shown in Fig. 5. However, there are alternative ways of satisfying this task, such as getting the description of the item before the auction, or getting the description during the auction. So a new problem is raised how we can model such alternative satisfactions. For solving this problem, the language includes the *AND/OR Decomposition* pattern.

AND/OR Decomposition

Context	You have identified all the high-level goals and tasks for an actor.
Stages	Early Requirements, Late Requirements
Problem	How can you break down a goal/task into simpler more specific goals/tasks?
Forces	— Too much detail can be confusing. — There can be multiple ways of achieving a goal. — Only goals and tasks can be decomposed.
Solution	Break down the component into smaller, more precise components. Two different techniques can be used to perform this. AND/OR decomposition allows developers to consider alternatives when decomposing the goals/tasks of an actor into sub-goals/sub-tasks. Whereas AND decomposition means that all the sub-goals/sub-tasks must be achieved for the root goal/task to be achieved, OR decomposition means that the achievement of one of the sub-goals/sub-tasks leads to the achievement of the root goal/task.
Consequences	When all goals have been dealt with to the satisfaction of the actors that want to achieve them, refinement is complete. Alternative ways of satisfying a goal derived using OR decomposition can be compared in terms of their impact using *Contribution Analysis*.
Known uses	IP management model [16] Buyer-driven e-commerce system [16] eCultural project [4] eSAP system [10]

The application of the pattern to the refinement of the Get Item Description task is shown in Fig. 5. In the Tropos notation, a decomposition is shown as a link with a bar crossing the link near the decomposed goal/task. As shown, Get Item Description is decomposed into the subtasks Before Auction and During Auction.

A common difficulty in applying Tropos is to know when to use means-end analysis vs. task decomposition. Strictly speaking, ends in means-end analysis must be (hard) goals, and means are either other goals, tasks, or resources. A goal always indicates that there are several possible ways (means) of satisfying it. Task decomposition, on the other hand, is, strictly, a way of expressing a mapping from larger, less specific goals/tasks to smaller, more precise subgoals/subtasks. Technically, goal decomposition is just shorthand for achieving the goal via some intermediary task using means-end analysis, and subsequently decomposing the task into goals.

The total effect of applying the various ways to *Refine Actor Goals* is shown in Fig. 6. This diagram shows the goal hierarchy for the Buyer actor inside a dashed circle representing the actor internals. In addition to the above, it includes one other

Fig. 5. Applying *AND/OR Decomposition* to the example

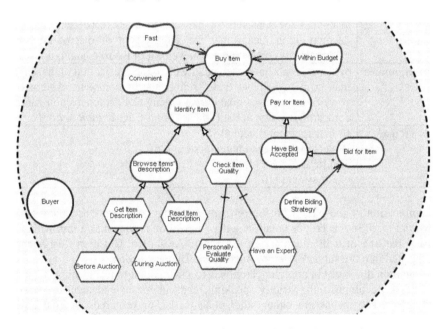

Fig. 6. Summary of applying *Refine Actor Goals* to the example

example of *AND/OR Decomposition* (different ways to Check Item Quality), and one other example of *Contribution Analysis* (refinement of Pay for Item).

The same analysis can be performed for all the actors. However, an important issue at this point of the development is the existence of some goals, softgoals and/or tasks that an actor cannot achieve on their own. Let us consider the Buyer actor. Our analysis so far has resulted in various goals, soft goals and tasks such as the Get Item Description and Pay Item. However, it is rather obvious that the Buyer cannot achieve these two on its own. In such situations, we are using the *Ask for Help* pattern.

Ask for Help

Context	An actor cannot achieve a goal/task by itself.
Stages	Early requirements, Late Requirements
Problem	How can actors satisfy goals for which they don't have the means?
Forces	—Actors cannot achieve all of their goals/tasks on their own. —As subgoals are generated, you will find goals that an actor cannot achieve at all or not as well as another actor. —New actors might be introduced that can achieve these goals.
Solution	Delegate such subgoals to other actors, and add dependency links between them and the actor. For each dependency link, the actor becomes the depender, the other actor the dependee, and the goal the dependum. The same solution can be used for tasks/resources.
Consequences	For each subgoal, the responsibility for achieving it is assigned to the actor itself, or delegated to another actor, while adding a dependency link. Sometimes this requires the introduction of new actors to which the actor delegates goals/tasks. By depending on the dependee for the dependum, the depender is able to achieve goals that it is otherwise unable to achieve on their own, or not as easily or not as well. On the other hand, the depender becomes vulnerable, since if the dependee fails to deliver the dependum, the depender is affected in their aim to achieve their goals. New goals, plans and resources are identified. Therefore, further refinement of these newly introduced entities might be required. When a new actor is introduced as part of goal delegation, also apply *Refine Model*.
Known uses	Health Care configuration modelling [15] eSAP system [10] Meeting scheduling [15] eCultural project [4] IP management model [16]

To get the item description the Buyer depends on an Auction House, whereas to pay for the item the Buyer depends on the Seller to provide him with payment options. Therefore goal dependencies are introduced between the Buyer, Auction House and Seller actors to indicate that the Buyer depends on these two actors to achieve the Item Description and the Payment Option goals as shown in Fig. 7. Similarly, new dependencies are introduced from Seller and Auction House to Buyer. In the Tropos notation, dependencies are represented by links with a –D– symbol. One link is between the depender and the dependum, the other between the dependum and the dependee.

Although not shown in Fig. 7, dependencies can also be between goals, tasks, or resources (of different actors). In the example, we could show the internal goals of the Buyer actor, including the Get Item Description task as shown in Fig. 6. The Item Description dependency between Buyer and Auction House, can then also be modelled

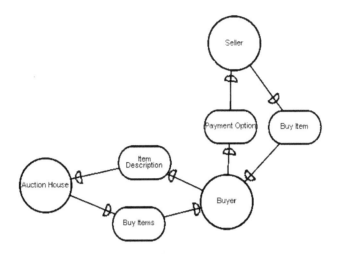

Fig. 7. Applying *Ask for Help* to the example

as a dependency between the Get Item Description task and Auction House. A key insight provided by the *Ask for Help* pattern is that goal refinement is tightly coupled to the discovery of actor dependencies. While in some cases we may determine a dependency in a top-down manner (that is, we model the dependency between two actors, before we have modelled their internals), we will often add new dependencies as a result of refining the goals of at least one of the actors in a dependency.

However, when *Ask for Help*, as is the case here, results in the introduction of a new actor, the existing models need to be revisited to make sure that no dependencies between the new actor (that is, Auction House) and the existing actors are missing. For this reason the *Refine Models* pattern is added on the pattern language.

Refine Models

Context	New actors are introduced to the model.
Stages	Early Requirements
Problem	How can we refine existing models?
Forces	— The actor and goal models produced should be consistent.
Solution	Revisit the existing models, and add new dependencies between the existing actors and the new actors as appropriate.
Consequences	Refining the dependencies and the social relationships of the actors, leads to a more precise definition of the *why* of the system functionalities, and as a last result, helps to verify how the final implementation matches the real needs [13]. When you are satisfied with the level of the analysis of the system's environment, you can start modelling the system itself as described in *System-to-Be*.
Known uses	eSAP system [10] Health care configuration modelling [15] Insurance claim modelling [15]

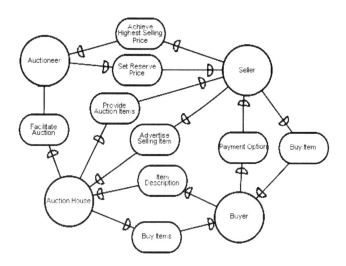

Fig. 8. Applying *Refine Model* to the example

The refinement of the case study is shown in Fig. 8.

As shown, new dependencies have been identified between the Auction House and the rest of the actors. Applying *Ask for Help* only resulted in the addition of dependencies involving the Buyer, but there are also new dependencies involving the Auctioneer, as well as the Seller.

When the developers are satisfied with the level of the analysis of the actors, and, therefore, the model of the system's environment, the next problem is to integrate the system-to-be within the existing analysis. Only at this point, when applying the *System-to-Be* pattern, we start modelling the actual system, and its internals.

System-to-Be

Context	The Early Requirements analysis is complete.
Stages	Late Requirements
Problem	How can you model the system-to-be.
Forces	– The System-to-Be claims responsibility for some of the goals of the existing actors. – The actor and goal models produced should be consistent.
Solution	Model the system-to-be as an actor, which has a number of dependencies with the actors identified during the early requirements stage. These dependencies indicate the obligations of the system towards its environment, and therefore define the system's functional and non-functional requirements.
Consequences	Some of the dependencies between the existing actors can be delegated to the newly introduced system actor.
Known uses	eSAP system [10] eCultural project [4] Buyer-driven e-commerce system [16]

The main goal of the system-to-be is to provide online auctions. This is a goal that the Auction House cannot achieve without an online system. Moreover, the introduction of the system means that some goals will be delegated to the system. As a result of applying *System-to-Be*, new dependencies are identified, or obligations are delegated, respectively, as shown in Fig. 9. As an example of the delegation of obligations consider the Item Description goal, which is now the responsibility of the Online System. Auction House has delegated this obligation to the Online System. This pattern captures an important goal of the Tropos methodology, which is to emphasise the need to understand *what* organisational goals are required. Before the system itself is designed, developers need to understand the context in which the system will operate. This is a realization of the interdependency of the system and its environment, that is, the system exists to meet the expectations of its stakeholders.

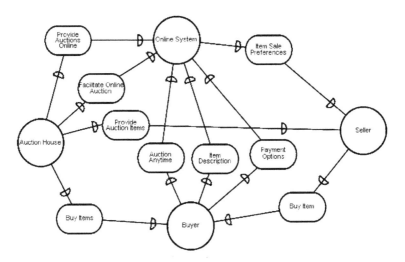

Fig. 9. Applying *System-to-Be* to the example

4   Conclusion

In this chapter we have introduced the Tropos approach in the form of a pattern language. The existence of such a language is important since it will provide a guideline through the various design challenges faced by developers when employing Tropos, especially those who do not have prior experience with the methodology. The proposed language satisfies multiple needs related to the Tropos methodology:

- It motivates the various modelling constructs (for example, what are the benefits of modelling the goals of the stakeholders affected by the system?).
- It justifies each of the stages (for example, why should developers model the environment first, and only then the system?).
- It addresses various specific problems (for example, how to select actors?).

As stated in the introduction, this work is not finished. Rather, our pattern language is an initial step towards a language that covers all Tropos development activities. In particular, our pattern language only consists of patterns covering the core modelling activities of the early and late requirement stages of the Tropos methodology.

Future work will involve the extension of the language with patterns derived from the other development stages as well as architectural patterns and styles. In addition, we are planning to introduce to our language patterns that provide guidance to specific modelling challenges, such as deciding whether to model an actor as a role or position, and the introduction of domain-specific patterns, such as security patterns.

References

1. Brescani, P., Perini, A., Giorgini, P., Giunchiglia, F., and Mylopoulos, J., Modelling Early Requirements in Tropos: A Transformation-Based Approach, Agent-Oriented Software Engineering, LNCS 2222, 151-168, Springer, 2002.
2. Brescani, P., and Giorgini, P., The TROPOS Analysis Process as Graph Transformation System, OOPSLA Workshop on Agent-Oriented Methodologies, 2002.
3. Bresciani, P., Sannicolo, F., Requirements Analysis in Tropos: a Self-Referencing Example, Agent Technology, Infrastructures and Applications for e-Services: NODe 2002 Agent-Related Workshops, LNCS 2592, 21-35, Springer, 2003.
4. Brescani, P., Perini, A., Giorgini, P., Giunchiglia, F., and Mylopoulos, J., Tropos: An Agent-Oriented Software Development Methodology, Journal on Autonomous Agents and Multi-Agent Systems, 8, 203-236, Kluwer, 2004.
5. Castro, J., Kolp, M., and Mylopoulos, J., Towards Requirements-Driven Information Systems Engineering: The Tropos Project, Information Systems, 27, 365-89, 2002.
6. Evitts, P.. A UML Pattern Language, Macmillan, 2000.
7. Fuxman, A., Giorgini, P., Kolp, M., and Mylopoulos, J., Information systems as social structures, Formal Ontology in Information Systems, 10-21, ACM, 2001.
8. Giunchiglia, F., Mylopoulos, J., and Perini, A., The Tropos Software Development Methodology: Process, Models, and Diagrams, Agent-Oriented Software Engineering, LNCS 2222, 162-173, Springer, 2002.
9. Kolp, M., Giorgini, P., and Mylopoulos, J., Organizational Patterns for Early Requirements Analysis, Conference on Advanced Information Systems Engineering, LNCS 2861, 617-632, Springer, 2003.
10. Mouratidis, H., A Security Oriented Approach in the Development of Multiagent Systems: Applied to the Management of the Health and Social Care Needs of Older People in England, PhD Dissertation, University of Sheffield, June 2004.
11. Mouratidis, H., Weiss, M., and Giorgini, P., Security Patterns Meet Agent Oriented Software Engineering: A Complementary Solution for Developing Secure Information Systems, Conceptual Modeling, LNCS 3716, 225-240, Springer, 2005.
12. Newell, A., The Knowledge Level, Artificial Intelligence, 18:87-127, Elsevier, 1982.
13. Perini, A., Brescani, P., Giorgini, P., and Mylopoulos, J., A Knowledge Level Software Engineering Methodology for Agent Oriented Programming, Autonomous Agents, 648-655, ACM, 2001.
14. Weiss, M., Pattern Driven Design of Agent Systems: Approach and Case Study, Conference on Advanced Information Systems Engineering, LNCS 2681, 711-723, Springer, 2003.
15. Yu, E., Modelling Strategic Relationships for Process Reengineering, PhD Thesis, University of Toronto, Department of Computer Science, 1995.
16. Yu, E., Liu, L., Li, Y., Modelling Strategic Actor Relationships to Support Intellectual Property Management, Conceptual Modelling, LNCS 2242, 164-178, Springer, 2001.

On the Use of Formal Specifications as Part of Running Programs

Giovanna Di Marzo Serugendo

University of Geneva (CUI),
Department of Information Systems,
24, rue Gnral-Dufour, 1211 Geneva 4 Switzerland
Giovanna.Dimarzo@cui.unige.ch

Abstract. Issues related to large scale systems made of autonomous components encompass *interoperability* among independently developed software and *adaptability* to changing environmental conditions. Formal specifications are traditionally used at design time for software engineering tasks. However, recently, several attempts of using formal specifications at run-time have been realised that let envisage a future use of formal specifications at run-time that will enhance interoperability and adaptability of autonomous components.

This paper intends to highlight the potentialities of the use of formal specifications at run-time as a support for the correct execution of such components. This paper reviews and discusses the use of formal specifications at run-time from different perspectives: software engineering, run-time code evolution, adaptive middleware, trust and security, or business applications. It highlights the potentialities of the use of formal specifications at run-time as a support for interoperability and adaptability of interacting autonomous components. It identifies as well application domains and open issues related to the combination of specifications and code in the framework of large scale systems.

1 Introduction

Formal methods are traditionally used at design time as a tool for defining systems, for analysis tasks, and for model checking.

However, current and future applications' needs are different than those of traditional software. Indeed, computing paradigms such as ubiquitous, pervasive computing, or service-oriented computing imply the use of a large number of autonomous components, services or agents interacting at run-time, possibly with decentralised control, independently developed, and acting on behalf of self-interested users. Off-line verification in these cases is impossible or of limited utility. Therefore, several works have emerged that combine the use of formal methods and programming languages at run-time, in order to benefit of some functional and quality assurances at run-time. This paper reviews (non-exhaustively) some of these works: from traditional ones allowing exception handling, to more recent ones supporting interactions among independently developed components. Even though this area of research is rather young and not

A. Garcia et al. (Eds.): SELMAS 2005, LNCS 3914, pp. 224–237, 2006.

yet mature enough for direct and efficient application into actual systems, this paper advocates that there is a large potential of interest and benefit of using formal methods at run-time, essentially due to run-time reasoning and decoupling of code from specification. Focus is given on large scale systems made of autonomous interacting components.

Section 2 briefly reviews different domains where formal methods are used at run-time and for different purposes. Section 3 describes the potential interest of having simultaneously formal specifications and executable code. Section 4 lists several domains where formal specifications at run-time may prove useful. Section 5 identifies several issues related to the use of formal methods at run-time. Finally, section 6 mentions some advantages and drawbacks of the use of formal methods as part of running programs.

2   Current and Emergent Practice

2.1   Design by Contract

The most popular and probably the earliest work using formal specifications inside programs is the "Design by Contract" paradigm of Meyer [24,25]. The idea is to attach to each function or routine of the program a list of pre- and post-conditions. Pre- and post-conditions are assertions or logical conditions that have to hold at the entry, respectively at the output of the corresponding routine. In addition to pre- and post-conditions applying to specific routines, invariants applying to a class as a whole, i.e. which have to hold for all instances of a class, can also be defined.

The "Design by Contract" paradigm serves different purposes. At design-time, it is used for testing, debugging and for quality assurance of the related software. The program runs are checked against the pre- post-conditions and the invariants. At run-time, it is used for exception handling. Exceptions occur when a routine cannot fulfil its contract: post-condition or invariant are violated, a called sub-routine fails, or the underlying hardware or operating system indicates an abnormal condition. Exceptions are handled by exception handlers whose goal is to restore the objects in a state where the invariants hold. If they cannot, the routine fails and throws an exception to its caller. The Eiffel programming language [23] has built-in features supporting the Design by Contract paradigm.

Trusted Components. Built on the notion of Design by Contract, the initiative of Trusted Components launched by Meyer et al. [27,26] aims at providing software components equipped with "specified and guaranteed quality properties". This notion covers both assessing properties of existing components and producing proofs of correctness of some properties (specified by the contract) for newly developed components.

2.2   Proof-Carrying Code (PCC)

With similar goals to the above notion of Trusted Components, but intended for run-time decisions instead of design time implementations, the Proof-Carrying

Code mechanism [29,28] allows a host system to determine if it is safe to execute a newly received untrusted binary program. The program comes with a proof that it validates some safety properties agreed in advance. The code producer creates such a proof, the code consumer (e.g. the host system that has to execute it) then simply checks that the proof is valid given the received binary program.

More precisely, a *safety policy* is specified in advance by the consumer, and expresses the conditions under which the consumer considers the program execution to be safe. The safety policy is made of: safety rules specifying operations and their pre-conditions; and interface calling conventions describing post-conditions and invariants that the code must establish. It is expressed with first-order predicate logic. The code producer performs a verification that the code she intends to furnish respects the safety policy, and provides a *proof* of the successful verification, realised through theorem proving. On receipt of the code, the consumer *validates* the proof received along with the code, through proof checking.

2.3 Run-Time Verification

Run-time verification encompasses both the use of lightweight formal methods at run-time to complement traditional methods for proving programs correctness at design-time, and the use of formal techniques for dynamic program monitoring [16,17,32].

Dynamic monitoring usually consists in executing the program and checking whether it conforms to a requirement specification. The most popular languages for expressing such specifications are either temporal logics, or state machines. Among the different proposals made in this field, we can mention [4], who provide a specification method for expressing the semantics (not only the syntax) of components' interfaces. The program runs concurrently with its specification and deviations from the expected specified behaviour reveals incorrectness in the program. This technique is realised without any instrumentation of the program. The interesting point here is that the component's interface specification not only describes the signature but it specifies the component's behaviour. This technique uses executable specifications written with the Abstract State Machine Language (AsmL), and the COM infrastructure for monitoring the execution of a component and checking the behavioural equivalence of the component and the concurrently executing specification.

An interesting verification tool for the logic-based alternative is provided by [10] for Java programs. In this approach, the programmer specifies Linear-Time Temporal Logic (LTL) formulae directly in the code under the form of metadata annotations. These annotations are compiled into Java bytecode as attributes; they are thus available together with the program, and subsequently used by verification tools. Another runtime verification system for Java programs, the Java PathExplorer, requiring instrumentation of the code, is provided by [18]. This tool monitors Java programs execution traces by checking them against a provided requirement specification written with Maude, a specification and verification system allowing implementation of rewriting logic. The instrumentation of the code serves to insert additional bytecode that send relevant events to an observer. The observer, which may reside on another machine, actually checks the event trace against the provided specification.

The commercial tool Temporal Rover [14] allows to insert LTL temporal assertions into a Java program under the form of comments. The Temporal Rover tool generates a new program file where these assertions are implemented, so that the validation of the temporal properties is executed as part of the program.

In an attempt to provide a kind of unifying logic encompassing the different proposals, [5] propose the temporal finite trace monitoring logic EAGLE and its Java implementation.

2.4 Ontologies

An ontology for a given domain is a description of some *shared* concepts and relationships among these concepts. Ontology usually defines a set of keywords for expressing the concepts, and for expressing the relationships among them. However, expressivity of ontology may vary from very large vocabularies to complete formal theories [15].

Ontologies are currently used as an interoperability tool for knowledge management in business applications, for autonomous agents, and for semantic Web services.

Meta-Ontologies. Meta-ontologies are algebra allowing definition of type theories, operations, and axioms. From that perspective, category theory [19], higher-order logics that define terms, operators, axioms, and provable or checkable theorems are meta-ontologies.

2.5 Trust-Based Management Systems

Trust management systems deal with security policies, credentials and trust relationships (e.g., issuers of credentials). Most trust-based management systems combine higher-order logic with a proof brought by a requester that is checked at run-time. Those systems are essentially based on delegation, and serve to authenticate and give access control to a requester [34]. Usually the requester brings the proof that a trusted third entity asserts that it is trustable or it can be granted access. Those systems have been designed for static systems, where an untrusted client performs some access control request to some trusted server [2,6]. Similar systems for open distributed environment have also been realised, for instance [22] proposes a delegation logic including negative evidence, and delegation depth, as well as a proof of compliance for both parties involved in an interaction. The PolicyMaker system is a decentralised trust management systems [3] based on proof checking of credentials allowing entities to locally decide whether or not to accept credentials (without relying to a centralised certifying authority).

More recently, an operational model for trust-based access control in highly dynamic environment has been defined by [11]. Interacting parties maintain trust values about each other. These trust values are updated dynamically depending on positive or negative behaviour of the corresponding principal. This schema allows trust to *evolve* with time as a result of evidence, and allows to adapt the behaviour of principals consequently.

2.6   Smart Labels/Smart Tags

Smart tagging systems are already being deployed for carrying or disseminating data in the fields of healthcare, environment, and user's entertainment. For instance, in the framework of data dissemination among fixed nodes, [8] propose a delivery mechanism, based on the local exchange of data through smart tags carried by mobile users. Mobile users or mobile devices do not directly exchange smart-tags; they only disseminate data to fixed nodes when they are physically close to each other. Data information vehicled, by smart tags, is expressed as triples indicating the node being the source of the information, the information value, and a time indication corresponding to the information generation. Smart tags maintain, store, and update these information for all visited nodes. A Bluetooth implementation of these Smart Tags has been realised in the framework of a vending machine [7]. In smart tagging systems, data remain structurally simple, and understandable by human beings, and does not actually serve as a basis for autonomous local decisions.

2.7   Self-configuring Systems

In the field of self-configuring systems, [9] propose a model based on a service-oriented middleware able to perform dynamic binding of components (or services) based on behavioural specifications *and* on contextually non-functional requirements. The selection and binding of the component is performed at runtime and is based on the adequacy of its functional description to the user's requirements. Once a component is selected, the underlying infrastructure allocates the resources necessary for the component to execute, based on the component's non-functional requirements. Several components can be composed together (sequentially, conditionally, or in parallel) based on an execution sequence specified by the user under the form of a dependency graph.

The component's functional description is expressed in IOPE format: Input, Output, Pre-condition and Effects. Input and Output serve to describe the parameters types of the interface, while pre-condition and effects are similar to pre-condition and post-conditions of the Design by contract paradigm.

Self-configuration is obtained through adaptation to changing user's requirements and changing environmental/contextual information, which is realised thanks to the decoupling of code from those requirements and information.

This is an ongoing work: the formal language to express the IOPE information and the implementation of the middleware are under way.

2.8   Specification-Carrying Code

Specification-Carrying Software. The notion of specification-carrying software is being investigate since several years [31,1]. This idea has been proposed initially for software engineering concerns, essentially for ensuring correct composition of software and realising correct evolution of software. Algebraic specifications and categorical diagrams are used for expressing the functionality, while co-algebraic transition systems are used to define the operational behaviour of components.

The visions of this team include as well run-time generation of code from the specifications.

Alternatively, [30] propose a version where the behaviour of a component is not fully specified in all its operational details, but sufficiently in order to be used for correct self-assembly of software at run-time. Indeed, moving from the traditional use of formal methods for testing and debugging, this approach intends to replace traditional APIs with full formal specifications, understood and checked at run-time by the different components or services involved in a computation. The specification becomes the primary element and the basis for communication and interaction. This approach is currently supported by a service-oriented middleware architecture implemented in Java, supporting specifications written either as regular expressions or in Prolog. Components offering services publish their specification, while components requesting services submit specification requests. The middleware then checks services specifications with service requests and seamlessly binds the service provider and the service consumer.

This approach has been applied to run-time code evolution [30] and as a potential solution to autonomic computing [13].

2.9   B2B Interoperability

At a larger scale, the Web-Pilarcos middleware [21] allows independently developed business applications to interoperate. The business applications are grouped into what the authors call a "eCommunity" whose structure is defined by roles and interactions between the roles. A business application is assigned a given role if it fulfils the corresponding conformance rules. A Business Network Model (BNM) semantically describes the collaboration rules requested by each partner and defines the structure of the eCommunity. A eCommunity contract, expressed as an XML-schema, comprises the BNM as well as additional information related to the format of messages, functional and non-functional (trust, QoS, security) aspects of the different services. The Web-Pilarcos middleware supports eCommunities by providing discovery of services, eCommunity's contract management and monitoring. It checks interoperability of the different business applications, their adherence to the BNM, and maintains interoperability at the collaboration, semantic and technical levels. The Web-Pilarcos approach goes beyond traditional unified virtual enterprise systems for B2B, where all business applications have to share the same interoperability model.

2.10   Summary

We can see from the different paradigms and approaches discussed above, that the range of use of formal methods at run-time varies greatly. We will compare them from the point of view of dynamic interactions of components at run-time.

The use of design by contract at run-time is currently limited to exception handling. Both parties of the contract have to share it in advance. For trusted components, proof of properties are based on contracts, however they do not serve interoperability purposes.

Proof-Carrying code is useful for checking safety properties, agreed in advance. Usually these properties are low-level properties; they do not express functional or non-functional requirements. The code consumer needs to know the kind of program it receives. However, as advocated by [12], proofs are not the ultimate solution, since even if a proof has been positively checked, a component may nevertheless fail due to changing environmental conditions (particularly in highly volatile environment). Therefore, a more adaptable schema, as one based on evolving trust, can be more efficient.

Run-time verification is essentially meant for checking deviations of the program execution from its expected execution. In addition, dynamic monitoring of program usually reveals only errors (as traditional model checking) but cannot guarantee that the program is correct in all cases, but only in the particular traces that have been checked against the specification.

Moving from purely software engineering concerns to interacting components or agents, ontologies serve interoperability purposes. They are based on a common shared domain of concepts. They act as a powerful tool for independently developed software provided there is a common ontology.

At a more dynamic level, trust-based management systems allow the different interacting components to take security decisions based on the evolving trust values.

Self-configuring systems, specification-carrying code are attempts to replace traditional well-agreed (in advance) APIs with formal specifications understood at run-time by some middleware infrastructure. This avoids the need of having shared ontologies, or agreed contracts, thus allowing a high-degree of interaction among heterogeneously designed components.

Following the same ideas, but a larger level of granularity, B2B middleware for interoperable business applications, are addressing similar concerns: allowing interaction and run-time evolution of independently developed business applications.

As a summary, we can observe that there is a shift from pure software engineering concerns to new communication paradigms for distributed systems based on formal specifications. In addition, we can observe that in the above described approaches, the more the specification is decoupled from the code, the more they apply to coarse grain components, and the more they allow dynamic interactions among the components.

3   Potential Interest

The potential interest, we foresee of the use of formal specifications at run-time, resides essentially in the *semantic interoperability* and *adaptability* possibilities they offer for large scale systems made of autonomous independent components. The potentiality resides in the one hand on the run-time reasoning that can be performed on the specification, and on the other hand on the decoupling of concerns between the code and the specification information.

3.1 Semantic Interoperability

Formal specifications allow going far beyond interface descriptions or shared keywords or concepts. Ideally, they allow: run-time understanding of the functionality of the components they represent (useful for self-assembly of components), on-the-fly deduction of component's properties, as well as compositions of properties on which to base composition of components for obtaining new functionalities (useful for automating the composition of components).

Design by contract, and similarly proof-carrying code techniques, allow a limited form of semantic interoperability: pre- and post-conditions allow run-time checking of expected properties, but APIs must be shared among the different components. Run-time verification tools essentially serve dynamic monitoring purposes (i.e., checking deviations from a requirement's specification), and therefore have a limited utility for supporting dynamic interaction among unknown components.

Ontology-based systems provide a semantic interoperability based on the sharing of common concepts, essentially keywords. Smart-tags provide an infrastructure for disseminating and handling tags at run-time among autonomous components. The tag is the support for interactions, however the type of tags remains limited to numerical or textual values, and do not benefit yet from richer descriptions based on formal specifications.

The most advanced techniques for realising semantic interoperability are those based on service-oriented computing, such as self-configuring systems (Subsection 2.7), specification-carrying code or B2B interoperability techniques (Subsection 2.9). An underlying middleware handles the decoupling of functional and non-functional formal specifications from services codes; of roles description from business applications. The middleware seamlessly retrieves corresponding services and applications based on the specified descriptions.

3.2 Adaptability

In addition to functional adaptability, captured by the above notion of semantic interoperability, formal methods may prove useful for satisfying non-functional requirements at run-time, particularly for systems evolving in changing environments, and needing to constantly adapt themselves.

Dependability. Covering several issues, from exception handling, to resilience to unexpected environmental conditions, dependability can be dealt with formal specifications. Indeed, as already mentioned, the design by contract favours exception handling at the level of classes. At a coarser level of granularity, non-functional requirements such as QoS, constraints, CPU requirements expressed as formal specifications may serve to guide the component's execution in order to maintain the component's requirement level of functionality. In the techniques reviewed above, Design by Contract, proof-carrying code, and run-time verification techniques allow to detect violations of expected conditions or properties, and support exception handling. More advanced techniques, such as those based on service-oriented techniques provide resilience to unexpected environmental conditions.

Uncertainty. Independently designed and developed components necessarily interact with unknown software, and necessarily deal with uncertainty in both the peer components and their environment. Proof-carrying code techniques allow executing a code only if a proof of correctness has been furnished for well specified agreed properties. Trust-based systems help components in taking run-time decisions related to both peers' or executing environment's behaviour. Those decisions are based on observations and experience. Specification-carrying code supports interaction with unknown software based on formal specifications only, and not on agreed APIs.

Security Issues. In a world where a high number of components have to interact together, do not know each other in advance, cannot fully or durably rely on peers, hosts or servers, a dynamic trust-based management system allows entities to take decisions on the basis of recent, own or shared, experiences. Such a framework allows run-time and autonomous adaptation of entities to insecure situations.

Run-time Code Evolution. Software that cannot be stopped nevertheless needs to be updated. Service-oriented computing combined with formal specifications of component's requirements and functionality provide a powerful tool for offering a 24/7 service while performing code changes.

Run-time policies. Individual components or whole workflow processes may define run-time policies or protocols related to: security, mode of operation, constraints, etc. Decoupling policies from the code, and having the policies expressed as formal specifications allows reasoning about the policies, on-the-fly understanding and checking of those policies, and more importantly allows run-time modification of the policies. For instance, in eSociety applications, such as eGovernment services, software is submitted to laws changes. Any change in the law, affects the way services have to work. For large software as those we can find in public administration, changing the software code to be compliant with the new laws, while still offering the service to the citizens, may become an impossible task. However, if policies are specified independently of the underlying code which is simply assembled so as to adhere to the policy given a user's requirement, a change in the law turns out to be a change in the corresponding policy, without any modification of the code. Service-oriented computing techniques such as self-configuring systems, specification-carrying code or the Web-Pilarcos middleware are among the techniques that better support the application of run-time policies through the decoupling of code and specifications provided as a built-in feature.

4   Applications Domains

Application domains that most likely will benefit the most from approaches based on the use of formal specifications at run-time are those made of a large number of autonomous components or devices, evolving in dynamic environments, and under uncertainty conditions. Among the techniques described in this paper, service-oriented computing techniques directly support these requirements, since the different components are independently equipped with all the necessary information (described through a formal specification) to interact with unknown software.

4.1   Ambient Intelligence

Ambient intelligence scenarios envisage devices and software agents, running in devices, that organise themselves for the wellness of their respective users: software agents interoperate and share knowledge or experiences, they gather information (e.g., road traffic), they automatically pay amount of money from e-purses, they customise rooms lights and temperature, requests for references, or build user profiles.

These applications are supported by an unobtrusive and invisible technology, which is able to take decisions, and initiatives, make proposals to the user, and negotiate. In addition, in order to fully support human beings without overloading them with requests and information, the underlying technology (devices, and agents) needs advanced means of communication for: understanding each other, gather and share knowledge, information and experience among each other, ensure their own security (data integrity, confidentiality, authentication, access control), and resources management. In distributed and decentralised environments, as those in which ambient intelligence systems will evolve, interoperable policies are closely linked with authorisation policies, or resource management.

Entities evolving in ambient intelligence systems will need to deal with different kinds of information. They are autonomous and not always able to rely on a central control entity dictating its behaviour. Therefore they must be provided with means for *understanding* and *adapting* their behaviour to changing situations and environment. Such a technology needs an infrastructure enabling agents' mutual understanding, and knowledge sharing for handling interoperability, security support, and resource management. Formal specifications provide an interoperability basis for ambient intelligence systems founded on *semantic* information exchange.

4.2   Autonomic Computing

There is currently a growing interest in biologically inspired systems, not only from researchers but also from industry. Recent interest by IBM, as part of their *Autonomic Computing* [20] program, and by Microsoft, as part of the *Dynamic Systems Initiative*, indicates the importance of self-organisation and self-adaptation for managing distributed resources. Formal specifications provide solutions addressing *self-management of autonomic components*. Indeed, coupled with the corresponding infrastructure, they enhance *self-protection* by checking proofs of access control or interoperable compatibility, or to refuse or accept an interaction with a component that appears to be faulty or malicious. Based on a provided or collected user profile (expressed as a theory), components can *self-configure* to customise their appearance or behaviour to the user.

Self-optimisation and *self-healing* are made possible by observation, experiences, and recommendations that allow, for instance, components to optimise the use of a pool of printers, or to alert users that faulty printers should be restarted, or refilled with paper or toner.

4.3 Services

On the one hand Web services represent a first step towards software services composition through the Web. On the other hand, efforts towards automating Web tasks have lead to the Semantic Web research works. Combined together, Semantic Web services are under investigation for allowing automating service composition on the Internet. Current Semantic Web services architectures rely on ontology for realising these automation tasks and on specific repositories. Replacing ontologies with more powerful formal specifications could allow any individual user to publish its own service on the Web (described through the specification) in a similar way as today Web pages are published, and any other system or user to use it (maybe anonymously) on the basis of required properties matching the ones of the published service. This would give rise to what could be called "Google-like" services, where instead of searching data, the user or the underlying software system searches for a particular service on the Web through a "Google-like" service browser.

5 Issues

We have identified the following issues related to the use of formal specifications at run-time.

Content. Functional description encompasses interfaces, signatures, contracts, operational behaviour. Non-functional descriptions encompass a larger range of information from QoS to constraints, to policies, to protocols, etc. The richer the information, the more powerful interactions can be envisaged, but the more power consuming the computation becomes.

Languages. From the above described approaches, we can observe that languages for expressing the information vary from simple keywords, to more structured ontologies, to algebraic specification, to different kinds of logics (temporal logics, descriptive logics, higher-order logics, etc.), and even to category theory. Here again the more expressive the language, the more powerful the management of the specifications can be, but the more difficult the corresponding automated tools are. In addition, there is no consensus yet or any emerging formal specification language allowing powerful reasoning with a reasonable need for specification processing power.

Specification Checker/Theorem Proving. In addition to the language for expressing the specification, it is necessary to have run-time efficient tools for processing them, either specification checkers or theorem provers.

Run-Time Infrastructure. Finally, it is necessary to define a run-time infrastructure supporting both the processing of formal specifications and the corresponding code execution. From the above described approaches, solutions seem to come from service-oriented architectures allowing varying degree of granularity for components (from classes to business applications), as well as a decoupled processing of the corresponding specifications (functional descriptions, policies, protocols, etc).

6   Advantages/Drawbacks

Formal specifications and automated reasoning solve interoperability problems: there is no need for compatible interfaces or exact declarations and queries. Specifications may express as well non-functional properties, (re)configuration policies, and interaction protocols allow tackling issues related to dynamic large scale systems such as adaptability to uncertain environments.

Formal specifications at run-time provide several advantages for run-time execution of decentralised autonomous software in general, for ambient intelligence scenarios and for autonomic computing systems. Among them we can cite interaction and interoperability with unknown entities, seamless integration of new entities and functionalities, possible combination of services, robustness against errors or failures.

However, there is a need for additional mechanisms and automated tools for checking the adequacy of a code with its published specification, for discovering errors, and propagating information about erroneous code, for correlating information and detecting malicious attacks.

In addition, the use of formal methods at run-time is currently slowed down because the tools (specification checkers or theorem provers) for dealing with formal methods are not efficient enough for a run-time computation of a program, or not enough automated (they still need human assistance). However, research in this field is advancing and we can foresee some advances in the use of formal methods at run-time.

7   Conclusion

This paper has reviewed different works from different domains and driven by different concerns, but with a common "conviction" that formal specification can be helpful if used at run-time: for designing correct software, for guiding executable software, for composing services and middleware services, as a powerful tool for autonomic computing, etc. Focus has been given on interactions among independently developed autonomous components. Current service-oriented computing techniques based on a middleware supporting a decoupling of code from specifications, describing functional, non-functional, or contextual information, seem the more promising for realising future efficient systems. As advocated as well by [33] in the context of middleware services, formal semantics and reasoning will most likely be the key to ensure the interactive management of resources and services, of large-scale interactive systems, all systems that are naturally exposed to dynamic changing conditions.

The different attempts at using specifications at run-time described in this paper show an increased interest in this field from different communities. This area of research is rather young; consequently there is currently no satisfying efficient solution. Tools dealing with formal specifications are becoming more powerful; this lets presuppose that the efficient processing of formal specifications at run-time will soon become possible.

Acknowledgements

This work is supported by Swiss NSF grant 200020-105476/1.

References

1. M. Anlauff, D. Pavlovic, and D. R. Smith. Composition and refinement of evolving specifications. In *Proceedings of Workshop on Evolutionary Formal Software Development*, 2002.
2. A. W. Appel and E. W. Felten. Proof-carrying authentication. In *6th ACM Conference on Computer and Communications Security*, 1999.
3. M. Balze, J. Feigenbaum, and J. Lacy. Decentralized trust management. In *IEEE Conference on Security and Privacy*, 1996.
4. M. Barnett and W. Schulte. Spying on components: A runtime verification technique. In *Workshop on Specification and Verification of Component-Based Systems*, 2001.
5. H. Barringer, A. Goldberg, K. Havelund, , and K. Sen. Rule-based runtime verification. In B. Steffen and G. Levi, editors, *Verification, Model Checking, and Abstract Interpretation: 5th International Conference, VMCAI 2004*, volume 2937 of *LNCS*, pages 44–57. Springer-Verlag, 2004.
6. L. Bauer, M. A. Schneider, and E. W. Felten. A proof-carrying authorization system. Technical Report TR-638-01, Princeton University Computer Science, 2001.
7. A. Beaufour. Using Bluetooth-based Smart-Tags for Data Dissemination. In *Pervasive Computing 2002*, 2002.
8. A. Beaufour, M. Leopold, and P. Bonnet. Smart-tag based data dissemination. In *ACM International Workshop on Wireless Sensor Networks and Applications (WSNA'02)*, 2002.
9. U. Bellur and N. Narendra. Towards a Programming Model and Middleware Architecture for Self-Configuring Systems. In *The First International Conference on Communication Systems Software and Middleware*, 2006.
10. E. Bodden. A Lightweight LTL Runtime Verification Tool for Java. In J. Vlissides and D. Schmidt, editors, *OOPSLA Companion*, pages 306–307, 2004.
11. V. Cahill and al. Using trust for secure collaboration in uncertain environments. *IEEE Pervasive Computing Magazine, special issue Dealing with Uncertainty*, 2(3):52–61, 2003.
12. G. Di Marzo Serugendo and M. Deriaz. A social semantic infrastructure for decentralised systems based on specification-carrying code and trust. In D. Hales and B. Edmonds, editors, *Socially-Inspired Computing*, 2005.
13. G. Di Marzo Serugendo and M. Deriaz. Specification-Carrying Code for Self-Managed Systems. In *International Workshop on Self-Managed Systems & Services*, 2005.

14. D. Drusinsky. The Temporal Rover and the ATG Rover. In *SPIN Model Checking and Software Verification*, volume 1885 of *LNCS*, pages 323–330. Springer-Verlag, 2000.
15. D. Fensel. *Ontologies: A Silver Bullet for Knowledge Management and Electronic Commerce*. Springer, 1998.
16. K. Havelund and G. Rosu, editors. *Proceedings of The Run-Time Verification Workshop (RV'01)*. Electronic Notes in Theoretical Computer Science 55 (2). Elsevier Science B. V., 2001.
17. K. Havelund and G. Rosu, editors. *Proceedings of The Run-Time Verification Workshop (RV'02)*. Electronic Notes in Theoretical Computer Science 70(4). Elsevier Science B. V., 2002.
18. K. Havelund and G. Rosu. An overview of the runtime verification tool java pathexplorer. *Formal Methods in System Design*, 24(2):189–215, 2004.
19. M. Johnson and C. N. G. Dampney. On Category Theory as a (meta) Ontology for Information Systems Research. In *International Conference On Formal Ontology In Information Systems (FOIS'01)*, 2001.
20. J. O. Kephart and D. M. Chess. The Vision of Autonomic Computing. *Computer*, 36(1):41–50, January 2003.
21. L. Kutvonen, T. Ruokolainen, J. Metso, and J. Haataja. Interoperability middleware for federated enterprise applications in Web-Pilarcos. In D. Konstantas, J.-P. Bourrires, M. Lonard, and N. Boudjlida, editors, *Interoperability of Enterprise Software and Applications*, pages 185–196, 2005.
22. N. Li, J. Feigenbaum, and B. N. Grosof. A logic-based knowledge representation for authorization with delegation. In *12th IEEE Computer Security Foundations Workshop*, 1999.
23. B. Meyer. *Eiffel: The Language*. Prentice Hall, 1991.
24. B. Meyer. Applying "Design by Contract". *IEEE Computer*, 25(10):40–51, 1992.
25. B. Meyer. *Object-Oriented Software Construction*. Prentice Hall, second edition, 1997.
26. B. Meyer. The grand challenge of trusted components. In *ICSE*, pages 660–667. IEEE, 2003.
27. B. Meyer, C. Mingins, and H. Schmidt. Providing trusted components to the industry. *IEEE Computer*, 31(5):104–105, 1998.
28. G. Necula. Proof-carrying code. In *The 24th ACM SIGPLAN-SIGACT Symposium on Principles of Programming Languages (POPL'97)*, pages 106–119, 1997.
29. G. Necula and P. Lee. Proof-carrying code. Technical Report CMU-CS-96-165, School of Computer Science, Carnegie Mellon University, September 1996.
30. M. Oriol and G. Di Marzo Serugendo. A disconnected service architecture for unanticipated run-time evolution of code. *IEE Proceedings-Software, Special Issue on Unanticipated Software Evolution*, 2004.
31. D. Pavlovic. Towards semantics of self-adaptive software. In *Self-Adaptive Software: First International Workshop*, volume 1936 of *LNCS*, pages 50–65. Springer-Verlag, 2000.
32. O. Sokolsky and M. Viswanathan, editors. *Proceedings of The Run-Time Verification Workshop (RV'03)*. Electronic Notes in Theoretical Computer Science 89 (2). Elsevier Science B. V., 2003.
33. N. Venkatasubramanian. Safe "Composability" of Middleware Services. *Communications of the ACM*, 45(6):49–52, June 2002.
34. S. Weeks. Understanding trust management systems. In *2001 IEEE Symposium on Security and Privacy*, 2001.

Adaptive Replication of Large-Scale Multi-agent Systems – Towards a Fault-Tolerant Multi-agent Platform

Zahia Guessoum[1,2], Nora Faci[2], and Jean-Pierre Briot[1]

[1] LIP6, Université Pierre et Marie Curie (Paris 6),
8 rue du Capitaine Scott, 75015 Paris, France
Zahia.Guessoum@lip6.fr, Jean-Pierre.Briot@lip6.fr
[2] MODECO-CReSTIC - IUT de Reims,
51687 Reims Cedex 2, France
faci@leri.univ-reims.fr

Abstract. In order to construct and deploy large-scale multi-agent systems, we must address one of the fundamental issues of distributed systems, the possibility of partial failures. This means that fault-tolerance is an inevitable issue for large-scale multi-agent systems. In this paper, we discuss the issues and propose an approach for supporting fault-tolerance of multi-agent systems. The starting idea is the application of replication strategies to agents, the most critical agents being replicated to prevent failures. As criticality of agents may evolve during the course of computation and problem solving, and as resources are bounded, we need to dynamically and automatically adapt the number of replicas of agents, in order to maximize their reliability and availability. We will describe our approach and related mechanisms for evaluating the criticality of a given agent (based on application-level semantic information, e.g. interdependences, and also system-level statistical information, e.g., communication load) and for deciding what strategy to apply (e.g., active or passive replication) and how to parameterize it (e.g., number of replicas). We also will report on experiments conducted with our prototype architecture (named DimaX).

1 Introduction

The possibility of partial failures is a fundamental characteristic of distributed applications. The fault-tolerance research community has developed solutions (algorithms and architectures), mostly based on the concept of replication, and notably applied to data bases. But, these techniques are almost always applied explicitly and statically, at design time. In such approaches, this is the responsibility of the designer of the application to identify explicitly which critical servers should be made robust and also to decide which strategies (active or passive replication...) and their configurations (how many replicas, their placement...).

A. Garcia et al. (Eds.): SELMAS 2005, LNCS 3914, pp. 238–253, 2006.

New cooperative applications, e.g., air traffic control, cooperative work, and e-commerce, are much more dynamic and large scale. Such cooperative applications are now increasingly designed as a set of autonomous and interactive entities, named agents, that interact and coordinate (multi-agent system). In such applications, the roles and relative importance of the agents can greatly vary during the course of computation, of interaction and of cooperation, the agents being able to change roles, strategies. Also, new agents may also join or leave the application (open system). It is thus very difficult, or even impossible, to identify in advance the most critical software components of the application. Furthermore, criticality can vary over run time.

In addition, such applications may be large scale. And the fact that the underlying distributed system is large scale makes it unstable by nature, at least in currently deployed technologies. This increases the needs for mechanisms for adaptive fiabilisation (improving robustness) of the application.

Our approach is consequently to give the capacity to the multi-agent system itself to dynamically identify the most critical agents and to decide which fiabilisation strategies to apply to them. This is analog to load balancing but for fiabilisation. In other words, we would like to **automatically** and **dynamically** apply fiabilisation (mostly through replication mechanisms) **where** (to which agents) and **when** they are most needed. To guide the adaptive fiabilisation, we intend to use various levels of information, system level, like communication load, and application/agent level, like roles or plans.

This paper is organized as follows: Section 2 presents the related work and Section 3 introduces our multi-agent monitoring architecture. Sections 4 and 5 introduce a dynamic and adaptive control mechanism of replication. Section 6 presents the DimaX platform that we developed to implement this solution and the realized experiments.

2   Related Work

Several approaches address the multi-faced problem of fault tolerance in multi-agent systems. These approaches can be classified in two main categories: corrective (e.g., [10],[5]) and preventive (e.g., [12],[11],[14]). The preventive approach deals with the ability to continue to deliver services when faults occur. In the corrective approach, the process consists of fault diagnostic and repair. Moreover, several works address the difficulties of making reliable mobile agents, that are more exposed to security problems [1] such as intrusion detection. This category is beyond the scope of this paper.

Kaminka et al. [12] introduce a monitoring approach in order to detect and recover faults. They use models of relations between mental states of agents. They adopt a procedural plan-recognition based approach to identify the inconsistencies. However, the adaptation is only structural, the relation models may change but the contents of plans are static. Their main hypothesis is that any failure comes from incompleteness of beliefs. This monitoring approach relies on agent knowledge. The design of such multi-agent systems is very complex. Moreover, the agent behavior cannot be adaptive and the system cannot be open.

Horling et al. [11] present a distributed system of diagnosis. The faults can directly or indirectly be observed in the form of symptoms by using a fault model. The diagnosis process modifies the relations between tasks, in order to avoid inefficiencies. The adaptation is only structural because they do not consider the internal structure of tasks. The different diagnosis subsystems perform local updates on the task model. However, performance is optimized locally but not globally.

The work of Malone et al. [14] on coordination relies on a characterization of the dependencies between activities in terms of goals and resources. These dependencies represent situations of conflict, and the different coordination mechanisms represent the solutions to manage them. The main contribution of this approach is the proposed taxonomy of these dependencies. The authors offer a framework of coordination study, that provides the basic stone to build a monitoring approach. However, this monitoring approach has not yet been developed. This work has been reused by Klein et al. [16] to detect exceptions in multi-agent systems.

These corrective approaches present useful solutions to the problem of monitoring in multi-agent systems. However, the monitoring component is often centralized and its design relies on the agents' knowledge [19].

The fault-tolerance research community has developed preventive solutions (algorithms and architectures), mostly based on the concept of replication, and notably applied to data bases. Replication of data and/or computation is thus an effective way to achieve fault tolerance in distributed systems. A replicated software component is defined as a software component that possesses a representation on two or more hosts [6].

Many toolkits (e.g., [6] and [18]) include replication facilities to build reliable applications. However, most of them are not quite suitable for implementing large-scale, adaptive replication mechanisms. For example, although the strategy can be modified in the course of the computation, no indication is given as to which new strategy ought to be applied; moreover, such a change must have been devised by the application developer before runtime. Besides, as each group structure is left to be designed by the user, the task of designing a large-scale software appears tremendously complex.

S. Hagg introduces sentinels to protect the agents from some undesirable states [10]. Sentinels represent the control structure of a multi-agent system. They need to build models of each agent and monitor communications in order to react to faults. Each sentinel is associated by the designer to one functionality of the multi-agent system. This sentinel handles the different agents that interact to achieve the functionality. The analysis of its beliefs on the other agents enables the sentinel to detect a fault when it occurs. Adding sentinels to multi-agent systems seems to be a good approach. However the sentinels themselves represent failure points for the multi-agent system. Moreover, the problem solving agents themselves participate in the fault-tolerance process.

A. Fedoruk and R. Deters [5] propose to use proxies to make transparent the use of agent replication, i.e. enabling the replicas of an agent to act as a same entity regarding the other agents. The proxy manages the state of the replicas. All the external and internal communications of the group are redirected to the proxy. However this increases the workload of the proxy, which is a quasi central entity. To make it reliable, they propose to build a hierarchy of proxies for each group of replicas. They point out the specific problems of read/write consistency, resource locking also discussed in [23]. This approach lacks flexibility and reusability in particular concerning the replication control. The experiments have been done with FIPA-OS, which does not provide any replication mechanism. The replication is therefore realized by the designer before run time.

The work by Kraus et al. [13] proposes a solution for deciding allocation of extra resources (replicas) for agents. They proceed by reformulating the problem in two successive operational research problems (knapsack and then bin packing). Their approach and results are very interesting but they are based on too many restrictive hypothesis to be made adaptive.

In the next section, we will introduce our monitoring multi-agent architecture, which allows to control automatically and dynamically the agent replication.

3   Monitoring Multi-agent Architecture

The deployment of large-scale multi-agent systems that must operate continuously faces several problems:

- the existing multi-agent architectures are often not well scalable [2],
- failures affect often a subset of the agents,
- the environment is often dynamic and the number of resources is limited.

One of the prime motivation behind the proposed monitoring multi-agent architecture is to improve the robustness of large-scale distributed multi-agent systems in dynamic environments and with limited number of resources. Monitoring consists thus in acquiring necessary information to dynamically and automatically apply replication to agents when it is most needed. This information may be based on standard measurements (communication load, processing time...) or multi-agent characteristics such as the roles of agents [8] or their interdependences.

3.1   Interdependence Graph

In a multi-agent system, each agent is defined as an autonomous entity. However, the agents do not always have all the required competencies or resources and thus depend on other agents to provide them. Interdependence graphs [3] [21] [22] were introduced to describe the interdependences of these agents. These graphs are defined by the designer before the execution of the multi-agent system. However, complex multi-agent systems are characterized by emergent structures [20], that thus cannot be statically defined by the designer.

In our architecture, a multi-agent system is therefore represented by a graph that reflects an emergent organizational structure. This structure can be interpreted to define each agent criticality.

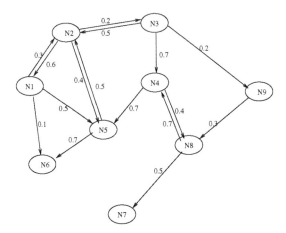

Fig. 1. Example of interdependence graph

For each domain agent[1], we associate a node. The set of nodes (see Figure 1), named interdependence graph, is represented by a labelled oriented graph (N, L, W). N is the set of nodes of the graph, L is the set of arcs and W the set of labels.

$$N = \{N_i\}_{i=1,n} \tag{1}$$

$$L = \{L_{i,j}\}_{i=1,n,j=1,n} \tag{2}$$

$$W = \{W_{i,j}\}_{i=1,n,j=1,n} \tag{3}$$

$L_{i,j}$ is the link between the nodes N_i and N_j and $W_{i,j}$ is a real number that labels $L_{i,j}$. $W_{i,j}$ reflects the importance of the interdependence between the associated agents ($Agent_i$ and $Agent_j$).

A node is thus related to a set of other nodes that may include all the nodes of a system. This set is not static: it can be modified when a new domain agent is added, or when an agent disappears, or when an agent starts interacting with another agent.

Our hypothesis is that the criticality of an agent relies on the interdependences of other agents on this agent. So, the agent $Agent_i$ is critical if the weights $wji_{j=1,n}$ are important. In this case, the failure of $Agent_i$ may be propagated to the agent $Agent_j$. It thus affects a subset of agents that form a connex component in the interdependence graph.

The interdependence graph is initialized by the designer. It is then dynamically adapted by the system itself. The proposed adaptation algorithms of the interdependence graph are described in Section 4. These adaptation algorithms are used by the monitoring agents that are described in the following section.

---

[1] In the following, we will name *domain agents*, agents from the application domain. In the following section, we will introduce other types of agents, named *monitoring agents*, to monitor them.

3.2   Multi-agent Architecture

In most existing multi-agent architectures, a monitoring mechanism is centralized. The acquired information is typically used off-line to explain and to improve
the system's behavior. Moreover, the considered application domains typically
only involve a small number of agents and *a priori* well-known organizational
structures.

These centralized monitoring architectures are not suited for large-scale and
complex systems where the observed information needs to be analyzed in real-
time to adapt the multi-agent system to the evolution of its environment.

We thus propose to distribute the observation mechanism to improve its
efficiency and robustness. This distributed mechanism relies on a reactive-agent
organization. These agents have several roles:

- Observe the domain agents and their interactions,
- Build global information,
- Update the interdependence graph,
- Use the interdependence to define the agent criticality,
- Use the agent criticality to manage the resources.

These roles are assigned to two kinds of agents: domain agent monitors (named
agent-monitors) and host-monitors (named host-monitors). An agent-monitor is
associated to each domain agent and a host-monitor is associated to each host
(see Figure 2).

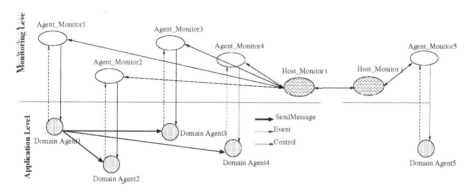

Fig. 2. Multi-agent architecture, domain agents are the agents of the application

An agent-monitor is thus associated to each agent of the application (named
domain agent) and a host-monitor is associated to each host. These monitoring
agents (agent-monitors and host-monitors) are hierarchically organized. Each
agent-monitor communicates only with one host-monitor. Host-monitors exchange their local information to build global information (global number of
messages, global exchanged quantity of information, ...).

After each interval of time Δt, the host-monitor sends the collected events and data to the corresponding agent-monitors. An agent-monitor has then the following behavior (see algorithm 1):

Algorithm 1. Agent-Monitor Behavior

1: Read the messages received from the host-monitor,
2: Update the local data and interdependences,
3: Compute the domain-agent criticality,
4: Determine the number of its replicas,
5: Inform the associated host-monitor of local changes that are important.

When the criticality of the domain agent is significantly modified, the agent-monitor notifies its host-monitor. The latter informs the other host-monitors to update global information. In turn, agent-monitors are informed by their host-monitors when global information changes significantly. Algorithm 2 describes the behavior of host-monitors.

Algorithm 2. Host-Monitor Behavior

1: Read messages received from the agent-monitors,
2: Update local statistics that define aggregation of the host-monitors parameters,
3: Send the new parameters to the agent monitors of the local host,
4: Send to the other host monitors the observed parameters that have significantly changed.

---

4   Adaptation Algorithms

Several parameters may be used to define the interdependences between agents such as communication load, executed tasks, roles of agents or their goals. An adaptation algorithm gives an outline of the adaptation mechanism of the interdependence graph. This adaptation relies on local information (communication load, cpu time ...) and on global information, which is defined as an aggregation of the local information of the various agents and hosts. The adaptation algorithm is thus used by each agent-monitor to manage the associated node of the interdependence graph (see Section 3.1).

Let us consider an interval of time Δt. The agent-monitors are activated each Δt. At each step, an agent-monitor executes an adaptation algorithm (see the two following subsections). However, the domain agents act continuously according to their goals and the evolution of their environment.

These algorithms are automatically used by each agent-monitor to update its interdependences with the set of agents. This set includes agents that communicate with it. Our hypothesis is that if an $Agent_i$ does not communicate with $Agent_j$ then then $Agent_i$ does not depend on $Agent_j$.

In this section, we propose two algorithms to compute the interdependence between two agents. The first one considers only the number of messages exchanged by agents and the second one deals with speech acts (performatives).

The first algorithm (see Algorithm 3) relies on the global number of sent messages $NbM(\Delta t)$, which is calculated by the host-monitor as follows:

$$NbM(\Delta t) = \sum_{i=1,n} \sum_{j=1,n \ i \neq j} NbM_{i,j}(\Delta t) \tag{4}$$

where $NbM_{i,j}(\Delta t)$ is the number of messages received by $agent_i$ from $agent_j$ during the interval of time Δt.

Algorithm 3. Basic adaptation of the interdependences

1: **for** each j different of i **do**
2:     Update the weights by using the following rule:

$$W_{i,j}(t + \Delta t) = W_{i,j}(t) + NbM_{i,j}(\Delta t)/NbM(\Delta t) \tag{5}$$

3: **end for**

Algorithm 3 is very simple, thus the cost of monitoring is very low. Consequently, it is useful for applications where the semantics of messages is not required. However, several applications rely on semantics of messages. So, we propose a new algorithm that deals with performatives. This algorithm is described in the following section.

The second algorithm (see Algorithm 4) relies on the semantics proposed by FIPA and the influence of the reception of a message on the receiver. Based on the work of Colombetti and Verdicchio [4], we propose the following six classes of performatives:

- class 1 =request, request-whenever, query-if, query-ref, subscribe
- class 2 = inform, inform-done, inform-ref
- class 3 = cfp, propose
- class 4 = reject-proposal, refuse, cancel
- class 5 = accept-proposal, agree
- class 6 = not-understood, failure.

To represent the influence of a message on its receiver, we use a graduation of the interval of possible variations $[0, 1]$, where:

- 0 corresponds to no influence,
- 1 corresponds to the maximum influence.

Table 1. Symbolic values of the six classes

Classes	Symbolic Value
classes 4, 6	Low
classes 2, 3, 5	medium
class 1	high

We propose then to represent influences by symbolic values such as *low, medium, high,* that correspond respectively to the intervals: $[0, 0.35],]0.30, 0.65]$ and $]0.60, 1]$. The average value of each symbolic value is the median of its interval. It is used to define the weight of a message.

Table 1 gives the symbolic values of the six classes.

Let us consider:

- ΔW: an aggregation of the variations of $W_{i,j}$, as defined below:

$$\Delta W(t) = \sum_{i=1,n} \sum_{j=1,n \; i \neq j} \Delta W_{i,j}(\Delta t) \tag{6}$$

- $S_{i,j}$: the set of messages received by $Agent_i$ from $Agent_j$.

The weight of a message is defined by the median of the interval corresponding to the fuzzy value of its performative.

Algorithm 4. Performative-based adaptation of the interdependences

---

1: **for** each j different from i **do**
2:     Update $W_{i,j}$ by using the following rule:

$$W_{i,j}(t + \Delta t) = W_{i,j}(t) + \sum_{m \in S_{i,j}} weight(m)/\Delta W(t) \tag{7}$$

3: **end for**

Algorithm 4 cost seems higher than that of the first Algorithm 3. However, the semantics of messages is very useful when dealing with interdependences in some application domains such as e-commerce.

5   Agent Criticality

The analysis of events and measures (system data and interaction events) provides two kinds of information: the interdependence and the degree of activity of each agent. To evaluate the degree of the agent activity, we use system data that are collected at the system level. We are considering two kinds of measures: CPU time and communication load. We are currently evaluating the significance of these measures as indicators of agent activity, to be useful to estimate agent criticality.

For an agent $Agent_i$ and a given time interval Δt, these measures provide:

- The used time of CPU (cp_i),
- The communication load (cl_i).

cp_i and cl_i may be then used to measure the agent degree of activity aw_i as follows:

$$aw_i(t) = (d_1 * cp_i/\Delta t + d_2 * cl_i/CL)/(d_1 + d_2) \tag{8}$$

where:

- CL is the global communication load,
- d_1 and d_2 are weights introduced by the user.

The estimation of the criticality of the agent $Agent_i$ is computed as follows:

$$w_i(t) = (a_1 * aggregation(W_{ij,j=1,m}) + a_2 * aw_i(t))/(a1 + a2) \qquad (9)$$

Where a_1 and a_2 are the weights given to the two kinds of parameters (interdependences and degree of activity). They are introduced by the designer.

Note that in our experiment (see Section 6), we do not consider the activity. So, $a_1 = 1$ and $a_2 = 0$.

For each Agent A_i, its estimated criticality w_i is used to compute the number of its replicas and decide where to replicate the agents (see our SELMAS'2005 paper [9] for the resources management problem).

6   Implementation and Experiments

This section gives an overview of the realized platform (named DimaX) that implements our adaptive replication mechanism. It then describes the example that we use for the experiments and give some results.

6.1   Overview of DimaX

DIMA [7] and DarX [15] [2] have been integrated to build a fault-tolerant multi-agent platform (named DimaX). DimaX provides multi-agent systems with several services such as distribution, replication, and naming service [15]. In order to benefit from fault tolerance mechanisms, the agent behavior is wrapped in a task of the DarX framework (see Figure 3). Moreover, for a dynamic control of replication, the monitoring architecture has been introduced. Figure 3 gives an overview of DimaX.

We consider a distributed system consisting of a finite set of agents $Ai = \{A_1, A_2, \ldots, A_n\}$ that are spread through a network. These agents communicate only by sending and receiving messages.

DarX provides global naming. Each agent has a global name that is independent of the current location of its replicas. The underlying system allows to handle the agent's execution and communication.

The failure of a machine or a connection often involves the failure of the associated DarX server. However, in our solution the fault tolerance protocols are agent-dependent, and not place-dependent, i.e. the mechanisms built for providing the continuity of the computation are integrated in the replication groups, and not in the servers. For instance, the monitoring agents are built as active components associated to the domain agents.

Moreover, DarX provides a fault-detection mechanism. A machine crash - server failure[2] - is handled in three steps within every replication group:

---

[2] In this work, we consider fail-silent (crash) model of faults.

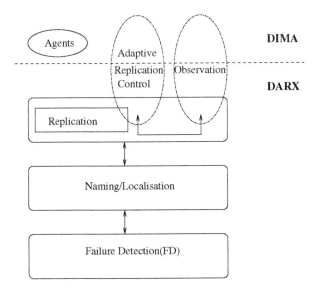

Fig. 3. Overview of DimaX

- detection of an eventual failure within the group,
- evaluation of the context: new criticality, leader failure, ...
- recovery: If the missing replica was the group leader, a new one is elected and an agent monitor is automatically activated. In the other case, it depends on the evaluation; a new follower/backup may or may not be instantiated.

Obviously, if a leader without any follower/backup fails, then it is not recovered. This derives from the original assumptions we made: the criticality of an agent evolves during the computation, and there are phases when an agent do not need to be fault-tolerant [15].

To validate DimaX, we realized several series of experiments. The first series evaluates the performances of the proposed multi-agent architecture and the proposed adaptation algorithms. The second one evaluates the robustness of the multi-agent systems that are based on the proposed monitoring architecture.

The following sections describe our example and the experiments.

Note: The experiments presented in this section were carried out on twenty machines with Intel(R) Pentium(R) 4 CPU at 2 GHz and 526 Mb of RAM.

6.2   Example

In our experiments, we consider the example of a distributed multi-agent system that helps at scheduling meetings. Each user has a personal assistant agent that manages his/her calendar. This agent interacts with:

- the user to receive his meeting requests and associated information (a title, a description, possible dates, participants, priority, etc.),
- the other agents of the system to schedule a meeting.

If the assistant agent of one important participant (initiator or prime participant) in a meeting fails (e.g., its machine crashes), this may disorganize the whole process. As the application is very dynamic - new meeting negotiations start and finish dynamically and simultaneously - decision for replication should be done automatically and dynamically.

6.3   Performances

The proposed monitoring multi-agent architecture is very useful to implement the proposed adaptive replication mechanism. However, the monitoring cost does not seem insignificant. So, our first series of experiments measures the monitoring cost in the proposed architecture. We consider, a multi-agent system with n distributed agents that execute the same scenario (a fixed set of meetings to schedule). We realized several experiments with various number of agents. For each n (100, 150, ..., 300), we considered m meetings (20, 40, ..., 80) and we realized two kinds of measures (with and without monitoring). We used 20 machines for each experiment and we repeated each experiment 10 times. We considered three cases: 1) a multi-agent system without monitoring, 2) a multi-agent system with monitoring based on *Algorithm 1*, and 3) a multi-agent system with monitoring based on *Algorithm 2*.

Figure 4 shows the average global execution time for these three different monitoring solutions. We found that monitoring cost is almost a constant function. The monitoring activity does not increase when the number of agents (domain agents and associated monitoring agents) increase. That can be explained by the proposed optimization within the multi-agent architecture, such as the hierarchical organization of monitoring agents and the communication between the agent-monitors

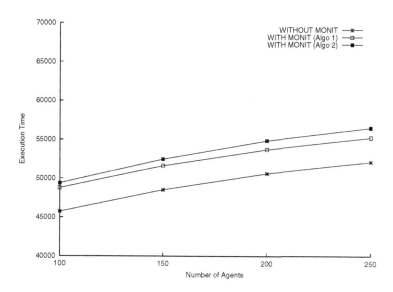

Fig. 4. Fault-Tolerant Multi-Agent Systems Costs

Table 2. Monitoring Cost and Comparison of the two Algorithms

Number of Agens	Monitoring Cost of Algorithm 1	Monitoring Cost of Algorithm 2	Difference
100	3025	3635	610
150	3094	3945	851
200	3089	4227	1138
250	3130	4387	1257

and host-monitors. These agents are organized hierarchically. For instance, to build the global information (global communication load ...), the host-monitors communicate only if the local information changes. Moreover, the host-monitors exchange local information only when there is an important change. Therefore, the number of communications between these agents is optimized.

6.4   Robustness

For this second series of experiments, we use a failure simulator. This simulator chooses randomly an agent and stops its thread. If the killed agent is critical then the multi-agent application fails. We considered a multi-agent system with 200 agents distributed on 10 machines. We run each experiment 10 minutes and we introduce 100 faults. We repeated several times the experiment with a variable number of extra resources Rm. Here, Rm defines the number of extra replicas that can be used by the whole multi-agent system. This experiment measures the rate of succeeded simulations SR, which is defined as follows:

$$SR = \frac{NSS}{TNS} \tag{10}$$

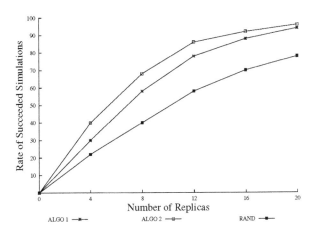

Fig. 5. Rate of succeeded simulations for each number of replicas with the two Algorithms

where NSS is the number of simulations that did not fail and TNS is the total number of simulations. Let us remind that a simulation fails when the fault simulator stops a critical agent that has not been replicated.

We considered three cases: 1) the replication is random, 2) the replication is based on algorithm 1 and 3) the replication is based on algorithm 2.

Figure 5 shows the success rate SR as a function of the number of extra replicas. It compares the two algorithms. It shows that algorithm 2 gives the best results for the considered application. Meanwhile the two algorithms require a number of extra resources that is at least equal to the number of critical agents.

Moreover Figure 5 compares the two algorithms with a random replication. In this case the agents criticality is defined randomly. We thus show that our algorithms for adaptive replication are more accurate than random replication.

6.5 Discussion

In the example, the monitoring cost of the second algorithm is more important than the cost of the first one. The difference corresponds to the cost of the message analysis. However, multi-agent systems using the second algorithm are more robust. Indeed, in our application the content of messages is important. This is not the case for some application domains such as network management where all the messages have the same weight. In this kind of application it is recommended to use the first algorithm to reduce the monitoring cost.

It is thus useful to study classes of application domains for each algorithm. The results of this study can be then used to help the designer to choose the most suited algorithm for his/her application.

7   Conclusion

This paper presented a new approach to make large-scale multi-agent systems reliable. This approach is based on the concepts of interdependence, where an agent criticality is estimated through its interdependences with other agents. The agent criticality is then used to replicate agents in order to maximize their reliability and availability based on available resources and their costs.

We thus proposed a generic architecture to extend an already built where an agent criticality is estimated through its interdependences multi-agent system with a basic adaptation mechanism to dynamically and automatically update the replication strategy. To make concrete this architecture, we have implemented a fault-tolerant multi-agent platform (named DimaX). DimaX is the result of an integration of the DIMA multi-agent platform [7] and the DarX replication framework [2].

The obtained results are interesting and promising. However, more experiments with a large-scale real-life applications and several local area networks (e.g. the one of our two teams : LIP6 and CReSTIC) are needed to validate the proposed approach and to analyze the proposed algorithms. Moreover, the proposed classification of performatives needs to be evaluated and compared with other classifications and different weights.

Finally, we are working on a methodology based on the Model Driven Architecture [17] to facilitate the design of fault-tolerant multi-agent systems and their implementation with DimaX.

Acknowledgment

The authors would like to thank the members of *Fault-Tolerant Multi-agent System* project of the LIP6 for their many useful suggestions regarding fault-tolerant multi-agent systems.

References

1. F.M. Assis-Silva and R. Popescu-Zeletin. An approach for providing mobile agent fault tolerance. In *Second International Workshop on Mobile Agents*, number 1477 in LNCS. Springer-Verlag, 1998.
2. M. Bertier, O. Marin, and P. Sens. Implementation and performance evaluation of an adaptable failure detector. In *the International Conference on Dependable Systems and Networks*, Washington, USA, 2002.
3. C. Castelfranchi. *Decentralized AI*, chapter Dependence relations in multi-agent systems. Elsevier, 1992.
4. Marco Colombetti and Mario Verdicchio. An analysis of agent speech acts as institutional actions. In *AAMAS'2002*, pages 1157–1164, 2002.
5. A. Fedoruk and R. Deters. Improving fault-tolerance by replicating agents. In *AAMAS'2002*, pages 373–744, Bologna, Italy, 2002.
6. R. Guerraoui, B. Garbinato, and K. Mazouni. Lessons from designing and implementing GARF. In *Object-Based Parallel and Distributed Computation*, number 791 in LNCS, pages 238–256, 1995.
7. Z. Guessoum and J.-P. Briot. From active objects to autonomous agents. *IEEE Concurrency*, 7(3):68–76, 1999.
8. Z. Guessoum, J.-P. Briot, O. Marin, A. Hamel, and P. Sens. *Software Engineering for Large-Scale Multi-Agent Systems*, chapter Dynamic and Adaptative Replication for Large-Scale Reliable Multi-Agent Systems, pages 182–198. Number 2603 in LNCS. April 2003.
9. Z. Guessoum, N. Faci, and J.-P. Briot. Adaptive replication of large-scale multi-agent systems - towards a fault-tolerant multi-agent platform. In *Proceedings of the ICSE'05 Fourth International Workshop on Software Engineering for Large-Scale Multi-Agent Systems (SELMAS'05)*, Saint Louis, U.S.A., may 2005. ACM.
10. S. Hagg. A sentinel approach to fault handling in multi-agent systems. In C. Zhang and D. Lukose, editors, *Multi-Agent Systems, Methodologies and Applications*, number 1286 in LNCS, pages 190–195, 1997.
11. B. Horling, B. Benyo, and V. Lesser. Using self-diagnosis to adapt organizational structures. In *5th International Conference on Autonomous Agents*, pages 529–536, Montreal, 2001. ACM Press.
12. G. A. Kaminka, D. V. Pynadath, and M. Tambe. Monitoring teams by overhearing: A multi-agent plan-recognition approach. *Journal of Intelligence Artificial Research*, 17:83–135, 2002.
13. S. Kraus, V.S. Subrahmanian, and N. Cihan Tacs. Probabilistically survivable MASs. In *IJCAI'03*, pages 789–795, 2003.

14. T. W. Malone and K. Crowston. The interdisciplanary study of coordination. *ACM Computing Surveys*, 26(1):87–119, March 1994.
15. O. Marin, M. Bertier, and P. Sens. DARX - a framework for the fault-tolerant support of agent software. In *14th International Symposium on Software Reliability Engineering (ISSRE'2003)*, pages 406–417, Denver, Colorado, USA, 2003. IEEE.
16. M.Klein, J.A. Rodriguez-Aguilar, and C.Dellarocas. Using domain-independent exception handling services to enable robust open multi-agent systems: The case of agent death. *Journal of autonomous Agents and Multi-Agent Systems*, 7(1-2):179–189, 2003.
17. OMG TC Document ormsc/2001 07-01. Model driven architecture (mda). Technical report, OMG, 2001.
18. R. Van Renesse, K. Birman, and S. Maffeis. Horus: A flexible group communication system. *Communications of the ACM*, 39(4):76–83, 1996.
19. N. Roos, A.t. Teije, and C. Witteveen. A protocol for multi-agent diagnosis with spatially distributed knowledge. In ACM, editor, *First Workshop on Programming Multiagent Systems: Languages, frameworks, techniques, and tools (ProMAS03), AAMAS'03*, pages 655–661, July 2003.
20. J. S. Sichman and R. Conte. Multi-agent dependence by dependence graphs. In *AAMAS'2002*, pages 483–490, Bologna, Italy, 2002. ACM.
21. J. S. Sichman, R. Conte, and Y. Demazeau. Reasoning about others using dependence networks. In *Actes de Incontro del gruppo AI*IA di interesse speciale sul inteligenza artificiale distribuita*, Roma, Italia, 1993.
22. J. S. Sichman, R. Conte, and Y. Demazeau. A social reasoning mechanism based on dependence networks. In *Proceedings of ECAI'94 - European Conference on Artificial Intelligence*, Amsterdam, The Netherlands, August 1994.
23. L. Silva, V. Batista, and J. Silva. Fault-tolerant execution of mobile agents. In *International Conference on Dependable Systems and Networks*, pages 135–143, 2000.

Author Index

Lecture Notes in Computer Science

For information about Vols. 1–3839

please contact your bookseller or Springer

Vol. 3890: S.G. Thompson, R. Ghanea-Hercock (Eds.), Defence Applications of Multi-Agent Systems. XII, 141 pages. 2006. (Sublibrary LNAI).

Vol. 3889: J. Rosca, D. Erdogmus, J.C. Príncipe, S. Haykin (Eds.), Independent Component Analysis and Blind Signal Separation. XXI, 980 pages. 2006.

Vol. 3888: D. Draheim, G. Weber (Eds.), Trends in Enterprise Application Architecture. IX, 145 pages. 2006.

Vol. 3887: J.R. Correa, A. Hevia, M. Kiwi (Eds.), LATIN 2006: Theoretical Informatics. XVI, 814 pages. 2006.

Vol. 3886: E.G. Bremer, J. Hakenberg, E.-H.(S.) Han, D. Berrar, W. Dubitzky (Eds.), Knowledge Discovery in Life Science Literature. XIV, 147 pages. 2006. (Sublibrary LNBI).

Vol. 3885: V. Torra, Y. Narukawa, A. Valls, J. Domingo-Ferrer (Eds.), Modeling Decisions for Artificial Intelligence. XII, 374 pages. 2006. (Sublibrary LNAI).

Vol. 3884: B. Durand, W. Thomas (Eds.), STACS 2006. XIV, 714 pages. 2006.

Vol. 3882: M.L. Lee, K.L. Tan, V. Wuwongse (Eds.), Database Systems for Advanced Applications. XXI, 923 pages. 2006.

Vol. 3881: S. Gibet, N. Courty, J.-F. Kamp (Eds.), Gesture in Human-Computer Interaction and Simulation. XIII, 344 pages. 2006. (Sublibrary LNAI).

Vol. 3880: A. Rashid, M. Aksit (Eds.), Transactions on Aspect-Oriented Software Development I. IX, 335 pages. 2006.

Vol. 3879: T. Erlebach, G. Persinao (Eds.), Approximation and Online Algorithms. X, 349 pages. 2006.

Vol. 3878: A. Gelbukh (Ed.), Computational Linguistics and Intelligent Text Processing. XVII, 589 pages. 2006.

Vol. 3877: M. Detyniecki, J.M. Jose, A. Nürnberger, C. J. '. van Rijsbergen (Eds.), Adaptive Multimedia Retrieval: User, Context, and Feedback. XI, 279 pages. 2006.

Vol. 3876: S. Halevi, T. Rabin (Eds.), Theory of Cryptography. XI, 617 pages. 2006.

Vol. 3875: S. Ur, E. Bin, Y. Wolfsthal (Eds.), Hardware and Software, Verification and Testing. X, 265 pages. 2006.

Vol. 3874: R. Missaoui, J. Schmidt (Eds.), Formal Concept Analysis. X, 309 pages. 2006. (Sublibrary LNAI).

Vol. 3873: L. Maicher, J. Park (Eds.), Charting the Topic Maps Research and Applications Landscape. VIII, 281 pages. 2006. (Sublibrary LNAI).

Vol. 3872: H. Bunke, A. L. Spitz (Eds.), Document Analysis Systems VII. XIII, 630 pages. 2006.

Vol. 3870: S. Spaccapietra, P. Atzeni, W.W. Chu, T. Catarci, K.P. Sycara (Eds.), Journal on Data Semantics V. XIII, 237 pages. 2006.

Vol. 3869: S. Renals, S. Bengio (Eds.), Machine Learning for Multimodal Interaction. XIII, 490 pages. 2006.

Vol. 3868: K. Römer, H. Karl, F. Mattern (Eds.), Wireless Sensor Networks. XI, 342 pages. 2006.

Vol. 3866: T. Dimitrakos, F. Martinelli, P.Y.A. Ryan, S. Schneider (Eds.), Formal Aspects in Security and Trust. X, 259 pages. 2006.

Vol. 3865: W. Shen, K.-M. Chao, Z. Lin, J.-P.A. Barthès, A. James (Eds.), Computer Supported Cooperative Work in Design II. XII, 659 pages. 2006.

Vol. 3863: M. Kohlhase (Ed.), Mathematical Knowledge Management. XI, 405 pages. 2006. (Sublibrary LNAI).

Vol. 3862: R.H. Bordini, M. Dastani, J. Dix, A.E.F. Seghrouchni (Eds.), Programming Multi-Agent Systems. XIV, 267 pages. 2006. (Sublibrary LNAI).

Vol. 3861: J. Dix, S.J. Hegner (Eds.), Foundations of Information and Knowledge Systems. X, 331 pages. 2006.

Vol. 3860: D. Pointcheval (Ed.), Topics in Cryptology – CT-RSA 2006. XI, 365 pages. 2006.

Vol. 3858: A. Valdes, D. Zamboni (Eds.), Recent Advances in Intrusion Detection. X, 351 pages. 2006.

Vol. 3857: M.P.C. Fossorier, H. Imai, S. Lin, A. Poli (Eds.), Applied Algebra, Algebraic Algorithms and Error-Correcting Codes. XI, 350 pages. 2006.

Vol. 3855: E. A. Emerson, K.S. Namjoshi (Eds.), Verification, Model Checking, and Abstract Interpretation. XI, 443 pages. 2005.

Vol. 3854: I. Stavrakakis, M. Smirnov (Eds.), Autonomic Communication. XIII, 303 pages. 2006.

Vol. 3853: A.J. Ijspeert, T. Masuzawa, S. Kusumoto (Eds.), Biologically Inspired Approaches to Advanced Information Technology. XIV, 388 pages. 2006.

Vol. 3852: P.J. Narayanan, S.K. Nayar, H.-Y. Shum (Eds.), Computer Vision – ACCV 2006, Part II. XXXI, 977 pages. 2006.

Vol. 3851: P.J. Narayanan, S.K. Nayar, H.-Y. Shum (Eds.), Computer Vision – ACCV 2006, Part I. XXXI, 973 pages. 2006.

Vol. 3850: R. Freund, G. Păun, G. Rozenberg, A. Salomaa (Eds.), Membrane Computing. IX, 371 pages. 2006.

Vol. 3849: I. Bloch, A. Petrosino, A.G.B. Tettamanzi (Eds.), Fuzzy Logic and Applications. XIV, 438 pages. 2006. (Sublibrary LNAI).

Vol. 3848: J.-F. Boulicaut, L. De Raedt, H. Mannila (Eds.), Constraint-Based Mining and Inductive Databases. X, 401 pages. 2006. (Sublibrary LNAI).

Vol. 3847: K.P. Jantke, A. Lunzer, N. Spyratos, Y. Tanaka (Eds.), Federation over the Web. X, 215 pages. 2006. (Sublibrary LNAI).

Vol. 3846: H. J. van den Herik, Y. Björnsson, N.S. Netanyahu (Eds.), Computers and Games. XIV, 333 pages. 2006.

Vol. 3845: J. Farré, I. Litovsky, S. Schmitz (Eds.), Implementation and Application of Automata. XIII, 360 pages. 2006.

Vol. 3844: J.-M. Bruel (Ed.), Satellite Events at the MoDELS 2005 Conference. XIII, 360 pages. 2006.

Vol. 3843: P. Healy, N.S. Nikolov (Eds.), Graph Drawing. XVII, 536 pages. 2006.

Vol. 3842: H.T. Shen, J. Li, M. Li, J. Ni, W. Wang (Eds.), Advanced Web and Network Technologies, and Applications. XXVII, 1057 pages. 2006.

Vol. 3841: X. Zhou, J. Li, H.T. Shen, M. Kitsuregawa, Y. Zhang (Eds.), Frontiers of WWW Research and Development - APWeb 2006. XXIV, 1223 pages. 2006.

Vol. 3840: M. Li, B. Boehm, L.J. Osterweil (Eds.), Unifying the Software Process Spectrum. XVI, 522 pages. 2006.